The Postmodern President

Also by Richard Rose
Taxation by Political Inertia, with Terence Karran
Ministers and Ministries: A Functional Analysis
Patterns of Parliamentary Legislation, with Denis Van Mechelen
Voters Begin to Choose, with Ian McAllister
Public Employment in Western Nations
The Nationwide Competition for Votes, with Ian McAllister
Do Parties Make a Difference?
Understanding Big Government
The Territorial Dimension in Government
United Kingdom Facts, with Ian McAllister
Can Government Go Bankrupt? with Guy Peters
What Is Governing? Purpose and Policy in Washington
Managing Presidential Objectives
Northern Ireland: A Time of Choice
The Problem of Party Government
International Almanac of Electoral History, with T.T. Mackie
Governing without Consensus
People in Politics
Influencing Voters
Politics in England
Must Labour Lose? with Mark Abrams
The British General Election of 1959, with D.E. Butler

Edited by Richard Rose
The Welfare State East and West, with Rei Shiratori
Fiscal Stress in Cities, with Edward Page
The Territorial Dimension in United Kingdom Politics, with Peter Madgwick
Presidents and Prime Ministers, with Ezra Suleiman
Electoral Participation
Britain: Progress and Decline, with William B. Gwyn
Challenge to Governance
Elections without Choice, with Guy Hermet and Alain Rouquié
New Trends in British Politics, with Dennis Kavanagh
Comparing Public Policies, with Jerzy Wiatr
The Dynamics of Public Policy
The Management of Urban Change in Britain and Germany
Electoral Behavior: A Comparative Handbook
Lessons from America
European Politics, with Mattei Dogan
Policy-Making in Britain
Studies in British Politics

The Postmodern President

The White House Meets the World

Richard Rose
University of Strathclyde

God grant us the serenity to accept things we cannot change, courage to change things we can, and wisdom to know the difference.
—Reinhold Niebuhr

CHATHAM HOUSE PUBLISHERS, INC.
Chatham, New Jersey

THE POSTMODERN PRESIDENT
The White House Meets the World

CHATHAM HOUSE PUBLISHERS, INC.
Post Office Box One
Chatham, New Jersey 07928

PUBLISHER: Edward Artinian
COVER DESIGN: Lawrence Ratzkin
COMPOSITION: BUREAU-GRAPHICS LTD.
PRINTING AND BINDING: BOOKCRAFTERS, INC.

LIBRARY OF CONGRESS CATALOGING-IN-PUBLICATION DATA

Rose, Richard, 1933-
    The postmodern president.

    Bibliography: p.
    Includes index.
    1. Presidents — United States. 2. United States — Foreign relations.   I. Title.
JK570. R67   1988   353.03'1   88-28525
ISBN 0-934540-74-8 (pbk)

Manufactured in the United States of America
10 9 8 7 6 5 4 3 2 1

Contents

Figures

Tables

Acknowledgments

This book has been a long time in the making. I began systematic research on Presidential politics at the height of Watergate in 1974, following two decades of examining comparative politics and public policy in Europe. The initial product was a study of White House relations with the agencies, *Managing Presidential Objectives*. It was followed by *What Is Governing? Purpose and Policy in Washington*. Differences in the way democratic leaders address common problems of directing government was the theme of *Presidents and Prime Ministers*, edited with Ezra Suleiman.

In 1983 Alexander Heard, heading a study of the American presidential selection process, asked me: What difference does it make that the American President is recruited in a very different way from the leaders of other democratic nations? The four-chapter monograph written in response to his question was the stimulus for this book. Along the way a variety of articles have been published about themes considered here. My wife and my wordprocessor can each bear witness that this is a freshly written book.

In carrying forward this study, it was especially helpful to be the Visiting Hinkley Professor at Johns Hopkins University immediately after the breaking of the Iran-*contra* affair. Baltimore offers a unique perspective, being outside the Washington Beltway yet making it easy to go back and forth between the world inside the Beltway and everyday American life. Useful feedback was obtained in talks about the Presidency at Yale, Princeton, George Mason, and Johns Hopkins universities, and at the Brookings Institution. Chapter 2 draws on a paper written with Robert J. Thompson.

Through the years various friends in government, think tanks and universities have been courteous and encouraging of my efforts to view Washington from an international perspective. Officials of foreign governments from Stockholm and Rome to Canberra and Tokyo have generously discussed common problems of giving direction to government. Kate Bateman of the U.S. Information Service was helpful in digging out promptly a variety of obscure references. John Hart, Karen Hult, George W. Jones, Bert A. Rockman, and Aaron Wildavsky commented on the book in draft.

Ms. Isobel Rogerson and Ms Anne Shaw looked after the office, and Rosemary Rose made the index. Drew Broadley of Bureau-Graphics contributed enormously to getting this book out.

Dedicated to
Richard E. Neustadt
Scholar, Gentleman, Democrat

Introduction: Approaching the White House

What does concern me in common with thinking partisans of both parties is not just winning this election, but how it is won, how well we can take advantage of this great quadrennial opportunity to debate issues sensibly and soberly.

Even more important than winning the election is governing the nation. Let's talk sense to the American people. Let's tell them the truth, that there are no gains without pains, that we are now on the eve of great decisions, not easy decisions.
—Adlai Stevenson

The easiest way to see the world closing in on the White House is to turn on the TV set. Day after day we see evidence of the impact on American life of actions elsewhere: an arms-control statement in Moscow, the kidnapping of Americans in the Middle East, and prices and jobs going up or down in response to changes in the dollar's value in Tokyo or Frankfurt. Events on the other side of the earth cannot be ignored by the President when they have a great impact on our lives. Nor can foreigners ignore what happens in Washington.

The past quarter-century has been very eventful for America, perhaps too eventful. As the central institution of American government, the years have also been eventful for the Presidency. The White House has been shocked by events in places as distant as Vietnam and Iran. It has been undermined close at hand, as in Watergate. The civil rights movement questioned generations of discrimination in the South and in the nation's capital itself. Assassins have repeatedly tried to intervene in the history of the Presidency, sometimes with success. In spite of the stresses imposed by such events, the American Constitution has maintained legitimacy and celebrated its bicentennial, a rare event in a troubled world. By contrast, the Constitution of the French Fifth Republic only dates from 1958, that of the Federal Republic of Germany from 1949, and Japan from 1947.

If a President is judged by responsiveness to public opinion and effectiveness in policymaking, then Ronald Reagan's four immediate predecessors have fallen short on one or both counts. Three Presidents have left office because they could not respond satisfactorily to the public. Jimmy Carter and Gerald Ford were rejected by the electorate, and Lyndon Johnson did not run

1

for reelection in 1968 because of domestic opposition to the Vietnam war. Richard Nixon won two elections, but suffered military defeats in Southeast Asia, inflation at home, and violations of the criminal law within the White House. John F. Kennedy was not in office long enough to leave a record that can be fully evaluated, but he was there long enough to learn that "the problems are much more difficult than I had imagined them to be" (quoted in Hirschfield, 1973: 134).

The postmodern President is not under pressure because American government has become weaker; the challenge arises because other countries have grown stronger. America is richer today than it was a quarter-century ago, and the armed forces are equipped with weapons that were then only visionary. But European countries and Japan have grown much richer, and oil-producing nations have grown rich by exploiting their natural resources. The vast populations of the Soviet Union and China have been mobilized into commanding military forces. Leaders of these countries see that America's President still stands tall. But foreign leaders can also stand tall. They want to advance their national aims, cooperating with the White House if appropriate or opposing the White House if necessary.

The Postmodern President

In two centuries, America has had three different Presidencies: a traditional President who had little to do; a modern President who had a lot to do at home and abroad; and a postmodern President who may have too much expected of him. As the world changes, our ideas must change, or we will become confused by applying the standards of one era to a different one. A modern President would not think of wearing a powdered wig, even though George Washington did so.

The traditional Presidency was designed two centuries ago to protect the American people against the abuses of an autocratic monarch and to guard against the emergence of an elected despot. For a century and a half, the White House was an office in a system of separated powers in which Congress and the Supreme Court each acted as a check on the Presidency and Congress was the leading branch. The traditional Presidency was not a driving force in government; with occasional exceptions, it was a dignified office of state.

The modern Presidency was created by Franklin D. Roosevelt's response to the depression of the 1930s. Although Roosevelt was not the first occupant of the Oval Office of the White House to believe in an active Presidency, he was the first to be an active leader in peacetime. To support his leadership, Roosevelt began the practice of appealing to the public for support through the new medium of radio broadcasting. Few Americans ever saw or heard the voice of Abraham Lincoln or Woodrow Wilson, but FDR's fireside chats made his voice familiar to every voter. America's involvement in World War II made President Roosevelt an international leader too. President Harry Truman placed America's world role on a permanent basis, deciding to drop the atomic bomb on Japan, and after 1945, committing American troops to the defense of places as far apart as Berlin and Korea. Because other nations were then devastated by war or had never been industrial powers, the modern President's eminence was at first a solitary eminence.

The military and economic eminence of America after 1945 resulted in American *hegemony* in the international system, that is, the United States was the dominant nation influencing what happened around the globe (cf. Keohane, 1984; Gilpin, 1987). The mobilization of American arms to contain the Soviet Union had a great impact because of America's vast population, double that of Japan and four times that of Britain, France, or Germany. The impact was enhanced by the development of new and increasingly sophis-ticated weapons' systems. Whereas the Soviet Union is also a military superpower and Japan is also an economic superpower, only the United States has been both a military and economic superpower. American money stimulated the economies of Europe and Asia, and products such as IBM computers, Xerox machines, and Coca-Cola penetrated every corner of the earth. U. S. policies sought to secure mutual defense and worldwide eco-nomic growth: "For Americans it was the ideal outcome: one could do well by doing good" (Russett, 1985: 228).

The difference between the modern and the postmodern Presidency is that a postmodern President can no longer dominate the international system. President Carter and President Reagan have each appeared as help-less victims of forces abroad: oil-exporting nations, foreign armies, small bands of terrorists, and bankers and businessmen profiting from problems of the American economy. *Interdependence* characterizes an international system in which no nation is the hegemonic power. The President is the leader of a very influential nation, but other nations are influential too. In an interdependent world, what happens in the United States depends on what happens in other countries as well as what happens at home. For example, if America is to increase its exports, then other countries must increase their imports. The line between domestic and international politics is dissolving.

While the White House is accustomed to influencing foreign nations, the postmodern President must accept something less appealing: Other nations can now influence what the White House achieves. Whereas the Constitution made Congress and the Supreme Court the chief checks on the traditional and the modern President, the chief constraints on the postmodern President are found in other nations. The White House depends on the cooperation of the Kremlin to deter nuclear war and for agreement in arms-control negotia-tions. It makes a big difference to the White House whether the Soviet Union

3

pursues a policy of *glasnost* or aggression. The White House looks to the Japanese government to act to reduce the American trade deficit, and it looks to the German central bank, the Bundesbank, to boost demand in Europe for American exports. When the President looks to the Middle East, he must wonder what next will disrupt White House hopes for stability in a region where instability is endemic.

Although America remains a world power, it is no longer the dominant power that it once was. The White House has not lost Britain or Germany or Japan, for these independent countries never belonged to the United States. Each remains an ally, but the terms of the relationship have changed. American support for other nations' development has met with such success that countries dependent on the United States shortly after World War II are now major players in the international system. As the United States becomes more integrated in the international system, it becomes more like other nations. America is no longer isolated geographically, as in the days of the traditional Presidency, or isolated by the preeminence of its power, as in the era of the modern Presidency.

In an interdependent world a President cannot always do what he wants, because policies cannot always be stamped *Made in America*.* A ruler with unchallenged authority could assume that to govern is to choose. A postmodern President must start from the assumption: *To govern is to cooperate*. A President has always needed to cooperate with Congress in order to succeed in a constitutional system that separates powers. What is novel is that a postmodern President must cooperate with foreign governments to achieve major economic and national security goals. Cooperation requires a mutuality of interests between nations. If this is lacking, then a postmodern President can face stalemate abroad, just as he can face stalemate in Congress. As Reinhold Niebuhr notes, the President requires strength to change those things that American government can change and a stoic sense to accept what he cannot change. Above all, a President needs the wisdom to tell the difference between what can be changed and what must be accepted.

If a postmodern President does not adapt to changes in the international system, then he is doomed to fail at home as well as abroad. The rise of other nations to economic and military power presents greater challenges to the postmodern President, and lessens the capacity of America to influence international outcomes. Whereas a modern President had international influence consistent with his responsibilities, a postmodern President does not. Hence political commentators have shifted from worrying about the Imperial Presidency, deemed too powerful for the nation's good, to worrying about an imperiled Presidency, too weak for the nation's good.

---

*Presidents are referred to as he, since every President has been a male, while countries as diverse as Britain, India, Israel, and Norway have had women as national leaders. To refer to Presidents by the phrase "he or she" would convey a misleading impression of gender equality.

The leading contemporary scholar of the Presidency, Richard E. Neustadt (1980: xi, 241), has asked: "Is the Presidency possible?" His answer is not encouraging: "Weakness is what I see." The standard for presidential success that Neustadt (1980: 210) offers is challenging but not impossible: A "minimally effective" President should match the achievements of President Truman; he adds that there is "nothing high-and-mighty about that." If Truman's achievement is taken as the standard for the Presidency, three-quarters of the country's leaders fall below this mark, in the judgment of historians (figure 13.3). It is particularly worrisome that historians do not rate any occupant of the White House as having reached this standard since Truman left office in 1953.

It is right to worry about the capacity of the President, for the man in the White House is not an ordinary officeholder. The President is unique in his claim to political authority; he alone is elected by the nation as a whole. Lincoln's idea of government by the people is simply not practical. When America has a population of 240 million people, big decisions about the economy and foreign policy cannot be taken in a New England-style town meeting. Nor can 535 congressmen give clear and coherent direction to government, individually or collectively. The job of a congressman is to represent his or her district in Washington. The job of the President is to represent the whole of the nation in an uncertain and sometimes hostile world.

The concern of this book is not with looking backward into history, but with history read forward. To look back longingly to a world in which the President stood as a colossus is to default on our obligations to the future. We are much closer to the twenty-first century than we are to the days of George Washington, Franklin D. Roosevelt, or John F. Kennedy. By the middle of the next century it will be easy to assess the successes and failures of the person inaugurated as Ronald Reagan's successor on 20 January 1989. Reading history forward is a challenge to understand under what conditions and to what extent a postmodern President can succeed in an international system in which he is not the only leader who counts, because America is not the only nation that counts.

An Overview

The success of the postmodern President depends on cooperation with leaders of other nations. This does not mean that a President can ignore public opinion or congressional opinion. It emphasizes that what the public and Congress think of the President depends, at least in part, on what the Japanese Ministry of Finance, the Kremlin, and diverse political forces in the Middle East think of the President. Any one of them can make the White

House look bad by imposing economic burdens or military setbacks on the United States. In an interdependent world, the President cannot avoid dealing with leaders in other nations; the question is whether the President plays his cards well or badly.

The biggest problem of the postmodern President is: *What it takes to become President has nothing to do with what it takes to be President.* A postmodern President must focus on complex economic, diplomatic, and military problems in the international system. But anyone who wants to be elected to the White House today must start campaigning years before a Presidential election is held. Instead of focusing on international problems, attention must be directed to parochial concerns of the counties of Iowa, where the first primary caucus is held, and of voters in New Hampshire, where a critical primary ballot is held. To win nomination for the Presidency requires great campaign skill and endurance. But it says nothing about the candidate's capacity to deal with the problems of an interdependent world in which the dollar is suspect, and friends and foes are not so easy to identify as once was the case.

An even more troubling prospect must be faced: *What it takes to become President actually makes it more difficult to be a successful postmodern President.* The demands of the campaign trail are such that in 1988 the Democratic party had difficulty in attracting respected Democratic leaders to enter the race. A contemporary presidential candidate is expected to demonstrate to voters that he cares about their views, and to the media that he has a chance of winning the nomination. Success in doing this is no proof that a candidate understands anything about the dollar in a volatile international economy, or about the troublespots that threaten national security. Years of campaigning have a high opportunity cost. A politician who dedicates his time to pressing the flesh on the campaign trail has little or no time to think about what he would do if he won the White House.

Personal character is important in determining who is nominated and elected President; compare the troubles of Gary Hart's candidacy or Senator Edward Kennedy's decision not to make the race for the nomination, with the ability of Ronald Reagan to smile through many problems. But the choice of President should not be reduced to a personality contest. Attempts have been made to apply insights from clinical psychology and personality theory to predict whether or not a President will be successful, but it is very difficult to relate differences in the personalities of Presidents with their performance in office (cf. Barber, 1972; Buchanan, 1987; Tulis, 1981). For example, by any conventional psychological standard, Abraham Lincoln was an oddball, but Lincoln was nonetheless a great President. To erect a superhuman standard for judging Presidents is to doom every White House occupant to failure. Since the typical President is likely to achieve some successes and some failures, his ups and downs are difficult to explain as the simple reflection of personality, which is a constant.

The immediate problem of a President is not what to do in his private life, but what to do about public issues that press on the Oval Office from the day he arrives. Jimmy Carter entered office with the simple belief that policy choices were between doing what was right or wrong, but found that presidential politics is about reconciling competing definitions of what is good. Lyndon Johnson entered office with a down-to-earth view that presidential ends justified any political means. The fundamental issue is not the personality of the President, but how he performs in office.

This book starts from the assumption that the Presidency can be understood only in terms of politics *and* government. Most studies of the Presidency concentrate on a single aspect of the Oval Office, such as the President's appeal to the electorate, his relations with Congress, the use of the media, or problems of managing White House staff. These concerns are means to the end of public policy. Although a President can never stop thinking about politics, neither can a President ignore the fiscal limits of the American economy or the impact of other nations on the success of a President's foreign policy.

The postmodern Presidency can be understood only by examining both the politics and the policy concerns of the White House. A public policy approach judges a President's success by what he does, as well as by how he deals with public opinion and with Washington. To succeed, a President must be effective as well as responsive. Responsiveness to the electorate is necessary if the authority of a President is to rest on the consent of the governed, a fundamental requirement of democracy. A President must be judged by the actual impact of his policies as well as by what he would like to do. Effectiveness is necessary if a nation's leader is to do more than declare good intentions. When push comes to shove, the test of a President is whether he acts effectively. The oath that the President takes to "preserve, protect and defend the Constitution of the United States" commits him to be effective in upholding the fundamentals of sovereignty: national independence in a troubled world, and the prerequisites of a sound economy (Rose, 1976a). Whereas a traditional President could be effective by doing little at home or abroad, a postmodern President can be effective only by acting in the international system.

Chapters of the Book

The first part of this study describes what the postmodern Presidency is, the imperatives for action in the White House, the standards for assessing the performance of Presidents, and how the Presidency differs from other forms of democratic government. In the second part, the tangible and intangible resources of the Presidency are analyzed. On close inspection, some of these resources turn out to be limitations. The third section considers the way in which economic problems and national security issues are dealt with in Washington and in an international system that America can no longer dominate. The concluding section evaluates how the American people judge a President, and how other countries view the Oval Office as the world closes in on the White House.

While the evolution from the traditional to the modern Presidency took a century, the shift from the modern to the postmodern Presidency has occurred within two decades. The transition to a world in which the President must bargain with leaders of other nations has occurred so abruptly that some presidential candidates have yet to notice it. Yet even the briefest consideration of America's position in the world economy makes it clear that the days are gone when President Kennedy could pledge that America would pay any price to lead the world. Chapter 1 describes the evolution of the Presidency from its traditional foundations and what this means when America is not the only elephant in the system. A President now cooperates and competes with other elephants to succeed in the Oval Office.

A postmodern President must respond to three different imperatives. To exercise influence within a system of separated powers, a President must go Washington, that is, learn how to bargain with congressmen, bureaucrats, and interest-group representatives who can make or break his policy initiatives. Going public is a second imperative; after an arduous campaign for election the President must continue campaigning for popular support for himself and his policies. Going international is the third imperative, involving bargaining with foreigners on whose cooperation the President depends for success in foreign and economic policy. Chapter 2 considers how the President may deal with each imperative on its own or simultaneously try to take charge of public opinion in Washington and the international system.

Because the President is a political figure, assessments vary about the proper role for the President; one school of thought favors an expansive role and another a more limited role. There is controversy about the direction in which a President leads: Those who approve of Ronald Reagan's policies are likely to disapprove of Lyndon Johnson's policies, and vice versa. Chapter 3 shows how an active President is praised as a leader if his policies are approved, but attacked as an overmighty Imperial President if his policies are disliked. A President who defines his role narrowly is praised as an exemplar of stoic virtue, if this fits with the political outlook of the evaluator, or criticized as imperiled if the President is thought to be too inactive. Assessments of a postmodern President need to consider how other nations respond to the President's efforts to take charge in the international system, influencing whether a President appears as a world leader, vulnerable, isolated, or a global failure.

Although the Presidency is regarded as normal in America, it is not the normal form of democratic government. Most democratic nations have a parliamentary system. The differences between the American system and the parliamentary system are set out in chapter 4. The American Constitution makes the Presidency one of three separate powers in Washington. By contrast, the parliamentary system fuses power in the hands of a Prime Minister and Cabinet that is accountable to a popularly elected Parliament. The independent strength of Congress, executive branch agencies, and interest groups create subgovernments that exclude the President from influencing many areas of public policy, whereas in a parliamentary system subgovernments must submit to the authority of government. The intent of the American system is to keep government weak, whereas the parliamentary system assumes that strong government is good government. The United States is thus represented internationally by a President whose power in government is far less than that of those with whom he must deal.

In order to understand what a President can do, we must first ask: How much does American government do? The surprising answer, given in chapter 5, is that it does not do much by comparison with mixed-economy welfare states of Europe. American government raises much less money in taxes, has relatively fewer public employees, and takes fewer legislative initiatives. Moreover, the federal system leaves Washington responsible for a much smaller proportion of the nation's resources than governments in London, Paris, and Tokyo. The checks and balances of the Constitution further limit what a President can effectively do. Sizing up the President's influence cuts the President down to size, for relatively few problems of public policy can be resolved by the White House acting alone.

Campaigning for the White House is necessary, but there is a political cost; the time spent in campaigning is not available for learning how to govern. The road to the White House typically attracts candidates who have no experience in the executive branch of government. Chapter 6 contrasts this with the experience of leaders in a parliamentary system. Before a British, French, German, or Japanese politician becomes Prime Minister, he or she must go government, gaining policymaking experience as a Cabinet minister, a civil servant in a major government department, or both. This is far more useful for policymaking than a presidential candidate's experience in playing the national media or baiting the executive branch as a Congressman. A newly installed Prime Minister has already learned how to govern; a President usually enters the White House an absolute beginner.

Once elected, a President must maintain popularity by continuously campaigning for support. Winning an election every four years is not sufficient in Washington, whereas in a parliamentary system a Prime Minister expects the governing party in the legislature to support difficult decisions throughout a term of office. Chapter 7 examines three reasons why the President must campaign continuously. First, there is no party system offering reliable support in Congress or public opinion. Second, a President must court the media, for TV newscasters can put the White House on trial any night of the week. A third need, courting Congress, is not a major problem in a parliamentary system, for party discipline normally leads the legislature to endorse what the Cabinet does. In Washington, legislation requires cooperation between Congress on Capitol Hill and the White House at the other end of Pennsylvania Avenue.

Once elected, the first priority of a President is to take over the White House. A newly elected President is expected to hit the ground running, using his fresh popular mandate to get legislation endorsed by an often recalcitrant Congress. This is easier said than done, for unlike a Prime Minister, a President is usually a stranger to the task of giving direction to government. Chapter 8 examines the problems the President has in taking and keeping control of the White House. A President needs staff to act as his eyes and ears, but staff members also have egos. Failure to control staff actions can lead to such abuses of presidential authority as Watergate and the Iran-*contra* affair. The strategic problem facing the President is organizing the White House so that he is kept informed about what concerns him without becoming buried in details and in political quarrels.

The President is a chief without an executive. Whereas a Prime Minister collaborates with Cabinet ministers and civil servants to steer the ship of state, the President is in charge of a collection of inexperienced campaign aides, strangers, and potential enemies. Only a few Cabinet ministers—in State, Defense, Treasury, and Justice—have much contact with the President. The rest are consigned to the bush leagues of the Outer Cabinet. However much zeal presidential appointees show, they often lack expertise in the programs and procedures of government. Hence chapter 9 examines how a President comes to terms with his political appointees and with expert civil servants. One way to do this is to use staff to keep him out of trouble, for keeping out of trouble is as important as acting effectively. In the course of a four-year term, a President cannot expect to alter the organized anarchy of the nation's capital; his aim is to intervene selectively in accord with his imperative responsibilities.

The President's problem in managing the economy is that the institutions of economic management often appear unmanageable. Chapter 10 examines the President's problem in holding the reins of a bucking bronco of an economy. Economic theories do not provide the White House with the certainty that astrophysics offers the National Aeronautics and Space Administration (NASA). Making the budget is a problem when tax revenues fall more than $100 billion short of spending commitments. In assisting the White House in meeting the deficit, the government's banker, the chairman of the Federal Reserve Board, must walk a tightrope between White House pressures and pressures from the international system. Whereas in a parliamentary system the Cabinet's budget is endorsed because it is a vote of confidence in the government as a whole, in Washington the President and Congress can disagree endlessly about how the federal government should spend more than a trillion dollars each year.

All Americans share a common interest in the nation's security in a troubled world, but a President finds no agreement about what should be done and who should be in charge. Many different agencies want to get into the act: the State Department, the Department of Defense, the Central Intelligence Agency (CIA), Congress, and representatives of public opinion. By contrast, in a parliamentary system government has the collective authority to respond to other nations with a single voice. Chapter 11 shows the President often relies heavily on his national security adviser, who can end-run Cabinet secretaries. By having his own foreign policy staff in the White House, the President can distance himself from bureaucratic infighting. The Iran-*contra* affair demonstrates the risk of an inexperienced White House operating without the warning signals provided by professionals in foreign policy.

As long as the United States was the only superpower in the world, the President could export many difficulties. Other countries were forced to adapt to whatever was done by the world's leading military and economic power. Today, America is no longer the sole power dominating the international system. Chapter 12 shows that the international system is collectively stronger than any President. There is interdependence between America and the Soviet Union in today's balance of power. The rise of other economies and the increasing difficulties of the American economy ended an era of American hegemony. The rise of Japan to international economic eminence has created American-Japanese "bigemony," in which the United States guarantees Japan's national security while Japan finances America's trade deficit. The postmodern President must now bargain in an open market, for there are insufficient common interests to encourage other nations to sacrifice their economic well-being for the sake of the United States. In a posthegemonic world, all major nations find that the international system is stronger than any national leader.

Evaluations of the Presidency involve a paradox: Everyone should consent to how the country is governed, yet voters disagree about who should govern. If the electorate is expected to approve of a President who is successful, then the majority ought to show disapproval when the President is unsuccessful. Thus, chapter 13 asks: How popular should a President be? Presidents usually enjoy the approval of a majority of Americans, and a significantly higher level of approval than Prime Ministers. But approval ratings go down as well as up. One reason is that approval depends on fluctuating conditions in the economy; another is that events, such as a military engagement, scandals, or a presidential initiative, cause popular evaluations to change. Even when a President is subject to widespread disapproval, a high level of support remains for institutions of government. But a President who does badly in going public is handicapped in Washington and the international system, whereas a Prime Minister can continue to exercise power without popularity.

As the world closes in on the White House, is the best President we've got good enough? The next President of the United States will not start with a fresh slate. Instead, he will inherit the Reagan legacy, including a budget deficit and a trade deficit that make the United States dependent on foreigners to finance the standard of living of American citizens by lending tens of billions of dollars to the United States. Chapter 14 outlines this legacy as it looks to foreign nations as well as to Washington. There is an asymmetry of knowledge, for foreign nations understand Washington far better than we understand them. The postmodern President must learn how to make interdependence work if the United States is to travel in the fast lane in the international system rather than on a collision course.

The Author's Perspective

There are many different ways of painting a portrait of the Presidency. A biographer may stress the life history of individuals; a political scientist, the impact of the President upon the institutions of Washington or the electorate; a social psychologist, the impression that a President makes on others; a legal historian might examine how the Presidency fares in the courts; and a public policy expert, the impact of the President on American society. A leading bibliography of writings about the Presidency divides the literature into twenty-one different headings and more than one hundred subheadings; the final section is headed "Additional Aspects of the Presidency" (Greenstein et al., 1977; see also Edwards and Wayne, 1983).

While conventional studies of the Presidency recognize that the President is not the only political animal in town, the Washington National Zoo is regarded as the only zoo that counts. The federal government is depicted as a menagerie of proud animals, each worthy of careful attention. To understand the postmodern Presidency we must learn to think in terms of comparative zoology and ecology, for there are many big beasts in the international system today. The author is a both a FONZ (a Friend of the National Zoo) and a traveler familiar with the behavior of political animals and institutions on other continents. The postmodern President must become familiar with these politicians and their political habitats too.

The author's starting point is that of a Missourian, a Truman Democrat who first visited Washington as a student in 1951, walking the whole length of the Mall from the Capitol to the Lincoln and Jefferson memorials. Washington has changed greatly since. One symbol of change was the election of John F. Kennedy in 1960. The rhetoric of Kennedy's inaugural address was a call to action in Europe, Latin America, Asia, and Africa as well as the United States. It made clear that Washington was becoming imperial in its political vision as well as its architecture. America was the champion of the world series of politics and of baseball for the same reason: Not many other countries played. Today, the record for most home runs in a lifetime is not held by Hank Aaron but by a Japanese slugger, Sadaharu Oh, and the record for most consecutive games played is not held by a first baseman for the New York Yankees but by a third baseman for the Hiroshima Carp in the Japanese Central League.

In keeping with the conventions of presidential scholarship, this study draws on the experience of the Presidency since World War II. Reflecting the author's experience in moving back and forth between America and Europe since 1953, it also draws on knowledge of government in other countries, and of how Washington looks to foreign leaders. This is appropriate when a postmodern President must spend as much time thinking about foreign countries as a candidate spends thinking about Iowa and New Hampshire.

As long as we understand how the world is changing, we can understand how the Presidency must change. The changes required are not so much institutional as intellectual. Just as we expect other nations to know what the White House wants, in an interdependent world we must learn how other governments think and what their interests are. We must also recognize that other nations can influence events in which the United States has an interest. A successful President learns to bargain in Washington. In an interdependent world, bargaining can also satisfy the mutual interest of all participants. Adapting to a world without hegemony does not require a postmodern President to sacrifice wealth or influence; it only requires a sacrifice of out-of-date illusions. This book seeks to contribute to this process by following the injunction of a Presidential candidate who never won the White House, Adlai Stevenson: "Let's talk sense to the American people."

PART ONE

Imperative Pressures for Success

1. The Emergence of the Postmodern Presidency

All politics is local.

—Thomas "Tip" O'Neill

There's a big difference between a bill being defeated and the country being wiped out.

— John F. Kennedy

The Constitution today incorporates elements of two contrasting eras, the eighteenth and the twentieth centuries. It was written when government was small and distances were great. Politics was local, for the national capital was several days' ride on horseback from Richmond or a journey of uncertain duration by boat from Boston. For George Washington, a trip to Connecticut or Georgia was the equivalent of a modern President going to London or Tokyo. Today, the White House is the home of a leader who sees the whole world as his bailiwick. Yet politicians such as Tip O'Neill, former Speaker of the House of Representatives, can continue to view politics from the other end of the telescope, seeing it in local terms. While a member of Congress may still think that the worst disaster is the defeat of a pork-barrel bill benefiting his district, the President sees the biggest danger as America being wiped out in a nuclear war.

A century ago, the view from the Oval Office was introverted; the President saw the nation's problems in terms of developments within the American continent. So too did the congressmen who dominated Washington politics. The development of the modern President made the White House seek to mobilize public opinion nationwide and then to look worldwide. As the world has gotten smaller and other countries have grown greater, the postmodern President finds that international events increasingly influence his domestic concerns. Although the price that we pay for gas at the corner service station is determined by events on other continents, the votes that elect the President and members of Congress are still cast locally, and no one in Washington can afford to forget this.

The emergence of the postmodern Presidency requires America's leader to respond to two very different audiences: the domestic audience on which

17

popular authority rests, and the international system that influences the effectiveness of major White House policies. When Ronald Reagan tells an American audience about "winning one for the Gipper," he can rely on it to respond to a classic anecdote from American football history. But as the world closes in on the White House, a President must think about another audience. The world championship of football is not decided in the Superbowl but in the World Cup, a soccer competition dominated by nations such as Brazil, Italy, and Germany, and not by the Washington Redskins. Foreigners are no more interested in being told about Knute Rockne of Notre Dame than a newly-elected President wants to hear stories of King Canute, who was expected to command the tides of the ocean.

A traditional President did not need to say anything, and a modern President could address his audience on a whistle-stop train tour or by radio. A postmodern President must be able to think and talk in terms that other countries understand. No one in the Nixon White House thought it odd when the President told his staff that he did not give an (expletive deleted) about the Italian lira. But a postmodern President *must* care about the yen and deutsche mark as well as the dollar because the values of all three currencies are now interdependent. What the President says about the dollar is today heard by a worldwide audience. If the words do not carry conviction around the globe, foreigners can sell the dollar short while the White House is asleep.

At each stage in its evolution, the Presidency has been shaped by three conditions. Constitutional doctrines of what the President can and cannot do have been first in importance. Doctrines establish expectations about the President's role in government. A traditional President was expected to do very little; a postmodern President may be expected to do too much. Second, urgent problems of public policy can force a President to act. Abraham Lincoln and Woodrow Wilson were different from traditional Presidents, but the wars they faced were not normal. When conditions returned to normal, the Presidency reverted to its traditional form. Third, government must have the resources that enable the President's actions to have a great impact. The taking of Americans as hostages in the Middle East or the international weakness of the dollar forces a postmodern President to face the fact that there are some things that the White House lacks the power to control.

From the Traditional to the Postmodern President

The Constitution tells us half of what we need to know about the Presidency. Its unchanging contribution is to create three separate institutions charged with executive, legislative, and judicial responsibilities. By establishing Congress and the Supreme Court as separate and equal to the executive branch, the President is prevented from dominating government. From the perspective of the Oval Office, the chief defect of the Constitution is not the powers conferred on the President but the substantial powers conferred on other branches of government.

Great changes have occurred in the Presidency because the constitutional grant of authority is so vague that it has been interpreted in very different ways. Article II opens with the sweeping statement: "The executive power shall be vested in a President." It enumerates a variety of powers and responsibilities of the President: commander-in-chief of the army and navy; making treaties; appointing heads of executive departments and judges subject to the advice and consent of the Senate; giving Congress information about the state of the Union; and taking care that laws are faithfully executed (see appendix). As a leading student of the subject emphasizes, the Constitution leaves the President a lot of room for maneuver.

> Article II is the most loosely drawn chapter of the Constitution. To those who think that a constitution ought to settle everything beforehand, it should be a nightmare; by the same token, to those who think that constitution-makers ought to leave considerable leeway for the future play of political forces, it should be a vision realized. (Corwin, 1957:3)

The constitutional formulas describing the President's office have not altered in two centuries, but the practice of the Presidency has altered greatly. Constitutional grants of authority are broad enough to cover the actions of a modern or a postmodern President, yet they have been interpreted so narrowly as to confine politicians to the role of a do-nothing President. Because the Constitution leaves so much open to debate, a contemporary President can justify his actions by choosing, among several contrasting constitutional interpretations, the one that suits his immediate political needs.

Development of the Traditional Presidency

As the first President, George Washington faced the challenge of establishing a completely unprecedented system of government in a world of monarchies, ineffectual principalities, and despotisms. The institutions at hand were minimal. There were only four government departments, State, War, Treasury, and the Attorney Generalship; activities were conducted in temporary accommodation in New York City; and Congress alternated between meeting in New York and Philadelphia while waiting for the capital to be built in the new District of Columbia. As the victorious general of the Revolution, George Washington brought great personal prestige and authority to the task of inventing the Presidency. By the end of President James Madison's term in 1816, the government had demonstrated its effectiveness, collecting federal taxes from citizens who had fought against taxation by

England, securing recognition of the new republic by European monarchs, and defending American soil against invasion by British troops in the War of 1812. Yet the government that did this was so small that when public papers were packed for shipment from New York to the new national capital on the Potomac, they could be contained in seven packing cases (Cunliffe, 1982, 1987; Ketcham, 1984).

The *traditional* Presidency was intended to be a do-nothing office because the Founding Fathers were on guard against an autocratic monarch or an authoritarian leader in the style of Napoleon. Congress, not the White House, was considered the representative of the people's will and the directing agency of government. The primary responsibility of the President was to see that acts of Congress were faithfully executed. Men whose names today mean little — John Tyler, Franklin Pierce, Rutherford B. Hayes, and Chester Arthur — had no difficulty in filling the Presidency, for the President was not expected to do much. Presidents who tried to play an active role stirred up controversy because the very idea of an active President was considered inconsistent with the dignity and nature of the office. Abraham Lincoln respected the doctrines of the traditional Presidency, invoking war powers on a temporary basis only, when challenged to act by the secession of Southern states. After the Civil War, the Presidency continued as before, an inconsequential position for inconsequential men.

The traditional do-nothing Presidency lasted for more than a century because there was very little that the White House needed or was expected to do; the prevailing doctrine was that the best government governed least. Washington's resources were few, whether judged in terms of tax revenues, personnel, or institutions. Politics was truly local. The public services that concerned people, such as education, police, and fire protection, were delivered locally, sometimes by part-time public officials and sometimes by private agencies acting in the public interest (Hall, 1982). The federal government's job was to stand guard on the nation's shores in the event of invasion and to maintain the financial credit of the federal government by economical taxing and spending policies.

The basic principle of America's nineteenth-century foreign policy was declared in George Washington's Farewell Address: Avoid entangling alliances with foreign nations. The Atlantic was an ocean barrier between America and Europe. In 1823, following the revolt of Latin American nations from Spanish and Portuguese colonial rule, the President's pronouncement of the Monroe Doctrine defined the Western Hemisphere as America's sphere of interest. In doing so President Monroe also limited America's international interests to an area remote from Europe. Immigrants who fled from autocratic European regimes welcomed isolation. Isolation was a practical policy, since slow transportation and communication made America distant from the centers of world power. European nations did not seek American intervention. The great Prussian Chancellor, Otto von Bismarck, viewed America's isolation sardonically: "God looks after fools, drunkards, and the United States of America."

For most of the history of the United States, the President has abstained from foreign affairs. In the first century of America's existence, only two foreign heads of state visited America: King Kalakaua of Hawaii and the Emperor Dom Pedro II of Brazil (Plischke: 1971, 1985). Until the beginning of the twentieth century, no President had ever traveled abroad while in office; it was even argued that the President lacked the legal authority to travel abroad. While the White House was occasionally compelled to negotiate with foreign powers, this was regarded as an exception to the usual practice of avoiding entanglement with foreign nations

At home, the westward expansion, the rise of industry, and the influx of immigrants did not challenge the traditional Presidency, for government's role remained very limited. Federal taxing and spending did not pass the $100 million mark until the Civil War, and did not reach the billion-dollar level until World War I. The income tax did not become effective until the ratification of the Sixteenth Amendment to the Constitution in 1913. The federal government spent less than 3 percent of the national product in 1902; two-thirds of public spending was undertaken by state and local governments. Throughout the nineteenth century, the federal government employed less than 1 percent of the nation's labor force. When Herbert Hoover was inaugurated President in 1929, federal employees constituted only 1.8 percent of the labor force (U.S. Bureau of the Census, 1960: chap. Y; Austin, 1986: chap. 6; Peters, 1985: tables 7.1-2).

Congress was the dominant force in the federal government. Congressmen did not want the President interfering in what they regarded as their responsibilities for giving direction to government. From Thomas Jefferson to the retirement of William Howard Taft, the President was not expected to deliver in person his constitutionally mandated annual State of the Union message to Congress. To do so would have suggested the pretension of a monarch's speech from the throne to Parliament. Parties dominated electoral politics, and party bosses taught aspiring politicians that politics is local. Presidential nominating conventions were national meetings of local barons. Like their medieval counterparts, these barons preferred a weak monarch at the head of government. In 1885 the youthful Woodrow Wilson published a scholarly critique of what he described as *Congressional Government*. When he left the White House a broken man in 1921, Wilson still had cause to lament the powers of Congress over the President, for his efforts to make the Presidency an active force were frustrated by Congress.

The Constitution was interpreted as imposing strict limitations on what a President could do. William Howard Taft, President from 1909 until 1913, summarized the prevalent doctrine of the President as a chief magistrate, responsible for carrying out the law and lacking the authority to do anything not specifically authorized or implied by the Constitution.

The true view of the Executive function is, as I conceive it, that the President can exercise no power which cannot be fairly and reasonably traced to some specific grant of power or justly implied and included within such express grant as proper and necessary to its exercise. Such specific grant must be either in the Federal Constitution or in an Act of Congress passed in pursuance thereof. There is no undefined residuum of power which he can exercise because it seems to him to be in the public interest (Taft, 1916: 139f).

To prove that he did not think the White House the zenith of a Washington career, in 1921 Taft was happy to accept appointment as Chief Justice of the United States.

Because the President had so little to do, he had no need of a large entourage. In the early 1900s a young reporter, Louis Brownlow, entered through the open White House front door looking for someone to give him information for a minor story; the only person he could find at home was the President himself. The relatively active Woodrow Wilson spent only three or four hours a day on the business of the Presidency. Calvin Coolidge expressed his commitment to the principle of a do-nothing Presidency by publicizing that he slept eleven of every twenty-four hours that he was in the White House (Hoover, 1934: 266, 268). In keeping with customs of local politics, up to the 1930s the President hosted a New Year's Day reception. Any Washingtonian could walk along to the White House to exchange best wishes and a handshake with the President.

Creating the Modern Presidency

The doctrine of the modern Presidency expresses a fundamental shift in political expectations in the White House, in Congress, and in public opinion. By contrast with the traditional Presidency, the modern President is expected to

1. Propose legislation and make budget recommendations to Congress, and secure congressional endorsement of his proposals.

2. Be active in defending and advancing America's interests abroad.

3. Be a visible national leader, projecting personality and ideas through the media.

4. Command the political and national resources to meet these expectations.

The modern Presidency effectively dates from Franklin D. Roosevelt's inauguration in 1933 (Greenstein, 1988). The stimulus to change was great: America was suffering from the Great Depression, and President Herbert Hoover believed that his job was to prevent the government from spending money to combat it. By contrast, President Roosevelt believed that government should act to stimulate economic recovery and that the White House should take the lead in doing so. The failure of the Hoover administration created conditions in which Congress was willing to try anything that might alleviate the depression. After four years spent opposing the constitutionality of major Roosevelt policies, the Supreme Court accepted that actions of a modern President were within the Constitution. While the modern Presidency was initially a response to domestic problems, from 1939 onward the Roosevelt administration faced the threat of world war. The Japanese attack on Pearl Harbor in 1941, followed by German and Italian declarations of war on the United States, committed the White House to a world role. By 1945, America was the dominant military power from Tokyo to the gates of Berlin. Instead of being a spectator in world affairs, the President was suddenly the central figure of the Big Three, courted by both Winston Churchill and Joseph Stalin.

The Roosevelt administration started a process that has transformed the resources of the federal government. In the 1920s, Washington spent less than 4 percent of the national product; by 1936, this figure had doubled; and World War II temporarily expanded federal spending to 45 percent of the national product. Peacetime spending has since grown under Republican as well as Democratic Presidents because of continuing statutory commitments to social security and health care, political commitments to a large military force, and the expectations of tens of millions of beneficiaries. Since 1953, federal spending has never been less than one-sixth of the national product and at times has approached one-quarter.

The modern President's resources for influencing public opinion have grown too. Initially, efforts were concentrated on influencing opinion in Washington; addressing opinion nationwide was a secondary concern. President Roosevelt made only occasional use of radio fireside chats, and his press conferences were informal discussions without tape recorders, photographs, or direct quotation of what he said. President Kennedy started the practice of televised press conferences, speaking directly to the electorate over the heads of questioning reporters. Political changes in Washington and in the nation, even more than changes in the technology of mass communication, have given the President great scope for appealing to public opinion for support that he can use to influence Congress to act as the White House wants (Kernell, 1986).

As resources have grown, so expectations of the President have grown. What was exceptional before FDR has become normal since. A President is now an active political leader in Washington and the nation. Congressmen look to the White House for leadership in the annual State of the Union address and the annual budget message. Congress may not vote in favor of what the President proposes, but no one on Capitol Hill questions the duty of the President to lead in legislation and in the budget. A President can try to influence events directly by lobbying Congress or by appealing to the mass public for support. Even a President inclined toward laissez-faire government finds the expectations of the Presidency are such that "nowadays he cannot be as small as he might like" (Neustadt, 1960: 5).

In one important respect the modern Presidency has been like the traditional Presidency: The power of the President is assumed to be determined by what happens within the United States. Furthermore, the President is thought to be more powerful abroad than at home because he is subject to fewer domestic checks when acting in the international arena. The President can claim the authority of head of state and commander-in-chief of the armed forces, committing American troops to action when and where he believes proper. The Supreme Court has put few checks on the war powers of the President, and Congress has grudgingly accepted that the President's effective authority is much greater in foreign policy than at home (cf. Frank and Weisband, 1979). In discussions of the Presidency, the influence of foreign nations on foreign policy is usually ignored or dismissed. It is argued that "few nations have latitude for independent economic action comparable to that of the United States...American decisions are constrained less by demonstrable realities than by beliefs" (May 1987: 38f).

Modern Presidents have invariably put foreign policy first; they have differed only in the extent to which they have paid attention to domestic issues as well (Kessel, 1974). Harry Truman's claim to greatness is based on his authorship of the Truman Doctrine, pledging the United States to defend Greece and Turkey against the threat of Soviet aggression; the promotion of the Marshall Plan to restore the economy of war-ravaged Europe; the creation of the North Atlantic Treaty Organization (NATO) to provide for the common defense of Western Europe and the United States; and the extension to Korea of the frontiers that America was committed to defend. While Dwight D. Eisenhower showed limited interest in promoting change in domestic policy, in the international field he ended the Korean war, kept the United States from becoming involved in war in French Indochina (subsequently known as Vietnam), and initiated the first postwar summit meeting with a Soviet leader.

John F. Kennedy and Richard M. Nixon agreed about one thing: Foreign affairs came first. President Kennedy reckoned that he spent four-fifths of his first year in office on foreign policy issues (Cronin, 1980: 146). He experienced a great failure at the opening of his Presidency, approving a plan to invade Cuba that ended in disaster at the Bay of Pigs. The following year he scored a great success, acting as commander-in-chief to prevent the placing of Russian missiles in Cuba. Lyndon Johnson entered office with domestic politics his primary interest; but after two years of promoting Great Society and civil rights programs he became enmeshed in the Vietnam war. President Nixon was more single-minded in his concern with foreign affairs. With the assistance of Henry Kissinger, Nixon carried out strategies that sometimes succeeded, such as the restoration of diplomatic relations with China, and sometimes failed, as in wars in Southeast Asia. Even though Gerald Ford entered the Presidency without any experience in foreign affairs, within three months he found himself in Siberia, discussing nuclear arms control with Soviet leader Leonid Brezhnev. The following year, the first summit meeting of Western leaders was held, with Ford representing the United States.

While the development of a global role for the modern President was hailed as evidence of the President's power, this was so only as long as America remained the hegemonic power dominating the international system. A President can order troops to defend regimes on other continents only as long as the United States has the effective military power to maintain order abroad. The White House can benefit from wealth only as long as the American economy has the money to lend or give to other nations. When President Kennedy in his inaugural address boasted that he would "pay any price" to advance American aims, he assumed that the United States had the money and the military might to do so. That era is now part of the past.

The Postmodern Presidency

The defining characteristic of the postmodern President is simply stated: *The resources of the White House are not sufficient to meet all of the President's international responsibilities.*

In order to succeed, the President now needs the freely given cooperation of foreign nations. The White House retains the attributes of the modern Presidency, but in a changing world these resources are no longer adequate. A postmodern President cannot secure success simply by influencing Congress and public opinion; the President must also influence leaders of other nations and events in the international system.

A postmodern President no longer enjoys isolation from other nations, whereas a traditional President could ignore the great powers of Europe, and a modern President could offer American leadership on terms that other nations were too weak to reject. Today, other major nations have gained strength. European nations that were destitute and demoralized by war when Harry Truman was President are now prosperous and politically much more confident. The Russians have developed weapons systems to counter the armory of the Pentagon and sophisticated diplomacy to advance their interests worldwide. Japan has spectacularly demonstrated that Asian nations can compete economically with America and can often win. The Organization of Petroleum Exporting Countries (OPEC) has found a way to hold the world to economic ransom for its oil.

The global scope of America's political commitments makes the White House vulnerable to troubles elsewhere. In Central America, old-fashioned gunboat diplomacy cannot secure White House aims. American-backed regimes are sometimes overthrown and American-backed guerrillas are not always successful. South American nations such as Brazil and Argentina have converted their debt into problems for the American banks that have loaned them money without adequate security. African colonies have achieved independence in international law and are now free to exploit America,

Russia, and international organizations in search of money and military equipment. The Middle East is a cauldron that can scald Americans when it boils over.

The emergence of the postmodern Presidency reflects a process of change in the postwar international system. While President Kennedy had global aspirations, he soon learned that the powers of the White House were not unlimited. At the mid-term of his Presidency, he told an interviewer:

> There is a limitation upon the ability of the United States to solve problems. We are involved now in the Congo in a very difficult situation. We have been unable to secure an implementation of the policy which we have supported. We are involved in a good many other areas. We are trying to see if a solution can be found to the struggle between Pakistan and India, with whom we want to maintain friendly relations. Yet they are unable to come to an agreement. There is a limitation upon the power of the United States to bring about solutions. (Quoted in Hirschfield, 1973: 134)

We cannot say that a particular President lost the modern Presidency, for such a statement assumes that the United States could have prevented other nations from growing in strength in order to maintain America's hegemony permanently. As Calleo (1987: 216) notes, "America's diminishing capacity to control events unilaterally results not from the failure of American postwar policy, but from its success." American efforts to revive the world economy and build new mutual security alliances have contributed to conditions in which other nations have prospered too.

The Vietnam war heralded the arrival of the postmodern Presidency. Everyone — from Saigon and Hanoi to the ordinary citizen on Main Street — could see that this was a war to which the White House was committed. Whereas President Truman's dispatch of troops to defend South Korea was a success, efforts by Kennedy, Johnson, Nixon, and Ford to defend South Vietnam finally met defeat. The Vietnam war also had important economic consequences. Financing the Vietnam war through a guns and butter fiscal policy caused inflation at home and finally a collapse of the Bretton Woods system of fixed exchange rates based on the dollar. We now live in an era in which the dollar is an international problem currency. In the world recession of 1975 America's national product actually contracted. The interdependence of advanced economies was recognized in 1975 by the first world summit of leaders from America, Britain, Canada, France, Germany, Italy, and Japan.

The transition from the modern to the postmodern Presidency is now complete. The United States can no longer dominate the world economy or use force to impose its will on every continent. Jimmy Carter has the unenviable distinction of being the first completely postmodern President. The Carter administration was upset by inflation at home, oil price rises, the seizure of Americans as hostages in the Middle East, and the Soviet Union's

invasion of Afghanistan. In retrospect, the problems of the Carter administration appear less a reflection on the man in the Oval Office and more as
symptoms of a structural shift from the modern to a postmodern President.*

The achievements and shortcomings of the Reagan Presidency illustrate
the critical difference between the modern and the postmodern Presidency.
In domestic politics President Reagan has been hailed for showing that the
Presidency was still "possible,"that is, a skillful politician could secure major
legislation from Congress, such as the 1981 and 1986 tax acts, and win reelection with an increased majority in 1984 (cf. Greenstein, 1983; Salamon
and Lund, 1985). Success is defined in terms of legislative and election
victories. A postmodern President must also be evaluated by his performance in the international system. President Reagan's successes, like his
failures, have depended on the response of other nations to White House
initiatives. The arms-control accord with the Soviet Union is a textbook
example of interdependence, for negotiations have succeeded to the extent
that the interests of the General Secretary of the Communist party of the
Soviet Union are in harmony with the interests of the President. Other
international events display the frustrations of the postmodern Presidency.
While American force was effective in Grenada (population 88,000), American arms and aid have not been able to secure White House aims in Nicaragua (population 2.9 million), even though the President has used novel
means to provide aid to the *contra* guerrillas there. The American economy
has boomed, but it has depended on foreign borrowing to finance the big
federal deficits created by tax cuts and massive trade deficits.

The President inaugurated on 20 January 1989 will inherit much more
than the powers of the modern Presidency. He will also be subject to the
traditional checks and balances of the Constitution. Many Americans still
put local politics first, and expect their member of Congress to do likewise.
Yet the pressures of the international system have been growing stronger.
The next President would like to dominate the international system, but
leaders of other nations from Moscow and Bonn to Teheran and Tokyo will
gradually teach him that this cannot be done. The Oval Office occupant must
learn to accept the limitations of the postmodern Presidency.

Learning to Live with Other Elephants

A generation ago the President had a trump card in dealing with foreign
nations: to act as if they were not there. Europeans characterized this with the

---

* Skowronek (1984: 114) similarly sees Carter as a President who had the misfortune to
take office at the final stage of an "enervated regime," ready to be superseded by another
regime. Skowronek's review of recurring cycles in the Presidency ignores changes in America's
place in the world, as if Carter's problems could be compared with those of Franklin Pierce.

saying: Having America as an ally is like being in bed with an elephant. Mammoth military and economic force gave the United States a unique displacement in the international system. When American foreign policy altered or the economy turned over unexpectedly, everyone else in the bed had to move quickly or risk being crushed accidentally by the American behemoth. The White House was confident of the global impact of its actions; no other nation was reckoned capable of countering the influence of the United States. This was recognized abroad too. When John F. Kennedy was assassinated, a leading British commentator, Bernard Levin, proclaimed to millions of British television viewers: "The President of the United States is the President of Britain."

Today, remarks are sometimes made as if nothing had changed. A distinguished Harvard diplomatic historian can declare, "Because of the size and power of the country, Presidents of the United States are able in unique degree to act to affect significantly the lives of people in other countries... relatively free from constraints imposed by other governments" (May, 1987: 41). It is suggested that foreigners might be given the right to make campaign contributions to presidential candidates in order to have a voice, though not a vote in choosing their (sic) leader. Other analysts are worried that too much has changed. The Carnegie Endowment for International Peace celebrated its seventy-fifth anniversary by commissioning a study of *Estrangement*, asking: "Are we caught in a system not of our own making, enmeshed in the webs and biases and disappointing reactions of others?" (Ungar, 1985: xi).

Whatever a postmodern President would like to believe, he soon recognizes that there are now few problems of significance to him that can be resolved by unilateral American action. The traditional President did not need to bargain with anyone, for his was a do-nothing role. The modern President had to bargain with Congress, for active White House leadership required the active support of Congress. The postmodern President must also bargain with leaders of other nations, for his success in an interdependent world depends on measures taken in a number of national capitals. For example, White House efforts to prevent domestic interest rates from rising require other nations to regard American economic policy as worth supporting in their national interest.

While the traditional President did not participate in the international system and the modern President could dominate it, the postmodern President has no choice but to cooperate and compete, since economic and national security problems are not contained within national boundaries. There is nothing novel in this challenge. Leaders of other democratic nations long ago learned the basic fact of life: To succeed in an interdependent world requires watching the rest of the world as well as one's own country. Treasury officials in many lands recognize that the prosperity of their national economy is affected by whether the world economy is booming or in recession. When America dominated the international system alone, other governments waited for Washington to act before making their own decisions.

Competition is inevitable. Common interests can sometimes encourage cooperation, as in the NATO military alliance. But cooperation is not always easy to achieve, even among allies, for the leaders of Britain, France, Germany, and Japan have *their* nation's interest at heart. The President can ask the Japanese Prime Minister to lower trade barriers in the interest of American exporters, but why should a Japanese Prime Minister agree to jeopardize the livelihood of millions of farmers who vote for his party by lowering barriers to the import of American farm produce? As Putnam and Bayne (1987: 12) conclude: "The fruits of contemporary interdependence are bittersweet, for it fosters foreign interference in matters once reserved for domestic decisions."

Competition is continuous, for the President must deal every day with leaders of foreign nations. The President is involved in bilateral meetings with heads of state who come to Washington from every continent. The President is involved in an annual summit meeting with heads of major friendly governments, and months are spent preparing and following up its agenda. Summit meetings with Soviet leaders are less frequent because they involve very important security concerns, and misunderstandings, such as at the 1986 Reykjavik summit, are disturbing. In a world of "crazy states" (Dror, 1980), many countries, small and large, can unexpectedly seize the attention of the White House.

In an interdependent world, the old political saying—How will this play in Peoria?—needs to be placed in a much wider setting. Today, a President must think not only about how a policy will play in Paris, Illinois, but also in Paris, France; in Tokio, Texas as well as Tokyo, Japan, and in the Moscow Kremlin as well as in the bowling alleys of Moscow, Idaho. One of President Reagan's press secretaries, Larry Speakes (1987), got it half right when he said that at every White House meeting there should be someone asking how a decision will play on the TV news and the next morning's newspapers. His error was limiting his thoughts to ABC, the *New York Times* and the *Wall Street Journal*. The White House press secretary forgot the BBC (British Broadcasting Corporation), the German *Frankfurter Allgemeine Zeitung*, and *Asahi Shimbun* in Tokyo.

The great challenge to the postmodern President is to be both responsive and effective. Responsiveness to a national electorate does not guarantee international effectiveness, for the qualities required to be elected President are not relevant to international success. Americans may think that a presidential candidate who frequently smiles is personable and may vote for a friendly face. A foreign leader may decide that a smiling face is the mark of inexperience or gullibility, and try to take advantage of a President. Americans may think that a President who talks about the need to defend the nation's economic interests abroad is saying the right thing. But a German or a Japanese Prime Minister has his country's economic interests to defend too.

Exchange is the normal form of politics in an interdependent world. Exchange can be profitable for all concerned when it involves buyers and sellers in the marketplace. It can express agreement, as in the conclusion of diplomatic negotiations. Or it can involve threats or violence, as in exchanges in the Middle East. A President knows that bargaining is an integral part of political exchange, for the White House is always bargaining with Congress, executive agencies, and interest groups. The novelty of the postmodern Presidency is that the White House must increasingly bargain with foreigners who run governments, central banks, or control hostages. A postmodern President may not welcome being in such a hot spot, but as President Truman once remarked: "If you can't stand the heat, stay out of the kitchen."

2. The Imperatives of the Presidency

A President's priorities are set not by the relative importance of a task, but by the relative necessity for him to do it. His time remains the prisoner of first-things-first. And almost always, something else comes first.

—Richard E. Neustadt

The President today faces three imperatives. In order to hold office, the President needs popular support. In order to direct government, he must influence other powerholders in Washington. To maintain America's national security and the economy, the President must influence the international system. Each imperative is a response to a different political audience. Going Washington is about village politics; the nation's capital is an intimate community continuously assessing its members. Going public has a TV audience, for the electronic media are the prime means by which a President campaigns for popular support. Going international addresses a global audience; space satellites and the jet airplane are the principal means of communication.

Imperatives concentrate attention politically and analytically. This is desirable because the President has many very different roles to play, some major and many that are minor. One scholar has enumerated forty-three different activities that the Oval Office can be involved in (Bailey,1966). Given so many competing claims for attention, a President must ration his time so that he can put first things first. The three concerns examined here are imperatives because a President *must* go Washington, go public, and go international. Otherwise, his political career, the country, or both are wiped out. Other studies enumerating roles of the President emphasize much the same imperatives (Rossiter, 1956; Corwin, 1957; Koenig, 1975; Seligman, 1980; Tatalovich and Daynes, 1984).

An imperative tells a President what he must do—boost his rating in the public opinion polls, win agreement with Congress, or keep the Russians from introducing arms into a previously neutral nation. But it does not tell him how to achieve these aims. In order to do this, we need models of presidential action, that is, systematic outlines of the way in which the President responds to imperatives. The models in the following pages outline what the President can do to influence public opinion, strike bargains in Washington, or influence international events. Whereas an analysis of roles restricts attention to what the President does, these models emphasize what is expected to happen as a result of presidential action.

On a day-to-day basis, the President's priorities are often not of his own choosing; the President is the prisoner of first things first. Many priorities are set by action-forcing dates: elections, summit meetings with foreign leaders, deadlines for the annual budget or State of the Union message to Congress, and so forth. Events can force the President to drop everything, if there is a threat of war in the Middle East, the loss of his popularity at home, or a bill on Capitol Hill. Outbursts of trouble are so frequent that Neustadt (1960: 155) concludes: "Trying to stop fires is what Presidents do first. It takes most of their time." Because a President has three different imperatives, this chapter looks at each in turn and then considers how the President can juggle all of them simultaneously.

Going Washington

Washington was once a small, closed community. Congressmen ate, drank, and slept together in boardinghouses, and sometimes voted as boarding-house blocs (Young, 1966). In many ways it is still a small community whose members depend on one another for success, though its commitments are now global in scope. Every politician is very conscious that there are others with whom he must bargain in order to achieve his own political ends. Since no one can alone determine what government does, every Washingtonian deals, as a matter of course, with friends, neighbors, and opponents in order to get things done.

A newly-elected President finds himself in an office that is only one of three separate branches of government. Whereas the decisions of a British Prime Minister and Cabinet effectively bind Parliament and the courts, a President cannot bind coequal branches of government. As Neustadt (1960: 33) emphasizes, the President cannot act alone, for the Constitution "created a government of separated institutions sharing powers."

The Washington community, as seen from the Oval Office, can be represented in a simple model of going Washington.* In order to strike a successful bargain with other powerholders in Washington, the President must influence Congress, the bureaucracy, and interest groups which collectively constitute the subgovernments of Washington (see figure 2.1). Congress is important because it can enact or refuse to enact the laws needed to authorize new programs; it appropriates money for existing as well as new programs; and its committees have oversight of actions by the executive

---

*This model reflects the inspiration of Richard Neustadt's classic study of *Presidential Power*, but it cannot present that author's complex outlook, best examined in Neustadt (1960, 1980); and discussed by critics (cf. Sperlich, 1975; Cronin, 1980: 121ff; Kernell, 1986: 14ff).

branch. Career bureaucrats must be influenced because they have much of the expertise required to develop new programs and respond to problems that concern the White House. High-ranking bureaucrats also work closely with the congressional committees overseeing their work. Interest groups cannot be ignored by the White House because they are listened to in Congress and by bureaucrats in executive branch agencies.

The intended outcome of going Washington is a *bargain among power-holders*. Bargains result from actions by Congress, by bureaucrats, and by interest groups as well as by the White House. Insofar as each has something that is needed for agreement, each gets a piece of the action. No one—including the President—is able to get everything that he wants; the bargaining process requires each person to yield concessions as the price of obtaining agreement. A President may launch a proposal with ambitious hopes, but the process of Washington politics whittles away at what the White House can obtain as more and more people must be cut into the deal to obtain support.

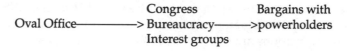

FIGURE 2.1

GOING WASHINGTON: THE PRESIDENT INSIDE THE BELTWAY

What is often described as the power of the President (as distinct from his legal competencies or powers) is actually his capacity to influence other institutions with whom he shares the authority of government. President Truman expressed clearly the importance of persuasion to the Presidency:

> The President may have a great many powers given to him in the Constitution and may have certain powers under certain laws which are given to him by the Congress of the United States, but the principal power that the President has is to bring people in and try to persuade them to do what they ought to do without persuasion. That's what the powers of the President amount to. (Truman, 1949: 247)

A President's ability to achieve a bargain on terms favorable to the White House is substantially influenced by previous success or failure. No one wants to be left out of a bargain with a successful President, just as no one wants to be committed to a President who has a reputation for backing losers.

To see the President's principal role as pursuing influence within Washington makes a political bargain an end in itself. While seeking consensus is reasonable in a system of shared powers, for a President to do nothing but seek consensus is an abdication of leadership (cf. Dahl, 1957). A President who simply wanted to secure agreement with Congress, bureaucrats, and pressure groups could adopt their measures as his own, without regard to his own preferences. If the White House is to influence a bargain, it must seek objectives that are not completely consensual, and use its influence to get others to agree to much of what the White House wants.

While the President has a large White House staff, only he can provide direction. Individual occupants of the White House differ in their way of dealing with Congress, but each must have a legislative strategy (Jones, 1983). Similarly, a President needs a strategy for dealing with the bureaucracy and with interest groups if he is to succeed in converting Oval Office intentions into bargains that commit the federal government to actions.

The first important assumption of this model is that Washington powerholders have a substantial leeway for bargaining. What happens inside the Washington Beltway is reckoned to be insulated from the pressures of public opinion. The views of the electorate as a whole are reckoned to give little positive direction to policy because most voters are not interested in or informed about issues of concern inside the Washington Beltway (Neuman, 1986). In such circumstances, elected representatives can advocate policies and strike bargains that reflect their own ideas of what voters will accept.

Second, going Washington assumes that powerholders are sufficiently few so that negotiations are easily conducted and everyone wants to reach agreements to keep the political poker game going. Each person is assumed able to deliver his share of a bargain. In a Congress where committee chairmen acted as barons, bargains were easy to strike because a chairman could deliver the votes of his committee.

Third, the model assumes that a President has no alternative to endless bargaining in the Washington community because others have what he needs. Congressmen vote on legislation, budget appropriations, and the confirmation of presidential appointees. Career bureaucrats are experts in the ways of their agency and have substantive knowledge about how programs work. Interest groups can deliver money needed for election campaigns, publicity in support of agreed policies, and trouble to politicians who oppose what they want.

Each of the foregoing assumptions about going Washington is less true today than it was a quarter-century ago. Public opinion outside Washington is far more readily mobilized by groups with an interest in an issue, and interest groups have the capacity to link evidence of popular support in the country with political activity inside the beltway. The media regularly report public opinion polls about controversial issues. For example, President Reagan's nomination of a conservative, Robert Bork, to the Supreme Court, was defeated in the Senate because Bork's opponents mobilized public pressure on senators to vote against his confirmation.

As power has fragmented in Congress, elite bargains are harder to put together. A veteran Washingtonian, former Secretary of State Dean Rusk, has described the change thus:

In the 1950s and 1960s we handled sensitive foreign affairs policy questions with the Congress by dealing with the "whales"—Rayburn, Vinson, men like that. They could make commitments. Now it is as if we were dealing with 535 minnows. (Quoted in Kernell, 1986: 49)

When economic problems are caused by trends in the world economy, there is even greater difficulty because there is no one there to bargain with. The movement of money and trade in the international economy is not determined in a few Oval Offices; it is determined in an international market with thousands of bargains being struck daily around the globe.

Going Public

The President now has an alternative to bargaining with other Washington powerholders. A White House faced with the prospect of fishing for the votes of hundreds of congressional minnows can turn to the publicity resources of the Oval Office to create public support for a proposal before it is discussed with Congress. If successful in this, a President need not bargain for votes; instead, members of Congress are forced to support a White House proposal by the tide of public opinion that the President has created. In international affairs, the President has prerogatives to act as commander-in-chief, moving troops into action anywhere on earth without first carrying a vote in Congress. Even if Congress does not like what the President does, it can voice complaints only after the fact.

The traditional doctrine was that a President should be seen but not heard, that is, he could superintend the executive branch of government, but not lecture Congress or the nation. It was thought that the President would be at a *dis*advantage in any appeal to the people because, as James Madison argued in *The Federalist Papers*, No. 49, he would be "personally known to a small part only of the people," whereas congressmen would be close to the voters in their district.

Twentieth-century Presidents have increasingly made the Presidency audible and visible, claiming that the White House speaks *to* the people on behalf of government and *for* the people in Washington. Theodore Roosevelt described the Presidency as a "bully pulpit." In 1913 Woodrow Wilson broke the custom of more than a century by delivering his State of the Union message to Congress in a well-publicized speech. Franklin D. Roosevelt produced twice as many words as Herbert Hoover in major public addresses in his first term of office, and Dwight D. Eisenhower doubled that figure again (Lammers, 1982). Today television has literally brought the Oval Office into the family room of every voter.

Going public—the President continuously publicizing himself and his views nationwide through the media—is now a necessary condition of a politician reaching the White House (Kernell, 1986). The decline in party organization and party identification means that the President is now on his own in running for the Presidency. Going public is also necessary between elections, so that a President can use public opinion to influence other powerholders in Washington too.

```
                    Press and              Public opinion and
    Oval Office———————>Broadcasting————————> Electoral behavior
                    Media
```

FIGURE 2.2

GOING PUBLIC: THE PRESIDENT IN THE NATIONAL MEDIA

When the President goes public, the goal is to influence public opinion, as measured by frequently reported opinion polls and periodic elections (see figure 2.2). The press and broadcasting media are the means to this end. The White House has no problem in securing publicity for the President; names make news and the President is the biggest name in Washington. In order to gain the maximum from the bully pulpit of the White House, the President today maintains a wide repertoire of staff resources, senior advisers whose primary expertise is in public relations. Ceaser et al. (1981: 165) note that the growth of speechwriters and publicists in the White House has created a paradox: "At a time when Presidents are judged more by their rhetoric, they play less of a role in its actual formulation."

Going public can be a political objective in itself, reducing governing to questions of media presentation, and altering the way in which the White House looks at national problems. Policies can be judged, not so much in terms of their intrinsic character, as in terms of their suitability for political marketing. In the words of Larry Speakes (1987), a press secretary to President Reagan: "It ain't good policy if the public won't buy it." In arguing for the press secretary to be involved in all major decisions, Speakes declared: "When we sit in the Situation Room in the White House and launch a policy initiative, let's judge it by how it would look if it showed up in tomorrow's headlines."

Going public can also be a part of a two-stage process of influencing powerholders in Washington (Kernell,1986: chap 2). As bargaining within the Beltway has become more difficult, it now makes sense for a President to go public *before* seeking to influence Congress. Since public opinion tends to be less informed and more suggestible than Washington opinion, it is far easier for a President to influence the public than to persuade experienced and knowledgeable Washingtonians. A President who rides high in public opinion can intimidate congressmen, or use public opinion polls taken after a White House media blitz as evidence that what the White House wants is also what the people want. If a President succeeds in this strategy, Washingtonians are reduced to watching a nationally televised spectacular. The visit of Soviet leader Mikhail Gorbachev to Washington in December 1987 to sign an arms-control agreement illustrates how the White House can stage a media event to disarm potential critics.

The Iran-*contra* affair illustrates how the President can appeal to public opinion rather than discuss issues with Congress. When news broke in November 1986 of the White House offering to swap arms for hostages in Iran and siphoning funds to *Contra* guerrillas in Central America, the wisdom or the legality of the action was deemed less important than the impact of the event on public esteem for the President. Reagan's approval rating dropped from 63 percent in the Gallup poll, just before the news broke in November, to 40 percent by February. The White House fought back, seeking means to make the President look "presidential," that is, appear in command of the government. Once televised hearings commenced, the media interpreted testimony in the light of public opinion polls about popular reactions to witnesses. Lieutenant Colonel Oliver North realized that his sworn testimony should not be directed toward convincing Congress, but at public opinion nationwide. His arguments in favor of the arms-for-*contra* mission were directed past congressional questioners to the TV audience. The media responded by commissioning opinion polls to measure the extent of his success.

The underlying assumption of the White House in going public is that presidential activities favorably influence public opinion. But this assumption is often wrong. Public opinion reflects many influences besides the words and actions of the President: fluctuations up and down in the economy, unexpected international events, and the exposure of scandals in the White House. A President who relies on opinion polls as proof of success is handling a double-edged sword. When the President's popularity is high or rising, the President benefits from increased influence over others in Washington. But when his popularity is low or falling, his influence will wane, and other powerholders in Washington will react against what an unpopular President wants (see chapter 13).

Foreign leaders have much less reason than congressmen to be impressed by polls of American public opinion, for they must respond to their own citizens. They do not expect an American President to worry about their problems in winning reelection in Britain, France, Germany, or Japan. Whatever the level of the President's popularity, foreign leaders are concerned first and foremost with their standing with publics that are foreign to the White House.

Going International

Governing is about being President as well as appearing presidential. A contemporary President must do more than bargain with other Washingtonians and influence American public opinion. A President must also go international, that is, participate actively in the politics of an open international system. A President can no longer do his job simply by staying at home. Whereas Herbert Hoover spent only three days abroad in his term of office and Franklin Roosevelt spent only nine days abroad in his first term, Richard Nixon spent fifty-nine days abroad in his first four years in office, and Jimmy Carter fifty-six days (Lammers, 1982: 160; Plischke, 1971: 755ff).

The reasons for the President's going international are rooted in politics and policy. Peace and prosperity are the central concerns of the Oval Office, and achieving these goals today requires international cooperation. The Vietnam war made evident links between domestic politics and foreign policy, and the budget deficit and the trade deficit show that there is no sharp distinction between domestic and international problems. Aaron Wildavsky once argued that the President's greater constitutional authority in foreign policy created two Presidencies, one for domestic affairs and one for international affairs. But this distinction is no longer tenable. For example, two of the four issues that Wildavsky (1975a: table 1) cited as domestic—natural resources and agriculture—are critically influenced by international supply and demand factors, and a third, labor, is now linked to America's trade in the world economy (see Peppers, 1975; Le Loup and Shull, 1979). In an open international system, the President must influence what happens in other countries because what happens abroad affects what happens at home.

When a President goes international, he is confronted by leaders of other sovereign states. Instead of speaking with the media, agency bureaucrats or members of Congress, the President engages in a dialogue between the White House and other Oval Offices (see figure 2.3). A President may not think that other nations' interests and policies are as important as American interests and policies, but foreign leaders can also give priority to their national concerns. Just as the White House is trying to make the American system work, so heads of foreign governments are trying to make the British, the German, the Japanese, the Soviet, or the Iranian system work. Agreement depends on a coincidence of interests between different countries.

The number of Oval Offices in the world has increased greatly since 1945. Of the 142 countries with which the United States has diplomatic relations today, more than half were not in existence or recognized by the United States before World War II (Austin, 1986: table 4.1). The President must pay attention to heads of governments scattered across every continent. In doing this, he is reflecting the concerns of the American public. More than half the American people think that the United States has vital interests in Europe (especially Britain, France, and Germany); the Middle East (Israel, Saudi Arabia, Egypt, and Iran); South Africa; Asia (Japan, China, Taiwan, the Philippines, and South Korea); and Latin America (Mexico and Nicaragua). Looming over nearly all these countries is the relation between the White House and the Kremlin (Rielly, 1987: table 3.1).

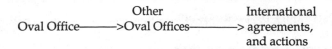

FIGURE 2. 3

GOING INTERNATIONAL:

THE PRESIDENT IN A GLOBAL SYSTEM

A new President is attracted by the prospect of going international, for the issues involved are of supreme importance; the President's powers are greater than in domestic policy, and dealing with world leaders is a welcome change from seeking votes in a primary state or from obdurate congressmen. However, a President soon learns that international politics can be even more frustrating than domestic politics. Foreign governments are sovereign powers, responding to influences very different from those that affect powerholders in Washington. Success is not so easily achieved when it depends on actions taken by foreign governments, corporations operating in international markets, and armed groups on many continents.

When dealing with allies—whether in NATO, in economic negotiations between central banks, or in world summit meetings—the White House starts from an assumption of common interests. But allies can differ about the best means of achieving common ends. For a decade the White House has sought to get Germany and Japan to alter economic policies to benefit the American economy, while the leaders of these nations have sought changes in American economic policy. Ironically, the Soviet Union's position as America's chief enemy strengthens the interdependence of the leaders of the two nations. If both are anxious to avoid a third world war, then each must avoid doing anything that would lead the other to launch a military Armageddon. The hotline telephone between the White House and the Kremlin is a symbol of the President's desire to maintain communication and of Soviet recognition that its success often depends on the American response to its initiatives.

A novel development of recent years is presidential concern with international troublespots where leaders do not want to talk to the White House, or there is no other Oval Office to talk with. Internal wars between states and foreign-backed insurrectionary groups concern the White House, but the chief participants often define the conflict as their own affair, and deny the White House opportunities for intervening in their civil war. Terrorist organizations are more interested in going public internationally by exploding bombs or kidnapping Americans than in conventional diplomatic discussions. The first problem of the President is to determine who, if anyone, can speak for terrorists, and whether or not it is advisable to negotiate with groups that are not governments in international law. There are also states such as Libya that have international recognition, but that deal with the

United States only by pressing nonbargainable demands or in unconventional ways.

When going international, the President claims to speak for the United States as a whole, but he knows how difficult it can be to deliver: "Ongoing disunity within the executive branch is one of the conspicuous hallmarks of American diplomacy" (Crabb and Mulcahy, 1986: 2). By contrast, in a parliamentary system the Prime Minister, the foreign secretary and the secretary of defense are bound by constitutional practice to enunciate a single line of policy abroad as well as at home. The only thing that an American secretary of state and secretary of defense are sure to share is the suspicion that their policies are being undercut by actions of the President's national security adviser (see chapter 11).

While going international, a President must continue to be concerned with Washington and with public opinion. If a negotiation culminates in a treaty, the White House has the task of selling it to the Senate, for a treaty requires approval by two-thirds of the Senate to become valid. If a President sends troops into action, he must worry about hostile statements by Congress and opinion polls, as well as about what happens when American troops meet an enemy. While every national leader must respond to domestic political pressures, the President is unique in the degree to which success in going international depends on what happens at home. The result is aptly summed up by Neustadt (1960: 3) as "emergencies in policy with politics as usual."

Juggling Imperatives

While each imperative requires White House attention, the relative significance of imperatives varies through time. A President has always had to go Washington in order to ensure that acts of Congress were faithfully executed. Until World War I, going Washington was both necessary and sufficient. The modern Presidency flourished as the White House expanded its scope by going public and going international. The postmodern President has increasingly been concerned with going international, but doing so is more difficult when the United States is no longer the only elephant in the international system.

Within a four-year term of office, the attention required by different imperatives tends to vary with the political calendar. There is an incentive to go Washington at the start of a term, using public support generated during the election campaign as a resource to prod Congress to adopt White House proposals during the President's initial honeymoon period. In his second year, the President is familiar enough with international routines to begin taking initiatives, or is forced to respond to the initiatives of other nations.

Mid-term elections make congressmen more than usually sensitive to public opinion. In the third year, a President must continue to go international and influence Washington while seeking to boost public support to frighten off potentially embarrassing challengers in primary contests, and to prepare a campaign for reelection (cf. Rockman, 1984: chapter 4; Quandt, 1986).

Within each year there is a cycle of action-forcing events demanding presidential attention. In late autumn and early winter the President concentrates on bargaining with other powerholders in preparation for his State of the Union address to Congress, proposing new legislation, and budget recommendations about federal expenditures. In late winter and spring the President promotes these policy proposals, going public and bargaining with the Hill. International affairs have a cyclical element too. The annual summit meeting of Western leaders in June requires preparatory activities in late winter and spring. Annual gatherings each fall at the United Nations in New York and the International Monetary Fund in Washington require planning for routine and nonroutine discussions.

Each of the President's days is full, starting with early morning meetings with White House staff, followed by meetings with other officials in the executive branch, telephone or face-to-face discussions with members of Congress, more internal staff meetings, public appearances or photo opportunities for the media, and calls from a variety of people outside the Washington Beltway (see table 8.1). The day ends with the President receiving a stack of papers to read before he falls asleep, before returning to action the next morning.

While a historian can retrospectively identify how the President has allocated his attention between priorities, the challenge to the President is prospective: to juggle competing imperatives as they arise, often unexpectedly and sometimes in unpleasant ways. As an experienced management consultant said of the White House: "This is the sort of place where everything hits the fan *before* 9 o'clock in the morning." A President has two ways to deal with multiple imperatives: keeping them separate by compartmentalization or linking responses in an effort to take charge.

Compartmentalization

One way to deal with many problems is to place each in a separate compartment, just as a juggler keeps only one ball in his hand at a time and others in the air. In the course of a day, a President will do many different things. In the absence of any reason to link these activities, each can be treated independently of the others. A President can be going international at a 9 o'clock morning meeting with his national security assistant; going Washington in a 10 o'clock phone call to a congressman; and going public in an 11 o'clock photo session with a popular celebrity. The likelihood of a President being able to compartmentalize a problem depends on three principal determinants:

1. *Autonomy of constituencies.* In order for a President to keep problems separate, the affected interests must be confined to a single constituency. Some public relations activities have narrow constituencies, for example, an association receiving a Rose Garden commendation that confers status on it. Even when an issue is controversial, for example, a dispute between senators from two states about where to locate a new federal installation, this can be compartmentalized if the agency concerned is relatively indifferent, and the support of the senators is not critical to other issues.

2. *Staff involvement.* Every problem that comes to the President is staffed out, that is, one or more units in the White House give the President background information, identify opportunities and pitfalls and supply options for response. Because the White House is organized into a large number of small units, the potential for involvement is very large. Most units confine their activities to a more or less well defined turf, since staff time is limited and so is presidential readiness to listen. Everyone wants to get into the act when it affects his turf, and not to waste time on an issue when it does not.

3. *Independence of outcomes.* A President compartmentalizes responses to imperatives best when the outcome of each action is independent of other outcomes. An issue that is only a problem of congressional relations (e.g., the wounded vanity of a committee chairman) can receive a compartmentalized solution, for example, inviting the congressman to a prestigious White House dinner. When a congressman's complaint is about a White House legislative proposal that affects many different groups, the problem cannot so easily be compartmentalized. While a congressman may see increased foreign imports in terms of its impact on a factory in his district, the White House is likely to view it as part of an interrelated set of international economic questions affecting many countries and, through its impact on American consumers, affecting the President's public standing too.

Compartmentalization is not easy to achieve, for many problems that merit presidential attention come to the Oval Office for resolution because there is an international, a Washington, and a public opinion dimension. Whereas a President's press secretary, national security adviser, and congressional liaison person can each take a narrow view of an issue, the view from the Oval Office tends to dissolve lines compartmentalizing problems.

> The President sits in a unique seat and works within a unique frame of reference. The things he personally has to do are no respecters of the lines between civil and military or foreign and domestic or legislative and executive or administrative and political. At his desk—and there alone—distinctions of these sorts lose their last shred of meaning. (Neustadt, 1960: 183)

The fact that the President can see many sides to a single issue does not mean that he can treat all of them equally. A President must always deal with first things first.

In such circumstances, a President can treat a problem *as if* it were compartmentalized, concentrating on a single imperative. As Lindblom (1965: 146) comments, "Forthright neglect of important consequences is a noteworthy problem-solving tactic." Once committed to push a bill through Congress, a President may give absolute priority to influencing other Washington powerholders. Once committed to an election campaign, a President can concentrate on going public. In his final year of office, a President may concentrate on achieving an international agreement that will make his name in the history books.

Giving priority to one imperative at a time does not deny that it has consequences for other imperatives; these are simply ignored. Those concerned with problems temporarily neglected by the White House must bear the consequences of neglect. For example, President Kennedy's concern with going Washington and going international led him to do nothing about civil rights for the first eighteen months of his Presidency. He was not prepared to jeopardize congressional support for his foreign policy by taking controversial initiatives on civil rights. The cost of this decision was externalized onto civil rights demonstrators in the South. Only after demonstrations had erupted into nationally televised disorder did the President decide to give civil rights issues a high priority, and accept the cost of losing support from pro-segregation congressmen (see Barber, 1972: 338ff).

Taking Charge

The President's ideal is to take charge of the nation's political agenda. A President takes charge by devising a policy to which the public, Washington and the international system each react. The linkage of different imperatives is seen as desirable; the outcome is that the President gets what he wants.

a. *International system*

President————>Congress————>International system
Public opinion

b. *Congress*

President————>Public opinion————————>Congress
International system

c. *Public opinion*

President————>International system——>Public opinion
Congress

FIGURE 2.4

GOING ON THE ATTACK: THE PRESIDENT TAKES CHARGE

When a President links different imperative concerns, he is free to decide which is the end and which is the means. Figure 2.4 shows three different ways in which the President can link concerns to produce a desirable outcome.

1. *International system.* When deciding international policies, a President knows that what he can do is limited by the support that can be mobilized from Congress and public opinion. For example, the 1947 British announcement of withdrawal of military protection from Greece and Turkey not only created a power vacuum there; it also revealed constraints on the exercise of presidential power. President Truman could not respond immediately by committing the United States to defend those countries against aggression. It was first necessary to mobilize support from public opinion and Congress. Kernell (1986: 153ff) uses the development of the Truman Doctrine to contain Soviet forces as a textbook example of how a President can go public and go Washington as the means to an international objective.

2. *Going Washington.* Given that Congress holds the power of the purse and that the Senate must approve or can reject international treaties, a President sometimes finds that the object of international discussions is to arrive at a policy that Congress will approve. If an agreement is shot down on the Hill, the President is a loser as well as foreign nations. Even if Congress will endorse only part of what the President wants, its endorsement assures an international commitment. When President Carter initially negotiated a treaty with the Panamanian government about the Panama Canal, he could not get congressional approval of the terms. The President had to return to the government of Panama to secure amendments desired by the Senate before the treaty was approved.

3. *Going public.* Events abroad can be viewed primarily in terms of domestic politics. This is most obvious when a President interrupts a trip to stop off in a foreign country such as Ireland, with a significant ethnic constituency in the United States. The recognition by President Truman of the State of Israel in spring 1948 was done with great speed. The President was less concerned with consulting foreign nations or Congress than he was with the presidential election campaign, for granting diplomatic recognition to Israel was expected to boost his approval by significant elements in American public opinion.

Although every President would like to take charge, this can occur only if three conditions are met. First of all, there must be a clear understanding of the cause-and-effect link between actions affecting one audience and their impact on others. Responses in Washington present the fewest problems of estimation, for the White House is continuously taking the political pulse of congressmen. Opinion polls provide a snapshot of public attitudes, but they are not certain guides about how the public will respond to events that have

44

yet to happen. Knowing how foreigners will react is even more difficult, for by definition they are remote, diverse, and free to react in accord with their own national imperatives.

A second requirement of taking charge is that the White House can actually influence events and institutions. Unfortunately for the President, a good cause-and-effect analysis, for example, of a Middle East troublespot, may show that the principal influences on the outcome are outside the control of the Oval Office. Even if there is a theoretical causal model for securing a White House goal, putting it into effect is difficult in circumstances in which a causal chain is only as strong as its weakest link. If the White House loses a critical vote in Congress, if opinion polls turn against the President, or if a foreign nation refuses to cooperate, then the cause-and-effect links are broken.

Third, the measures needed to satisfy one audience may create dissatisfaction with another. This risk does not arise when issues are treated as compartmentalized because only one audience is of concern. But when a President wants to act on the federal deficit in ways that satisfy both international and domestic opinion, difficulties arise if the measures required to reassure foreign lenders, such as boosting taxes and interest rates, are likely to be unpopular with American public opinion.

Any response that a President makes to a political imperative is likely to impose costs as well as promise benefits. An economist may regard this as a simple problem of calculating costs and benefits. Costs can be externalized onto others as long as the benefits accruing to the President are greater than these costs. Positively linking different imperatives can be considered worth the effort as long as benefits to the President outweigh the costs. But a simple arithmetical balance sheet does not work well in the White House, for the President's concern is with maximizing benefits and avoiding costs (cf. Weaver, 1987). When political costs are high, the ideal strategy for the White House is to avoid entanglement with an issue. But because the President's major responsibilities are imperatives, he is forced to make choices in unfavorable as well as favorable circumstances. For this reason, "choices are the means by which he dissipates his power" (Neustadt, 1960: 179).

3. Assessing the Presidency

Paint my picture truly like me and do not flatter me at all; but remark all those roughnesses, pimples, warts and everything as you see me.
—Oliver Cromwell

Presidents have an interest in their own demystification if they are to keep from falling into the perennial trap of seeking overachievement and accomplishing dismal underachievement.
—Fred Greenstein

Portraits of the Presidency can be painted in three different ways. The old-fashioned textbook picture of the Presidency was flattering to the point of being unreal; the President was depicted as wielding power for good at home and abroad (Cronin, 1980: chap. 3). The Vietnam war and Watergate showed that the President could also use power for disputed or illegal ends. The reaction was iconoclastic, the debunking of idols. Portraits of Presidents began to emphasize warts and pimples to the exclusion of all else. The esteem shown Ronald Reagan by his landslide reelection in 1984 created a problem for the iconoclasts. Reagan appeared to be showing a "failure to fail"(Horowitz, 1987: 21). The Iran-*contra* affair revived the faith of the iconoclasts that each President is bound to fail.

The overall effect is confusion rather than understanding; balanced portraits are relatively rare. Furthermore, scholarly monographs about one aspect of the Presidency have the defects of their virtues. Only one dimension of the Presidency is presented. What we need is a means of assessing the Oval Office in the round. Demystification is in the interest of the Oval Office in order to avoid the futile cycle of treating the President first as a savior and then as Satan (Greenstein, 1978: 85).

In order to assess a President, we need to distinguish between what a President intends to do and what he achieves in office. Campaigning for office forces a presidential candidate to state intentions and raise expectations about what will happen. Statements of intention are often treated as evidence of leadership, showing where a candidate would like the country to head. Leadership is not only about stating grand intentions; it is also about mobilizing others to follow in the direction that the White House leads, and the mobilization of support must start by winning elections.

Judgments can be made about presidential actions directed at the political process and about actions influencing policy outcomes. As professional politicians, Presidents can be judged by how well they manage the political process. Political scientists and journalists covering the White House are quick to note when a President is skillful in dealing with his staff, with Congress, and with the media, and when he makes mistakes. From a public policy perspective, the process is only a means to the end of producing substantive policy outcomes. How a President handles Congress is not so important as what he gets from it. The enactment of a presidential recommendation that lands the economy in trouble is not a success. Nor can sending American troops into action abroad be treated as evidence of leadership if troops are withdrawn in defeat.

Assessments of Presidents inevitably reflect political values. The White House describes the President's intentions as good and the results as success, but there are always detractors describing his every action as a failure. As an institution, the Presidency attracts partisan supporters too. Most political scientists who write about the Presidency favor an active role for the incumbent in the White House; the more a President intends and achieves, the higher he is rated as President. Given that Franklin D. Roosevelt was both the first modern President and the proponent of liberal policies, the advocacy of an active role for the White House is particularly congenial to Democrats.

As the White House has been in the hands of Republican Presidents for sixteen of the past twenty years, students of the Presidency have had to face the fact that sometimes a President will lead in directions that they do not want to go. For example, many social scientists opposed the escalation of the war in Vietnam by Presidents Johnson and Nixon, and President Reagan's domestic policies have relatively few friends among political scientists. Yet a President who twice wins the majority of the votes of the American people can claim the right to decide the direction of public policies and can ask political scientists to confine their judgments to how well he handles the political process. Conservative Republicans are under pressure to change their views too. After decades of denouncing a Democratic-controlled White House for becoming too powerful, Republicans now argue that the President ought to be the unchallenged leader of government and blame a Democratic Congress for failing to follow a Republican President's lead.

Success within the United States was sufficient for a modern President, assuring success internationally as well. By contrast, a postmodern President's standing is influenced as much by what happens in the international system as by what happens at home. Foreign governments, foreign banks, and events abroad affect his standing in ways that the White House cannot be sure of controlling. The first part of this chapter assesses Presidents in domestic terms: How expansive or limited is the job seen to be, and how popular or unpopular is the performance? On this basis, a particular President can be described as a leader or a careful guardian, or as Imperial or

47

imperiled. When evaluating postmodern Presidents, foreign as well as domestic actions must be taken into account in order to determine whether the Oval Office occupant is a world leader, isolated, vulnerable, or a global failure.

Conflicting Standards for the Modern President

In a democracy, it is tempting to say that a President's role is to do what the people want. A President can claim that election victory is a popular mandate that makes what he says tantamount to what the people want. But popular demands for peace and prosperity only demonstrate the obvious: that a President who produces war and depression will be a failure. The public wants the President to succeed in achieving these widely valued goals, but it leaves to the White House the difficult task of translating general goals into immediate policy objectives and determining how to achieve popular results.

Clarifying Controversy

Since politics concerns conflicting opinions about what government should do, the President's job definition is inevitably a cause of controversy. Since 1933, there has been recurring controversy about the scope of the Presidency. Although no President would wish to return the White House to the days of the somnolent Calvin Coolidge, liberals and conservatives disagree about whether the President should try to do more or do less. Most liberals favor expanding the scope of the White House as part of a general preference for greater involvement by government in American society. In contrast, most conservatives favor a limited role for government, including the Presidency.

Any assessment of the President almost invariably contains a judgment about the desirability or undesirability of the actions taken by the man in the Oval Office. For example, we cannot assess President Nixon without reference to his role in the Watergate cover-up. Assessments of President Johnson are controversial depending on a person's views about the expanded scope of Great Society domestic programs and the war in Vietnam. A President who actively pursues goals favored by a critic will be praised as a leader, and a President who fails to do this will be criticized.

Combining normative judgments about the scope of presidential action and approval of what is done produces a fourfold typology of Presidents since 1933 (see figure 3.1). Two very different kinds of Presidents can be deemed desirable, according to the political values of the assessor. A *leader* is a President who views the Oval Office in expansive terms and does what is considered desirable. Positive judgments of the leadership of Franklin D. Roosevelt thus assume a favorable assessment of the New Deal. The conservative ideal is the President as a *careful guardian*, doing a limited number of things that are obligations of the Oval Office and refraining from actions that expand the role of government. Dwight D. Eisenhower is praised by his supporters for what he did *not* do. After two decades of Roosevelt and Truman in the White House, Republicans wanted to guard against further expansion of the power of the Presidency.

Scope of Presidency	Assessor's Views of Actions	
	Approves	Disapproves
Expansive	LEADER	IMPERIAL
Limited	GUARDIAN	IMPERILED

FIGURE 3.1

NORMATIVE CRITERIA FOR ASSESSING MODERN PRESIDENTS

A President can be deemed unsatisfactory for carrying leadership too far, or not carrying it far enough. An *Imperial* President is a leader inasmuch as he has an expansive view of what the White House should do. But if a President directs government in ways that are regarded as undesirable, such as the Vietnam war, or even illegal, such as Watergate, this is considered as an abuse of power. An *imperiled* President is undesirable because his intentions are limited, and his achievements are few and undesirable. The Presidency is imperiled because the President interprets his role in so limited a fashion that he refuses to act when he has the capacity to do so; this criticism was frequently levied by liberals against President Eisenhower. The Presidency may also be imperiled when the Oval Office attempts little and has difficulty in achieving that which it seeks to do, a criticism made of President Gerald Ford.

From Leadership to Careful Guardianship
The creation of the modern Presidency meant the rejection of the traditional idea that the President's role in government was very limited. Herbert Hoover's self-denying approach to his job in the Great Depression led to rejection by the electorate in 1932. Franklin D. Roosevelt's great expansion of the role of the Presidency and the federal government initially stirred up great controversy. His novel activities were denounced as an unwarranted reinterpretation of the Constitution by Republican opponents and by Supreme Court justices. By the time of Roosevelt's campaign for an unprecedented third term in 1940, a few of his early supporters were accusing him of being an Imperial President, claiming too much power. Roosevelt became the model for the modern President because nearly all scholars writing on the

subject approve of his policy goals and the way in which he expanded the role of the Oval Office in the pursuit of these ends.

President Truman saw himself as a leader in the style of Roosevelt, advancing America's global commitments and proposing a Fair Deal expansion of government's domestic role. Congress rejected his proposed social measures while backing an extension of the White House's role in the international system. Contemporary evaluations of Truman were often negative, for he lacked the stimulus of a Depression to justify his expansive approach to government. Opponents claim that Truman was trying to do too much in the Oval Office. Congress, the Supreme Court, and the electorate each imposed restrictions on his capacity to lead because they believed he was not careful enough in exercising self-restraint.

Dwight D. Eisenhower entered the White House in 1953 with the intention of being different from his two Democratic predecessors. As a person whose views on domestic politics were formed well before the New Deal, Eisenhower favored government doing less and saw himself as a careful guardian, consciously restricting his role in Washington politics. By accepting the global commitments inherited from Roosevelt and Truman, Eisenhower confirmed that there would be no return to the traditional role of a do-nothing President. But by limiting his role to that of a careful guardian, Eisenhower took half a step back from the activist conception of leadership. This approach to the Presidency did not appeal to many scholars. Richard Neustadt (1960: 180, 194) characterized Eisenhower as an *"anti-politician"* and quoted approvingly the Democratic Speaker of the House Sam Rayburn's words: "No, won't do. Good man. Wrong profession." Subsequent scholarship has provided an alternative interpretation. Greenstein (1982: 57ff) describes Eisenhower as a "hidden-hand President," carefully avoiding involvement in disputes, yet engaged in behind-the-scenes intervention in pursuit of the goals of an effective guardian of limited government.

From Leader to Imperial President

John F. Kennedy campaigned for the Presidency by proclaiming that he would restore leadership to the White House. Eisenhower's guardianship was rejected with the statement, "A restricted concept of the Presidency is not enough." Kennedy told the National Press Club in Washington that "only the President represents the national interest." Kennedy pledged an expansion of the scope of the Oval Office, asserting that the President should "exercise the fullest powers of his office—all that are specified and some that are not." The nation was said to need "a Chief Executive who is the vital center of action in our whole scheme of government," a leader who would master great problems, originate bold plans, and vigorously and capably fight for what he believed in (Hirschfield, 1973: 128-33). The commitment was reaffirmed in the bold rhetoric of Kennedy's Inaugural Address.

50

Kennedy's call for leadership from the White House was supported by Richard Neustadt's influential 1960 study *Presidential Power*, which Kennedy read before entering the Oval Office. Assassination cut short the record required to assess Kennedy as a leader. Contrary to his rhetoric, for much of his period in office Kennedy was careful and cautious. This reflected the fact that Kennedy was elected President with less than half the popular vote, and his support in Congress was weak. President Kennedy was much readier to act expansively in the international arena, invoking all the powers specified in the Constitution and some that are not, thus paving the way for what has become known as the Imperial Presidency.

The Johnson Presidency began a fundamental reappraisal of the President's powers. In his first several years, Lyndon Johnson's success in expanding social legislation led liberal supporters to hail him as a great leader in the tradition of Franklin D. Roosevelt. Concurrently, he was denounced by the 1964 Republican candidate for the nomination, Barry Goldwater, as threatening to undermine the Constitution. Goldwater pledged to return the White House to the traditional role of a guardian imposing self-restraint on government; he lost in a landslide. When Johnson expanded leadership to involve an increasing commitment to war in Vietnam — where Eisenhower had refused to commit troops and Kennedy had taken the first steps of involvement — he came under attack from antiwar liberals. Those who disapproved of the Vietnam war charged Johnson with being too powerful.

The Nixon Presidency showed that Republicans as well as Democrats could take an expansive view of the White House. President Nixon's concentration on foreign policy meant that he was able to invoke broader powers than a President could claim in domestic policy. He used the expansive international powers of the Presidency to the hilt in pursuit of war aims in Southeast Asia and in secretly negotiating the reopening of diplomatic relations with China. At home, Nixon was prepared to stretch the power of the Presidency in efforts to shore up a flagging dollar. In the Watergate break-in, the President overstretched his claim to power, trying to cover up criminal acts in furtherance of electoral interests. Election victory was claimed to legitimate whatever the Nixon White House chose to do. One Nixon White House staff member, Patrick Buchanan, dismissed the Watergate charges with the statement "61 percent," the share of the vote that Nixon won in securing reelection in 1972. Buchanan charged that complaints about criminal activity in the White House were the sour grapes of those who had lost a national plebiscite placing the White House in Nixon's hands. Nixon developed a theory of the *unlimited* power of the Presidency which he explained in a 1977 television interview with David Frost.

> *Frost*: What you're saying is that there are certain situations where the President can decide that it's in the best interests of the nation or something, and do something illegal.

Nixon: Well, when the President does it, that means that it is not illegal.
Frost: By definition.
Nixon: Exactly. Exactly. If the President, for example, approves something because of the national security, or because of a threat to internal peace and order of significant magnitude, then the President's decision enables those who carry it out to carry it out without violating a law. (Quoted in Hinckley, 1985: 256)

A full-blown indictment of the Imperial Presidency was published by Arthur Schlesinger Jr., a sometime proponent of presidential leadership, and biographer of Franklin D. Roosevelt and John F. Kennedy, and a Kennedy White House staff member. Schlesinger (1974: 10ff) used the phrase "Imperial Presidency" to describe the President's claim that his broad powers as commander-in-chief could justify almost anything that the White House sought to do. Schlesinger traced the overexpansion of power through World War II and Korea to Vietnam, describing Johnson as "the Presidency rampant" and the Nixon Administration as a revolutionary Presidency, systematically trying to destroy the checks and balances of the Constitution. He concluded: "The Presidency has gotten out of control and badly needs new definition and restraint." As a liberal Democrat, Schlesinger did not want to replace what he called a runaway Presidency with a careful guardian, whom he pejoratively and inaccurately dismissed as a messengerboy. Instead, Schlesinger called for "a strong Presidency *within the Constitution*" (1974: 12; italics in the original).

Some writers believe that the President can use his media visibility to develop support for Imperial actions taken without constitutional authority. Theodore Lowi (1985: xi) argues that the Presidency has become a "plebiscitary office," meaning that the President can manipulate public opinion through the mass media so that "the masses give their noisy consent to every course of action." Unlike critics of the Imperial Presidency, Lowi impartially attacks Presidents of both parties since Franklin Roosevelt. Lowi (1985: 20) argues that the results are not problematic, but certain and undesirable: "As presidential success advances arithmetically, public expectations advance geometrically. And this is the pathology. The desperate search is no longer for the good life but for the most effective presentation of appearances." A President who initially whips up support for what he wants to do is eventually forced to attempt what no President can achieve.

The Imperiled Presidency

Gerald Ford entered the Oval Office in 1974 intending to reject the activities that had caused his immediate predecessors to be attacked as Imperial. In an apt pun at the swearing-in ceremony, he remarked that he was a "Ford, not a Lincoln." As a Republican coming to office by accident and succeeding a man driven from office by excesses, Ford favored a guardian conception of the Presidency. Ford took office within months after the first oil price shock, and in his first full year there the economy went so deeply into recession that it actually contracted. The only thing that grew was the inflation rate. In his 1976 State of the Union message President Ford rejected on pragmatic grounds the case for an expansive government, saying too much had been tried because "we became overconfident of our abilities." Defeat in his only bid for election meant Ford had no opportunity to establish a full-fledged record for himself. In retrospect, Ford (1980: 30) declared that the problem was not that of an Imperial Presidency but the opposite, "an imperiled Presidency. Under today's rules, which include some misguided reforms, the Presidency does not operate effectively."

Analysts of the modern Presidency agree on one point: The powers of the Presidency are global in significance. Greenstein (1988: 352) concludes his study by imputing a godlike power to the White House, quoting the words of an old spiritual: "He's got the whole world in his hands." It follows from this assumption that the problems of the modern Presidency are caused by domestic constraints. Assessing the President solely in domestic terms is reasonable in a world in which America enjoyed political hegemony, but it ceases to be so when America is no longer the only elephant in the international system.

The Postmodern President: Between World Leadership and Global Failure

In an interdependent world, the President's actions are not the only things that count, nor does a decision in the White House guarantee a desired policy outcome. Actions abroad influence what happens in the United States, just as actions in Washington have an impact on every continent. To assess a postmodern President, we must consider whether or not he can take charge of many major problems that affect the Oval Office. A postmodern President can exert formidable influence upon other nations, but in an interdependent world, he is only one player in the game. If he succeeds in his actions, then he appears a world leader, but if not, then the White House is a failure on a global scale.

A Player but Not in Charge

Because students of the Presidency normally concentrate on the influence of the White House, the President is seen as being in charge, whether trying to influence Congress, public opinion, or the international system (cf. figures 2.1-2.4). In social science language, the President is regarded as the independent variable, the primary influence on a policy. Concentrating on the President's role in policymaking gives the impression that he is the one who counts most.

53

If we ask what determines public policy outcomes, the picture is very different. The White House is not the only place to look for an answer, for the President is only one among many influences on events. A given policy outcome is usually the result of a multiplicity of influences. Some are personal, such as the position of the President or members of Congress, and others are impersonal, such as the state of the economy. When urban problems are the issue, the influences are restricted to the United States. National security issues and most economic problems ranging from those of auto workers or dirt farmers to major banks, involve foreign influences too. The greater the number of influences that must be taken into account, the less important any one is likely to be. As the White House must take Congress into account when deciding domestic policy so the White House cannot dictate actions in the international system. Many checks and balances constrain what the United States can do. A postmodern President remains subject to domestic political constraints, but his actions are even more subject to international constraints.

Independent variable	Intervening variable	Dependent variable
Domestic crisis		
	Urban community	
Race riot——>	Local police, politicians	———> Urban
	State guard	order/disorder
	White House	
Economy		
	International oil producers	
	International money markets	World
Oil price shock——>	U.S. oil consumers	————> recession
	U.S. industry, labor	
	White House	
	Federal Reserve Board	
	Congress	
National security		
	Muslim factions	
	Christian factions	
Civil	Muslim neighbors	
war in——>	Israel	————————> Outcome of
Lebanon	Soviet role	fighting
	European role	
	White House	
	Other Americans	

FIGURE 3.2

THE PRESIDENT AS AN INTERVENING VARIABLE

The limits on the power of the Presidency today can be illustrated by considering what can and cannot be done by the White House in response to three problems of presidential concern: an urban race riot, a recession triggered by an oil price rise, and fighting in the Middle East. In each case, the independent variable is a shock external to Washington. The President is forced to respond to imperative pressures, but his actions are not the only actions that count. The White House position is that of one among a number of intervening variables (see figure 3.2).

1. *Domestic order.* The President's influence on domestic problems is limited in four major ways: by constraints on the White House within Washington, by federalism, by social and economic forces, and by international influences. An urban race riot is a distinctly American problem that can claim the attention of the President. Even though it is a domestic problem, the White House is a remote influence on the outcome of a race riot. If the immediate objective is defined as securing order, then the local police and conditions in the riot area will be the most important variables. If the objective is reducing underlying causes, such as racial discrimination, the courts and congressional legislation will be important. If the objective is defined as reducing economic insecurity, then international as well as national market factors will be critical. In each case, it is possible for the President to exert some influence, but presidential action is neither necessary nor sufficient to achieve a desired outcome.

2. *The economy.* The postwar era has seen the American economy become integrated in an open international system in which many nations are involved. The 1973 and 1979 oil price increases were determined jointly by member nations of OPEC: Iran, Iraq, Kuwait, Saudi Arabia, Venezuela, Algeria, Ecuador, Gabon, Indonesia, Libya, Nigeria, Qatar, and the United Arab Emirates. The consequence was a major shock to the world economy because the price increases produced a great transfer of funds to the oil-producing nations and disrupted the assumptions on which the American economy had been running. Because the problem was profoundly international in character, every nation was much affected by OPEC decisions. While advanced industrial nations differed in their responses, each suffered as part of a global recession. Presidents Ford and Carter were correct in blaming a portion of America's economic difficulties at the time on foreign nations. Within the United States, the President depended on the cooperation of industry, labor, the Federal Reserve Board, and Congress. The extent of White House dependence on others could excuse the President of much blame for economic conditions, but his slight influence also meant that he could not claim to be a leader.

3. *The international system.* In a world with many nations pursuing their interests, a host of different countries can influence a single troublespot. The White House faces particular difficulties when the immediate participants to a dispute do not accept the United States as central to its resolution. This is particularly true where wars reflect historic internal divisions, for example,

Vietnam, Nicaragua, South Africa, and the Middle East. In the civil war in Lebanon, the critical issue for the White House was whether American involvement could make any difference. President Reagan tested this by sending in a contingent of U.S. Marines, only to find the troops caught in crossfire between local groups. Following the killing of more than two hundred Marines by the bombing of their Beirut compound, President Reagan withdrew forces that had had no positive effect.

The challenge to the postmodern President is to influence outcomes by influencing others to cooperate in pursuing mutual aims. A world recession is a challenge to the leaders of many nations with a common interest in reviving world demand and thus their own national economies. In diplomatic negotiations, the President sometimes finds other leaders ready to cooperate, as Mikhail Gorbachev was in 1987, but some leaders can be very uncooperative, for example, Colonel Qaddafi in Libya. The one thing a postmodern President cannot do is ignore the influence of other nations.

Assessing Postmodern Presidents
While a postmodern President must worry about domestic political debates when acting in the international system, an equally important concern is the position of other nations. Just as a modern President knows that what he can accomplish is limited by what Congress will support, so a postmodern President knows that what he can do internationally depends on whether Oval Office actions are in harmony or conflict with those of other influential nations. As the international system becomes more important, the standards for assessing the postmodern President alter. One criterion is the influence of the President on American policy; the other is the influence that other nations have on American policy. If other nations act consistently with White House goals, this reinforces the President's lead. If foreign influences are opposed to White House goals, then the President's chances of success are much reduced (see figure 3.3).

President's influence on policy	Foreign influence on policy	
	Reinforcing	Opposing
High	WORLD LEADER	VULNERABLE
Low	ISOLATED	GLOBAL FAILURE

FIGURE 3.3
ASSESSING A POSTMODERN PRESIDENT

A President can be a *world leader* if two conditions are met: He exerts a major influence on policy, and what he does is reinforced by actions of other major nations. The history of America's relations with its NATO allies reflects the way in which the common interest of European nations and America in deterring a Soviet invasion of Western Europe has made the President the world leader of a vast military alliance. But a President cannot count on other nations automatically following where he chooses to lead.

A postmodern President is a *vulnerable* leader if his influence on American policy is high but his actions are opposed by other nations. This situation was unlikely when America was a worldwide hegemonic power; a lead from the President was sufficient to secure support from other nations. There is no assurance, however, that a trade policy formulated by the White House will receive agreement from nations such as Japan, that must accept it if it is to be effective. The President is vulnerable to frustration or defeat when measures that he advocates as a consensus of Washington opinion are opposed by other nations.

Isolation occurs if a President acts in accord with other national leaders, but fails to carry Washington. Isolation is an inevitable hazard of leaders of small nations, who cannot stand against a stampede of elephants. A postmodern President will be isolated if he agrees with what foreign governments advocate but cannot get other Washington powerholders to agree with him on, for example, a harsh package of economic measures designed to win international support for the dollar. Leaders of nations that have lost hegemony have lots of experience in supporting measures that are domestically unpopular but internationally necessary. The Carter administration showed how the Oval Office can appear in Washington when it is isolated domestically because of international pressures.

If a President fails to influence American policy and his actions are simultaneously opposed by other nations, then he becomes a *global failure*. It would be a very rash or unlucky President who managed to unite everyone against him, both at home and abroad. The phenomenon is familiar in other lands, for example, where a leader having difficulty with foreign nations is finally deposed by a military coup at home. An American President is not subject to violent ejection from office, but failure in advancing American interests in the international system can nonetheless doom him to election defeat at home.

Applying these ideal-type categories to our two postmodern Presidents, Jimmy Carter and Ronald Reagan, illustrates the difference in the way in which we should evaluate a postmodern as against a modern President. There is nothing imperial about a postmodern President, for his leadership in the world depends on cooperation with leaders of other nations. Equally, any perils that the President faces at home are likely to be less troubling than opposition from other nations.

Carter: Isolation and Failure

Conventional interpretations of the Carter Presidency have tended to confound two very different points. One reason for regarding Carter as a failure is that he lacked skill in going Washington and going public. The defeats he suffered in Congress and his rejection by the American electorate in 1980 are cited as evidence of Carter's inadequacy as a politician. It follows from this that if President Carter had not been inadequate, he could have had a successful tenure of the White House.

An alternative interpretation is that Carter was a victim of the "imperiled" Presidency. The difficulties of the Carter administration—even the fact that he, rather than someone more knowledgeable about Washington, won nomination and election—are regarded as symptomatic of underlying faults in the Presidency, faults that make it difficult for any President to succeed for long in going public or going Washington, and that predict failure in going international. The Presidency is said to be in a "no-win" position (Light, 1982; Neustadt 1980: 215ff). From this perspective, Ronald Reagan's apparent success, rather than Carter's failure, appears to be the aberration.

Carter could not be a world leader because he was not an American leader. For example, the President's energy policy, addressing an issue of global significance, could not secure support within Washington and from the public. Carter did not know Washington before he was elected, nor did he want to learn Washington ways until after suffering many domestic defeats. When OPEC nations imposed a second major price rise, the failure of the United States to adopt major energy-saving measures became a global failure. Domestic inflation and the weakness of the dollar internationally caused the American economy to contract in 1980 instead of grow — failure on a global scale.

Yet President Carter was sometimes able to reach agreements with foreign nations while isolated from Congress. This was dramatically illustrated when Carter negotiated a Panama Canal treaty acceptable to the Panamanian government but rejected in the first instance by Congress. In June 1979 Carter agreed to SALT II, an arms-limitation treaty with the Soviet Union, but he was isolated by congressional opposition to the document. When the Soviet Union undermined it by invading Afghanistan at the end of the year, Carter appeared a global failure. The closest President Carter came to acting as a world leader was in being the broker between Israel and Egypt in their peace negotiations at Camp David, an important step forward in the Middle East but of limited concern within the United States.

Reagan: A Vulnerable World Leader

By the standards of the modern Presidency, Ronald Reagan has been a leader, winning congressional and public approval for major policy priorities, such as tax cuts and increased defense spending. President Reagan's activism is in marked contrast to the careful guardianship of Eisenhower's approach to the Presidency. Reagan's skill in winning support for policy initiatives is in contrast with the imperiled Presidency of Gerald Ford. Critics charge that Reagan has been too active, making the White House into an Imperial Presidency, palace intrigues and all.

As a postmodern President, Ronald Reagan must be judged by the influence that foreign nations have on his policies as well as by domestic achievements. By the standards of a postmodern President, Ronald Reagan is sometimes a world leader and sometimes vulnerable. Vulnerability is evident in the economy. Reagan's consistent support of big-ticket defense and social security spending and consistent opposition to tax rises have maintained a big boom in the consumer economy, but the boom has been financed by foreign nations. Moreover, imports from abroad have grown much faster than American exports, thus producing a massive trade deficit financed by foreign lending. Foreign loans have financed both budget and trade deficits. When the dollar has been under great pressure in foreign exchange markets, it has been supported by foreign central banks. As long as it is in the interests of foreign nations to sustain the American economy, then President Reagan appears a world economic leader. But if countries such as Japan and Germany decide to raise the price for funding American deficits, the White House would become vulnerable.

The arms-control agreement signed by President Reagan and Soviet leader Mikhail Gorbachev in Washington in December 1987, and reaffirmed in Moscow in May 1988, is a positive example of world leadership by a post-modern President. President Reagan can claim credit for the agreement as the fruition of a policy of strengthening defense to increase America's capacity to bargain for arms control. But success depended on Gorbachev too; agreement could be reached only if his objectives coincided with those of the White House. Reagan and Gorbachev depended on each other for success. In negotiating with the United States, Gorbachev had to take care not to demand so much that Reagan would be left isolated, without congressional support for the treaty. Equally, Reagan could not demand so much that Gorbachev would be overthrown and replaced by a Soviet hardliner. In an interdependent international system, world leadership is a cooperative exercise.

The Iran-*contra* affair illustrates that the vulnerability of a postmodern President can at times lead to global failure. In seeking to exchange arms for hostages with Iran, the President lacked the support of Congress and was rejected by Iranian authorities as well. The White House policy toward Nicaragua has also been a record of failure, for the President has turned to private funding for *contra* guerrillas because Congress is against a substantial government commitment to the rebels. The failure of the rebels to win power in Nicaragua is evidence of the ability of the government there to defy the White House.

In an interdependent world, we cannot confine the assessment of a President to what he does at home. Success in going Washington and going public is necessary but not sufficient for a postmodern President. The responsibilities that make the President so important also make him dependent on what happens in other nations, even as other nations depend on what happens in Washington. A postmodern President cannot expect to be a world leader all the time, any more than he can expect to be successful in dealing with Congress on every issue. After winning an election, the President-elect is immediately vulnerable to foreign pressures. The worst fate that could befall him is to lose support both at home and abroad, becoming a global failure. The next worst is to become isolated by failing to communicate to Congress and the public reasons why agreements must accommodate the interests of other nations as well as American interests. Only if the President can win American *and* foreign support for his policies will he succeed as a world leader.

4. Widening the View from the Oval Office

Oh would some power the giftie gi'e us
To see ourselves as others see us!
It would from many a blunder free us,
and foolish notion.
—Robert Burns

To be an effective leader in the international system, a postmodern President must understand the imperatives that drive other national governments. A traditional leader could ignore how other countries governed themselves, and the modern Presidency made it imperative for other nations to understand how the American system works. Today, the White House can no longer count on other nations doing what the President wants simply because this is deemed in America's national interest. A postmodern President must be the leader of a coalition in which other nations have concerns and institutions that must be considered. Just as the White House must take into account the needs and foibles of congressmen in order to secure commitment by the American government, today it must also take other countries into account. A President must learn to see America as other nations see us, for as the Scottish poet Robert Burns notes, this can free us from many a foolish notion and blunder.

The fundamental political question facing every country is not whether it will be governed but *how*. Nations differ greatly in the way in which they organize political authority; some are democracies and others are dictatorships. Many countries governed by a President are dictatorships; a dictatorial President concentrates authority in a single person, free of constitutional checks and balances. Most democracies are parliamentary systems. A presidential system is neither necessary nor sufficient for democratic government.

Many contemporary comparisons between the Presidency and parliamentary systems are based on misunderstandings. Europeans and Japanese usually think that the Presidency centralizes power, because it concentrates authority in one person instead of placing it in the collective hands of a Cabinet and Parliament. The President is seen as a person who can take charge without any constraints. Foreign observers often fail to appreciate the significance of the separation of powers. White House decisions are mistakenly assumed to be endorsed by the legislature and the courts with the same readiness shown by these institutions in parliamentary systems. When an Englishman refers to Margaret Thatcher as "presidentializing" the British parliamentary system, the idea is that the Prime Minister's power is being strengthened, not that it is being shared with Parliament as a President must share power with Congress. Foreign diplomats who must come to grips with Washington are under no illusions: They see the White House as a symbol of the fragmentation of authority in a system of separated powers.

The object of this chapter is to compare and contrast the central features of the Presidency with leadership in parliamentary systems. This is not done because of a belief in the inadequacies of the American system in itself (cf. Robinson, 1985). The reason for doing so is practical. Because America is increasingly involved in the international system, a postmodern President must spend more and more time dealing with allies governed by a parliamentary system. The first part of the chapter considers the ways in which parliamentary systems differ from the Presidency; the second considers how the power of subgovernments flourishes in Washington by comparison with parliamentary systems; and the conclusion examines the "responsibility gap" that faces a President with greater tasks and fewer institutional resources than leaders of other major nations.

An Alternative to the Presidency

The American Presidency is unique, but it is not the only democracy in the world today. Most democracies—that is, countries with free elections, competitive political parties, freedom of speech, and the rule of law—do *not* have a President as the leader of government. The political leader is a Prime Minister, who is head of a Cabinet consisting of ministers in charge of the major departments of the executive branch. The system is described as parliamentary, because the Prime Minister and Cabinet must command the confidence of a popularly elected Parliament.* The Prime Minister is usually the leader of the majority party in Parliament, or leads a coalition of parties with a majority. Notwithstanding significant differences among parliamentary systems, there remains an ocean of difference between the American Presidency and parliamentary systems of government (Rose and Suleiman, 1980). Other democracies may not be governed better, but they are certainly governed differently from America.

* In a previous study (Rose, 1980b: 290ff), I referred to parliamentary systems as Cabinet systems. The terminology has been changed to avoid confusion with what is sometimes inaccurately labeled Cabinet government in Washington. The President's Cabinet is as different from the Cabinet of a parliamentary system as a California state college campus is from the colleges of Oxford and Cambridge.

From an American perspective, we can view the parliamentary system as an alternative to the Presidency. But in an international perspective, it is more accurate to see the parliamentary system as the norm for democratic government. Among advanced industrial nations, the United States is an exception because it has a presidential system. Six of the seven national leaders at world summit meetings have a basis for understanding the system of government of other leaders because they too lead a parliamentary system. The President must learn how to deal with parliamentary leaders without this experience.

Separation of Powers versus Fused Powers

Differences between the presidential and the parliamentary system are organic. While the fundamental requirements of government are universal, power is not organized in Washington as it is in countries with parliamentary systems. In a parliamentary system, it is normal to speak of "the state," emphasizing collective and durable institutions. The Washington equivalent, a reference to a particular President's administration (e.g. , the Reagan or the Carter administration), emphasizes what is personal to the President and therefore transitory, expiring when a President leaves office.

The *separation of powers* is the essence of the American system. The American Constitution divides government into separate branches—the Presidency, the Congress, and the Supreme Court—in order to create checks and balances on the exercise of authority. A President can be checked by Congress, and the views of Congress are balanced by the White House. The Supreme Court can check an excess of legislative or executive authority, balancing its interpretation of the Constitution against the views of popularly elected politicians.

Power in Washington is distributed horizontally between the three branches of government (see figure 4.1). The President is not superior to the Congress. If geography is any guide, the Founding Fathers valued Congress more, for the Capitol is on top of the hill dominating Washington; the Supreme Court initially met there too. By contrast, those charged with seeing that laws are faithfully executed, the White House and bureaucrats in federal agencies, are downtown, beneath the hill. Since most acts of government require laws and money appropriated by Congress, actions by executive agencies, and approval by the courts, the federal government can act only by cooperation between its coequal parts, each of which is subject to checks and balances. The executive agencies are formally subordinate to the President, but because they are also subject to Congress and the courts, they can sometimes be insubordinate. Because the parts of government are divided, cooperation is uncertain. Corwin (1957: 171) describes the Constitution as "an invitation to struggle" for the authority of government.

The *fusion of powers* is the defining characteristic of a parliamentary system of government. Power is fused because a single authority is responsible for the executive and legislative sides of government. The vertical nature of authority reflects the fact that a parliamentary system has normally succeeded monarchical rule; a king was at the top in such a system, and all organs of government depended on the throne. Because a king claimed to do no wrong, courts could not check his authority. The rise of popularly elected Parliaments has removed the monarch as an effective part of government and confirmed Parliament as its foundation; authority remains vertical.

a. *Separation of Powers* (America)

b. *Fusion of Powers* (Parliamentary systems)

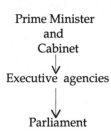

FIGURE 4.1

SEPARATION OF POWERS VS. FUSION OF POWERS

The Prime Minister and Cabinet are at the top of the parliamentary system. Collectively, they are responsible for giving direction to all the executive agencies and organizing the business of Parliament, which normally endorses what the Cabinet does. Individual members of Cabinet are ministers in charge of particular departments, such as Defense, Agriculture, and Education. Each minister has substantial responsibility within his department, and each collectively shares responsibility for what other departments do in the name of the government. The fusion of power is so complete that it is misleading to describe Parliament as a legislature; the making of laws is actually in the hands of Cabinet departments, which can be confident of parliamentary endorsement for what they propose. The Prime Minister speaks authoritatively for government as the chair of the Cabinet and leader of the largest party in Parliament. For a Prime Minister, managing the parliamentary party is very much less a restriction on maneuver than is the President's need to defer to Congress, because parliamentary parties are disciplined to vote as a bloc.

64

Free elections are common to America and parliamentary systems, but there is a big difference in the offices for which people vote. A national election in the United States is really two separate elections, one to elect local representatives to Congress and the other to elect a President. Since the President appoints the Supreme Court and other federal judges, subject to the consent of the Senate, elections indirectly affect the courts as well. The Constitution set the terms of office for members of the House of Representatives at two years and senators at six, as against a four-year term for the President. Each politician can thus run separately from the others and can seek votes from a different constituency. While a congressional election takes place every two years, the President is not a candidate in the mid-term election that determines the fate of the Congress he must deal with for half his period in office.

In a parliamentary system there is only one election and one vote that counts: the vote for members of Parliament. The Prime Minister is not chosen by popular election; instead the Prime Minister is chosen by a vote in Parliament. At a national election, a voter simply has a choice between parties seeking to represent him or her in Parliament. The use in most parliamentary systems of proportional representation to convert votes into seats effectively severs the link between an individual member of Parliament (MP) and voters. The decision about who represents a party locally is largely in the hands of the party organization (Bogdanor and Butler, 1983). The leader of the party that elects the most MPs normally becomes the Prime Minister.

While presidential candidates run as Republicans or Democrats, in practice the American system is characterized by *party indiscipline.* The primary contests that determine which candidate will receive a party's nomination split people into supporters of competing members of the same party. The decisive bloc of votes that determines who wins the White House is in the hands of independent voters who identify with no party. Presidential and congressional candidates tend to campaign independently of one another, since their electoral constituencies differ greatly. Since 1952, one or both houses of Congress have usually been in the hands of the party opposed to the White House. In such circumstances, a President can be sure of support only if there is party indiscipline. Only if some members of Congress in the majority party vote along with the minority party will the President get what he wants.

By contrast, *party discipline* dominates a parliamentary system. All MPs practice what Benjamin Franklin prescribed on 4 July 1776: "We must all hang together." A Prime Minister does not have to negotiate with MPs as members of a separate branch of government; the MPs on whose votes the government depends share a common party allegiance and a common electoral fate. A Prime Minister will campaign hard for the election of all the party's candidates for Parliament, knowing that a party majority is needed there for the leader to take charge of government. Once a minister has the endorsement of Cabinet for a departmental policy, he can be confident that Parliament will endorse it by voting along party lines. An MP who disagrees with what the government is doing can try to get the party to choose a new leader. But as long as a Prime Minister remains leader of the majority party, dissatisfied MPs must follow the party line or risk electoral suicide by losing the endorsement of the party at the next election.

A Prime Minister leads a team of partisans, and like a baseball manager, must rely on others to score runs. By contrast, an American President is like a tennis star, an individual competitor who wins or loses by his own performance. As a team captain, a Prime Minister stands or falls with colleagues in Cabinet and Parliament. Cabinet members are expected to be capable ministerial heads of their departments, and parliamentary colleagues are encouraged to work for the party's reelection nationwide. A President's success or failure depends on his own efforts.

National Variations on the Parliamentary Theme

The differences between parliamentary government and the American system are so sharp that variations among parliamentary systems are minor by comparison. While no short summary can do justice to the nuances of each national system of government, it is useful to consider salient characteristics of the parliamentary systems of Britain, France, Germany, and Japan. These four nations will frequently be compared with the American Presidency; they are major allies with which the White House must consistently deal. They are major military or economic powers and each is a democracy with a parliamentary system.

In *Britain* the power of government is doubly centralized, for as well as fusing the legislature and executive in Cabinet, central and local authority is fused in a unitary state. The party in control of Parliament and Cabinet has authority over the finances, powers, and boundaries of local as well as central government. Backed by a disciplined majority in Parliament, the Cabinet can secure any legislation that it wants. Within the Cabinet, the Prime Minister is conventionally described by the Latin phrase *primus inter pares* ("first among equals"), because all members of Cabinet are collectively responsible for government. But as Sir Winston Churchill once said: "There can be no comparison between the positions of number one, and numbers two, three or four." Whereas Americans complain about the President being too weak, in Britain the usual complaint is that the Prime Minister has acquired too much strength as against other Cabinet members (cf. Rose, 1980a; King, 1985). The courts regard an act of Parliament as supreme, and cannot strike an act down as unconstitutional. The official head of state is a monarch, but when Queen Elizabeth II speaks on affairs of state, she does so on the instruction of the duly elected government. Checks on the power of government are meant to come from the electorate. Because authority is concentrated in the hands of the governing party, it cannot avoid blame when things go wrong.

The 1958 Constitution of the Fifth *French* Republic was enacted to create a strong central authority within a unitary state. The Fifth Republic has greatly limited the power of the Assembly (the French term for the chief chamber of Parliament) because the Fourth Republic had been racked by divisions between a multiplicity of parties in Parliament, resulting in frequent changes of a coalition Prime Minister. Under Article 38 of the Constitution, the government may ask Parliament to give it the power to legislate by decree for a limited period of time. The Cabinet can also propose laws deemed to be approved by Parliament unless a vote of no confidence is moved within twenty-four hours, and promptly passed. The President is directly elected for a term of seven years; the Assembly has a maximum term of five years. Until 1986, the majority in Parliament was of the same political tendency as the President. The Prime Minister was thus less important than the President because both were of the same political allegiance (Massot, 1979: chapters 3-4; Hayward, 1983). After the Right won a majority in the Assembly in 1986, a period of "cohabitation" commenced between a Socialist President, Francois Mitterrand, and an anti-Socialist Prime Minister, Jacques Chirac. Prime Minister Chirac used the constitutional powers of his office and the Cabinet to dominate government, as he claimed the legitimacy of an electoral majority in Parliament. In 1988, President Mitterrand secured a fresh electoral mandate, and his party became the largest in Parliament and a Socialist again became Prime Minister.

The parliamentary system of the Federal Republic of *Germany* emphasizes powersharing. In reaction against the experience of Hitler's Reich from 1933 to 1945, constitutional checks were introduced to guard against the dictatorial exercise of power. In reaction against the "too weak" Weimar Republic from 1919 to 1933, a parliamentary system was adopted to fuse the power of the legislature and the Cabinet. Since authority is decentralized in a federal system, the German Parliament has two chambers, a popularly elected *Bundestag*, and the *Bundesrat*, which consists of representatives of the various German states. A Constitutional Court is another check on the abuse of executive authority. The use of proportional representation to elect MPs means that no party normally has an absolute majority of seats; a coalition is usually formed with a small third party, the Free Democrats. Either a Christian Democrat or a Social Democrat holds the office of Chancellor *(Bundeskanzler)*, the German equivalent of Prime Minister. A distinctive feature of the Constitution is the constructive vote of no confidence; the *Bundestag* can vote a Chancellor out of office only if, in the same resolution, it agrees on the name of another Chancellor. In practice, the Chancellor is secure in office. The head of state, the Federal President, is a figurehead chosen by a special electoral college of members of the *Bundestag* and of state legislatures (cf. Mayntz, 1980; von Beyme, 1983).

Collective authority in *Japan* is best characterized as party government, for the Liberal Democratic party (LDP) has controlled the popularly elected House of Representatives of the Parliament, known as the Diet, since the LDP was formed in 1955. Because the Prime Minister and Cabinet require the confidence of the majority in Parliament, the leader of the LDP becomes the Prime Minister. The politics of the LDP is based on factionalism; each faction head is a politician who is a candidate for election as LDP leader, and thus Prime Minister (MacDougall, 1982; Hrebenar, 1986). The factions resemble those that used to characterize many states in the American South (cf. Key, 1949). But because the parliamentary system fuses the legislature and executive, the competition between factions does not turn government into as big an arena for conflict, as in Washington. The Emperor is only a figurehead, but the political culture continues to emphasize unity. Consensus is normally sought before government acts, and it requires a process of lengthy consultation. While widespread and detailed consultation is also needed in Washington, Tokyo is different, for "when consensus is finally reached, there is a high degree of support among members of an organization for the decision, and greater willingness to implement it" (Vogel,1979: xxiii; Richardson and Flanagan, 1984: 192ff).

A Different Intent
The contrast between the American Presidency and a parliamentary system is not an accident; it reflects a historic difference in intent. America began as a governmentless agglomeration of people, divided among thirteen colonies. There was politics aplenty among the scattered colonies. The American Revolution was a protest against the unresponsiveness of the English Crown, and the Articles of Confederation of 1781 made no allowance for an executive branch or even a central authority. The Founding Fathers erected the Madisonian system of checks and balances, based on the separation of the legislature from the executive, because they wanted to prevent the concentration of authority. The tradition of putting politics before government remains to this day. As Justice Brandeis said in a 1926 Supreme Court decision, the purpose of the Constitution is "not to promote efficiency but to preclude the exercise of arbitrary power."

The American people like the way that authority is subject to checks and balances. When a public opinion poll asks people whether they would prefer the division of Congress and White House between two opposing parties "to give balance to our government" or for the two institutions to be in the hands of the same party "to enact laws efficiently and quickly," 51 percent favor dividing responsibility for government between competing parties, as against 36 percent endorsing concentrating authority in the hands of one party, as is the intent of a parliamentary system (Lipset and Schneider, 1983: 380). When voters support candidates of one party for Congress and another for the White House, they are not voting for stalemate. They are casting a vote of confidence in the Founding Fathers, refusing to trust all the powers of government to a single office or institution.

Most Americans accept a system of lawmaking in which the President can propose a variety of policies, and Congress has the power to decide how much or how little will be enacted into law. When the Gallup poll asks people whether the President, Congress, or both should have major responsibility for economic policy, foreign policy and energy policy, in each case the median respondent does *not* want the President to have sole responsibility for policymaking. In economic and energy policy more Americans would like to concentrate responsibility in Congress than in the White House; in foreign policy more people favor giving primary responsibility to the President (see table 4.1).

TABLE 4.1

POPULAR SUPPORT FOR THE SEPARATION OF POWERS

(IN PERCENT)

Policy Should Be Set by	Economic policy	Foreign policy	Energy policy
Congress	40	27	40
Both Congress and President	20	18	19
President	34	49	35
Don't know	6	6	6

SOURCE: Calculated from report of Gallup poll survey in Wayne (1982), 19.

By contrast, parliamentary systems evolved in predemocratic societies with a traditional emphasis on government as the expression of a unitary political will, the Crown in England, the State in France, the Nation in Germany, and very much older and strong group loyalties in Japan. The idea of frequent resort to the electorate for popular approval or direction was not popular with rulers who wanted to preserve central authority for their own use. Louis Napoleon, elected French Emperor by a manipulated plebiscite, described election as like baptism: "It was absolutely essential to do it once, but one wouldn't want to spend all one's life in the baptismal font." The existence of a strong central authority *before* democracy has left a legacy of respect for authority today. The historic problem facing European countries and Japan has been the creation of political institutions that are responsive to the views of ordinary subjects, as well as to aristocrats, the church, and servants of the Crown. The process of doing this began in England in the seventeenth century; it was completed in Germany and Japan only after World War II.

While both presidential and parliamentary systems are democracies, authority is exercised differently. A parliamentary system fuses authority through the integration of party, Parliament, and Cabinet. Although the Prime Minister is restrained by the need to maintain collective authority, heading an integrated set of institutions confers collective authority. In Washington, the President has only a piece of the action. In order to get things done he must gain the support of those who hold other pieces, whether in Congress, interest groups, or the courts. The fragmentation is not accidental; it is the result of a belief in the virtues of the separation of powers. Each system has its characteristic vices as well as virtues. These are described by David Broder (1987a) as fusion placing so much power in the hands of the Cabinet that it risks "parliamentary absolutism," whereas the Madisonian system, with too little power in the hands of the President, has a tendency to deadlock.

Subgovernments and Government

Every modern organization, including government, is divided in order to carry out specific tasks; specialization leads to differentiation. A business corporation or a military unit can be envisioned as a pyramid of authority, with a single individual at the top having the final say, a commanding officer in the army, or a chief executive officer (CEO) in a corporation. But a pyramid is too simple to describe government. Even in dictatorships, a government is subject to internal divisions and pressures that must be balanced by a leader. For example, in negotiating with President Reagan, Mikhail Gorbachev had to look over his shoulder to make sure that he was not going further than Soviet critics would accept (Tarschys, 1977). A government is like a range of mountains; it has more than one peak and the peaks differ in their height and distance from each other.

The term *subgovernment* originated in Washington to describe the way in which interests and institutions divide. A subgovernment is (1) focused on a particular policy area, such as education, defense, or transportation; (2) includes representatives of more than one branch of government; (3) is relatively stable through time; (4) involves continuous bargaining among its members; and (5) tends to resist direction from outside by organizations such as the White House (cf. Freeman, 1955; Ripley and Franklin, 1980; Freeman and Stevens, 1987). Subgovernments are not so much concerned with the big headline issues as they are with the less dramatic activities that account for 90 percent or more of public spending.

Subgovernments arise because separate institutions must combine their actions in order to get anything done—or to veto unwanted change. A subgovernment is not part of Congress or the executive branch; it creates links between those in different institutions who share a common policy concern: congressmen on committees dealing with an issue; bureau chiefs responsible for relevant programs; interest groups that benefit from a measure; and free-floating experts and policy analysts with knowledge and views. Subgovernments are particularly suitable to maintain the congressional practice of log-rolling or reciprocal noninterference (Schattschneider, 1935). Each is prepared to let other subgovernments go their way, as long as it can secure what it wants. When a dispute arises, an attempt is made to resolve it within the confines of the subgovernment, where everyone knows and understands each other.

The President, as the one officeholder elected to represent the whole of the nation, is concerned with government, that is, linking concerns divided up among many subgovernments or left out of their calculus altogether. The President is more likely to see overarching national considerations because of the nationwide electoral constituency of the Oval Office. For example, a President is concerned with advancing the nation's security by measures that appear appropriate in the circumstances. He is not concerned, as subgovernments are, with the distribution of the next round of defense contracts for ships, planes, and missiles. Because the President does not share the narrow interests of subgovernments, the participation of White House staff in such deliberations is usually unwelcome.

In seeking to exercise influence on subgovernments, the basic problem of the President is simple: There is no government there (Rose, 1980b). The President does not have in his own hands the authority to override the preferences of subgovernments in the name of broader national interests. Worse than that, many officials in executive branch agencies are themselves on the side of subgovernments, for the security and advancement of their particular agency interest depend on going along with congressional committees and interest groups. When White House officials try to exert pressure upon a particular subgovernment, they learn why these groups are often called *iron triangles*. They show strong resistance against the White House interfering in the arena of the subgovernment. In default of the authority to order Congress and independently-minded bureau chiefs to do what the President wants, the White House is reduced to pressure politics and seeking to mobilize public opinion, or the President may decide to ignore routine concerns of subgovernments, in order to concentrate selectively on international and national crises (see chapter 9).

Parliamentary systems have subgovernments too, although they are sometimes called by other names, such as policy communities, iron triangles or, in Japan, *zoku*, which is translated as "policy tribes" (cf. Pempel, 1987: 289ff; Jordan, 1981). But in a parliamentary system there is government as well as subgovernments (Rose, 1980b: 290ff). As head of an executive department each minister is involved in subgovernment politics on a daily basis, but the Cabinet has the collective authority to hold subgovernments in check. A minister cannot promise new and controversial legislation without Cabinet approval, or spend more money without first securing approval from the budget minister. Furthermore, a subgovernment cannot "end run" the finance minister by appealing to Parliament because votes in Parliament follow Cabinet directives. Cabinet guidelines set limits within which individual departmental ministers must work. A minister armed with the authority of Cabinet can stand up against pressure groups and MPs lobbying on behalf of sectional policies. The line of policy comes down from the Cabinet and from ministers, instead of being formulated in relatively remote and impenetrable committee meetings reflecting bureaucratic and interest-group influences.

The parliamentary system's fusion of executive and legislative authority integrates government and subgovernment, with the former in command. The parliamentary system does not eliminate politics. The critical difference from Washington is that the Cabinet resolves problems centrally with the binding authority of government. By contrast, when pressures converge on the White House, it is because subgovernments want to use the President to their advantage. Even if they fail there, they can always try somewhere else, for Washington is an open house for pressure politics. A comparative review of Cabinet politics in parliamentary systems concludes:

> Certainly, compared with the United States, parliamentary systems with Cabinet structures have a very high capacity for coordination, conflict resolution and authoritative decision making *within the executive.* (Mackie and Hogwood, 1985: 35; italics in the original)

The Responsibility Gap

The position of the American President is more difficult than that of a Prime Minister in two respects. First of all, the United States is by far the most important government in the Western world. Washington is a front-line government in international diplomacy, in military security, and in the international economy. On every continent, political groups are trying to make the United States do what they want. By contrast, the Prime Minister of the average European country is mostly concerned with problems of other European nations that are its neighbors and trading partners. The size of the American economy is so large that what happens to the dollar is followed by bankers from London and Saudi Arabia to Tokyo. By contrast, the position of the Dutch guilder or the Austrian schilling is of limited concern outside the Netherlands or Austria. Difficulties of smaller European economies may upset a nation's treasury minister and cause anxieties to its Prime Minister, but they will not upset the world economy.

Second, the political resources available to the President are fewer in relation to his problems because of the checks imposed on the White House by the separation of powers. While a small country such as Denmark does not command great resources, its responsibilities in the world are few, for a Danish Prime Minister does not have to worry about how his army will deter the Soviet army, or about the impact upon the international economy of changes in the value of the Danish kroner. Countries that are major powers without being superpowers, such as Britain, France, and Germany, have fewer economic and military responsibilities and resources than the United States yet they have the capacity to commit the authority of government to advance their interests internationally. Japan takes longer to make commitments because of the intricacies of its domestic political bargaining process, but when Japanese government does meet other nations, it can act with great collective authority.

The responsibility gap is between the global responsibilities of the Oval Office and the influence that it can exert within Washington. This was not so great a problem for a modern President, who could rely on America's economic and military might to ensure that other nations followed. However, a President cannot use the nation's military and economic might in a "war" against Congress or the bureaucracy. In addition, a postmodern President is subject to checks and balances abroad as well as at home. The responsibility gap between what the President would like to do and what he can do has widened. International responsibilities remain great, but the United States can no longer be sure that other nations will fall into line once decisions are taken in Washington. The need to wheel and deal rather than dominate other nations ought to come naturally to a President who is always bargaining with Congress. But it represents one more unwelcome check on a President who likely feels that there are already many domestic restrictions upon his capacity to do what he thinks best for the United States.

When the Founding Fathers drew up the Constitution, they gave the President powers sufficient to his tasks. Because the responsibilities of American government were then very few, his authority could be checked in many ways. The postmodern President lives in a world that James Madison could never have envisioned. His responsibilities are unparalleled in American history, or in the history of any other democratic government. While the President's responsibilities have become much greater, the constitutional checks on authority have remained in place. As the world closes in on the White House, allies as well as potential enemies now have resources that they can use to advance their interests in cooperation and competition with the White House.

PART TWO

Tangible and Intangible Resources of Leadership

5. Resources and Constraints of Government

No man ever saw a government. I live in the midst of the government of the United States, but I never saw the government of the United States.
—Woodrow Wilson

Government is not the solution to our problem. Government is the problem.
—Ronald Reagan

If government is defined as the problem, then anarchy is the logical solution, yet no one who wants to be President would advocate anarchy. The whole point of winning the White House is to give direction to government. The paradox of an "anti-Washington" politician such as Ronald Reagan is that in order to get rid of the problems diagnosed, it is necessary to go Washington. An activist President depends to an even greater extent on effectively using government resources for success. Nevertheless, both activist and antigovernment Presidents soon learn that the expanse of government is very different from the Oval Office. After four years in the White House, Woodrow Wilson said that he had never seen the government of the United States, for the separation of powers and the nationwide ramifications of federalism make much of government remote from the White House.

By contrast, in a parliamentary system, the Prime Minister and Cabinet can take a broad view because they are collectively responsible for everything done in the name of government. In unitary states, the Cabinet can answer for activities of local and regional government, the health service, and public utilities, as well as government ministries. The great range of policies for which the Cabinet is responsible enables politicians to take credit for many benefits. It also forces them to face up to many difficulties. The breadth of responsibilities is evident at budget time; the Cabinet in a European parliamentary system makes decisions about how to spend twice as much of the national product as is the concern of the Presidency.

All systems of government rely on three principal resources: laws, money, and public employees (Rose, 1984a). Laws are an impersonal resource; like everyone else, public officials are meant to be under the law. Money is important, for every action of government has some cash cost, and some programs cost tens of billions of dollars. But government can spend large sums only if it can collect large sums in taxes. Public employees must be mobilized in order to deliver major public programs. The typical public employee is not a pointy-headed intellectual but soldiers and sailors, nurses and teachers, policemen and tax collectors (Rose, 1985a). Without millions of such employees, modern government could not exist as we know it today.

Government has grown by expanding popular social programs. Social security and health programs account for a substantial proportion of the budget of every modern government. Education is a big-ticket item too, although it is not a federal government responsibility. America's global defense commitments require the mobilization of hundreds of billions of dollars and millions of men and women. Most programs involve a mix of resources. Some are law-intensive, such as the regulation of environmental pollution; others are money-intensive, such as the payment of social security; and some are labor-intensive, such as defense.

The fewer the checks and balances on government, the fewer the institutional constraints on governments adopting new programs or altering existing programs. The White House is far more inhibited in mobilizing resources than are leaders in parliamentary systems. Conservative Americans welcome the separation of powers as a check on the growth of government, making it difficult for a liberal President to act. But the separation of powers also makes it difficult for an antigovernment President to cut back public spending.

When strength is measured by the government's power to allocate resources for peaceful purposes in society, the President appears much weaker than the Prime Ministers of mixed-economy welfare states of Europe. Successive sections of this chapter show that the resources of American government are relatively small by comparison with governments in other advanced industrial nations, and this is the case whether one looks at taxes, public employees, laws, or spending on public programs. Moreover, the federal system reduces Washington's influence on the totality of government in America. Within Washington the President's effectiveness is further whittled down because he must share powers that are fused in a parliamentary system.

How Much Does Government Do?

America is a "big" society in material wealth as well as in population and geographical area. The country's gross national product is the largest in the world, double that of the Soviet Union, which has a similar population, and more than four times that of such major European nations as Britain, France, and Germany. When gross national product per head is calculated, America remains a wealthy country by the standards of the average member of the United Nations and by the standards of advanced industrial nations. American society has vast resources that could be mobilized for public policies—if the federal government acted to do so.

The federal government today mobilizes far more resources than in the 1920s or 1880s. But by comparison with contemporary European mixed-economy welfare states, the President heads a *not so big* government (Rose, forthcoming). A European Cabinet controls far more of its national resources than does the entire federal government. Whether the measure is laws, money, or public employees, the conclusion is the same: The programs of an American President are less important in American society than are the programs of his European counterparts. This is made evident in two ways: European states claim a larger share of their national resources than all levels of government in the United States, and within the American system the federal government claims a smaller share of public resources than do central governments in Europe. Thus, a European parliamentary government has a much greater influence on the economy and welfare of its citizens than the White House and Congress put together.*

Laws

The power to enact laws is a unique resource of government. Without a law, government cannot act, for bureaucrats require legal authorization for what they do. Once a law is enacted, it will remain in force for decades or generations, for legislatures repeal very few laws, even when the party in control of government changes hands at a general election. A President who can persuade Congress to enact legislation registers a durable impact on American society. Long after the President leaves the White House, laws passed in his term of office will still be in effect. The growth of government has resulted from the persistence of statutory commitments to spend money on social security, health and education, and the accumulation of amendments expanding these social programs (Rose, 1986a).

In a parliamentary system, the Cabinet is collectively responsible for the bulk of legislation enacted by Parliament. Because the Cabinet must have the continuing confidence of the majority of MPs, Parliament will endorse the great bulk of bills that the government brings forward. The proportion of government-sponsored bills approved ranges from 97 percent in Britain to 77 percent in Japan (see table 5.1). In a country such as France, the head of government also has substantial powers to issue decrees that have the force of law without a positive vote of approval by Parliament.

*The relationship between a parliamentary system and a big government is empirical not theoretical; Japan is a conspicuous exception in having a parliamentary system and a not so big government (Rose, forthcoming). Therefore, this chapter compares America with parliamentary systems in Europe.

The legislative role of Parliament is nominal, since measures introduced by individual members of Parliament usually deal with unimportant concerns or nonparty issues. Measures introduced by opposition parties are often intended for publicity purposes, since the minority in Parliament cannot wheel and deal to win votes, as in Congress. Nongovernmental measures are a small proportion of total bills introduced. In Britain, for example, only 14 percent of private members' bills are enacted, as against 97 percent of government bills.

TABLE 5.1

SUCCESS OF GOVERNMENT IN ENACTING LEGISLATION

(IN PERCENT)

Country	Government-sponsored bills		Members' bills	
	Enacted	All laws	Enacted	All laws
Britain	97	81	14	19
Germany	87	81	57	19
France	82	91	6	9
Japan	77	86	41	14
United States (federal)	33	4	n.a.	96

SOURCES: Britain (Van Mechelen and Rose, 1986); France and Germany (Inter-Parliamentary Union, 1986: table 31); Japan (Pempel, 1986: table 4.3); United States (Wayne, 1978: table 5.2, 1969-75; Inter-Parliamentary Union, 1986: table 31).

The President has far less power over legislation than does a Prime Minister. In Washington, only a very small percentage of the legislation enacted by Congress each year consists of measures put forward as part of the President's program. Two-thirds of the measures the President puts forward are rejected outright by Congress. Of the third that are approved, many are subject to amendments that are forced on the White House as a part of the process of bargaining for votes on the Hill. Members of Congress assert their independence of the President by introducing and carrying into law the bulk of statutes enacted each year. Congress also shows its power by voting down measures proposed by the White House.

An American President's influence on legislation is even weaker than is indicated by the comparative statistics in table 5.1, for congressional committees also use their legislative power to influence bureaucrats working in executive branch agencies (Kaufman, 1981). Congressmen can suggest that if officials do not use their discretion to interpret laws as Congress wishes, then legislation will be introduced compelling them to do so, or that their appropriations will be cut. A President cannot sack a civil servant in an executive agency who does what Congress wants in defiance of what the White House wants.

Federalism establishes a system of concurrent legislation in fifty state legislatures as well as Congress, making every citizen subject to at least two sets of laws. On average, a state legislature enacts nearly 600 laws a year (Council of State Governments, 1982: 86-89, 206ff). These measures can concern many controversial matters, such as education, abortion, or right-to-work legislation affecting unions, and often differ from what the White House desires. The power of the states to legislate represents an additional limitation on the White House capacity to mobilize laws to presidential ends.

Tax Revenues

A government that collects a large proportion of the national product in taxation is powerful—some would argue too powerful—in society. The impact of taxes is measured as the proportion of the gross national product that government collects. By this criterion, government is relatively small in the United States. Whereas from 38 to 45 percent of the national product is raised in taxation in European parliamentary systems, in the United States all levels of government collectively account for 29 percent of the national product in taxation (see table 5.2). Among the twenty-three member nations of the Organization for Economic Cooperation and Development (OECD), the United States ranks nineteenth in the proportion of the national product levied in taxation; only Turkey, Japan, and Spain rank lower. Furthermore, the political resistance of American citizens has resulted in taxation growing more slowly in the United States than in European countries. While American government appears powerful when military might is the measure, it appears weak when judged by its ability to claim tax revenues from its citizens.

TABLE 5.2

TAX CLAIMS ON THE NATIONAL PRODUCT

(AS PERCENTAGE OF GROSS DOMESTIC PRODUCT)

	Central	Regional and Local	Total
France	41.6	3.9	45.5
United Kingdom	34.4	4.1	38.5
Average	30.5	6.6	37.1
Germany	26.2	11.5	37.7
Japan	20.3	7.1	27.4
United States	20.0	9.0	29.0

SOURCE: Derived from OECD (1986a), 82, 204.

American federalism further limits the taxing capacity of Washington, and with it the resources that the President can use for his purposes. The taxing power of state and local governments is more important in the United

States than in most OECD countries. For example, in France central government collects 91 percent of total tax revenues, whereas the federal government collects only 69 percent of the lower total tax revenues in America. The German federal system gives state and local governments virtually the same percentage share of total tax revenues as in the United States, but because tax effort in Germany is nearly one-third higher, the total collected by the federal government in Bonn is much higher than in America. Moreover, state and local taxation in Germany is much more subject to federal authority than in the United States.

Notwithstanding complaints often voiced about Washington collecting too much money in taxes, in comparative perspective Washington appears weak. It claims only $2 in $10 of the national product. France, by contrast, often scorned as a government incapable of enforcing tax laws, claims more than four francs in ten in taxation. Even in low-tax Japan, where the Prime Minister's office is so much against public spending that they have a saying, "Free is evil," central government collects a larger share of the national product than does Washington. In the average OECD nation, central government claims 30.5 percent of the national product; this is more than is collected by all levels of government in the United States.

The weak taxing power of the federal government can be gotten around for a period of time by borrowing. President Reagan has shown how White House dislike of taxation combined with an unwillingness to cut big-spending programs such as defense and social security can sustain a budget financed by high levels of borrowing. But the rapid growth of the federal deficit under Reagan has created another problem: how to pay for the deficit. The inability of the White House and Congress to agree on this is evidence of the ability of each end of Pennsylvania Avenue to block the other.

Public Employment

Government needs people as well as money; a large portion of the budget of every government is devoted to paying public employees. The growth of government in the past half-century has been paralleled by the growth of public employment, and this occurs nationwide (Rose, 1985a). The representative public employee is not a federal bureaucrat shuffling papers in a mammoth Washington office building, but someone providing a service locally: a teacher, a policeman, or a worker in the county hospital. Because public employees are meant to follow orders from above, a large number of them can enhance the impact of a political leader. As the nation's chief executive, a President's formal influence increases as the federal government employs more people to execute the laws for which he is responsible.

Public employment as a proportion of the labor force is not so high in America as in Europe (see table 5.3). In the United States, only 18.3 percent of workers are employed by one or another level of government; in European countries the proportion rises to 32 percent in France and 38 percent in

Sweden. Only Japan resembles the United States in having a limited fraction of the labor force in public employment; however, Japanese data is not comparable with that available for Europe (cf. Rose, 1985a; Heller and Tait, 1983). Moreover, differences between the United States and European countries have been increasing since the early 1950s. Public employment in the United States has been virtually constant at around 18 percent of the labor force since 1951; in France and Germany, public employment has increased by more than half in the postwar era (Rose, 1985a; 11).

TABLE 5.3

PUBLIC EMPLOYMENT BY LEVEL OF GOVERNMENT

(AS PERCENTAGE OF NATIONAL WORK FORCE)

	National[a]	State and Local	Total
Sweden	17.6	20.6	38.2
France	25.1	7.5	32.6
Britain	19.2	12.2	31.4
Germany	15.2	10.6	25.8
United States	5.5	12.8	18.3

a. Includes publicly owned industries and health service.

SOURCE: Rose (1985a), table 1.9. Comparable statistics not available for Japan..

From the perspective of a President or Prime Minister, the most important public officials work for the central government. Only these employees are directly in the line of authority that starts in the Oval Office or at a Cabinet table. Here too, the relative weakness of the Presidency is apparent, for twice as many Americans work for state and local governments as for the federal government (see table 5.3). Collectively, local governments constitute the biggest portion of American public employment. Federal civil servants constitute less than 2.5 percent of all public employees; only by adding in the military does the proportion reach 5 percent. Japan has a limited portion of employees working for the central government, but a unitary system of government ensures more coordination than American federalism.

A European Prime Minister and Cabinet have a far larger portion of the labor force working for them than does the White House. In France, more than one-quarter of the total labor force works for the central government. The President, America's nominal chief executive, is in charge of only 5 percent of the American labor force. In the German federal system, the central government has three times this proportion of public employees. Whereas the central ministry of a government in Europe or Japan can give direction to education by directly employing teachers or through central legal and fiscal powers, the President cannot do so. Since education is

83

organized by state laws, teachers are employees of local government and local school boards.

In addition to the constraints that Congress imposes on the President's capacity to direct public employees, there are constraints from the private sector. So weak is American government that in many fields of public policy, most people providing services do *not* work for any level of government; instead, they are employed in the private sector, for example, in private security firms or in nonprofit organizations that receive a substantial amount of funding from government, such as hospitals and universities (Peters, 1985: table 7.7).

Public Programs

When we look at the programs that government provides, here again the President appears much less important than his European counterparts. In the past quarter-century public spending as a proportion of the national product has risen slowly in America by comparison with Europe. Total expenditures by all levels of American government are little more than one-third of the national product, whereas they are nearly half the national product in France, and in the OECD world as a whole they average a quarter higher than in the United States (table 5.4). When the division of programs between federal, state, and local governments is taken into account, the President's responsibilities are further diminished.

TABLE 5.4

PUBLIC EXPENDITURES ON MAJOR PROGRAMS

AS PERCENT OF GROSS DOMESTIC PRODUCT

	Social[a]	Defense	Debt interest	Other	Total
France	34.5	4.1	2.6	8.2	49.4
Britain	21.5	5.3	4.9	13.2	44.9
Germany	26.2	3.3	3.0	10.9	43.4
United States	18.1	6.5	4.6	6.1	35.3
Japan	16.5	1.0	4.4	5.0	26.9
OECD average	24.5	3.0	5.1	11.1	43.7

a. Includes education, health, social security and social services.

SOURCES: Total public expenditure: *OECD Economic Outlook* No. 41, (1987) table R7. Social: Updated from OECD (1985). Defense: *SIPRI Yearbook* (1986). Debt interest: *OECD Economic Outlook* No. 36 (1984), table 5. GDP: *OECD Observer* No. 145 (1987). Data normally for 1984.

If the power of the Presidency is evidenced by programs intended to help people, then the White House appears ineffectual or uncaring by comparison with European countries. Total spending on social programs, such as education, health care, and social security, is more than one-quarter below the OECD average—and it is falling further behind with the passage of time (Rose, forthcoming). Only one major social benefit—the payment of pensions to older people through the social security system—is directly in the hands of the federal government. While the President likes to claim credit at election time for protecting or increasing social security benefits, claiming credit for what happens does not mean that the President causes pensions to rise. Pension increases are mandated by law to increase according to changes in the cost-of-living index. The federal government spends a lower proportion of the national product on health care than do European governments. Spending on education at the federal level is extremely low; education is preeminently a state and local responsibility.

In only one area of public policy can the President claim to be more powerful than his European counterparts: defense. Whether the White House is in the hands of a Republican or Democrat, America spends a much larger proportion of its national product on defense than do other OECD nations. In 1981, before the Reagan defense boom started, America was spending nearly double what the average OECD nation spent on defense. Because America's aggregate population and national product are much larger than any other OECD nation, American defense expenditures are even bigger in absolute terms. Since Japan's postwar constitution forbids it to have a standing army, American defense spending is particularly great in comparison with the world's second largest economy. Only if the power of the Oval Office is measured in terms of weapons of war is the President the most powerful leader among advanced industrial nations.

The substantial and growing sums of money that America must spend in paying debt interest is a sign of White House weakness. It shows that the President is incapable of cutting public expenditures to reduce borrowing or raising taxes to finance current levels of federal spending. In the 1980s, the cost of financing these debts has risen, as the dollar has weakened in the world economy and the White House has depended more and more on foreign nations to finance a deficit it is unable to control.

When the President's resources are compared with what is available to European political leaders, they appear smaller and different. A President has relatively less money, fewer people, and less control over laws than a European Prime Minister and Cabinet. The President's resources are also qualitatively different. A President has fewer responsibilities to help people, for the federal government spends much less on social programs than do European governments. Because of high spending on military defense, a President has more resources to deal with problems abroad than at home. However, massive force is less important today than in world wars of the past, for the characteristic military engagement is now a conflict in which a small, and often rebellious force creates difficulties for much larger opposing forces. A White House that avoids the so-called "jungles" of the cities and tries to influence warfare in jungles on other continents is not showing strength but vulnerability.

Government as a Constraint

Because success is relative we must ask, What can a President *do*? as well as what a President does. This is particularly important when comparing the Presidency with a parliamentary system, for the basic assumption of the American Constitution is that the President should be subject to far more constraints than his European counterparts. By contrast, parliamentary systems that have evolved from monarchical regimes assumed a concentration of authority in government. In Europe, politicians of all parties see government as a strong force in the nation.

Whereas all the resources of government are available to the Prime Minister and Cabinet through the fusion of powers, in the Madisonian system the President is not so advantaged. The President finds that powers of one part of government can be used against the White House. Instead of government being a resource, it is often a constraint upon the White House. The most prominent constraints are those of judicial review, federalism, and methods for delivering public services.

The Courts

The role of law imposes three limitations upon a President that are often lacking in other systems of government. First, Congress determines legislation; the most the President can do is veto a bill that he does not like, and his veto can be overridden. Laws that bind executive agencies are not authorized by the President, but are acts of Congress. By contrast, in parliamentary systems the laws that bind government are written in executive ministries; acts of Parliament confirm what the Prime Minister and Cabinet want. Acts of Congress, or the unwillingness of Congress to legislate, often constrain what the White House can do (Fisher, 1978).

Second, the federal government operates in a very legalistic culture. In an executive agency, the office of the general counsel is important because it advises presidential appointees about what they can and must do, and what they cannot do under the law. The adversary character of the American system means that a White House official who does something without an indisputable guarantee of legal authority may be hauled into the courts to answer for his or her action. Actions taken by the President himself are also subject to challenge in the courts. By contrast, from Britain to Japan, politicians who have won a general election have a mandate to do what they think proper, and the courts rarely constrain their actions. In Britain, the absence of constraint can be explained by the absence of a written constitution.

86

Notwithstanding American influence on the drafting of the 1947 Japanese constitution, it, too, is an example of the absence of a legalistic culture. Langdon (1967: 178) comments: "In spite of a legal system almost completely Western in origin, very little recourse is made to litigation; the lawyer plays a minor political role."

Litigation is a form of pressure-group activity limiting the White House, for it brings the courts into subgovernments (Shapiro, 1981). The courts are different from congressional committees, and unlike other groups involved there, the courts speak with binding authority. The process starts by Congress passing a law granting an entitlement to a particular group of citizens, for example, handicapped children. The executive branch agency enforcing the law and writing detailed regulations is not accountable to the White House; it is immediately accountable to interest groups representing beneficiaries and to congressional committees that oversee their actions. If the agency does what the interest groups wish, all is well. If it does not—for example, if the White House gives it a specific direction—then the interest group can challenge this in the courts. The ultimate decision about what the agency does is in the hands of a judge appointed for life, and usually, by a predecessor of the serving President. As Congress confers more statutory rights on groups, judicially oriented subgovernments have expanded as a constraint on the President's influence within the executive branch.

Third, the Supreme Court has the power of judicial review. It can hear cases challenging an action by the President and prevent the White House from doing what it wants by declaring an action unconstitutional. In the era of a traditional Presidency, there were few challenges to the President's authority because do-little Presidents followed a narrow construction of the powers of the President. The rise of the modern Presidency made both Congress and the White House seek to expand the powers of government. The Supreme Court rejected as unconstitutional a number of major laws approved by Congress and supported by President Roosevelt, but the Court came to accept as constitutional the expansive role of a modern President. Simultaneously, the Court began to define an activist role for itself, expanding its influence on measures that it deems constitutional. The President is not usually a party to the case before the Supreme Court, but the President can have a view about what the decision ought to be concerning segregation and antidiscrimination cases, police powers, or abortion. When the President disagrees with the opinion of a majority of the Supreme Court, he cannot veto it, but he can try to alter the outlook of the Court by appointing justices with a political outlook congenial to his own. Ideology is not the only test; party loyalty, personal friendship, and patronage are other considerations. The Senate must confirm nominations. Occasionally a nominee is rejected because he fails the "sleaze" test. In 1987, a nominee was rejected on political grounds: A majority of senators held that the views of Judge Robert Bork, a former law school professor, were so right-wing as to be a disqualification.

President Reagan thus had to nominate a less controversial person to the Court.

Courts exist in parliamentary systems, but they do not so constrain the executive. Britain is an extreme example of untrammeled executive power. Historically, Parliament was deemed the highest court of the land, and judges acted as agents of Parliament. As the rise of party government has allowed the Cabinet to dominate Parliament, it has also gained ascendancy over the courts. In reaction against the excesses of Hitler's Reich, Germany has a Constitutional Court with the power of judicial review, but unlike the American courts, it is not often used as a forum in which groups pursue political ends through litigation.

Federalism

In a unitary state, the central government is the supreme authority in the land. Local and regional institutions of government are normally granted taxing and spending powers by an act of Parliament instead of deriving authority and money from a constitution. The powers of local authorities can be drastically altered by central government, whether local authorities like it or not. The government of the day may use its parliamentary majority to reduce powers of regional and local authorities; pass legislation altering taxing powers; change local government boundaries drastically; or even abolish local government units. The British Conservative government led by Margaret Thatcher has done all these things since 1979 (cf. Gunlicks, 1981; Page and Goldsmith, 1987).

By contrast, the powers of American states are entrenched in the federal Constitution. The White House must accept their permanent status as partners in the federal system. Moreover, the position of cities is determined by each state's constitution. In the era of the traditional Presidency, the federal government did so little that grounds for conflict with states and cities were few.

As governor of California, Ronald Reagan could complain about the powers of the federal government, and as President of the United States, he can complain about the powers of state and local governments. In neither office could he control, by legislation or by executive action, what the other level of American government did.

The growth of government programs, concurrent with the rise of the modern Presidency, has created the need for continuous contact between federal, state, and local agencies. The terms of the relationship can be described in many different ways, such as cooperative, creative, or competitive federalism. The President himself devotes very little time to the problems of the federal system; his imperatives are international. So variegated are the interests of different states, of big cities as against suburbs, and of rural areas, that it is even difficult to secure a consensus that the President can endorse (Wright, 1982: chaps. 3, 5).

State and local governments concentrate their attention on Congress and on executive agencies permeable by congressional influence. The separation of powers gives authority to a Senate with two members from each of the fifty states, and each member of the House of Representatives normally identifies with a limited part of a state and sometimes with a single city (cf. Fenno, 1978). A President can make a major impact on state and local governments only with the consent of Congress. Congressmen are sensitive to lobbying by governors and mayors. Even more, they are sensitive to pressures from their own constituents. Federalism thus adds a vertical dimension to subgovernments that are constraints on the White House.

Delivering Public Policies

The growth of government in the twentieth century has changed the scope of government in two senses. First, government today does many more things than it did half a century or a century ago. Second, the characteristic services of contemporary government—education, social security, and health care—must be delivered in a local community or to individual households. The delivery of services is not determined by whether a system is unitary or federal, presidential or parliamentary. The actual delivery of services takes place in *local* schools, hospitals, and police stations. The growth of government thus involves a shift from government at the center to government nationwide (Rose, 1985b).

In a unitary state, all agencies delivering services anywhere in the country can be considered building blocks in a pyramid of authority, with the Cabinet and Prime Minister at the top. France is the most centralized of the countries examined here. The French Ministry of Education employs teachers, determines the curriculum of schools, and pays for education from central government taxes. The Department of Education in Washington does nothing like this; its role is primarily advisory and symbolic, accounting for less than 5 percent of expenditures on education at all levels of government. The Department of Education is also a focus for state and local education lobbies wanting to press policies forward in the federal government. The national health service and state-owned industries are also subject to the legal and financial control of the central government.

The growth of the modern Presidency has been paralleled by the growth of an activist federal government. In 1932, state and local governments accounted for more than two-thirds of all government expenditures; today, the federal government accounts for more than two-thirds. In dollar terms, Washington is now the largest partner in the federal system, but for the most part it is only a money-moving organization. The federal government does not deliver large numbers of services to individuals; it delivers checks, sometimes to individuals, sometimes to state and local governments, and sometimes to defense contractors or other nongovernmental agencies. Some checks are relatively small, such as social security payments, whereas others are big, such as debt interest payments to foreign banks. Social security does not bring government into personal contact with the elderly; checks are produced by a computer in Baltimore and delivered through the mail. The traditional service-delivery agency of the federal government, the Postal Service, was deemed of so little importance that it was removed from the President's Cabinet and turned into an independent agency of the executive branch in 1970.

The distribution of public employment illustrates the extent to which service delivery is in the hands of state and local governments, not the federal government. More than half of all public employees work for municipal, county, and other local jurisdictions. State governments employ almost as many people as the federal government. The federal government is a big employer only in defense; it has fewer civilian employees than do the governments of the fifty states. The importance of local government in service delivery is illustrated by the fact that more than one-third of all public employees are teachers and other workers in local and state education systems (Peters, 1985).

The most important policy imperative for the postmodern President— advancing America's interests in the international system—is not shared with mayors and governors. The one thing that the President alone can authorize delivering—a nuclear attack—looms larger in the literature of presidential power than it does in the history books. While often cited to illustrate the awesome power of the Oval Office, only President Truman has ordered the use of nuclear weapons, for two air raids that precipitated the end of World War II. We must therefore ask: What does the President deliver when he is not delivering nuclear attacks? The answer is: Not much.

Sizing Up Resources Means Cutting the President Down to Size

"More means better" describes the view of government in much of contemporary Europe. A government, including its Prime Minister, is judged by the benefits it provides for its citizens such as education, health care, and social security. Social policies today account for up to two-thirds of public expenditures in mixed-economy welfare states, and one-quarter of the national product. Socialist governments are judged by whether they can deliver the "good" goods of government; if they falter, their opponents are willing to accept this challenge. The electorate expects a right-of-center Prime Minister such as Margaret Thatcher to maintain social benefits. High taxes are accepted as the price that must be paid for a high level of benefits.

"Less means better" is a common American judgment of the role of government, particularly the federal government. The less money that government collects in taxation and therefore the fewer services it provides, the better governed the country is thought to be. In Europe the big question is— Who rules? Americans still debate the issue: How much rule? Europeans normally divide into two groups, those who are content with the present scale of government activities and those who want government to do even more. Americans face the opposite direction; differences in opinion tend to be between supporters of the status quo and those who want government to do less (ACIR, 1983: 17; cf. Hadenius, 1985).

The roots of contemporary American opposition to big government go back two centuries; the result is that the President is responsible for doing much less for fellow citizens than are his counterparts in Europe. A President is not responsible for taking $2 in every $5 produced by the national economy. The White House is not responsible for a national health service looking after every citizen. The states, not Washington, are responsible for education, and more than two-thirds of public employees work for state and local government.

President Reagan has played on American antipathy to "too much" government by making generalized attacks on the government he heads, telling anecdotes intended to show incompetence and waste in Washington. Opinion surveys show that his views reflect majority opinion; 62 percent think the federal government creates more problems than it solves (*Public Opinion*, 1987: 25). The President's comments assume that government is always and everywhere incompetent. But the actions of European mixed-economy welfare states show that government *can* act effectively on a scale well beyond what is deemed possible in Washington. If the critics of the federal government are correct, then the infirmities complained about are not inherent; they are limitations of government in the United States.

The Force of Political Inertia

Granted the limited resources that the President has, the fact remains: Government moves. Political inertia is the principal force propelling government forward (Rose and Karran, 1987). Inertia is here a force in motion, more or less routinely maintaining activities of government without any direction from the White House. Public laws enacted by Congress remain in effect whether the President likes them or not. Executive branch agencies are established by statute, and their officials will see to it that the laws for which they are responsible are carried out with or without direction from the White House. Appropriations for many programs are more or less "uncontrollable," following from statutory commitments to pay social security benefits, provide health care, pay interest on the national debt, and meet the salaries of federal employees and the armed forces. The expectations of citizens that government will maintain public services reinforces inertia.

Political inertia is particularly important in the American political system, insofar as the separation of powers makes it harder to change the direction of public policy. Without any interest being shown by the White House and without any positive intervention by the President, the great bulk of activities of the federal government are propelled forward. Political inertia is also a constraint on the President. In order to redirect government, the President must mobilize a force that is at least equal and opposite to the force moving in a direction of which he disapproves.

When the President takes the oath of office, he pledges to see that laws are faithfully executed. In doing so, he accepts the constraints of the Constitution and all the constraints imposed by an inheritance of past legislation, administration, and appropriations. The continuing commitments of government are vast by comparison with the personal resources of a newly elected President. A President can respond to the imperatives of office only by letting most actions of government continue as before, propelled by the force of political inertia (chapter 9). The programs for which the President is nominally responsible appear large in an absolute sense, but by comparison with European welfare states, the resources of the White House are small. Sizing up the President's resources cuts the Presidency down to size.

6. Learning to Campaign or Learning to Govern?

The Presidency is no place for amateurs
—Richard E. Neustadt

The campaign for the White House is an educational process; a candidate learns to go public by competing in a grueling round of primary elections. The chief resources that a newly elected President brings to the White House are personal: the political skills developed by political campaigning, and previous experience in public office. Election victory is proof that the President has what it takes to become President. Being President is different from running for the Presidency, however. Once in office, a President must learn how to go Washington and how to go international. Otherwise, his record will be a disappointment to himself, and to everyone who voted for him.

While it is easy to understand Richard Neustadt's dictum that the Presidency is no place for amateurs, it is not so clear what qualifies an individual as a "professional" President. A White House hopeful does not qualify for the job as a doctor or lawyer qualifies for a profession; there are no examinations or licensing bodies to declare a person capable of being President. The constitutional requirements are few and formal. The President must be a natural-born American citizen, resident in the United States for fourteen years, and at least thirty-five years old. Since governing is the most important responsibility of a President, the conventional way to learn the job has been to go Washington:

> Expertise can hardly be acquired without deep experience in political office...
> An expert in the White House does not guarantee effective policy, but lacking
> such an expert every hope is placed in doubt (Neustadt, 1960: 181, 193).

The one characteristic a President usually lacks is experience in the White House. A President is likely to gain his political experience in Congress or as a governor, positions where the White House is often seen as the opposition.

The first priority is winning a pair of elections—the primary ballots that lead to the nomination of a candidate and the November vote. To be elected

President, a politician must learn how to campaign, responding to the concerns of those he seeks to represent. In primaries, candidates are evaluated primarily in terms of their personal attributes and not according to their positions on issues (Miller et al., 1986). Success in campaigning is a necessary *pre*condition of facing the challenges of the Oval Office. By contrast, for a politician wanting to become Prime Minister in a parliamentary system, learning to govern is the first requirement.

Governing is very different from campaigning, and even more important. Effectiveness in government requires a postmodern President to be able to deal with other governments in the international system, as well as with other powerholders in Washington. A President who has spent years learning how to go public may not be competent in going Washington or going international, for time spent in practicing the arts of campaigning subtracts from the time that a politician can use to learn about Oval Office problems. By contrast, a Prime Minister normally has had years of experience within government as a Cabinet minister, senior civil servant, or both. Once placed in the highest office in a parliamentary system, a Prime Minister is ready to act, for he or she has already gained a lot of experience about how government works.

This chapter examines what politicians learn on the road to the White House by comparison with what politicians must do to get to the top in Britain, France, Germany, and Japan. The conclusion is clear: An American President learns far more about campaigning than about the practice of effective government, while Prime Ministers learn much more about governing effectively. When Presidents and Prime Ministers meet in world summits, the President's public relations staff is the most elaborate and the most professional, for a President is addressing the American public whether in Tokyo, Bonn, or Washington. Leaders of foreign nations do not require such an elaborate front, for they are usually more at home discussing problems of government.

Coming In from the Outside

A contemporary President enters the White House as an outsider; in the poignant words of former Georgia governor Jimmy Carter (1982): "We came to Washington as outsiders...We left as outsiders." The major difference is the degree to which candidates have been distant from the Oval Office. The vice-presidency is a difficult observation post, for the occupant is required to give uncritical loyalty to the President, while the President can more or less ignore him, as the experience of George Bush illustrates. A seat in Congress gives a politician a position of influence and incessant campaigning experience, but the vantage point of the Hill is miles away from that of the White

House, as John F. Kennedy learned. A governor's chair is even more distant from Washington. A state legislature is normally weaker than Congress, and the problems of a governor—education, crime, and urban and rural development—are very different from international problems facing the President.

To describe the President as an outsider is not to suggest the insecurities of a social isolate. The social origins of Presidents are very diverse. We do not classify Presidents by whether they grew up rich (Franklin D. Roosevelt, John F. Kennedy) or sons of dirt farmers (Harry Truman, Dwight Eisenhower, Lyndon Johnson, Jimmy Carter); by whether they display Irish wit and charm (John F. Kennedy, Ronald Reagan) or a Germanic capacity to fracture syntax and make meanings obscure (Dwight D. Eisenhower); or by whether they graduated from Harvard or Yale (John F. Kennedy, Gerald Ford), Whittier or Eureka colleges (Richard Nixon, Ronald Reagan) or attended the "university of life" (that is, like Harry Truman, had no college education). We judge a President by what he does once in office, not by what he did in childhood or what his parents did.

In order to evaluate how well prepared a President is, we must relate political experience to the imperatives of the Oval Office. A President is prepared for governing insofar as he brings to the Oval Office skill in campaigning (going public); in the politics of government (going Washington); and in managing the economy and national security (going international). In an ideal political system, the candidates of both major parties would be well qualified to juggle all the imperatives of office. In such circumstances, the White House would be in capable hands, whoever won the election. Alternatively, the parties could compete by nominating different kinds of candidates, one appealing as a campaigner responsive to the public and the other as an effective governor. In the worst case, neither candidate would be up to the demands of office; whoever won, the country would be the big loser.

Going Public

Prior experience in running for elective office is the common attribute of the sixteen Americans nominated for the Presidency by the Democratic or Republican parties since 1945 (see table 6.1). Dwight D. Eisenhower, a career military official, was the sole exception, but he was no novice in the arts of mobilizing support, having led armies in Europe in war and peace. The average presidential candidate is likely to have fought at least half a dozen elections and held elective public office for a dozen years before entering the Oval Office. Of the sixteen candidates, ten had been elected to Congress, five had been elected governor, and six ran in the vice-presidential slot before making a bid for the Presidency in their own right. A simple count of the number of times a President has previously run for office understates involvement in electoral politics, for American politicians are accustomed to incessant campaigning.

Most White House aspirants have started their political lives campaigning at the grass roots as a candidate for local or state office. This develops skill in dealing with ordinary people and their concerns, and in avoiding topics

TABLE 6.1

POLITICAL EXPERIENCE OF AMERICAN PRESIDENTIAL CANDIDATES

| Presidents | Years | Elected Offices | | Executive Branch | | |
		Congress	State Local	Inter-national	Eco-nomic	Other
Harry Truman	1945-52	10	12	0	0	1 VP
Thomas Dewey	1944, 1948	0	2	0	0	0
Dwight Eisenhower	1952-60	0	0	35	0	0
Adlai Stevenson	1952, 1956	0	4	6	0	1
Richard Nixon	1960; 1969-74	6	0	0	0	8 VP
John F. Kennedy	1961-63	13	0	0	0	0
Lyndon Johnson	1963-68	25	0	0	0	3 VP
Barry Goldwater	1964	12	4	0	0	0
Hubert Humphrey	1968	16	6	0	0	4 VP
George McGovern	1972	14	0	0	0	2
Gerald Ford	1974-76	25	0	0	0	1 VP
Jimmy Carter	1977-80	0	8	0	0	0
Ronald Reagan	1981-88	0	8	0	0	0
Walter Mondale	1984	12	4	0	0	4 VP
George Bush	1988	4	0	4	0	8 VP
Michael Dukakis	1988	0	18	0	0	0
Median		8	3	0	0	1
Average		9	4	3	0	2

NOTE: Names of Presidents appear in italics except for 1988. Dates indicate years in White House or year of campaign.

that are remote from local or state concerns, for example, the complexities of foreign policy or of international economic relations. Five post-war candidates have used the governorship of their state as the launching pad for a presidential campaign. In running for the White House from the State House of Massachusetts, Michael Dukakis hopes to emulate President Jimmy Carter and President Ronald Reagan. Being governor gives a politician a sense of how to deal with bureaucrats in state agencies, and with members of the state legislature, both skills relevant to the White House. But being a governor provides no experience in dealing with the major substantive problems facing a President: diplomatic negotiations with foreign powers, adapting the nation's defense to a changing environment for national security, managing an economy that is open to international influences, and overseeing a federal budget that spends more money in a state such as Massachusetts than the state government does itself.

Experience in running for election cultivates skills that a President needs for going public: the capacity to make a good impression when addressing a large audience and when dealing face-to-face with small numbers of important people, such as campaign backers. To run for governor or the Senate requires the ability to exploit the mass media, for a governor of New York, Illinois, or California can communicate with millions of electors only through television and the press, and a senator cannot press the flesh of every voter in his state.

As the nature of campaigning has changed, so too there have been big changes in what a politician must learn to campaign effectively. When nomination to the Presidency was in the hands of party caucuses and conventions, a presidential aspirant had to learn how to impress party leaders. For example, Harry Truman was a party politician of the old school, a product of the machine politics of Boss Tom Pendergast's Kansas City. Truman went to the Senate in 1934 as a machine nominee. When Dwight D. Eisenhower won the nomination and election in 1952 by projecting his personality through television in a nonparty campaign, old-style professionals held this against him, regarding it as an indication that Eisenhower was not fit for office (Neustadt, 1960: 194).

Today the ability to go public through the national electronic media is of first importance in campaigning for office. It is difficult to conceive of Harry Truman winning the nomination, for his rural Missouri twang and manners were more appropriate to a small-town Rotary Club than the national media. John F. Kennedy was a transitional politician, having a feel for old-style Boston machine politics and the wit and good looks that were appropriate for an age of TV campaigning. Ronald Reagan is the prototype of a modern media President, deploying the skills of an actor through television to communicate with the electorate on what appears as a personal basis. Personal popularity is now a necessary, and perhaps sufficient condition for running for the Presidency. The emphasis on personal appeal was aptly summed up by a Carter aide's comment during the 1976 presidential campaign:

> Issues. Issues. Issues! Can't political scientists ever think of anything else? The issues take care of themselves. Everybody who counts knows where Jimmy is, except the press who parrot back whatever some idiot Republican tells 'em. Issues are not our problem now. We've got to have good advance, good and precise targeting, good media, better polling, and a hell of a lot more on turn-out. We've got one major goal between now and November: to show Jimmy and Mondale as leaders whom voters will trust. *They are the issue.* (Quoted in Wayne, 1980: 183; italics in the original)

97

Going Washington

Prior experience of Washington is not necessary in order to run for, or to be elected, President. In the wake of the Vietnam war and the Watergate scandal, Jimmy Carter benefited in 1976 from his lack of Washington experience, for it meant that he was untouched by the failures of people who knew only too well how the system worked. Ronald Reagan has campaigned against the Washington view of the world, which he caricatures as remote from the lives of ordinary Americans. In 1988 Michael Dukakis campaigned with the argument that State House experience could easily transfer to the White House. Unfamiliarity with Washington is no barrier to winning the Presidency.

In the past four decades, eleven of the fourteen presidential nominees have been familiar with Washington before running for the biggest job in town. Lyndon Johnson and Gerald Ford each spent a quarter-century in Congress. Even a nominee with relatively little experience, Adlai Stevenson, had spent seven years in Washington. The average period of Washington experience for candidates is fourteen years.

Washington experience is almost invariably Hill experience. Congress is a superb place to learn how to bargain with other politicians in order to get things done in a system of divided powers. A senator soon learns that he or she is only one among 100 egos in the Senate, and a member of the House of Representatives is only one among 435 egos in the House. A congressman soon learns that his views are not the only views on an issue, and there is an incentive to get a bargain, whatever the content, rather than worry about the substance of an issue. A President must be more concerned with the substance of a policy.

Nevertheless, Congress is at the *other* end of Pennsylvania Avenue from the White House, operating very differently from the Oval Office. The move from one end of the avenue to the other may seem a small step, but it is much greater than moving from one baseball team to another. It is more like switching from playing baseball for the St. Louis Cardinals to playing quarterback for the football Cardinals. Being President means giving up the luxury of blaming the other end of the avenue for all the things that go wrong in the federal government. Whereas a congressman can pick and choose what issues to address without responsibility for outcomes, a President must see problems in the round. President Kennedy put the difference as follows:

> There is a big difference between those who advise or speak or legislate, and the man who must select from the various alternatives proposed what will be the policy of the United States. It is much easier to make the speeches than it is to make the judgements. Unfortunately your advisers are frequently divided. If you take the wrong course, and on occasion I have, the President bears the burden of the responsibility. (Quoted in Hirschfield, 1973: 135)

98

After three decades of experience in Washington and a year of experience as President, Lyndon Johnson concluded, "The Presidency looks a little different when you are in the Presidency than it did when you are in the Congress" (quoted in Hirschfield, 1973: 147).

A congressman specializes in micropolitics, dealing with particular issues of constituency concern or a single aspect of a complex problem. By contrast, the President must concentrate on macropolitics, the interconnection of the interests of different constituencies represented in Congress, between different economic goals such as employment and stable prices and between national security concerns on different continents. A congressman enjoys the luxury of passing the buck to the President. Often a congressman will go public with a demand that the White House do something about a problem. A congressman does not have to specify what a President ought to do. In a committee hearing, a congressman can cross-examine presidential appointees about their failures without having to show what he would have done differently.

The 1985 Gramm-Rudman-Hollings Act to reduce the federal deficit is an excellent example of Congress passing the buck to the President. Congressmen did not want to take the political responsibility for cutting spending on popular programs or increasing unpopular taxes. They wanted to dump the burden on the White House, or the General Accounting Office. Congressman William Gray (1985), chairman of the House Budget Committee, described the Gramm-Rudman Act as violating "the most fundamental principles of congressional responsibility and accountability, the precepts of economic policy, and plain common sense."

As Congress changes, the value of experience changes too. In the first decades after World War II, a congressman could serve an apprenticeship in Hill politics, for the system of giving substantial power to the chairmen of congressional committees chosen on the basis of seniority provided incentives for individuals to specialize in well-defined policy areas. The big figures in Congress, such as House Speakers Sam Rayburn and Tip O'Neill, saw themselves as congressional politicians, not as presidential aspirants. Today, members of Congress are under great pressure to go public as well as to go Washington.

Going International
The experience of presidential candidates in managing the economy and international affairs is easily described: None. No one who has served as secretary of state has subsequently become President since Buchanan entered the White House in 1856. George Bush was briefly U.S. representative to the United Nations, and then to Peking, and head of the CIA. It is characteristic of American politics that this has not made him appear as experienced or successful in executive politics as a governor of Massachusetts, Michael Dukakis. Moreover, as Vice-President Bush has been handicapped by being only

intermittently informed on national security matters and, in the case of the Iran-*contra* affair, the more he knew, the worse it would be for him politically.

A presidential aspirant is more likely to have worked in a city hall or a state capital than in the State Department, the Department of Defense, or the Treasury. When a mayor or governor thinks of money problems, he thinks only in dollars. When the President worries about money, he must also think of deutsche marks and yen. To a mayor, security is a problem of crime on the streets; to a President, it is a question of American and Soviet weapons in space. The road to the White House—via Iowa and New Hampshire, Super Tuesday and carefully staged TV appearances—gives candidates no knowledge of the international system.

A President normally learns about national security *after* entering the White House. A congressman cannot negotiate with foreign nations or experience the diverse pressures that flow into the Oval Office from every continent on earth, in addition to conflicting pressures from the State Department, the Defense Department, and the Central Intelligence Agency (CIA). A Governor is even more remote from foreign affairs. Nor has a presidential candidate normally had the experience of living in a foreign country as a student or a businessman, learning how people in other countries work and think. The demands of building a career in Congress or state politics and of a national campaign prevent extensive foreign travel—except as a carefully calculated part of campaigning for the presidential nomination.

The accidents of war account for most of the international exposure that a President has before entering the White House. Only Harry Truman in World War I and Dwight D. Eisenhower in World War II actually saw what problems of national security are like on the ground by fighting on foreign soil. Jimmy Carter showed that a Naval Academy education is not a guarantee of familiarity with foreign affairs. George McGovern took a post in Food for Peace because he needed a presidential appointment after being unsuccessful in a Senate race in 1960. In the past century only one President, William Howard Taft, had previously been a Cabinet officer concerned with military matters.

No postwar presidential candidate has been directly involved in the management of the economy, and no Secretary of the Treasury has subsequently moved to the Oval Office. Knowing banking is a qualification for the secretaryship of the Treasury, but a disqualification for the White House. The typical presidential candidate is a self-employed full-time politician, who may have acquired a law degree to assist in following a political career. The problems examined in papers from the Treasury, the Federal Reserve Board, and the Council of Economic Advisers are often completely new to a President. Even more alien are the problems of international economic policy. Congressional experience in the micropolitics of budgeting, looking at particular appropriations for specific programs in one department, is no preparation for looking at the bottom-line totals of the budget.

Death, assassination, and resignation have resulted in three postwar vice-presidents becoming President, but the vice-presidency is not an office used as a training for succession (cf. Goldstein, 1982). For an active politician such as Lyndon Johnson, the vice-presidency was an agony, withdrawing him from a powerful role in the Senate and making him subordinate to a President junior in Washington politics. Only Richard Nixon could be said to have gained substantive policy experience as a traveling ambassador on behalf of the White House. Two vice-presidents—Hubert Humphrey and Walter Mondale—could not translate their experience in the vice-presidency into election to the Presidency, nor could Richard Nixon when he first ran for the White House in 1960. For George Bush, eight years as vice-president was a handicap in 1988.

The field of hopefuls who sought the Democratic and Republican nominations in 1988 displayed the same political careers as earlier candidates: Congressional experience was common, and a candidate was as likely to have been without government experience as to have served in the executive branch. Of the six Republican and seven Democratic candidates who received federal funding for contesting primaries, two had no previous experience in government: Jesse Jackson, a civil rights activist, and Pat Robertson, a preacher. Three made their name as governors: Michael Dukakis, Bruce Babbitt, and Pete du Pont. Six of the candidates were congressmen or former congressmen. Robert Dole and Richard Gephardt were "insider" congressmen, concerned with building coalitions on the Hill; and Albert Gore, Gary Hart, Jack Kemp, and Paul Simon were not. Only two candidates could boast of experience in the executive branch. George Bush, a two-term vice-president, and briefly before that ambassador to the United Nations and to China and was briefly head of the CIA, and General Alexander Haig, a career soldier who had served as national security assistant in the White House and as secretary of state.

In a parliamentary system of government, persons with the government experience of George P. Shultz (present secretary of state, former treasury and labor secretary, and former head of the Office of Management and Budget [OMB]) and Joseph P. Califano (a former assistant to President Johnson, an assistant secretary of defense, and secretary of health, education, and welfare) would have been very visible candidates for the nation's leading post. In the presidential system, people who have spent years learning how the federal executive and White House work appear to be disqualified for the job.

Do What You Must, or Do What You Can?
A management consultant might suggest recruiting a President by first identifying the qualities needed and then searching for politicians who had the right aptitude. This is not possible, for becoming President is determined by electoral competition. We must instead take an inductive approach; given

the skills that candidates have, what can they do once in office? The one thing a President-elect is sure to be good at is going public. But campaigning is out-door work, undertaken in places distant from the problems that must be faced within the Oval Office. Learning to campaign is about spreading hope and good feeling. As John F. Kennedy soon learned, making speeches that inspire people is much easier than facing hard choices between uncertain international alternatives.

A President enters office with both amateur and professional creden-tials. Election is proof of credentials as a professional campaigner. In some cases, a President is also a pro on the Hill, but he is an amateur in the international system. While spending a short time in service he may have learned how to fire a gun, but not the diplomatic skills needed to avoid firing a nuclear missile. As a campaigner, he will have learned how to raise millions of dollars for campaigning, but not how to deal with a trillion-dollar budget. In the course of time, a President can gradually lose his amateur status and earn the respect of professionals by relating concerns of Washington and public opinion to international issues. But while learning by doing, an amateur is likely to make mistakes, and the mistakes of a postmodern President can be costly for the nation.

Another Way: Going Government

The American way to the top is very different from the career of politicians in parliamentary systems. Instead of going public, a European or Japanese politician must first go government. To succeed, a leader must do more than get a positive response from the electorate; he or she must also learn to be effective in government. Fusing control of the legislature and executive in a Cabinet accountable to Parliament focuses the attention of elected officials on what government does. The immediate responsibility of Cabinet ministers is to deal with substantive problems of government (see figure 6.1). An effective minister is deemed successful especially when what the minister does is also popular with the electorate. A minister of finance responsible for a booming economy can be considered a potential Prime Minister, just as a minister who is in charge when unemployment and inflation rise suffers a big career setback. A Cabinet that is ineffectual will lose electoral support and be attacked in Parliament.

To secure action on policies, a Prime Minister and Cabinet colleagues must influence two groups: high-ranking bureaucrats in the ministries and the governing party. Bureaucrats have substantial knowledge of the prob-lems of formulating and implementing policies; it is no good proposing a policy that is popular in the party but that cannot be effectively implemented (Rose, 1987a). A minister who wants to be effective takes into account the advice of officials expert in the substance of policies. By contrast with Washington, there is much less opportunity for bureaucrats and interest groups to play off MPs against the Cabinet and, civil servants serve their minister since their loyalties are not divided by a separation of powers.

Prime Minister	Bureaucracy	Policy
and Cabinet————————>Parliamentary————>outcomes
action	party

FIGURE 6.1

GOING GOVERNMENT: THE PRIME MINISTER IN OFFICE

In a parliamentary system, party is the tie that binds together members of Parliament and Cabinet ministers. Except in a major political crisis, the majority party in Parliament will vote for government proposals for legislation and expenditure. Given a disciplined parliamentary majority, a Prime Minister can regard votes in Parliament as a means to the end of enacting public policies. By contrast, White House staff often view winning a vote in Congress as an end in itself.

Because each Cabinet minister is immediately and personally responsible for a particular field of policy, his career prospects tend to rise or fall with success in a ministry. A Cabinet minister wants to convince the public that policies are desirable. To do so, he must also convince Cabinet colleagues, Parliament, and the country that they are effective. The Prime Minister is concerned with the overall balance of government, seeking to combine measures in ways that produce effects popular with the majority of the electorate. Central collective authority in government makes it easy for a Prime Minister to think in terms of goals for the government as a whole.

Going government is very different from going Washington (cf. figures 2.1 and 6.1). Washington politics is a continuous process of bargaining between more or less independent powerholders. The task of the President is to learn how to assemble support from disparate voices on terms acceptable to everyone. The object is a bargain that enhances the status of the President and therefore his ability to exert influence in another round of bargaining. Since a bargain is a necessary condition of action, achieving agreement can become an end in itself. By contrast, a Prime Minister does not have to reduce policymaking to the lowest common denominator acceptable to the legislature, the bureaucracy, and interest groups outside government. With a secure majority in Parliament, a Cabinet can concentrate on the substance of government.

Going government is also very different from going public (cf. figures 2.2 and 5.1). Whereas a President's characteristic mode of communication today is through television, where listeners are remote and cannot talk back, in a parliamentary system politicians are in continuous face-to-face discussions and debates in Cabinet and Parliament. Whereas a President can go public to appeal over the heads of Congress, a Prime Minister cannot. Maintaining the confidence of Cabinet and Parliament and of the party linking the two is a necessary condition of remaining in office. The leaders of a parliamentary system are constantly tested in discussions with other politicians around them, while still having the authority to make effective decisions.

Going international is a task of Prime Ministers as well as Presidents, but they approach international responsibilities differently. A Prime Minister is usually experienced in international negotiations. In order to become Prime Minister, a politician usually has previously had a job that includes negotiations abroad, either as a foreign minister or as a minister dealing with other member nations of the European Community. By contrast, an American presidential aspirant does not negotiate with foreigners because he has no authority to do so, and foreigners do not vote in primaries. A Prime Minister is certain of being able to commit his or her government when making an international agreement, whereas a President must simultaneously negotiate with other powerholders in Washington and with foreign governments.

Britain: Apprenticeship in Office

Political leaders in Britain serve decades in a parliamentary apprenticeship. To get to the top, a politician must enter the House of Commons at a youthful age in order to gain a series of increasingly important political appointments in ministries (see table 6.2). At each step, an aspiring politician must demonstrate skill in dealing with problems of government as well as party politics. When a party leader enters 10 Downing Street for the first time as Prime Minister, he or she is not a stranger in a strange house in a strange city, as with some Presidents entering the White House. A new Prime Minister has been in and out of Downing Street for years, attending twice-weekly Cabinet meetings. Cabinet ministers have far more opportunity to observe the work of a Prime Minister at close quarters in Cabinet than a member of Congress has to observe the President. In opposition, a British politician can learn by testing his or her wits against the Prime Minister twice a week in Question Time in the House of Commons.

A politician must be elected to the House of Commons before being considered for the Prime Ministership, since this job goes with being leader of the majority party in the Commons. A British politician has on average spent twenty-three years as a member of the House of Commons, the elected chamber of Parliament before becoming a party leader. Instead of running for the leadership in primary contests remote from the seat of government, the Conservative leader is chosen by the vote of MPs* and the Labour leader is chosen, by an electoral college dominated by MPs and trade union leaders. By the time a British politician gets to the top, he or she has been in Parliament for more than twice as long as the average presidential candidate has been in Congress. Since a minister is simultaneously an MP, serving in Parliament is not a substitute for government experience, as is the case in Washington.

TABLE 6.2

POLITICAL EXPERIENCE OF BRITISH MAJOR PARTY LEADERS

| Leader | Years | Elected Office | | Executive Ministry | | | Civil |
		Parlia-ment	Local	Total	Inter-national	Eco-nomic	Ser-vant
Clement Attlee	1935-55	23	8	8	7	0	0
Winston Churchill	1940-53	39	0	25	14	7	0
Anthony Eden	1955-57	32	0	21	21	0	0
Harold Macmillan	1957-63	31	0	11	4	4	0
Hugh Gaitskell	1955-63	10	0	6	0	4	5
Harold Wilson	1963-76	18	0	6	0	6	5
Alec Douglas-Home	1963-64	32	0	16	9	0	0
Edward Heath	1965-75	15	0	13	3	2	1
Jim Callaghan	1976-79	31	0	12	3	3	11
Margaret Thatcher	1975-	16	0	7	0	0	0
Michael Foot	1980-83	30	0	5	0	2	0
Neil Kinnock	1983-	13	0	0	0	0	0
Median		27	0	10	3	2	0
Average		23	1	11	5	2	2

NOTE: Italic letters indicate party leaders who have also been Prime Minister. Years in office as of date of first being elected party leader.

The apprenticeship of an aspiring Prime Minister starts by learning how to discuss practical problems of government in parliamentary debate with senior figures of the Opposition, gaining a good name in the media, and building up a following in the party. Promotion to a ministerial post is not won by an election campaign; it is a decision of the Prime Minister, who wants ability in giving direction to government and loyalty to the party and its leader. A politician with a foot on the lowest rung of the ministerial ladder has every incentive to work for promotion. Every two or three years, a

---

*The term MP is short for member of Parliament. It is used only for members of the House of Commons, and not for members of the nonelected House of Lords. A politician must be a success as a government minister in order to advance up the career ladder.

minister will either be promoted to a higher-ranking post or be turned out of office by the Prime Minister as ineffective in government. Whereas an American presidential aspirant can treat the job of governor or congressman as simply a springboard for the Presidency, an ambitious British politician must be a success as a government minister in order to advance up the career ladder.

Usually a leader has had experience in going international. The average British party leader has served five years in the Foreign Office or Ministry of Defense and two years in an economic ministry *before* making a bid for the Prime Ministership. As foreign secretary of a major power in the European Community, a permanent member of the Security Council of the United Nations, and a postimperial nation linked with Commonwealth countries on every continent, a British foreign secretary will quickly become familiar with problems and personalities in all corners of the world. In a major economic post in a country that must export to pay for imported food, a British minister learns about dealing with a national economy subject to what happens elsewhere in the international system.

The average British party leader has spent eleven years as a minister *before* becoming party leader. Four party leaders—Hugh Gaitskell, Harold Wilson, Edward Heath, and James Callaghan—had also been civil servants before running for elective office, further broadening their knowledge of Whitehall, where government offices cluster. A British politician must simultaneously establish a career in the House of Commons and in Whitehall, whereas a congressional career is *not* an apprenticeship to giving direction to the Pentagon, the State Department, or the Treasury. The time and effort that an American President invests in going public is invested by British politicians in going Whitehall. The public to which British politicians play is an elite public, a small circle of Cabinet colleagues, headed by thePrime Minister. A good name in the House of Commons is important, for the media tend to take their cues about who is a good or bad politician from what is said in Parliament. Knowledge of the substance of government activities is necessary to hold one's own in a parliamentary debate involving other MPs who have previously been in the same ministry, or hope to gain the job in the future. What the public hears and sees about politicians tends to be an echo of opinions voiced by political elites.

The contrast between the careers of British Prime Ministers and American Presidents is extreme. While British politicians differ from each other in many ways, they are alike in having learned to go government before entering Downing Street. The two postwar party leaders with the least experience in government, Labour's Michael Foot and Neil Kinnock, each suffered a disastrous electoral defeat. Before entering office, a Prime Minister has already become familiar with the substance and problems of government.

TABLE 6.3

POLITICAL EXPERIENCE OF FRENCH PRESIDENTS AND PRIME MINISTERS

| | | Elected Office | | Executive Ministry | | | |
| | | Assem-bly | Local | Civil service | Min-istry | Inter-national | Econ-nomic |
Leader	Years						
Charles de Gaulle	Pres. 1958-69	0	0	30	5	35	0
Michel Debré	PM 1959-62	0	0	9	1	0	0
Georges Pompidou	PM 1962-68 Pres. 1968-74	0	0	0	0	0	0
M. Couve de Murville	PM 1968-69	0	0	28	10	18	10
J. Chaban-Delmas	PM 1969-72	23	22	2	1	1	0
Pierre Messmer	PM 1972-74	4	0	15	13	28	0
Jacques Chirac	PM 1974-76, 1986-88	7	0	8	7	0	12
V. Giscard-d'Estaing	Pres. 1974-81	2	0	4	12	0	14
Raymond Barre	PM 1976-81	0	0	11	6 [a]	5	12
F. Mitterrand	Pres. 1981-	35	0	2	7	7	0
Pierre Mauroy	PM 1981-84	8	14	0	0	4 [a]	0
Laurent Fabius	PM 1984-86	6	0	5	3	0	3
Michel Rocard	PM 1988-	7	0	8	4	0	10
Median		4	0	8	5	1	0
Average		7	3	9	5	8	5

a. Includes Barre's five years as a commissioner of the European Community and Mauroy's four years as a member of the European Parliament.

NOTE: Political experience prior to the creation of the Fifth Republic in 1958 included; symbolic posts as mayor of a small commune in constituency are omitted.

France: Technocratic Training

The dominant characteristic of French politicians who get to the top is technocratic skill. A French President or Prime Minister does not have to learn about government after entering office, for he normally starts his career as a civil service expert in economic or foreign affairs. If anything, he will be an amateur in the art of going public.

The typical political leader of the Fifth Republic is a technocrat recruited into the civil service by an extremely competitive examination and trained at l'Ecole Nationale d'Administration (the National School of Administration). *Enarques* (i.e., graduates of ENA) gain experience of government immediately on completing their higher education. The best and the brightest normally head for the ministries of foreign affairs or finance. By the age of thirty-five, they have a decade of experience in dealing with the substance of international diplomatic, military, and financial problems, and will be experienced in representing national interests in the twelve-nation European Community, in Moscow or Washington. By contrast, an American politician is likely to have spent these years glad-handing voters or doing whatever it takes to prove that he is not an expert technocrat.

Since the foundation of the Fifth French Republic in 1958, thirteen men have been President or Prime Minister; and three-quarters have followed a technocratic route to the top (see table 6.3). The founder of the Republic, General Charles de Gaulle, abhorred party politicians; he had been a career military officer before France's military defeat in 1940 catapulted him into politics in exile. Prime Minister Jacques Chirac is a representative example of a political leader on the right in the Fifth Republic. Immediately after completing studies at ENA in 1959, Chirac became a Ministry of Finance official and then worked as a civil servant in the Prime Minister's office. After being elected to Parliament in 1967, he became a junior minister. In 1974, Chirac was first named Prime Minister under President Georges Pompidou, in whose private office he had previously been a civil servant. Since 1981, President François Mitterrand has named three Premiers from the left; two of these, Laurent Fabias and Michel Rocard, have been classic technocratic graduates of ENA, more at home in the ministries than in the elected Assembly.

In France, a civil servant can easily move into government because continental European political systems do not enforce a distinction between politics and administration (Suleiman, 1984). Both elected officials and civil servants are regarded as in the service of the state. Civil servants have the right to go on leave from their post to stand for Parliament or take a partisan appointment. In Paris, becoming a civil servant opens doors to political preferment because it gives an individual the chance to practice skills in government and the opportunity to catch the eye of the President or Prime Minister, who can offer patronage important in reaching the top.

By contrast with Britain, the French Prime Minister is not allowed to be a member of the National Assembly. Hence, a Frenchman pursuing a political career can move from being a civil servant to becoming a minister without ever having to contest an election. High office requires the President or Prime Minister's confidence that an individual has the technical capacity to run a major department of government. Five of the leaders of the Fifth Republic never sat in the Assembly. The median French leader had served longer as a civil servant than as an elected Assembly member, whereas the median American presidential candidate has spent time in Congress but never in the executive branch.

The process by which a Frenchman goes government has a parallel in Washington, where there are bright and ambitious young people who seek a high-level job in the executive branch without running for elective office. The talents demonstrated as a special assistant to a Cabinet secretary or in a White House staff post may lead to a senior appointment in a subsequent administration. But an American technocrat cannot go all the way to the Oval

Office, for experience in running government is not a qualification for becoming President. By contrast, a Frenchman who has worked as a civil servant may become Prime Minister or President in his own right.

A French leader differs fundamentally from an American President in *not* being trained in going public. It is possible for an individual to become Prime Minister without ever having run for elective office; the patronage of the President was the route by which Georges Pompidou, Couve de Murville, and Raymond Barre reached the Prime Ministership. Since 1965, the President has been popularly elected. The weakness of parties and the use of a two-ballot system of popular election, in which the leading candidates in the first round compete in a runoff in the second round, make it necessary to go public to become President. But in order to qualify as a candidate for the Presidency, an individual must first establish a national position in government (de Gaulle, Pompidou, Giscard d'Estaing) or in opposition in the Assembly (Mitterrand).

Germany: Going the Rounds

A German gets to the top by going the rounds in government, gaining experience at more than one level of the Federal Republic (*Bundesrepublik*), and in party and Parliament as well as government. Experience outside the national capital, Bonn, makes German leaders resemble American presidential candidates. But a German leader differs in that the parliamentary system makes it normal for a leader to participate in Bonn as well as at the *Land* (state) level before becoming Federal Chancellor (see table 6.4). The German equivalent of "going Washington" might be described as "going *Bundesbahn*" (federal railway), riding the train from Munich to Hamburg, wheeling and dealing with other political elites in a system that is federal in party politics as well as government.

Of the leaders who started their political careers in postwar Germany,* nearly all have learned the ways of Bonn well before becoming leader. The average candidate for the German Chancellorship has had more experience in the elected chamber of Parliament, the *Bundestag*, than American counterparts have had in Congress. Unlike candidates for the White House, a party leader has also been a minister for an average of five years. Two Chancellors, Ludwig Erhard of the Christian Democratic Union and Helmut Schmidt of the Social Democratic party used their success as finance minister to become Chancellor. German leaders are less likely to have held important posts in foreign affairs or the Treasury than British politicians. By contrast with France, it is unusual for a German political leader to have begun his career as a civil servant in Bonn.

---

*The first four leaders to contest the Chancellorship—Adenauer, Schumacher, Ollenauer, and Brandt—had been born in the Kaiser's regime, and faced the extreme challenge of surviving in exile or within Germany during Hitler's Reich.

TABLE 6.4

POLITICAL EXPERIENCE OF MAJOR PARTY LEADERS IN GERMANY

Leader	Years	Elected Office		Executive Office			
		Federal Parliament[a]	State and Local	Federal Ministries			State and Local
				Total	Inter- national	Eco- nomic	
Ludwig Erhard	1963-66	14	0	14	0	14	0
K.G. Kiesinger	1966-69	9 (+8)	8	0	0	0	8
Willy Brandt	1969-74	8 (+9)	11	3	3 (+12 exile)		9
Rainer Barzel		15	0	1	1	0	0
Helmut Schmidt	1974-82	17 (+4)	4	5	3	2	8
Franz Josef Strauss		31	0	12	6	3	0
Hans-Jochen Vogel		11 (+1)	14	9	0	0	22
Helmut Kohl	1982-	6 (+7)	17	0	0	0	7
Johannes Rau		0 (+16)	17	0	0	0	17
Median		11 (+4)	8	3	0	0	8
Average		12 (+5)	8	5	1	2	8

a. Figures in parentheses are years as member in nonelected upper chamber, the *Bundesrat*, representing a state government in which elective office held.

NOTE: Names of party leaders who have served as *Bundeskanzler* are in italic.

Concurrently, German politicians often have grass-roots experience of government, useful in a country where state and local governments are important in making and delivering public policies. The average German candidate for the Chancellorship has four times the state and local government experience of an American presidential candidate. Leaders of state governments simultaneously gain experience of federal politics as ex officio members of the nonelected upper chamber of the federal Parliament, the *Bundesrat*; the average leader has spent five years there in addition to a dozen years as an elected member of the lower house. Since members of the upper chamber of Parliament vote on important federal legislation, Bonn politicians must pay more attention to state political leaders than the White House pays to governors. A politician who is primarily known as the head of a state is also knowledgeable in Bonn. While Chancellor Helmut Kohl built his career at the state level, he spent six years as leader of the parliamentary opposition in the *Bundestag* before getting the top job in government.

The geopolitical position of Germany between Eastern and Western Europe makes international issues a part of domestic politics. Every leader has lived through the trauma of Hitler's Third Reich, defeat in World War II and military occupation, and the division of Germany between a Russian-controlled East German regime and a Federal Republic dependent on American military protection. To be born a German before 1945 is to experience the fragility of peace, the economy, and public order. The European Community was founded on a joint German and French desire to create a political alliance that would replace a century of strife between the two nations. German politicians are well aware of the need to judge the international implications of domestic political statements, given their vulnerable position on the border between the Soviet and Western blocs. As mayor of Berlin, former Chancellor Willy Brandt learned the problem firsthand when the Russians put up the Berlin Wall.

An ambitious German politician must cultivate the confidence of party officials, for nomination to the leadership is determined by party conventions and not by American-style primary contests. There are three major leadership posts in the Christian Democratic and Social Democratic parties. the party chairman, the head of the party in Parliament, and the party nominee for the Chancellorship. A candidate for high office must cooperate with other very important officeholders within the party, including potential challengers for his job. Party management thus has a much higher priority than in Washington. The federal system also gives German leaders substantially more experience in going public than their British or French counterparts, for party leaders are concerned with the outcome of state as well as federal elections, and state elections are staggered, occurring at different times during the life of a Parliament.

Superficially, the recruitment of a German Chancellor may appear to resemble the road to the White House because less time is spent in central government than in the British or French system. But the structure of the German system means that party, Parliament, and state government focus on the federal government's politics and policies. A newly-elected Chancellor is not coming in from the outside, as in Washington, but rising higher in a system that he has been working in all his political life.

Japan: Party and Bureaucracy

"Going" party is a necessary condition of reaching the Prime Minister's office in Japan, given the dominance of Parliament by the Liberal Democratic party. Election as leader by the parliamentary representatives of the LDP is tantamount to election as Prime Minister. Campaigning within the LDP is intensive, for the party is divided into factions that compete with one another in a leadership election every two years. Each faction has a permanent organization, dozens of members of Parliament, and lots of money to finance campaigning. Factions are far more stable than the personal followings that American presidential aspirants assemble. Each faction is in effect a party within a party (Tomita et al., 1986: 248ff). Since no faction has a majority within the parliamentary party, a leader must mobilize the support of a coalition of factions.

Japanese politics places a high premium on going public, for ballots are frequent and the form of ballot—a single vote is cast for one candidate in a

111

district electing several members to the Diet—forces LDP members to run against each other in districts that can be as populous as an American state. Campaigning in Japan emphasizes personality, local benefits, and expensive campaign techniques. An aspirant for the party leadership not only campaigns for his own election to the Diet, but also campaigns for the election of other Diet members who belong to his faction. Because a Japanese Prime Minister is elected by the parliamentary party, he has an interest in the success of the party (and faction) as an institution, as well as in his own career (Curtis, 1979: 42ff).

Going government is important too. A similar number of LDP Prime Ministers have started their political career as an elite civil servant instead of starting in party politics (see table 6.5). Before the American occupation in 1945, those who governed in the name of the Emperor, including most Prime Ministers, were career officials; the attempt in the 1920s to establish the principle of party government was not sustained. Following Japan's defeat, former civil servants were an important source of politically experienced recruits to the new Diet and Cabinet. Moreover, their conservative temperament was in accord with the dominant outlook of the electorate (Pempel, 1984: 79ff). Since the Liberal Democratic party (LDP) has governed without a break since 1955, most civil servants have spent their whole working life under an LDP government.

As in France, a Japanese politician can build a career by starting as a high-status civil servant within an important ministry, use the status and contacts acquired there to become elected to the Diet, then become a Cabinet minister, a faction leader, then party leader and Prime Minister. Civil servants who make this progression are not low-level bureaucrats; they are graduates of elite institutions such as the Tokyo University Law Faculty, and have often served in the ministry of finance. Since retirement is possible at an early age and candidates elected to the Diet are often older, party politics offers a second career to some civil servants. The LDP welcomes former civil servants; up to one-half of Cabinet ministers have been ex-officials and more than one-fifth of LDP Diet members are former civil servants (Baerwald, 1986: table 1.14; Shiratori, 1988; Pempel, 1986).

In the 1950s and 1960s Prime Ministers had often spent more time as a civil servant than as a member of Parliament. For example, Hayato Ikeda, head of government from 1960 to 1964, had spent more than two decades as a civil servant in the Ministry of Finance prior to the creation of the postwar parliamentary system. He then spent four years as the Minister of Finance and in MITI (Ministry of International Trade and Industry) before becoming leader. At the start of the 1980s the Prime Minister, Masayoshi Ohira, had spent an equal period of time as civil servant and member of Parliament, bringing to the highest office in government twenty-four years of experience as a civil servant in the Ministry of Finance, and five years as the Cabinet Minister of Foreign Affairs.

TABLE 6.5

POLITICAL EXPERIENCE OF JAPANESE PRIME MINISTERS

Prime Minister	Years	Elected to Diet	Executive ministry			
			Civil Service	Min- ister	Inter- national	Eco- nomic
Ichiro Hatoyama	1954-5	3	0	4	0	0
Tanzan Ishibashi	1956-57	5	0	5	0	5
Nobusuke Kishi	1957-60	9	21	3	3	21
Hayato Ikeda	1960-64	13	20	5	0	24
Eisaku Sato	1964-72	16	24	7	0	2
Kakuei Tanaka	1972-74	25	0	5	0	4
Takeo Miki	1974-76	37	0	9	2	2
Takeo Fukuda	1976-78	24	19	10	6	20
Masayoshi Ohira	1978-80	26	26	7	5	28
Zenko Suzuki	1980-82	33	0	3	0	0
Yasuhiro Nakasone	1982-87	35	2	8	2	2
Noboru Takeshita	1987-	29	0	8	0	6
Median		25	1	6	0	5
Average		24	9	6	1	9

NOTE: Experience in government prior to 1946 included; parliamentary vice ministries not included.

SOURCE: Data compiled by Masaaki Kataoka, 1988.

The three most recent Prime Ministers—Suzuki, Nakasone, and Take-shita—have reflected a shift in the LDP toward choosing leaders who are career MPs. Each has had more than a quarter-century of experience in the Diet and in LDP politics before becoming leader. In addition, the three have had an average of five years as minister. Like Congressman Tip O'Neill, the current Japanese Prime Minister, Noboru Takeshita, endorses the sentiment that all politics is local politics. But because Takeshita's career has been in a parliamentary system, he has been a Cabinet minister too. From 1982 to 1987 he was Minister of Finance, watching the ups and downs of the U. S. dollar and America's rising trade deficit with Japan. The Japanese Prime Minister does not need to fly to Washington to be told about the American economy, for he has already had ample briefings from U.S. Treasury secretaries, seeking Japanese help in dealing with America's deficits.

Politics in Japan is at least *two* full-time jobs, campaigning in the party and participating in Parliament and government. Going party is an impera-tive in building the factional support necessary to be elected LDP leader and thus Prime Minister (cf. Tsurutani, 1977: 95; Hayao, 1985). Politicians who succeed in becoming party leader spend a quarter-century in Parliament, half a dozen or more years in government office as a minister, and often have had a high civil service post as well. Confronted with the classic Confucian Chinese problem of choosing between a career that is "red" (i.e., dominated by political expedience) or one that is "expert" (dominated by technocrats unresponsive to concerns of the electorate), the Japanese have sought leaders who can work both systems (Pempel, 1984: 75ff).

Comings and Goings of Leaders

Going public is the first priority of an American President, whereas going government is the first priority of the people with whom he must work in the international system. When Americans evaluate a President, it is first of all in terms of his success in running for office. But when the President discusses economic, diplomatic, and military concerns at a world summit meeting, he is evaluated for what he knows about problems of government.

In a democracy, gaining the highest political office should require electoral support, but the American way of preparing a politician for the White House is not the only way in which a democracy can recruit a leader. One major difference is the American emphasis on virtually continuous campaigning. There are congressional elections every two years and a presidential primary and general election every four years, plus instant judgment by public opinion polls and the media. When campaigning becomes incessant and an end in itself, it imposes costs. According to a scholar of political parties, Austin Ranney: "It puts a premium on sitting in someone's living room and being a pleasant fellow. But that isn't what a President is supposed to do" (quoted in Taylor, 1987).

Parliamentary systems have another way of recruiting leaders. Before an individual can be considered as a Prime Minister, he or she must serve more than a decade as an apprentice in government. The experience varies from country to country. In France and Japan, apprenticeship is often in the civil service. Only after winning a position as an insider in the ministries does an individual begin to appear in public as a party politician soliciting votes. In Britain and Germany, success in electoral politics is the first but not the last step to the top. An individual must also demonstrate a capacity to give direction to government. In all parliamentary systems the importance of party as against the American concern with personality gives politicians more opportunity to concentrate on government.

Experience in dealing with substantive problems of government—foreign policy, economic policy, and the intersection of the two—is an asset for a national leader in the international system. The winner in a campaign for the White House is pitchforked into the international system, ready or not. For the first time, he must think about international issues, and foreign

114

political systems and personalities are new to him. However many promises a candidate scatters when campaigning, to put words into action often means going international. To succeed, a President must deal with leaders of other nations who have more experience in government. Having long had an American elephant as an ally, other leaders are usually better able to understand the United States than a new President is able to understand their country and its concerns.

When Richard Neustadt argued against an amateur President in 1960, he cited economic and international problems as a reason why the Presidency should no longer be a place for amateurs. Nevertheless, major changes since then have made it more likely that Americans will elect a President who is an amateur in government. Nominations are no longer decided by party conventions, with the knowledge and incentives to pick a candidate whom they think can be elected *and* do a good job in government. Today, presidential nominees are chosen in a sequence of primary contests that constitute the longest political marathon in the world. Since those who vote in primaries have no particular knowledge of government, the contests become a test of personality and character, or even something as fortuitous as early success in a primary, generating the "big momentum" that media correspondents look for to favor a candidate as the potential winner. The effort required to run for the nomination—and its irrelevance to many activities of government—has led many experienced congressmen and governors to avoid the race for the White House. The result, according to David Broder (1987a), is that the present system "forces us to accept repeatedly and inevitably, people who are less than the best qualified individuals for the job they seek."

By definition, the winner of a presidential nomination is a professional campaigner. By the time a candidate reaches the White House, he is certain to know a lot about Iowa and very little about Iran, a lot about Super Tuesday but very little about super budgets and super weapons. Parliamentary systems have their limitations, even insulating politicians from the electorate, but they do this in order to emphasize professionalism in government. A President-elect only realizes after winning election that while campaigning is important, it is not a preparation for effective government.

7. Perpetually Campaigning for Support

Too many good people have been defeated because they sought to substitute substance for style.

—Pat Caddell

What happens when a President spends so much time thinking about speaking and so little time thinking about thinking?

— Roderick P. Hart

Voters need leaders, for the ordinary voter has neither the time nor the inclination to come to grips with the many problems of government. As V.O. Key (1964: 544) has noted: "The voice of the people consists mainly of the words 'yes' or 'no,' and at times one cannot be certain which word is being uttered." The President is perpetually campaigning for popular support because endorsement by the electorate is his biggest political asset. Armed with this support, a President can present recommendations to Congress as the will of the people, give direction to appointees in government departments, and meet foreign leaders as the nation's undoubted representative. When a President is unpopular, his political authority is diminished.

While every democratic political leader ultimately depends on popular support, the means of assuring support differ greatly between Washington and a parliamentary system. A Prime Minister works from the inside out, first maintaining support among those who are closest: Cabinet colleagues, the governing party's members of Parliament, and the extraparliamentary party organization. A leader who has their confidence will almost invariably be reported favorably in the national media and have a positive rating in public opinion polls too.

A President works from the outside in, using support won by going public to influence other powerholders in Washington, who are "vulnerable to any breeze from home that presidential words can stir" (Neustadt, 1980: 238). As the journalist Sidney Blumenthal explains:

> Once elected, candidates have to deal with shaky coalitions held together by momentary moods, not stable party structures. They then must try to govern through permanent campaigns. It is something more than the selling of the

President—even of a telegenic President able to project an attractive image. It has become an inescapable necessity for Reagan, and probably for his successors.

The President's strategists are at the center of the new political age. At the end of the day, they become spectators, seeing their performance tested by the contents of the television news programs. *For the Reagan White House, every night is election night on television.* (Quoted in Kernell, 1986: 138)

Perpetual campaigning is an invention of the modern Presidency. Nineteenth-century political doctrines "proscribed the rhetorical Presidency as ardently as we prescribe it" (Tulis, 1987: 5). Presidents emphasized ceremonial activities, and their infrequent speeches stressed what united the nation rather than divisive issues. When Congress sought the President's opinion, he deliberately communicated it in the form of a written and reasoned statement. Consistent with this doctrine, Abraham Lincoln neither sought nor received top billing when he spoke at Gettysburg in November 1863. When Lincoln said, "The world will little note nor long remember what we say here," he was voicing the conventional view that a President was seen but not heard, and the press initially ignored his Gettysburg Address. Lincoln's successor, President Andrew Johnson, broke the conventions of the time by appealing to the people through rabble-rousing stump speeches. One of the charges in his impeachment by Congress was that "unmindful of the high duties of his office and the dignity and propriety thereof...he did make and deliver with a loud voice certain intemperate, inflammatory and scandalous harangues." Tulis (1987: 46) describes the traditional Presidency as involved in political discussions that were "*public* (available to all) but not thereby *popular* (fashioned for all)."

Today, campaigning is central in the job description of the postmodern President. Unlike a parliamentary leader, a President does not have a strong party ready to support what he does. In the White House, he is surrounded by campaign aides whose experience of politics is campaigning, and nothing but campaigning. Budget Director David Stockman (1986: p. 88f) said of President Reagan's trusted advisers, "For Mike Deaver and the others in the Reagan White House, reality happened once a day on the evening news. They lived off the tube." There is a cost in perpetual campaigning. The more time spent thinking about campaign style, the less time there is to think about the substance of government. Perpetual campaigning can become an end in itself rather than a means to the end of going Washington.

To understand why perpetual campaigning is necessary and important, this chapter examines three features of the Presidency that distinguish it from a parliamentary system of government. Whereas a Prime Minister is the head of a party government, the President must mobilize support in a no-party system. The mass media is central to a President; he goes public in default of support by a disciplined party. A Prime Minister can rely on party discipline to produce parliamentary endorsements of government proposals, whereas a President must campaign hard to win the support of Congress.

Leading a No-Party System

Words can cause confusion; nowhere is this more true than in the description of the President as the leader of a party, and voters as choosing between Republican and Democratic party candidates. The fact that a candidate calls himself a Republican or Democrat indicates that the symbols of a party retain some relevance in electoral politics, albeit far less than a generation ago. But when a President goes Washington, there is limited value in being the nation's top Republican or Democrat, for there is no party there to lead. Neustadt's comments (1960: 33f) are even more true today: "What the Constitution separates our political parties do not combine."

Members of Congress are separately elected and party institutions organized independently of the White House. There are separate party organizations in each of fifty states and in thousands of cities and counties, each concerned with elections for their own level of government. The national committees of the two parties are committees of fifty state party organizations, and the presidential nominating conventions are organized by state delegations. By contrast, in a parliamentary system the Prime Minister is chosen because he or she is the leader of the majority party in the legislature. Elections are fought nationwide, and the electorate responds to national party appeals. A comparison of the resources of party available to a Prime Minister with those available to a President justifies a description of America today as a "no-party system" (Ranney, 1978: 213).

If the idea of a political party is to have meaning, it must refer to something more than a verbal label or such traditional symbols as the Democratic donkey and the Republican elephant. Political parties exist as effective organizations only if they are durable institutions nominating candidates to contest elections and mobilizing voters to elect a President with a program for government. Durability distinguishes a party from a temporary collection of campaigners gathered around a candidate or an individual officeholder. In the conduct of party government, elected officeholders should advance common policies rather than act independently of one another.

Nominating Candidates

The American President is unique among national leaders in being nominated by the votes of the mass electorate. Like baseball, the primary system is an American invention that has not been successfully exported to many countries. The use of primaries as the principal means of selecting presidential candidates is recent, dating only from the 1960s. Although few politicians publicly advocate abolishing the primary system because this would mean reducing popular participation, professional political scientists are often critical of the primary system (Polsby, 1983).

The most important point about the primary is that it succeeds in its aim. It lets ordinary voters choose candidates for the Presidency. George Bush became the Republican nominee in 1988 by winning the most votes in GOP primaries, and Michael Dukakis relied on primary votes to become the Democratic nominee. Membership in the Republican or Democratic party is not a condition for voting in a primary, and the primary is not a ballot organized by the party. It is a public ballot in which all properly registered electors are able to vote. Most states and most delegates to presidential nominating conventions are now elected in primaries. The once-in-four-years presidential conventions ratify the nomination of the winner of the primaries, and rally the support of TV viewers for the nominee (see Polsby and Wildavsky, 1984). The doctrine of direct democracy—in a primary, the people choose their candidates and in a general election, their President—is in marked contrast with parliamentary systems, where leaders are chosen by the parties, and the leader of the largest party in Parliament becomes the Prime Minister.

Tens of millions of Americans use primaries to express their preference for a presidential candidate. In 1984, 18 million voted in a series of Democratic primary contests, and another 6.5 million in the virtually uncontested ballot to renominate Ronald Reagan. In 1980, when the Republicans had a primary contest, 12.6 million people voted in Republican primaries (Scammon and McGillivray, 1985: 42ff). State primaries are held at different times, and as candidates concentrate attention on the early primaries, establishing momentum as a winner is critical in the race for the nomination. Whereas in baseball or football the league championship is clinched at the end of the season, in the primaries it is usually gained by victory in early contests. Two states with less than 3 percent of the population, Iowa and New Hampshire, have received 31 percent of media coverage, and forty-six states with 79 percent of the population received less than half the media coverage (Adams, 1987: 45). The media concentrate attention on the early primaries because the momentum gained by the winners there tends to determine who will be the final winner of the five-month primary marathon.

The primary process does not make a party nominee the choice of a majority of those voting in the primaries. A candidate does not need to win as many as half the votes to secure the party nomination; the more candidates running for the nomination, the more likely that the party's nominee is the first choice of a minority of primary voters. For example, when five principal candidates sought the Democratic nomination in 1984, Walter Mondale emerged as the winner with little more than one-third of the Democratic primary vote. Given the arbitrary sequence in which states varying greatly in size hold primaries, a voter in a state holding an April or May primary may find that the candidate favored has already been eliminated in a March primary.

In a European party, only a few hundred or a few thousand people are directly involved in casting votes for a party leader. The simplest system, used by the British Conservative party, is that Conservative MPs elect one of their number as leader. In the dominant Liberal Democratic party in Japan, party members are first given the opportunity to ballot for a variety of candidates; at the second stage, LDP members of Parliament choose the leader between the two front-runners. The choice of leader is made by a caucus of committed partisans, each of whom has a long-term involvement in the party. Therefore, candidates for the party's leadership are judged not only by what they say in media appearances but also by their performance over the years within the party organization, in Parliament, and in government.

In order to run in the presidential primaries, a politician must develop a personal organization of media handlers, experts in making TV spots, fundraisers, pollsters, and advance men who prepare the ground for a candidate to make a lightning visit to a district. There are a large number of professional campaigners who have specialist skills, moving from candidate to candidate and election to election, and each candidate mobilizes people who want to become skilled campaigners, and do so by campaigning for a primary candidate. No sooner is one election over than presidential aspirants begin to lay the groundwork for a possible campaign four years later. The first year or two will be devoted to test marketing, seeing whether there is sufficient support to finance and staff an individual's campaign. If the response is positive, the second stage, starting up to two years before the actual presidential election, will be devoted to cultivating popular support. This is going public to the exclusion of almost everything else.

The American primary system disrupts party organization because in primaries leading members of a party run against one another. Candidates are only interested in mobilizing resources for their own use. They are not interested in contributing anything to state and local party organizations which are no longer able to deliver convention votes. By definition, a primary contest divides people within a party; Republicans run against Republicans, and Democrats run against Democrats. Loyalty is not to the national party but to a party within a party, dedicated to a particular candidate or personality (e.g., a Kennedy) or to a cause (born-again Christians). The tens of millions of dollars and campaign hours spent by candidates who lose the race for the White House impose further costs; this is money and effort that is not available to build up a national party.

An aspiring party leader in a parliamentary system will concentrate on government, building his or her reputation dealing with problems of government in ministries and Cabinet and in confrontations with the opposition party in Parliament. In order to win the support of committed party members, a political leader must contribute to building up the party program and electoral support. If successful in doing so, a leader benefits from the party's strength. A parliamentary party leader is a team captain; election to the party leadership is the climax of a lifetime career in the party. By contrast, a President is a self-employed politician.

Winning Election

The presidential nominee does not ask what he can do for the party; instead, he asks: What can the party do for me? The answer usually is: Very little. The fight to secure the nomination forces a candidate to build a personal campaign organization: the Kennedy mafia, the Georgians, or the Californians, depending on the background of the candidate. It makes the candidate skeptical of the effectiveness, or even the existence, of party organization at the local level and distrustful of party luminaries who opposed him. After the nominating convention, the nominee can coopt some who previously had backed opponents, if he thinks this will strengthen his personal machine.

In appealing for votes, American presidential candidates play down their party labels, for the support of partisan Democrats or Republicans is not enough to win election. The median American voter, the person whose vote is critical in deciding the election outcome, identifies as a political independent, voting for the best person for the job. In 1984, 34 percent identified as independents, 37 percent as Democrats, and 27 percent said they were Republicans (Austin, 1986: 388). Moreover, the proportion of Americans who identify with a political party is falling; less than one-sixth of the electorate consistently reports a strong party identification from one election to the next (Asher, 1984: table 3.5; Kessel, 1984: table 9.1). To win the White House, a presidential candidate needs to combine support from those who normally identify with his own party, a large chunk of independents, and some who identify with the opposing party.

It is hardly surprising that party identification is so weak in the United States, for American parties are weak too. The very concept of an independent is unknown in Europe, where there is no alternative to voting for a party because it is the party that nominates candidates, contests elections, and forms a government. For example, in Britain at the 1987 general election, 85 percent of the electorate identified with a political party.* Relatively strong links between class, religion and other elements of social structure strengthen party identification in Europe; so too do party values and ideologies. Any parliamentary candidate who has a party's endorsement can count on a

---

*American academic surveys classify party identification on a scale ranging from strong to weak to so-called independent partisan. The idea of an independent partisan is a contradiction in terms in Europe. In Britain, the three choices offered in surveys—very strong, fairly strong, not very strong party supporter—reflect the higher degree of partisan commitment in the system as a whole (Rose and McAllister, 1986: table 8.10).

substantial vote from party loyalists. As the British saying has it, a lot of people would vote for a baboon if you painted its bottom in the party colors.

A national party system imposes collective political discipline on all its elected representatives. In a parliamentary system, the new leader's party is not his or hers in the sense of being a personal creation; there is an established organization with continuing institutions and loyalties. The electorate expects a party to be united, and if there are recurrent fights about the leadership, it will suffer electorally. Elections are nationwide competitions between parties about which one will control government. Members of Parliament accept that their electoral fate is collectively determined by a nationwide ballot. The ballot forces an individual to vote for a party; an elector cannot vote separately for a member of Parliament and for the Prime Minister. Only members of Parliament are subject to direct election. The choice of the Prime Minister is determined by which party wins a majority of seats in Parliament.

In the United States, a voter is confronted with a long ballot for seats in Congress, and for state and local posts that are decided in the same November election. Since voters mark their ballot separately for congressional seats, members of Congress usually campaign independently of the President and of their own party. Whereas it is impossible to split a ballot in a parliamentary system, in the United States, split-ticket voting, favoring Republicans for some offices and Democrats for others, is growing. In the 1920 election, the Republicans secured a majority of votes for the White House and for the House of Representatives in 97 percent of congressional districts. Split-ticket voting began to rise slowly after World War II, and further after the election of Dwight D. Eisenhower as a nominally Republican President. In 1984 the Democrats won a comfortable majority of seats in the House of Representatives, but 75 percent of Democratic congressmen saw their district simultaneously give a majority to Ronald Reagan for President. Wattenberg (1984: 20f) concludes from voting surveys from 1952 to 1980 that ticket splitting between the Presidency and the House of Representatives has increased from 12 to 34 percent of voters.

If a President is to make members of Congress indebted to him electorally, then he should poll more votes in their district than they do. In theory, the President's greater national visibility makes it easy for him to do so. In fact, this is not the case. Even when a district favors the same party's candidate for the White House and Congress, the President is as likely to run *behind* the congressional candidate of his party as to run ahead. George Edwards (1983: 86; see also Jacobson, 1983: 131ff) calculates that, at most, a President's popular appeal accounts for ten seats, less than 2 percent of the membership of the House of Representatives. In other words, 98 percent of all congressmen do not owe their election to the appeal of the President. By contrast, in a parliamentary system, the electoral fate of MPs and the Prime Minister are yoked together by the system.

The President has been a leader in promoting the practice of running for reelection as a nonparty candidate. Within the White House he maintains a team of public relations and campaign specialists to work continuously on his behalf. A President can create an organization outside the White House to raise funds and build support. In 1972 President Nixon preferred to rely on CREEP (the Committee to Re-Elect the President) rather than party regulars. CREEP was "in name and action an antiparty, nonparty national political machine" (Lees, 1987: 72). It was also central to the Watergate break-in and the eventual resignation of President Nixon.

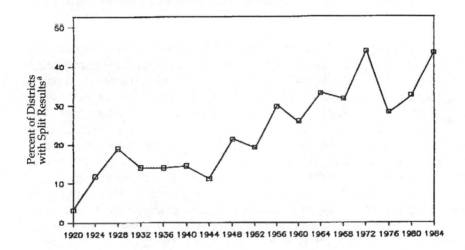

FIGURE 7.1

THE RISE OF SPLIT-TICKET VOTING

a. Congressional districts carried by a presidential candidate of one party and a house candidate of another party.

SOURCES: Adapted from Bibby, Mann, and Ornstein (1980), table 1.13, and Ferejohn and Fiorina (1985), 100.

Incumbents at all levels of government have been quick to follow the lead of the White House, building up a personal campaign organization based on the advantages of incumbency, such as the capacity to do favors for people in the district, to gain publicity, and to exploit the staff and funding advantages of having both a Washington and a district office.

No matter who runs for President or what happens to the economy or the world order, the great majority of congressional incumbents will survive. To do so they deemphasize the platform of their party and their allegiance to the President and emphasize instead their personal relationship with their constituents. (Ferejohn and Fiorina, 1985: 94)

Nominal party allegiance is a source of conflict when ticket splitting places Congress in the hands of one party and the White House in opposing hands. For most of the time since 1952, the President has been a member of the minority party in Congress. The Republicans have held the White House for twenty-four of the past thirty-six years, but in only two years have they had a majority in both houses of Congress. The Democrats have normally been the majority party in the House and the Senate, but have controlled the White House for only twelve of the past thirty-six years.

A no-party system replaces the cohesion of an organized party with the incoherence of individualistic politics. A member of Congress usually considers himself better able to assess what the electors of his district want than can a remote White House. A presidential nominee may prefer to campaign for national support without having to back hundreds of congressional candidates. But once in office, a President soon finds that success in campaigning does not guarantee him a legislative majority, as is the case in a parliamentary system. Arguably, the big loser from the decline of party is the public itself, for an American national election does not offer a choice between alternative teams seeking to govern the nation. Instead, it is an election in which electors cast a multiplicity of votes for people who, if elected, can claim some influence in a system in which it is impossible to hold any one person accountable for what the federal government does.

The discipline of a European party system frustrates individual initiative, but this is done in order to impose collective discipline on politicians. It offers voters a choice between teams of partisans competing for government, each with a leader experienced in government (Schumpeter, 1952; Lipset, 1960: 45ff). While opportunities for voting are reduced, government can be strengthened, insofar as parties choose leaders qualified to govern by their past experience and support in Parliament. A no-party system not only requires extraordinary talents in campaigning but also extraordinary talent to use an election victory when going Washington. The net effect of the primary system has been

> to separate completely the process of building the coalition needed for nomination from the process of building the coalition needed for governing. The winner has little or no contact with his party's leaders in Congress and owes them nothing for his victory. By the same token, they owe him nothing. Accordingly, when a President takes office in the 1980s, he has to build his governing coalition from scratch. (Ranney, 1983: 143)

Courting Mass Popularity through the Media

The vacuum left by the collapse of organized parties has been filled to a substantial extent by the media. The media, rather than party organizations, inform voters about who the candidates are, what they are like as individuals, and where they stand on issues. In place of face-to-face campaigning conducted at the precinct level by ward organizations of the parties, voters learn about elections from television and the press. A staffer for Congressman Tip O'Neill, former Speaker of the House of Representatives, complained:

> At a dizzying pace the TV news networks have absorbed many of the democratic functions traditionally held by political parties: the elevation of key public issues, the promotion of new leaders, the division of executive and legislative authority, and the constitution of political opposition.
>
> Today, network executives make these decisions on a rational mix of news judgment and commercial savvy. For better or worse, the nation's dogged two-party system has been challenged by a three-network system that runs at much higher voltage. (Quoted in Ladd, 1986)

An Open House for Publicity
The increasing importance to the President of going public has been matched by the media increasingly going Washington. The city is now the mecca of television and news reporters, and there has been a great influx of foreign reporters too. The First Amendment to the Constitution protects the media's right to free speech. The separation of powers is a second asset of the media: It institutionalizes access to competing sources of information about government. The dispersal of information among competing Washington institutions means that if news is not issued officially, it is likely to be leaked.

By contrast, parliamentary systems can use the fusion of powers to prevent leaks to Parliament and the press. In Britain, what happens within government, such as Cabinet discussions of major economic and social issues, can be treated as official secrets and none of the public's business (Bennett, 1985). A study of the making of the British government's annual budget was aptly titled *The Private Government of Public Money* (Heclo and Wildavsky, 1981). Radio and television have been subject to strict licensing, and interviewers are expected not to harry politicians. The separation of powers institutionalizes free access to information, for Congress can demand what the White House wants to know. In addition, subgovernments provide channels for passing information from executive agencies to Congress and the press.

Because information is free and plentiful, much of it is of low value. The daily concerns of congressional committees and executive agencies do not make the headlines. Thus, subgovernments can carry on routinely, dealing with matters that do not interest the press or television unless there is great controversy or evidence of corruption. Because names make news and the President is the biggest name in American government, the activities and personalities of the White House are, by definition, news.

The philosophy underlying political reporting in America is that of ideas competing in the freedom of the marketplace. The assumption is that if everybody is allowed to say what he or she wants to say, then the truth will be discovered. Since there is no equivalent of the Pure Food and Drug Act covering what politicians or media commentators say, the marketplace of political debate must have as its motto *Caveat emptor* ("buyer beware"). Openness makes it likely that lies will be found out. The pragmatic rule for a politician is—Don't tell lies—but there is no need to tell the whole truth. For example, during the Iran-*contra* affair White House Press Secretary Marlin Fitzwater was confronted with a series of quotes from President Reagan that contradicted each other. When a reporter prompted: "We're asking you what the reality was?" the President's press secretary answered: "They're going to stay in conflict" (Blundy, 1987).

The centrality of legal procedures in American politics often makes the pursuit of the truth an adversary process, with a prosecutor and a defendant. When scandals arise, such as Watergate, a special prosecutor, Congress, and journalists share a similar approach in establishing facts that may be used as an indictment on a criminal charge or impeachment of the President. The Iran-*contra* hearings were also "fact-finding" hearings, conducted in a quasi-judicial manner by Congress. The important points were deemed to be matters of fact rather than of political principle: Was the United States pursuing a sensible policy in Iran or in Central America?

Politicians and journalists have a love-hate relationship, for each needs the other. A good story for a journalist may be an embarrassment for a politician, and a good story for a politician may be produced by making a journalist believe something that is intentionally misleading. Former Senator Gary Hart showed he knew how to use the media to his advantage in his "near miss" campaign for the 1984 Democratic party nomination. But in 1987 he found that misleading the media about his private life could lead to the exposure of womanizing that caused him to withdraw from the race. When he decided to reenter the race in December 1987, name recognition from media publicity immediately made Hart a front runner in opinion polls about preferences in a Democratic field of Seven Dwarfs. In a candid moment, Hart (1988) admitted: "We are all the press; the distinction between producer and consumer, where news is concerned, is practically nonexistent."

Media Priorities

The media are not in business to provide political education; the business of television, radio, newspapers, and news magazines is to make money by providing entertainment and information and selling advertising aimed at well-defined audiences. For example, the *Wall Street Journal* is directed at well-to-do readers wanting financial news, whereas the evening TV news programs are directed at less knowledgeable mass audiences. This affects how the news is presented. Neuman (1986: 135) dramatically concludes: "The American polity conducts its business on borrowed time. It is borrowed from a commercial, entertainment-oriented media system."

Journalists *are* interested in politics and *do* want to tell their audience what they believe is important for citizens to know. Professional values, organizational pressures, and the constraints of technology give journalists criteria for deciding whether or not something is worth reporting as news (Hess, 1981). If a dog bites a person, this is not news because it is can be expected to happen. Similarly, if the government routinely pays hundreds of billions of dollars in social security benefits without difficulty, this is not news for it, too, is expected to happen. If a public official diverts $100,000 for personal gain, however, this is deemed news, for it is an illegal departure from normality.

Common professional norms are reinforced by the tendency for journalists to work in packs, following what other journalists are reporting as the big story. For this reason, the Iran-*contra* story was revealed in Beirut, not Washington; before the story broke, there was little motive for "pack journalists" to look for it (cf. Randolph, 1987). Because the pack is always under pressure to concentrate on the big story of the day, there is limited continuity in reporting.

A good story to a journalist may make the President look bad, but White House staffers deem newsworthy only the particular stories that make the President look good. The result is that the relationship between the President and journalists is a love-hate relationship, and therefore unstable (Herbers, 1976). Reporting of President Reagan illustrates how emotions can blow hot and cold on both sides. President Reagan initially played up to the media. As an accomplished actor and public speaker, he felt more at home as a communicator than as chief executive of government. After years of reporting the sometimes irascible Jimmy Carter, the dull Gerald Ford, and the suspicious Richard Nixon, the media welcomed a personable President who made quotable wisecracks and was good in front of a camera. The breaking of the Iran-*contra* affair in 1986 produced a reversal of judgments. Reporters began publishing stories revealing the President's apparent ignorance of what was happening in his administration, and his limited capacity to understand complexities of government and public policy. While President Reagan's limitations had long been known within the national capital, they were not widely reported when the President was popular outside the Beltway.

Loving or hateful, the President and the media need one another. The President needs publicity in order to reach the mass public, and Washington journalists need to report what the White House is doing because it is the most important office in government. Reporters can be agreeable to White House officials in return for good stories, and the White House can take steps to improve relations when they are sour. President Lyndon Johnson described the process of continuous quarreling and reconciliation as "throwing them a piece of meat when they are nipping at your ass" (quoted in Grossman and Kumar, 1981: 10).

The Media as the Means of Going Public

Because going public is so important to the President, relations with the media are a central White House concern. In the words of Richard Cheney, a former staff official for President Ford and now a congressman:

> There is no way to do the job as President if you are not willing to think about the media as part of the process in the same way that Congress is part of the process. Consciously or unconsciously, the press often becomes an actor in the scenario. (Quoted in Grossman and Kumar, 1981: 4)

Walter Mondale won the Democratic nomination for the Presidency in 1984 because he was successful in going Washington. But he was unsuccessful in going public and lost the race for the Presidency. Afterward Mondale explained:

> Modern politics requires television. I've never really warmed up to television. And in fairness to television, it never warmed up to me. I don't believe it's possible anymore to run for President without the capacity to build confidence and communications every night. (Quoted in Kernell, 1985: 118)

The whole of the White House is an institution for communicating on behalf of the President. Because the audiences that the President addresses are varied, the means by which the White House communicates are multiple: press, television, telephone calls, memoranda and mail, and face-to-face meetings. The press secretary, who briefs the media daily, is the primary source of public information about White House views. There are also specialized units concerned with the White House news summary, which monitors how well the President is presented by the media; liaison with specialist media important to the incumbent President (e.g., business, labor, or ethnic publications); a TV coordinator; advance men who promote favorable publicity for the President's travels; speechwriters; special projects groups; and officials communicating with interest groups. The White House is like an ice cream factory, producing many different flavors of the President's message to suit many different public tastes.

Many events involving the President are only media events, being staged to attract positive publicity. The White House staff likes to stage-manage such events as dinners with owners of newspapers and broadcasting companies, in hopes of generating goodwill affecting media reporting. A meeting with a popular nonpolitical figure can also generate goodwill. Well-publicized meetings on noncontroversial topics with prominent Protestant clergymen, Catholic bishops, and Jewish leaders may be organized to improve the President's standing with Protestants, Catholics, and Jews. Travels can highlight a particular geographical constituency. The President's wife, children, hobbies, and pets can also be mobilized to produce sympathetic TV or press copy (Hart, 1987).

By comparison, a Prime Minister must treat Parliament as a principal forum for communication, for MPs insist that important political statements are first made there. Unlike a President, a Prime Minister is less likely to be kept in isolation from the media by a ring of security staff. When attending party or parliamentary meetings, a Prime Minister is usually accessible to party colleagues, who relay their discussions to the media, and journalists. The organization of the press and broadcasting media is simpler than in America, and after years in Parliament, a Prime Minister will be on familiar terms with veteran reporters. Specialized appeals for group support are usually dealt with by the party organization, whereas in Washington they are the concern of the White House.

A White House press conference is the best-known example of the President gaining media attention. In favorable circumstances, a President can use the occasion to speak straight to the camera, secure in the knowledge that the TV networks will give good billing to what he says. The President will be prepared by his staff with responses to anticipated questions; friendly questions will get friendly answers, and awkward questions will be dealt with evasively. With a seating chart in front of him and a chance to scan his audience by closed-circuit television before a meeting, the President can identify reporters he believes sympathetic and can ignore others. If all else fails, the President can use rhetorical tricks to answer a question that was not asked, or to avoid the point of a question that could not be answered easily. The President talks over the heads of journalists to the TV cameras, in order to address the public directly (Lamar, 1987; Denton and Hahn, 1986: 250ff). Journalists looking for hard news now expect little from Presidential press conferences.

The transformation of the President's press conference reflects a fundamental shift in presidential priorities. Franklin D. Roosevelt's meetings with the press were frequent, informal, and off-the-record. He saw reporters almost twice a week; President Truman continued in much the same vein. As Presidents found that they could speak directly to the people via television, their meetings with the press declined to once every two weeks under Presidents Eisenhower, Kennedy, and Johnson. There was no need to talk to these knowledgeable Washingtonians when a President could go public without them. As press questioning increasingly addressed awkward problems, Presidents began to avoid the press. Richard Nixon held a press conference once every two months, and his successors, including Ronald Reagan, have also limited press conferences to a very few (Kernell, 1986: 69).

The rise of the modern Presidency and the rapid and easy global transmission of news gives the President a global audience when he is addressing the American people. On occasion this may be exploited by the White House. For example, the Reagan-Gorbachev signing of an arms-control agreement in December 1987 was featured internationally, and the President appeared on Russian television. At times, foreign reporting is bound to make the

President look bad, for example, news of the Iran-*contra* affair. There are also occasions when there are conflicts between the assessments of different audiences. President Reagan's references to "Rambo," intended to encourage American patriotism, can lead foreigners to think of him as a mindless user of violence.

Because the Presidency is a political office and politics is about the articulation of conflict, the man in the Oval Office is subject to *un*favorable as well as favorable reporting. A President who engaged only in ceremonial activities and avoided public controversy, like a figurehead monarch abroad, would avoid unfavorable publicity, but by going ceremonial, a President would remove himself from influencing government. A President who is a politician must expect to be attacked as well as praised, and to be reported unfavorably when events place the White House in a bad light.

A review of White House coverage by the *New York Times, Time* magazine, and CBS News found that since the Eisenhower Administration favorable stories have been much more frequent than unfavorable reporting. In *Time*, favorable stories outnumbered unfavorable ones by more than two to one; in the *New York Times*, by almost two to one; and on CBS, the median report was neutral (Grossman and Kumar, 1981: chap, 10). The President cannot blame personal unpopularity on a failure of the media to report him favorably. Nor can he blame unpopularity on the failure of White House staff to secure ample coverage. When a President is unpopular, it is likely to reflect the substance of what he is doing (see chapter 13).

Impact on Government
The attention given the media tends to overrate its influence on the electorate (cf. Robinson and Sheehan, 1983; Patterson, 1980). As the name emphasizes, the media are only a link between politicians and the public. The public has predispositions that affect how much political news is noticed, and how it is evaluated. The amount of time spent viewing or reading political news is limited and it is not a voter's sole source of political knowledge. What a politician says and what government does—a big rise in inflation or the shooting down of an American plane—are actions that can speak louder than any White House gloss. Neuman (1986: 142) concludes: "The message is the message."

The media are increasingly important because they reinforce the tendency of Presidents and presidential aspirants to go public in ways that avoid problems of government. The most popular medium, television, has the most limited capacity to convey information. A White House report will usually last a minute or two, the equivalent of about five paragraphs of a newspaper story. New technology in editing filmed interviews makes it possible to shorten the time given to an individual. In the late 1960s, the average duration of a film clip of the President speaking was 44 seconds; today, the average news "bite" in which the President speaks is 9 seconds

(Randolph, 1987). In order to make an impact on television, a President has to develop the art of the one-liner, a quick quip that evokes a positive response from the audience but need not convey any information or ideas, beyond the point that the person speaking is a good guy, sincere, or quick-witted.

Presidential elections are less and less about how America should be governed and more and more about campaign events carefully staged with an eye to the camera. Journalists often choose to make the primary news story how the candidate is organizing his campaign, who the people behind him are, and whether he is ahead or behind. Little attention is given to evaluating the position of the candidates on substantive issues of government. Reporting the horse race aspect of elections is particularly prevalent in primaries, where identifying the likely presidential nominees is considered the big story. Candidates play along in hopes of getting a favorable mention. As Jody Powell, Jimmy Carter's press secretary has recalled: "You're really running for President of the United States the way you would run for county school superintendent or state senator" (Arterton, 1984: 8).

TABLE 7.1

CHANGES IN TELEVISION COVERAGE OF PRESIDENTIAL CAMPAIGNS

(IN PERCENT)

	1968	1972	1976	Change 1976-68
Campaign events	26	60	63	+37
Foreign affairs	37	12	10	-27
Domestic politics	19	18	14	- 5
Social problems	9	4	4	- 5
Economic policy	9	5	9	0

SOURCE: Adapted from Graber (1980), 179.

While the modern President's policy responsibilities have become more important, media attention to policy has declined greatly. From 1968 to 1976 the proportion of TV coverage devoted to domestic and international policy fell from 74 percent to 37 percent. The time devoted to campaign events rose from 26 percent to 63 percent (see table 7.1). In 1976, only one minute in five of TV coverage was devoted to the two biggest issues that the President must deal with, foreign policy and the economy. The trend is very similar in the press (Graber, 1980: 179; cf. Entman, 1981: 85ff).

When television was new, fears were expressed that politicians might use the medium to brainwash the electorate (cf. Kelley, 1956). Today, the greater danger appears to be that the medium can mislead the President.

Every President since John F. Kennedy has been very attentive to the way that TV reports his actions and personality. The White House can confuse doing something about the media with doing something about a problem. Lyndon Johnson would blame the media rather than the formidable army of North Vietnam for his troubles in Southeast Asia, and Richard Nixon blamed the media rather than White House staff and himself for his downfall in Watergate.

A President who concentrates on winning popular approval can manage a no-party system successfully. But a President who concentrates on going public may neglect substantive problems of government and the international system. Because Prime Ministers are not directly elected by the public, they have less need to cultivate popularity for its own sake. Success in government is considered the best guarantee of popular success. The neoconservative journalist Norman Podhoretz (1987) contrasts President Reagan's second term, "less and less devoted to anything other than the boosting of his poll ratings" with Prime Minister Margaret Thatcher, "for all her personal unpopularity," using the authority of office to carry out a program of government.

Courting Congress

The President is compelled to court Congress in order to achieve his goals. Without the approval of Congress, the legislative requests in the State of the Union message remain a dead letter. Without the approval of Congress, the President's budget has no legal authority. Without the consent of the Senate, the President's appointees to executive agencies and the Supreme Court cannot hold office. Moreover, congressional oversight of executive agencies gives it influence with bureaucrats who are nominally supposed to take their direction from the White House. After two years in the White House, ex-Congressman John F. Kennedy reflected:

> I think the Congress looks more powerful sitting here than it did when I was there in the Congress. But that is because when you are in Congress you are one of a hundred in the Senate or one of 435 in the House, so that the power is divided. But from here I look at a Congress, and I look at the collective power of the Congress, particularly the bloc action, and it is a substantial power. (Quoted in Hirschfield, 1973: 140)

Changes since that time have made Congress even harder for the White House to deal with. Instead of power being concentrated among a small number of congressional barons who chair key committees and could deliver on agreements made with the White House, it is now dispersed among hundreds of peasants concerned with district interests that are difficult to aggregate and deliver as a package in a deal with the White House (e.g., Jones, 1981; Ornstein, 1983: 204ff).

Congress is a fundamental and continuing influence on what the President can do. The federal government operates according to a doctrine of concurring majorities: The White House *and* Congress must agree in order to sustain most major programs. When a President goes Washington, his object is to win the concurrence of Congress for what he wants to do. But what the President wants to do is not only a matter of deciding what policies he would like. The White House must also worry about whether Congress will buy what the President wants to produce. Even an expert wheeler-dealer such as David Stockman, Ronald Reagan's director of OMB, recognized that it was the end of the line for budget changes when congressmen asked privately: *"When is the White House going to learn something about the political facts of life? You're not going to get a consensus for anything very big or meaningful"* (Stockman, 1986: 332f; italics in the original).

In a parliamentary system, the Prime Minister and Cabinet can think first about adopting policies that they believe best for the party in government. Parliament *must* endorse the legislative program offered by the Cabinet; MPs agree to do so as a condition of securing nomination. A Prime Minister can threaten a member of Parliament who persistently votes against the party with expulsion and virtually certain electoral defeat because of the loss of the party's endorsement. A former British Labour Prime Minister, Harold Wilson, compared a dissident MP with a barking dog, adding that if an MP steps out of line often, "he may not get his dog license renewed when it falls due" (quoted in Rose, 1985e: 108). As a party leader, the Prime Minister must manage Parliament, retaining the confidence of the majority of MPs there. This is a far less difficult task than bargaining with an independent assembly of barons and peasants.

Differences in Political Self-Interest
In the no-party American system, individual politicians are on their own; this is true of members of Congress as well as the President.

> Senators and Representatives are in business for themselves. From the initial decision to seek the nomination and the rigors of the first primary and general election campaigns all the way to eventual retirement or defeat, they are political entrepreneurs in their states and districts, ...They are all likely to view themselves first and foremost as individuals, not as members of a party or as part of a President's team. (Mann, 1981: 53)

The self that a congressman seeks to advance is much more narrowly defined than the President's sense of political self. A member of the House of Representatives represents a district that is 1/435th of the nation, and a senator, 1/50th of America. By contrast, a President must try to appeal to all congressional districts and to all the states. A member of the House of Representatives must run for reelection every other year, and prepare for running in the alternate years. A member of Congress perceiving a clash between district and White House interests will normally vote his district, for it is to the district that he owes his place in Congress. The strength of congressional individualism means that there is "a limited capacity of national elections to impose a programmatic vision on a constituency-minded Congress" (Ferejohn and Fiorina, 1985: 93).

A congressman's day involves concern with subgovernment issues; it also tends to insulate him from broader concerns of government. A member of Congress has no responsibility for America's relations with foreign nations, as the President does. Nor does a congressman have a responsibility for the national or international economy; what concerns him is employment in his district, and the prosperity of local factories and businesses. A member of Congress defends a district of about half a million people; the turf that the President defends is the United States in an uncertain world.

Although all the institutions of American government derive from a common Constitution, the view of how the system works differs from one end of Pennsylvania Avenue to the other. Gerald Ford, a congressman for two decades before becoming President, reflected:

> When I was in the Congress myself, I thought it fulfilled its constitutional obligations in a very responsible way, but after I became President my perspective changed. It seemed to me that Congress was beginning to disintegrate as an organized legislative body. It wasn't answering the nation's challenges domestically because it was too fragmented. It responded too often to single-issue special interest groups, and it therefore wound up dealing with minutiae instead of attacking serious problems in a coherent way. (Ford, 1979: 150)

While Congressman Ford accepted the world of district interests and subgovernments, President Ford wanted a legislature that could be disciplined like Parliament to support the President's national perspective.

Alternatives in Approaching Congress
Ironically, the chief constitutional power that the President has in dealing with Congress is the right to ignore it under certain very limited circumstances, for example, when acting as commander-in-chief of the armed forces. The veto is a second formal power, but it is an indication of failure to win support on the Hill. A bill that the President vetoes will not become law unless his veto is overridden by a two-thirds vote in each house of Congress. A veto is usually not overridden by Congress, for a President expects to have the backing of a third of Washington and of much of the public before acting so controversially. While vetoes are often threatened by a President in dispute with Congress, they are not often used.

Whereas the traditional President was committed to ask little from Congress, modern and postmodern Presidents are expected to lead Congress. White House leadership requires cooperation with leaders in Congress. Everyone in the White House is expected to be sensitive to congressional opinion. The White House Office of Congressional Relations is continuously looking after the concerns of individual members of Congress with their district, their policy priorities, and their egos. When important votes come up on the Hill, White House staff alert the President of the need for action to secure the support of individual congressmen on the committee having jurisdiction on a measure and to influence waverers who could be decisive in votes on the floor of the House or the Senate.

The President is the senior White House person dealing with Congress. A President will telephone or meet with congressmen at the White House in efforts to win their support on the merits of the issue, by flattery, and by appeals to self-interest. If a congressman wants something from the White House (a federal judgeship for a friend or a contract for his district), then the White House can offer to trade patronage for votes. For example, in return for Senator Albert Ellender of Louisiana providing support for the administration on a crucial civil rights bill, President Johnson saw that a nuclear frigate the navy did not want was built in a Baton Rouge shipyard. Later, he taxed an aide: "Which do your liberal friends think is more important, voting rights or a nuclear frigate?" (quoted in Roche, 1985: 188).

A President's relations with Congress are affected by whether or not he belongs to the party with a majority in the House and Senate. *Everything else being equal*, members of Congress will be inclined to vote along party lines. Since the Democrats are usually in control of Congress, each Democratic President starts with an advantage in dealing with the Hill. But since the Democratic party is a coalition of many disparate groups and there is often disagreement among Democrats about what should be done, a Republican President can play on these divisions to secure support for his measures. For example, Ronald Reagan secured vital support for 1981 budget measures from southern congressmen known as boll weevils, who had more in common with his views of the economy than with those of liberal Democrats. Party indiscipline can benefit a Republican President, whereas a Democratic President tries to discipline an often undisciplined Democratic majority.

The relations of Presidents with Congress are also affected by their view of the Hill. Lyndon Johnson and Gerald Ford had spent most of their adult life as congressmen before entering the Oval Office. Johnson could view the Hill as a former Senate majority leader, and Ford had many years as a leader of the Republicans, the House minority party. By contrast, neither Ronald Reagan nor Jimmy Carter had ever served in Congress, and neither Richard Nixon nor John F. Kennedy had ever sought to be accepted as an insider by the senior congressmen who exercised leadership while they served there.

Presidential styles in dealing with Congress can be classified according to whether or not the President's party has a majority in Congress and whether or not the President sees himself as a partner of Congress or an outsider (see figure 7.2). Presidents Johnson and Ford each saw Congress as a partner, but they differed in their ability to use party loyalty as an argument for support. The 1964 election not only gave Johnson a landslide presidential majority but also a big Democratic majority in Congress. By contrast, the 1974 post-Watergate congressional election was a disaster for the Republicans, reducing further the Republican minority in Congress. Hence, President Ford often turned to vetoes to assert his policy views against Congress.

Position of President's party in Congress

	Majority	Minority
View of Congress	President as:	
Partner	Majority leader (Johnson)	Minority leader (Ford)
Outsider	Estranged (Nixon)	Fugitive (Carter)

FIGURE 7.2

ALTERNATIVES FOR PRESIDENTIAL DEALINGS WITH CONGRESS

SOURCE: Freely adapted by the author from Jones (1983, 1985).

Both Jimmy Carter and Richard Nixon saw themselves as outsiders in relation to Congress. Carter's sense of estrangement was so great that he had bad relations with a Congress in which his party was a majority. Carter's successor, Republican Ronald Reagan, won good marks from Democrats by treating them with more respect than his Democratic predecessor. As a partner of Congress, President Ford knew how to appeal to the vanity of congressmen. The significance of the President's personal touch is illustrated by an anecdote contrasting Ford and Carter.

> When Gerry Ford would sign a bill, he'd use nice metal pens with his name on them, and then he'd pass them out to the members who had worked on the bill. But Carter signs bills with a felt-tip pen and then he puts the pen back into his pocket. (Quoted in Davis, 1983: 77)

President Nixon was a fugitive from Congress. As a Republican, he could not appeal for votes on grounds of party loyalty. As a lone wolf by temperament, he was ill at ease in the camaraderie of the Senate cloakroom. The policies that most interested Nixon were international measures, such as the Vietnam war, and negotiations with the Soviet Union. In these international fields, the

Oval Office enjoys a substantial measure of discretion. On domestic issues, Nixon took administrative actions to prevent the spending of funds voted by Congress, rather than negotiate with the Hill.

It is not possible to classify Prime Ministers as we do Presidents, for a Prime Minister necessarily commands the confidence of Parliament. Except for France, a Prime Minister will normally have spent years or decades in Parliament; Prime Ministers differ only in the time spent learning the ropes of Parliament before going government. Each Prime Minister can normally be placed in the same category; he or she is an insider with the support of the majority party in Parliament.

Winning (and Not Winning) Support

While the White House proposes, Congress disposes. A simple index of the President's success in dealing with Congress is the reaction of the Hill to legislative proposals put forward from the White House. On average Congress refuses to approve more than half the measures that the President recommends (see table 7.2). In the period from Eisenhower through Ford,

TABLE 7.2

CONGRESSIONAL RESPONSE TO PRESIDENTIAL PROPOSALS

	Submitted N	Approved N	Approved %
President, Congress same party			
Dwight Eisenhower, 1953-54	276	182	66
John F. Kennedy, 1961-63	1054	413	39
Lyndon B. Johnson, 1964-68	1902	991	52
Total	3232	1586	49
President, Congress opposing parties			
Dwight Eisenhower, 1955-60	1283	610	48
Richard Nixon, 1968-74	979	333	34
Gerald Ford, 1974-75	220	68	31
Total	2482	1011	41
(Overall total)	(5714)	(2597)	(45%)

SOURCE: Adapted from *Congressional Quarterly* data as reported by Edwards (1980), 14.

for which the most complete data are available, the best record was compiled in President Eisenhower's first term, when 66 percent of legislation was approved, and the worst in the abbreviated Presidency of Gerald Ford, when only 31 percent was approved. One reason why the President fails to secure his aims is that one or both houses do not even vote on what is proposed; the President thus loses by default. While Congress more often than not supports a presidential recommendation if it comes to a vote, like the vote itself, such support cannot be taken for granted (Edwards, 1980: 15ff). Every President can be sure of having some successes to boast about in Congress, but he will also suffer some defeats. In anticipation of defeat, the White House will avoid putting forward proposals for which the time is not ripe, and trim others in hopes of making them more acceptable to Congress. In a parliamentary system, by contrast, the Prime Minister and Cabinet are certain that their proposals will be brought to a vote, and reasonably certain that they will be approved (cf. table 5.1).

Party control of Congress has a limited impact on what happens to presidential proposals. When Congress and the President are of the same party, a President is likely to see Congress reject a majority of measures that he puts forward. This is also true when Congress is in the hands of the opposing party. The difference in success is only 8 percent; Presidents working with a Congress of their own party can get through only 49 percent of their legislative proposals. A President making recommendations to a Congress of the opposing party on average gets through 41 percent of his measures (see table 7.2).

The President must rely on party indiscipline in order to secure the enactment of his proposals because a substantial fraction of members of his own party will vote against what the White House proposes. From 1953 to 1983, Democratic Presidents had an average of 31 percent of House Democrats vote against their proposals, and 39 percent of Senate Democrats. Similarly, Republican Presidents have suffered the opposition of 35 percent of House Republicans, and 32 percent of Senate Republicans (Edwards and Wayne, 1985: 321). Given defections of this magnitude, a Republican President must secure a substantial portion of Democratic votes to get a measure through, and even a Democratic President with a nominal majority in Congress needs some support from the Republican minority to offset the consequence of Democratic defections.

Congressmen do not see themselves as defecting when they vote against a President of their own party. The view from the Hill is that each member of Congress should vote on the basis of an individual calculation, reflecting the views of the district, personal political beliefs, and commitments to other congressmen and pressure groups, as well as on party inclinations, and White House views. The President is always sure to have some support, and some opposition. The White House problem is that it cannot predict how much support it will have on a given measure until after a proposal has gone forward. The actual outcome of a vote in Congress reflects forces "largely beyond the President's control" (Edwards, 1988).

By comparison with Prime Ministers, a President's legislative record places him in the second division. When courting Congress, Presidents usually finish below .500, losing more proposals than they win. By contrast, a Prime Minister expects to finish over .800, winning four out of five or better of the government's legislative proposals. In a parliamentary system with strict party discipline such as the British House of Commons, a government can have a .990 record on its bills (cf. table 5.1). A British Prime Minister can rely on the party whip to drive measures through the Commons with majority support by his parliamentary colleagues. As a Cabinet minister once commented, "It's carrying democracy too far if you don't know the result of the vote before the meeting" (quoted in Rose, 1985e: 106).

In order for a President to be sure of placing his vision of the national interest on the statute book, a fundamental change would be necessary in Washington. Ex-congressman and Reagan budget director, David Stockman (1986: 159) concludes: "The world's so-called greatest deliberative body would have to be reduced to the status of a ministerial arm of the White House," giving "rubber stamp approval, nothing less," What Stockman is complaining about is that the national leader that he served is a President rather than a Prime Minister in a parliamentary system.

8. Taking Over the White House

Everyone believes in democracy until he gets to the White House, and then you begin to believe in dictatorship because it's so hard to get the job done.
—Anonymous White House aide

If the President cannot control the White House, then he cannot expect to have much influence anywhere else in Washington. But taking charge of government is not as simple as it appears; it can defeat autocrats as well as democrats. Traditionally, the Japanese Emperor was treated as so unapproachable that, for many centuries, affairs of state were effectively in the hands of a hereditary shogun. Purges by Russian and Chinese leaders show that keeping control of a communist regime is uncertain too. As the White House staff has increased in number, the President has increasingly been under pressure to organize and control his helpers. If he cannot do that, there are narrow limits to the influence that the President can exert on what is, at least in name, his government.

The creation of the modern Presidency under Franklin D. Roosevelt meant the end of the White House as a home like the residence of an eighteenth-century European monarch. A committee under veteran administrator Louis Brownlow (1937: 5) concluded: "The President needs help." Help was forthcoming; a handful of staff assistants was authorized. Roosevelt wanted staff to act as an extension of the Oval Office, providing eyes and ears for a President accustomed to using others to do the "leg work" of investigating problems, while he was bound by polio to a wheelchair. Everyone was expected to work closely together under the President's personal direction. Gradually, additional personnel and new units were added in the White House and next door in the Old Executive Office Building. By the end of the 1960s, helpers were needing help too. A modern tower block, the New Executive Office Building, was erected across Pennsylvania Avenue to house the expanding staff of the Presidency.

The emergence of the postmodern Presidency has changed the use of the White House staff and extended its scope from the domestic to the international arena. The greatly enlarged staff of the postmodern Presidency acts as insulation; the many layers between the lowest-ranking presidential assistant and the Oval Office prohibit frequent personal contact between the average staffer and the President. As the great majority of staff members are

140

now specialists, for example, in directing publicity at the ethnic media, analyzing the risks and effects of inflation, or writing speeches, staff members now have very little in common with one another. As Presidents have increasingly concentrated on international problems, many issues of domestic policy are placed in the hands of White House personnel to find out what, if anything, the President should or can do about a problem. President Ford (1980: 31) summed up the situation when he stated: "A Presidency really is a combination of the individual President and his staff."

Formally, the President is at the top of an organization chart that has two complementary types of institutions (cf. *Federal Register*, 1986: 817). The *White House Office* employs people who are very much at the personal service of the President. They arrive at 1600 Pennsylvania Avenue when he does, work as he wishes, and leave when he leaves. Within the White House Office, staff persons have a wide variety of functions, from looking after the President's wife to looking after the political fortunes of the President. The positions include counselor to the President, press secretary, Cabinet secretary, congressional liaison, public affairs and public liaison, planning, speechwriting, advance preparation for travels, communication, intergovernmental affairs, private-sector initiatives, counsel, correspondence, scheduling, and personal photographer. There are more than fifty different miniunits within the White House Office.

A second set of institutions are within the *Executive Office of the President*. These units have continuity, as they are established by act of Congress. The heads are presidential appointees, but many staff members are civil servants. Units include the Office of Management and Budget, the National Security Council, Council of Economic Advisers, Office of the U. S. Trade Representative, Council on Environment Quality, Office of Policy Development, Office of Science and Technology Policy, Office of the Vice-President, and the Office of Administration.

The institutional Presidency—that is, the White House Office plus the Executive Office of the President—is advisory, not executive. Officials in its many units can analyze problems of Oval Office concern and make recommendations to the President, but no one in the institutional Presidency can bind the one person who counts, the President. The President alone is responsible for acting in the light of information from many different individuals and units that serve him.

To describe the President's problem as a management problem is misleading, for it leaves politics out. Successive Presidents have tried to reorganize the White House and the executive branch. But reorganization plans without a sense of political purpose confuse means with ends, and the symbols of activity with the purpose of government. The typical reorganization proposal is launched with a fanfare and consigned to the footnotes of history without being implemented (cf. Arnold, 1986; Szanton, 1981; March and Olson, 1983). When there is a political intent behind organizational changes, they will be controversial (cf. Seidman and Gilmour, 1986).

Because the President is a single individual with a finite number of hours to work each week, his own time is his scarcest resource. Much time is pre-empted by what Neustadt calls the law of first things first. Reactions are required more or less instantly to a host of events, some trivial and some of international significance. The White House term firefighting captures the urgency and unpredictability of many claims on the President's time.

Presidents differ greatly in the hours they work. President Johnson was a workaholic; he wanted to be awakened in the middle of the night for news from other parts of the globe. By contrast, President Ronald Reagan has said only half in jest, "It's true hard work never killed anybody, but I figure why take the chance."

The President *must* delegate, but the problem is: Whom can he trust? (Rose, 1980b: 327ff). One answer is: Nobody. But a President who trusts no one must find a way of institutionalizing distrust in order to keep an eye on staff to whom tasks are delegated. Inevitably, a President gives a measure of trust to staff bound to him by personal loyalties forged in years of campaigning for the White House. The White House is conspicuously lacking in the impersonal loyalty found in parliamentary systems, where a group of experienced and skilled higher civil servants normally fill many important advisory positions close to the Prime Minister (Suleiman, 1984). In Washington, virtually all posts close to the President are political appointments in the White House Office.

Each President enters the White House a beginner, and a governor is an absolute beginner in Washington. The first section of this chapter considers the immediate priority of a President-elect, hitting the ground running, that is, making use of the momentum generated by election victory to take successful initiatives immediately after inauguration (Pfiffner, 1987). Second, the chapter examines what the President must do to control his own time, and to control the White House staff he appoints to serve his ends. While directing the White House is about managing people, the staff of the White House is now so large that the President has to have a strategy for ensuring that he learns what he wants to know and can avoid what he wants to escape.

Hitting the Ground Running:
Energy in Search of Direction

A President-elect betrays the virtues and shortcomings of an amateur. He is full of energy and knows that he must run hard in the first few months of office. But as Meltsner (1981: 301) remarks: "There are no schools for Presidents." On the campaign trail there is no time to direct candidates' energies to preparing detailed programs, or even to prepare a strategy for going Washington. By contrast, decades of participation in Parliament give a Prime Minister a good education in government, and activity in the governing party provides a clear sense of direction. A Prime Minister selects a Cabinet from party colleagues whose strengths and limitations are known from years of working together. A newly installed Prime Minister faces problems, but being in government is not the problem, as it is to a President-elect.

Campaign Commitments

In running for office, a candidate is asked to make many commitments and soon becomes adept at avoiding being too specific about what he would do in office, for fear of offending one group by pledging support to others. Yet a candidate must promise to do something about some issues. Otherwise, voters are given no substantive reason for supporting him.

The party platform adopted by the convention that nominates a candidate is a lengthy statement of what the President and his supporters would like to do in office. Studies by Fred Grogan (1977) and Jeff Fishel (1985: 33) of domestic campaign promises by every elected President since John F. Kennedy divide campaign promises into four different categories:

1. One-fifth of promises are detailed and specific pledges to action. For example, a pledge to create a new government department to deal with programs of concern to a group of interests, such as education.

2. Two-fifths are reasonably clear statements of priorities for action. For example, a pledge to protect farmers from the threat of foreclosure on farm mortgages.

3. One-third are generalized expressions of concern without an indication of what might be done. For example, a show of concern about meeting needs for health care.

4. One-tenth are pledges to continuity in government policy. For example, maintaining social security.

While about half the platform commitments are reasonably clear pledges to do something within the power of government, the other half are relatively vague statements, reflecting uncertainties in the candidate's own mind.

A list of campaign promises is important for what it leaves out as well as what it includes. A candidate whose supporters are divided on a major issue will try to avoid the subject or discuss the issue in vague or meaningless terms. Because the national security and economic aims of a postmodern President can be achieved only with the cooperation of other nations, a

President-elect has little idea about how realistic or unrealistic are his intentions for dealing with these imperative responsibilities of office.

"Ignorance and Hopefulness"

After years of tailoring remarks to what voters want to hear, a President-elect faces a completely different task: selecting goals that are "do-able" within the constraints of Washington. Writing about John F. Kennedy's entry to the White House, Neustadt (1980: 223) describes the President-elect as having "two striking features, ignorance and hopefulness. The ignorance was tinged with innocence; the hopefulness with arrogance." Ignorance reflects the fact that the President-elect believes that winning a very grueling election campaign is sufficient to bend government to his will. The belief is innocent in intent, but it is also ill founded. Optimism becomes arrogance insofar as it encourages the belief that the difficulties that beset his predecessors will not trouble him. A President-elect is prone to believe that although predecessors failed, he cannot fail. While every new President may not commit a major error such as John F. Kennedy's early approval of the ill-fated, U.S.-backed invasion of the Cuban Bay of Pigs in 1961, each new President is likely, in Neustadt's phrase, to be responsible for at least a "piglet."

The first thing a President-elect learns is that "the virtues needed in the crucible of a campaign are almost the opposite of the preparation needed for life within the White House" (Patterson, 1982: 109). The President-elect is largely ignorant about how to steer the federal government in the direction he would like it to go. Theodore Sorensen, a staffer who went with John F. Kennedy from the Senate to the White House, has commented:

> There's no question that the world looks very different from inside the White House than from outside. You can be a good Senator or Congressman or politician if you make a strong speech or if you raise the right question or if you sound the alarm. None of that does you any good at all when you are in the White House and you are responsible for running the show. You have to come up with the answers. (Quoted in Kernell and Popkin, 1986: 91f)

The President-elect has about ten weeks in which to make the transition from campaigning to being President, subsidized by a federal appropriation of millions of dollars for staff, travel, and associated expenses. The President-elect must organize a mammoth personnel operation in order to recruit hundreds of people as presidential appointees, and commission task forces to advise how his new administration might tackle problems. By comparison, in Britain, control of government literally changes hands overnight, as the winner of a general election held on a Thursday takes over Downing Street on Friday evening. A parliamentary politician has far fewer difficulties in making this overnight transition to power, for the institutions of government are already familiar. A President-elect needs months, not weeks, to become familiar with the practice of the Presidency.

The biggest asset of a President-elect is intangible: public goodwill. This goodwill can be used to mobilize donations of time, money, and ideas from many who did not support his campaign. The President-elect's popularity is likely to rise in public opinion polls, as some who voted against him rally around the winner. Since the election of Dwight D. Eisenhower in 1952, a newly installed President's Gallup poll rating goes up by an average of 13 percent by the time of inauguration (Edwards, 1983: 217).

Staffing Government with Strangers

In the world of political campaigners, people come before policies. The first concern of a President-elect is staffing government with his people. Policies come afterward, for until people are in place in the Cabinet and other important posts there is no one to carry out the program of the President—whatever that might be. The election winner is surrounded by people who are eager to learn what victory means for their chances of landing a top presidential appointment. Journalists, too, focus on personalities; it is far easier to characterize the personalities seeking major government jobs than to analyze the problems that face them.

The populist tradition in American democracy makes the President-elect responsible for appointing some 4000 officials, and tens of thousands of names are put forward for these jobs. Throughout American history, democracy has been interpreted as meaning a big change in government jobholders with every swing of the electoral pendulum. This is considered fair—to the victor belongs the spoils—and desirable, as making government more responsive to the electorate. The historic underrepresentation of women, blacks, and other minority groups at the higher levels of the federal government adds a contemporary justification for the generous use of the President's appointment power to give jobs to politically favored groups.

By contrast, in parliamentary democracies most top officials remain in post from administration to administration, because they are civil servants. Even though there is no necessary link between a parliamentary system and a higher civil service skilled in policymaking, empirically, the two almost always go together. High-ranking civil servants, often only one or two levels below Cabinet ministers, are normally extremely able people, recruited by highly competitive examinations. Very senior civil servants have political tact as well as administrative skills. Unlike the Presidency, a Prime Minister is not forced to search for thousands of people to fill government offices; senior civil servants continue to contribute their expertise when party control of government changes. A Prime Minister has a few dozen jobs of major importance to fill, and another hundred or so jobs change with the election results. Because the distribution of jobs can be settled quickly, there is more time to devote to questions of policy.

Staffing the White House seems easy because key appointments typically go to familiar faces, individuals whose personal loyalty has been tested in years of campaigning before entering the White House. Their commitment to the President is undoubted, for when he goes, they go. There is only one difficulty: The President's new staff members find the White House as strange as he does. Their experience and skills are appropriate to going public and, if they have worked for a member of Congress, to going Washington, but not to going government. Appointing people able to handle the President, his press relations, interest groups, and congressmen still leaves a need to staff the government, that is, the agencies of the executive branch.

Many of the most important agency appointments the President makes are given to strangers (Heclo, 1977; Mackenzie, 1981). John F. Kennedy explained why: "I don't know any people for the Cabinet. I only know voters" (quoted in Schlesinger, 1965: 127). President Kennedy did not know Robert McNamara, his secretary of defense, or Dean Rusk, his secretary of state, before he asked them to join his Cabinet in crucial positions. In every administration, many Cabinet and sub-Cabinet members start as strangers to the President and to one another. The people President Kennedy felt comfortable with were the "Kennedy mafia," personal friends and relations. President Reagan had a choice between individuals who knew him but did not know Washington (e.g., the Californians) or individuals who knew Washington but did not know him (who were carryovers from the Nixon and Ford administrations). Experienced Republicans who were unacquainted with President Reagan were criticized by the Heritage Foundation for having "what might be best described as a tenuous relationship to a conservative presidential agenda" (Rector and Sanera, 1987: 331). Some committed Reaganites had problems because of their ignorance of government agencies, programs, and ethics.

The President invariably appoints strangers to many Cabinet and sub-Cabinet posts because he is looking for people who appear capable of handling the task at hand. For example, the chairman of the Council of Economic Advisers is an economist, and the secretary of the treasury is a person who can get on with Wall Street. The importance of nonparty qualifications for going government was made evident in the Carter administration. Before the 1976 election, in which Jimmy Carter ran against Washington insiders, his senior staff man Hamilton Jordan said:

> If, after the inauguration, you find a Cy Vance as Secretary of State and Zbigniew Brzezinski as head of national security, then I would say we failed. And I'd quit. But that's not going to happen. You're going to see new faces, new ideas. (Quoted in Cronin, 1980: 20)

Nevertheless, when President-elect Carter went looking for people with appropriate experience for secretary of state and national security adviser, he did not name Georgians but Brzezinski and Vance. Jordan ate his words and spent four years in the White House trying to learn what old hands already knew about government.

146

Action-Forcing Events

Within weeks of entering the White House, the President must deliver a State of the Union message that heralds his legislative program. But campaigning for the Presidency allows neither time nor political incentive for preparing detailed policies. At most, presidential candidates will have a few trusted friends do some preparatory work, but not too much in case this proves bad luck, a political embarrassment, or simply a dismal waste of scarce resources. By contrast, a parliamentary party leader will be entering office with the experience of years of debating issues in Parliament and making policy proposals subject to challenge there by experienced ministers.

The second action forcing deadline is even more difficult. sending a budget message to Congress that details how the federal government ought to spend more than $1 trillion. A President-elect can take small comfort in the fact that the uncontrollable programs of the budget, such as social security commitments and defense contracts, will go ahead without any action on his part. A new President's initial budget recommendations are important, for proposals made shortly after inauguration must wait until October before coming into effect, when the federal fiscal year begins. If changes are not made at the beginning, then two-fifths of a term of office is spent before the President makes an imprint on the budget.

To make the budget of his second year in office truly reflect his own priorities, a new President must go into action even before he is officially in the White House (Pfiffner, 1987: chap. 6). An incoming President faces three difficulties. The first is that his lame-duck predecessor can put forward a budget message containing unrealistic proposals about taxing and spending with the intent of making his own proposals look less attractive politically. Second, a President-elect does not have the assistance of the several hundred expert budget examiners of the Office of Management and Budget. Third, the incoming President has not spent the preceding months in discussions in which agency heads debate with one another and with senior presidential staff about competing claims for scarce public revenues.

While international actions are not predictable, the importance of foreign affairs requires the President-elect to give a high priority to national security appointments. If international issues have been prominent in the election campaign, the President-elect will be under a self-imposed pressure to launch whatever initiative has been promised. But national security issues are complex and involve confidential communication with foreign nations, who must still treat the lame-duck President as the head of government. There is thus very little that the election winner can do internationally until after inauguration. Once in office, the world will not wait for an amateur in the White House to become proficient in international affairs. A former adviser to President Carter comments: "A newly elected President may well have the authority, the power and the inclination to address foreign policy issues, but he rarely has the experience necessary to form sound judgments" (Quandt, 1986: 828). Harry Truman was faced with a decision about dropping the first atomic bomb within a few months of acceding to the Presidency, and John F. Kennedy with a decision about whether or not to permit a U.S.-backed invasion of Cuba (Mosher et al., 1987).

The Honeymoon Opportunity

Immediately after inauguration a President must run harder still, for he has a unique opportunity to use electoral goodwill to secure congressional approval of major legislative and budget initiatives, before the honeymoon spirit evaporates, and the President has to bargain hard with other power-holders in Washington. Whereas a parliamentary party leader can look forward to as much as five years in office, an American President can be stalemated after a year because of his own mistakes, or because events conspire to make him unpopular by the time of the mid-term congressional elections. President Johnson saw the need to hit the ground running:

> You've only got one year. No matter what your mandate and your vote is, you've only got a year because in the second year you will have done a lot of things that will make even people in your own party want to put distance between themselves and you. And then in the third year you've lost a lot of your votes usually in the mid-term election, and you lose a lot of your strength in the Congress. The fourth year is all presidential politics. (Quoted in Kernell and Popkin, 1986: 96f)

Johnson spoke with unintended foresight, for after enormous success in securing legislation from Congress in 1965, his popularity plummeted so much as the Vietnam war escalated that by 1968 he withdrew from the primary race for renomination.

A simple statistic illustrates the importance of hitting the ground running. Of legislative proposals put forward by a President in the honeymoon period of the first three months of office, 72 percent are enacted by Congress. This is far above the overall success rate that the President can expect for his term of office (cf. table 7.2). Of proposals put forward between April and June of the first year, only 39 percent are enacted, and the proportion falls to 25 percent of those presented in the last six months of his first year in office (Light, 1982: 45). In a parliamentary system, the government can take a year or more to prepare legislation carefully, knowing that once a bill is put forward, a disciplined majority of MPs will vote for it.

Within the constraints of the crash-course introduction of the President-elect to government, some Presidents do better than others (see Pfiffner, 1987; Buchanan, 1987: 110-35). President Carter secured the minimum in his first year of office because the White House mishandled other Washington powerholders, and the President did not focus promptly on a small number of priority issues. By contrast, the Reagan administration put through a major series of budget changes in its first few months of office, cutting taxes and shifting the direction of military and civilian spending. It did so by having a limited number of priorities, a small number of people around the President who agreed about immediate objectives, and a readiness to cultivate other powerholders in Washington in order to take full advantage of the honeymoon with Congress. Subsequent difficulties of President Reagan in getting measures through Congress show how brief is the honeymoon period. In 1982 President Reagan was stalemated in Congress, fell below 50 percent approval in the Gallup poll, and the Democrats scored major successes in the mid-term congressional election.

The dilemma of a President is that the more he learns about how to give direction to government, the less capacity he has to influence it. Neustadt (1980: 149) emphasizes the positive side. In the first two years of office, an amateur in the Oval Office will learn a lot about how government works and how the White House can direct it to the President's ends. The enthusiasms and confusion of the honeymoon period will gradually be superseded by a better understanding of policies. The third year is regarded as a time when the President is best able to govern, since the fourth year is spent in campaigning for reelection. If reelected, a President will be experienced in going Washington and going international and can benefit for two years, before the approach of another election relegates him to lame-duck status. According to Neustadt's method of reckoning, a President has only been able to be fully on top of things in Washington for a maximum of fourteen of the forty-four years since 1944. The country has had a President operating below full effectiveness for at least two-thirds of the postwar period.* Sundquist (1986: 107) argues that this deficiency has been true for seventy-seven of the eighty-eight years of this century.

The increased experience of the President is offset by the decreasing willingness of other Washington powerholders to cooperate with the President. When a President best understands government, he has least chance of being effective. According to one Nixon White House aide:

> The more we seemed to learn about the domestic system, the less we could do. We had our best shot at the start of the term, but didn't have the organization to cash in. By the time we had the organization, the opportunity was closed. (Quoted in Light, 1982: 36)

By contrast, in a parliamentary system, a Prime Minister can count on being consistently effective in votes in Parliament and maintain a Cabinet that has a judicious mixture of very experienced ministers and an injection of fresh faces and ideas.

*The number of effective years credited are as follows: Truman 3, Eisenhower 3, Kennedy 1, Johnson 1, Nixon 2, Ford 0, Carter 1, and Reagan 3. Given that Eisenhower's health was already a cause of problems by year five and Reagan's year six included the Iran-*contra* affair, the foregoing estimates are generous.

Keeping Control within the White House

While the President has a unique position within the White House, he cannot do his job alone. In order to conserve time, energy, and political capital, a President must rely on White House staff to investigate problems and review policy options with executive branch, congressional, and interest-group officials before issues receive Oval Office attention; follow up on problems as directed by the President; monitor subjects that do not require his personal attention; and protect the President from unwanted paperwork and people. The White House staff must be organized so that it does what the President wants done and keeps him in control of what is most important to the Oval Office.

Organization is a means to an end, not an end in itself; the word is derived from the Latin word for "instrument." Because the President is in politics, not business, conventional business school theories of organization offer no guidance about how to manage the White House. In the words of a former Johnson staff assistant, Bill Moyers: "The White House staff reflects the personal needs of the President rather than a structural design. There is no pattern to it that can be fitted to a chart" (quoted in Edwards and Wayne, 1985: 201f). Because political form follows political function, in order to organize the White House the President must decide: What do I want done?

Organizing Information In, and Organizing It Out

In order to do his job, the President needs information in many shapes, and forms. He needs information about international events and about economic trends. He also needs information about what members of Congress are thinking and doing, and about executive agency actions affecting presidential priorities. Furthermore, he needs information about public opinion and his standing with the public.

We can think of the White House as a vast information-processing machine. Two broad streams of information flow into the White House, one concerning "hot" issues in which the President has a personal interest and another concerning more or less routine matters that the White House keeps under surveillance because they may sometimes become hot. For example, while every country in the world can potentially present a problem to America's international interests, at any given moment only a few countries are at the boiling point, requiring Oval Office attention.

Because the volume of information flowing into the White House each day is vast, information processing is a primary responsibility of White House staff. Information processing goes far beyond sorting documents into two piles, one pile for the President's attention and another for routing elsewhere. If a memorandum concerns a hot political topic, then a staff official must determine whose interests are affected by the memo and how widely the memo should be circulated for comment before it goes to the

President. Alternatively, a staffer can decide that a document is routine, and divert it to other White House staff or answer it without referring it to the President.

Information is influence. A President cannot bring his authority to bear on actions that he does not know about; others will make policy when he is left in the dark. One of the oldest tricks in the bureaucratic trade is to drown a superior in paper, producing so much information that essential points are lost in a deluge of detail. In an effort to save the President's time, staff members often prepare a short summary of longer documents. Henry Kissinger, an experienced national security adviser, employed the "Option B" tactic to advance his arguments. By setting out three options and making A and C unattractive, this left Option B (Kissinger's preferred alternative) the obvious choice.

The perennial dilemma of the President is that he wants to know only what he needs to know, but he cannot be sure that what he is not told will not hurt him. In response to this dilemma, Presidents have evolved a variety of strategies to filter information flowing toward the Oval Office. At one extreme, White House staff can be encouraged to screen out details, reducing problems to a few essential points that focus on options for presidential action. At the other extreme, White House staff can be encouraged to let the President examine the details of a problem for himself, or a President may use multiple and competing channels of influence so that different staff members act as checks on each other.

Investing Each Day

Every President is limited in what he can do by the clock. This is as true of a workaholic President as of an aging or ill President. The things a President does *not* do and the people he does *not* see reveal more about his priorities than an organization chart. The basic rule is simple: If a President devotes time to going public, he cannot devote it also to going international. If a President devotes time to foreign affairs, he cannot use the same time for domestic issues. Since the President's time is the scarcest commodity in the White House, the President guards it carefully.

A detailed analysis of how President Carter spent his first year in the White House, prepared at his own request because he was concerned with using time to good advantage, gives a fair insight into the way in which a President rations time. Even when working a seventy-hour week, in an average week the President does not see most of his White House Office staff, or most of his Cabinet.

The President's daily routine is dominated by meetings with senior White House staff, not by meetings with Cabinet secretaries and heads of executive agencies. Of the total time logged, President Carter spent 42 percent in individual or group discussions with senior White House staff (see table 8.1). The President was scheduled to see only three people each day, and each was on the White House staff. With Zbigniew Brzezinski, his national security adviser, the President considered the international system. With Press Secretary Jody Powell, the President reviewed how he was going with the public. The President's concerns with going Washington were dealt with in discussions with congressional liaison officer Frank Moore (Kraft, 1977: table C). The lack of records for many meetings with Hamilton Jordan, who eventually was designated chief of staff, reflects Jordan's ease of access to the Oval Office.

TABLE 8.1

DEMANDS ON THE PRESIDENT'S TIME

	Average Hours	
	Weekly Hours	Percentage of Total
Senior White House staff	29.5	42%
Group meetings	7.1	
Brzezinski, National security	6.0	
Mondale, Vice-President	4.0	
Schultze, McIntyre, Economy	2.0	
Powell, Press secretary	4.0	
Jordan, Political	1.5	
Moore, Congressional liaison	2.6	
Eizenstat, Domestic policy	1.5	
Other	0.8	
Cabinet and other officials	10.8	15.5
Foreign visitors	5.2	7.5
Members of Congress	5.1	7.5
People, ceremonial, other	2.4	3.5
Press conferences, interviews	1.4	2
Special interest groups	1.1	1.5
State and local officials	.6	1
Other political leaders	.7	1
Private lunches (e.g., Mrs. Carter)	1.6	2
Oval Office private working time	11.5	16.5
	69.9	

SOURCE: Adapted from Kraft (1977). Tabulation is for President Carter's working week in Washington; excludes travel, and work outside the official timetable.

Presidential appointees in executive agencies claimed only 15 percent of the President's time. While there were dozens of presidential appointees who thought they had come to Washington to undertake tasks important to the President, few saw him with any regularity. The secretary of state was sure of the President's attention at a weekly foreign policy breakfast, but

Secretary of State Cyrus Vance finally resigned in protest against his views being ignored in important meetings about the attempt to rescue hostages in Iran. The treasury secretary was sure of seeing the President at a monthly economic policy luncheon, but that turned out to be too much for Carter, who subsequently fired Treasury Secretary Michael Blumenthal. All Cabinet secretaries could see the President at Cabinet meetings, but these became fewer and fewer through the President's term, as Carter regarded them as a waste of time by comparison with meeting his own people in the White House.

The timetable is also revealing about what the President chose to *ignore*. For example, economic policy was of minor concern. Whereas the President saw his national security adviser every day, he was timetabled to see his chairman of the Council of Economic Advisers and the director of the Office of Management and Budget only once a week. Overseas visitors rated more time than members of Congress. Discussions with congressmen were a higher priority than the discussion of domestic policy with executive branch officials. Notwithstanding the importance of state and local government in delivering many federal policies and the traditional roll of state and local parties in delivering support, the President spent less than an hour a week talking with these officials.

Most of the tasks that a President undertakes each week would be familiar to a Prime Minister. Every national political leader spends a lot of time talking with personal advisers and with other officials in government, communicating with heads of other nations, and attending to public opinion. But a parliamentary system involves a Prime Minister in far more group discussions with ministers and officials directly responsible for major programs. The staff with whom a Prime Minister spends much time consists of permanent civil servants expert in the policies of government, rather than the campaign staff with whom a President often surrounds himself. A Prime Minister talks to party colleagues who share a common desire to see the government remain in office. By contrast, a President meets many Washington powerholders who have incentives to pursue their interests without regard to him.

Staff as Eyes, Ears, and Egos

Because a President cannot be personally involved in every issue of White House concern, he must find ways to staff out problems. White House staff members are important because they are the eyes and ears of the President, gathering information that can be distilled into briefings for him, identifying policy options, and keeping an eye on the implementation of presidential decisions. Like the President, most of the staff members that he appoints are amateurs in the White House.

Presidential staff members differ in the routes that lead them to a White House job. Some are there because they are loyal aides who joined his entourage years before they, or he, ever thought it possible to reach the White House. Others are ambitious people ready to do whatever the President wants done in the belief that doing so will advance their own careers as well as his. A third group consists of "migratory technocrats who offer their skills to whatever chief executive occupies the office" (Holden, 1986: 27). Henry Kissinger was a national security adviser ready to offer his expertise to any President who requested it, and the chairman of the Council of Economic Advisers is usually an economist who has worked with many politicians.

The people whom the President appoints to serve in the White House have only one quality in common, dependence on the President. When he goes, they expect to leave the White House too. Most White House staffers share a second characteristic: No one else has ever offered them so important a job as their present post. The combination of gratitude and insecurity encourages staffers to agree with the President even when they think he is wrong. Chester Cooper, link man during the Vietnam war between President Johnson and the CIA, found that however much one may disagree with the President—and even dream about voicing this disagreement to him—when the President goes around the room and asks each staff member individually whether or not he agrees with the President's policy, one does not say no to the President (Cooper, 1970: 223).

White House staffers do have political views, and these views carry weight when expressed to Cabinet officers, executive agency officials, and the media. By influencing the memos put to the President, they also influence him. Staff views on issues tend to reflect the views of the President (Kessel, 1975, 1983, 1984b). Reagan staff members are conservatives, Nixon staff members were moderate conservatives, and the average Carter staffer was all over the ideological map, being liberal on civil rights, moderate on international policy, and moderate conservative on economic measures. Members of the Carter staff were likely to split three ways, one group on the liberal side, another on the conservative side, and a third group taking a middle-of-the-road position. The readiness of Reaganites to be in agreement about conservatism encourages harmony in advice, but it also substantially narrows the policy options discussed.

A few senior staff members act as political lightning rods, taking criticism away from the Oval Office, for it is much easier to attack a staff official than the President himself. One way in which staffers show loyalty is by being prepared to absorb criticism in order to protect the President. In the blunt words of H.R. Haldeman: "Every President needs a son of a bitch and I'm Nixon's. I'm his buffer and I'm his bastard. I get done what he wants done and I take the heat instead of him" (Page and Petracca, 1983: 169).

The strength and the weakness of White House staff members is that they are driven people, identifying their job with the President's purpose.

Bradley Patterson (1982: 107ff) characterizes hard-driving White House staffers thus:

> They have been asked by the President to work for him, to sacrifice a great deal, to help turn their country around in a short time. They come to Washington eager to meet that kind of challenge and they tend to be "don't get in my way" people. This does not set them up particularly well in their relationships with the bureaucracy or with one another.

The drive carrying a person to the White House can lead a staffer to forget that his power and influence is derivative from the Oval Office. The more junior the staff member, the more ego satisfying it is to ring up a Cabinet official and announce: "This is the White House calling." (The proper bureaucratic retort is: "Buildings don't make phone calls," a polite way of saying: "Who the hell are you?") A leading assistant to Lyndon Johnson describes how working in the White House can unbalance judgment:

> You sit next to the Sun King and you bask in his rays, and you have those three magic words: The President wants. And all of a sudden you have power unimagined by you before you got in that job. And if you don't watch out, you begin to believe that it is your splendid intellect, your charm and your insights into the human condition that give you all this power.
>
> I'm telling you, this is like mainlining heroin. And while you are exercising it, it is so blinding and dazzling that you forget, literally forget, that it is borrowed and transitory power. (Jack Valenti, quoted in Berman, 1987: 114)

At the extreme, White House staffers can believe that they need not obey the law of the land, as in Watergate and the Iran-*contra* affair

The loyalty that staff give to a President is often reciprocated. A President whose support is low in opinion polls and in Congress knows that his staff will still support him. In a lonely job, this support can be emotionally very satisfying. It explains why a President will stand by loyal staff appointees when they are under fire for showing bad political judgment or are investigated for accepting bribes.

Political Strategies for Organizing the White House

There is a conflict between the public administration doctrine about White House staff and the use that the President makes of such staff. The doctrine, often asserted by persons after they have left the White House, is that staffers should be few in number, anonymous, act as brokers rather than proponents of policies, and not exercise authority over Cabinet members and executive agencies. This doctrine has been rejected by successive Presidents; there has been a swelling of the Presidency in every sense. The names and faces of White House staff members appear frequently in the media. Staffers use their proximity to the President to cultivate and assert power over executive agencies and Cabinet secretaries. The distance between the President himself and the median member of a White House staff of hundreds bothers many students of public administration, but it does not bother the President. He has never wanted the number of staff limited—as long as they do what he wants done (cf. Price, 1982).

Because the White House is a focal point of politics, many conflicts are represented there. National security staff members are likely to dismiss domestic policy staff as dealing with trivia. Staffers concerned with developing new policies are likely to take a different view than budget staff trying to hold down the growing cost of established policies. Those responsible for projecting the President's public image will regard going international as just one more media trip, and specialists in congressional relations will point out that winning the applause of foreign Parliaments does not help a President carry measures on the Hill.

A President seeking to resolve conflicts effectively in ways economical of his own time and political capital cannot turn to theories of public administration, for there does not appear to be any significant correlation between particular ways of organizing advice and substantive policy outcomes (Barilleaux, 1985). He can try one (or all) of three different strategies for organizing the White House: hierarchy, multiple and competing channels, and collegiality (cf. Johnson, 1975; George, 1980: chap. 8).

Hierarchy Under a Chief of Staff

The basic principle of a hierarchy is a large number of organizations and officials are at the base and very few are close to the person on top. Work is meant to be organized into units with reasonably well-defined responsibilities, each reporting to a superior. When disputes occur or more than one unit or agency is involved in a problem, these should be dealt with by interagency committees, with a White House staff person chairing, or acting as an influential secretary. As papers and problems rise up the hierarchy, the perspective from which they are viewed becomes broader than those of particular subgovernments. Insofar as a hierarchy is a pyramid, as problems approach the top, the concerns of very different interests—spending and budgeting, domestic and international, congressional and electoral—are brought together. If White House staffers do their job, by the time a file reaches the President, people with many different responsibilities and views will have been consulted.

Although the President is inevitably at the top of the hierarchy, he usually has someone designated as a chief of staff conveying information to and from the Oval Office with the informal authority to tell others what the President wants (Kernell and Popkin, 1986). While the title and personality of the individual in this role varies, the usual practice is for one person to be in a position to review most of the documents that go to the President, and to add to a document whatever comments he wants. President Nixon relied upon H.R. Haldeman to see that issues were properly staffed out before being presented to him in the form of written memoranda. In 1985-86 President Reagan had as chief of staff Donald Regan, who saw himself as the chief executive officer of a corporation, with the President as the part-time chairman of the board.

A hierarchical system saves the President time and insulates him from political conflict (see table 8.2). A great deal of time and controversy are absorbed in going through interagency discussions before a problem approaches the desk in the Oval Office. A chief of staff can screen out a large amount of information of no interest to the President and condense much more information into the essential points of a single memorandum. Insofar as the system creates pressures among disputants to agree among themselves rather than risk the President ignoring disputatious views, the system may also produce committee consensus. Greenstein's (1982) study of what he calls the "hidden-hand Presidency" of Dwight Eisenhower emphasizes his use of Chief of Staff Sherman Adams as a screen behind which the President quietly maneuvered to influence events without publicly risking his own political capital.

The limitations of the hierarchical system are substantial. First, there is the risk that too much information will be screened out in the process, leaving the President ill informed about substantial arguments within his administration about major matters of policy. A bland review listing options for presidential choice conveys far less about the character of an issue than does a face-to-face discussion with senior officials who disagree about what should be done. Another major weakness is the extent to which the President must depend on the character and skill of a single member of his staff. With experience in the military and in Washington, President Eisenhower was able to use Sherman Adams as a staff officer who handled a great deal of sensitive work for his boss, but remained subject to orders from above. Donald Regan's imperious behavior under a lackadaisical Ronald Reagan produced press headlines such as "How Donald Regan Runs the White House" (Weinraub, 1986).

Multiple and Competing Channels

A President who wants to maximize the amount of information flowing into the Oval Office can organize multiple channels for staff communication. The logic is similar to that of the constitutional concept of the separation of powers; political ambition can check political ambition. This form of organization is sometimes described as a "spokes in the wheel" system, with the President at the hub of advisers each of whom separately channels information and advice (cf. Campbell, 1986: 83ff). The system invariably produces conflicting views about what should be done, because advisers in different positions are likely to differ in what they think the President should do. Instead of conflicting views being smoothed over in meetings chaired by a chief of staff, they are passed up to the Oval Office for the President to resolve.

TABLE 8.2
ALTERNATIVE STRATEGIES OF WHITE HOUSE ORGANIZATION

	Benefits	Costs
Hierarchical	Orderly process Saves time	Depends on single chief of staff Forecloses information, alternatives
Multiple Channels	Multiple views advocated Involves more participants	Confusion of direction Takes more time Generates friction
Collegial	Multiple views advocated Favors consensus	Limits debate Forecloses information Personality dependent

A multiplicity of information channels is likely to widen the President's scope for effective choice, by exposing him to the views of a multiplicity of advocates (George, 1980). Each advocate is a presidential appointee who can claim to be viewing a problem in terms of what is best, and to be well-briefed in giving reasons why the Oval Office should adopt a recommended course of action. Franklin D. Roosevelt was renowned for using staff assistants and unofficial advisers as competing sources of information in order to have diverse recommendations from which he could then try to forge a policy that would have the broadest base of political support. As former congressmen, Truman, Kennedy, and Ford were accustomed to the expression of differing points of view on the Hill. They also learned there how to spot political weaknesses in a case being made by the advocate of a particular point of view.

The problem with multiple channels of advice is that it offers a President who has made up his mind suggestions that he does not want to hear. While Lyndon Johnson was happy to listen to different points of view on subjects about which he had not formed an opinion, he demanded complete commitment once he had made up his mind, for example, on Vietnam. The encouragement of conflicting ideas within the White House can also signal uncertainty or confusion to others in Washington: "Attempts to keep all options open prevent the persistent pursuit of any one of them. A foreign policy whose chief characteristic is a plethora of unclosed options is not much of a foreign policy at all" (Hughes, 1967: 676; see also Kozak, 1980). Within the White House, competition intensifies personal frictions and jealousies between staff, turning policy disputes into emotionally trying disputes between staff. A President confronted with too much conflict is likely to decide that he would rather run a government than a debating tournament.

Collegial Advice
By definition, a collegial structure relies on several people, each of whom has direct access to the President. This avoids the risk of a President having ideas and information distorted by the perceptions of a single chief of staff. Because the number of people involved are few—often a *troika* (threesome)—a President is saved from the incessant claims on his time that can be made by many spokes in a wheel. As long as the small group includes people with diverse experiences, interests, and points of view, a collegial structure can provide the President with more diverse outlooks than a chief of staff at the top of a hierarchy. Because a collegial system emphasizes harmony among the threesome, different opinions may be impersonally analyzed rather than reach the President as unresolved arguments from individuals advocating their personal view, as can happen with multiple channels.

The first Reagan administration had a collegial organization under a *troika* of Edwin Meese, James Baker III, and Michael Deaver. Meese, a California friend of the President, represented conservative views on policy questions. James Baker was a knowledgeable political hand capable of dealing with Congress and the agencies, but not a loyalist, having backed the President's 1980 primary opponent, George Bush. Michael Deaver, another California loyalist, was especially sensitive to the President's personal psychology. By reducing the number of people to a very few, President Reagan was able to reduce his workload to what he found manageable. By having more than one person to whom he could immediately turn for advice, the President was not dependent on the judgment of a single chief of staff.

Collegial systems have their limitations, too. There is a danger that a *troika* can become closed, with the three members ironing out differences among themselves and presenting the President with a single agreed-upon view that becomes very difficult to reject. Alternatively, each member of a collegial system may take an expansive view of his personal responsibilities, resulting in personality and policy conflicts that cause the group to disintegrate. Moreover, a President who has three senior advisers can find that they require more of his time than a single chief of staff.

Because there is something to be said for each method of organizing information flows, a President can try more than one method during his tenure of the White House, as Ronald Reagan did, first organizing the White House as a collegial *troika*; then, under a hierarchical chief of staff, Donald Regan; and finally, an unstructured system encouraging competition, under Howard Baker. President Ford had different methods for dealing with particular types of problems. Henry Kissinger was, in effect, a chief of staff on national security matters; there was an Economic Policy Board to act as a collegial group; and legislative matters tended to involve the President receiving advice from a multiplicity of channels.

A President who is certain about goals will tend to favor a hierarchical structure, whereas a President uncertain about objectives will be readier to have a collegial sifting of opinion (Walcott and Hult, 1987). Problems confronting the President differ in important political characteristics. There may or may not be widespread consensus in diagnosing what a problem is or what can be done to reach White House objectives. If everyone in the White House agrees about what the problem is and what can be done about it, then there is no need for competing channels of information and advocacy. Uncertainty or disagreement about the cause of a political problem will stimulate many voices to speak out and make an effort to put their conflicting views before the President, whether or not the formal organization encourages this.

A Prime Minister has a much easier job than a President in organizing staff because most staff are a permanent part of government, high-flying civil servants. At London's 10 Downing Street, the most important officials sifting documents and screening visitors for the Prime Minister are a handful of civil servants who share two adjoining rooms, with the door open between them. Each knows what the other is doing, a recipe for collegial cooperation (Jones, 1987). In Germany, the Chancellor's office is bigger, but it too is staffed by experts in the practice of government. In parliamentary systems, the job of a Prime Minister is not to micromanage a problem but to indicate or endorse the direction in which the ship of state should be steered and then let others in Cabinet get on with that job. The constitution of the Federal Republic of Germany explicitly recognizes this, giving the Chancellor the authority to set guidelines for policy (*Richtlinien der Politik*) and Cabinet ministers the authority to direct the affairs of their own department (*Ressortprinzip*) (Mayntz, 1980).

Delegation and Arrogation
While a President cannot formally delegate his legal powers, he can effectively identify others as having the authority to act in his name. Since a President cares more about what is done than about how it is done, he is ready to allow White House staffers, executive agency heads, or even persons with no official status to speak in his name—as long as it is to his advantage. From the President's point of view, delegation has two advantages. First, it places awkward political problems in the lap of others, for example, questions about the role of the dollar in the international monetary system. Second, delegation offers a chance to multiply the President's achievements—as long as what is done is what the President would have endorsed had he been involved.

The risk in delegating responsibility is that White House staffers will regard this as an opportunity to go into business for themselves, arrogating the authority that belongs to the President. The problem increases as the number of staff members increases. For example, President Carter's national security adviser, Zbigniew Brzezinski, appointed his own congressional liaison man and had his own press secretary. In the 1985 Reagan White House the President's chief of staff, Donald Regan, had a deputy; his deputy chief of staff also had a deputy; and there was an assistant to the deputy chief of staff as well! Joseph Califano, a staff assistant to President Johnson and a member of President Carter's Cabinet, describes the consequences as follows:

> As the size of the White House staff expands, the ability of the President to maintain taut control is weakened. Senior presidential aides, who themselves supervise large staffs, find it difficult to control the use of the President's name by their own staff members. Large numbers provide fertile soil for mistakes and excesses that crop up out of perceived views of what the President wants or what would be good for the President. (Quoted in Patterson, 1976: 74)

A more succinct description has been given by a veteran of a time when the White House staff was small: "Now there are too many people in the White House who are trying to bite you with the President's teeth" (quoted in Rose, 1976b: 148).

161

9. The President: A Chief but Not an Executive

I agree with you, but I don't know if the government will.
— John F. Kennedy

If we're speaking of "running the government" that is a somewhat simple-minded conception of how power works in the American political system. Power is highly fragmented, much more than in just the civics text version of separation of powers.
—Richard Darman

Our view of the Presidency is bedeviled by what an early political scientist called "the one-man idea" (Goodnow, 1910:198). As the only politician elected by the nation as a whole, the President has a unique claim to voice what the people want. But his position of eminence is lonely, for the President is only one among 2 million employees in the executive branch of government. Moreover, executive agencies are not simply agents of the President; they are institutions created by acts of Congress, funded by congressional appropriations, and administered by career civil servants who have been running their bureaus long before a particular President enters the White House, and who will remain there after he has left. By himself, a President can do little. For the most part, the record of a President's administration is a record of what others do in his name.

The President is undoubtedly the chief political figure in Washington, but he is a chief without an executive. A President is *apart from* rather than a part of the executive branch of government. The President's title of chief executive is a misnomer; he can more accurately be described as a non-executive chief (Rose, 1977: 6ff). He is a chief in the old Irish sense of the leader of a small band of people kept together by personal loyalty to "the big man," the head of a clan (Farrell, 1971). John F. Kennedy did not see himself as a Prussian general, a French bureaucrat, or the CEO (chief executive officer) of a large business corporation; he saw himself as the head of a band of people trying to take over government.

One of the first things a President learns after entering the White House is that he is a leader who has few certain followers within government. As

President Kennedy explained to a visitor, the endorsement of a policy by the Oval Office doesn't necessarily mean that the U.S. government will do what he would like (quoted in Berman, 1987: 99). Republicans have had the same experience. Conscious of the limits on White House action, Ed Meese gave visitors pleading a cause pencils stamped with the motto "My heart is with you but my hands are tied."

The executive branch of the federal government is a collective noun, but it is not a collective organization. No one is in charge of all the executive agencies that require 586 pages to list in the *United States Government Manual*. The President has his institutions, such as the National Security Council and the Office of Management and Budget, but the Congress has "their" institutions, including executive branch agencies such as the Army Corps of Engineers, which dispenses pork-barrel benefits in the form of visible public works in many congressional districts. At one time, the Federal Bureau of Investigation was effectively a law unto itself. The President can claim greater individual eminence than a Prime Minister, but he is not so central in government. As former White House official Roger Porter (1987: 87) emphasizes: "The concept of a group of people being collectively responsible for policy is simply not there."

The gulf in Washington is not between the executive and the legislative branch but *within* the executive branch, separating agency officials oriented toward subgovernments from those who put the President's priorities foremost. Most bureaucrats think first of the affairs of their bureau, usually an operating division within a Cabinet department. Cabinet appointees are concerned with their immediate responsibilities, which inevitably involve them with the subgovernments. More than two-thirds of elected politicians and bureaucrats see Washington as an arena of group conflict about subgovernment benefits (Aberbach and Rockman, 1977: table 7).

Because the President stands apart from subgovernments, he therefore stands apart from most of the people he appoints to head the agencies that collectively constitute his administration. Most of the people the President appoints are strangers when they receive their commission from the White House. The longer presidential appointees work in Washington, the more they are likely to become estranged from the White House and put agency interests first. Career civil servants are even more remote from the President, identifying closely with the long-term interests and values of the agency in which they serve. Whereas a Prime Minister takes office sharing many values and experiences with Cabinet colleagues, the President must come to terms with two sets of strangers, the people whom he appoints to head agencies, and long-serving bureaucrats expert in programs and subgovernment politics (Heclo, 1977).

A President can avoid constant conflict with agencies by the simple device of ignoring them. A postmodern President has a particular incentive to do so, for his time is very much committed to the international system, whereas most federal agencies are concerned with domestic policies, such as housing, transport, energy, or labor. If their activities affect the President's interests, he can still keep his distance by using White House staffers to oversee their work and give them direction. If the staff members succeed, then the President can claim a success. If they fail, the wasted time and effort is theirs, not his.

This chapter first sets out the structure of the inner and outer Cabinet, and the ambiguous relation of the President with Cabinet secretaries and expert bureaucrats. Since the President is more a taster and filter of ideas than a maker of policies, the second section considers where the President's policies come from. Given that many problems of government are a distraction from the imperatives of the postmodern President, the third section considers the devices by which the President keeps out of time-consuming problems of government. The concluding section is called organized anarchy, because of the persistence of stable policy networks without any final authority in Washington. In such circumstances, the President is not so much laying down the law as he is selectively seeking to make policies where and when he can.

Coming to Terms with the Executive Branch

There is no such thing as a challenge to a President on his home ground, but there are plenty of challenges outside the White House. Because the President is a chief without an executive, the Oval Office is always subject to challenge by other parts of government, with their own political interests to pursue and the constitutional authority to advocate opinions different from the White House.

The independence of the President from executive agencies is an ambiguous asset. It frees the President from getting bogged down in problems that he does not understand or care about and that have no effect on his standing in Washington, in public opinion polls, or in the international system. Many problems are dealt with in the agencies by political executives (i.e., presidential appointees and ranking bureaucrats) and by subgovernments. When an issue arises that the President does care about, the White House can become so frustrated in trying to push things through executive agencies and Congress that some White House staff members begin to speak longingly about the attractions of dictatorship (cf. Cronin, 1970).

White House frustration is not the result of an occasional system failure; it is an indication that the checks and balances of the Constitution are working as intended. A parliamentary democracy avoids such frustration because authority is fused. After Cabinet ministers dispute policies with one another, they must collectively agree on a line to take in order to maintain their personal position in Cabinet and the authority of Cabinet. The policy put to Parliament is then endorsed, thanks to party discipline, and the controversy resolved. By contrast, presidential appointees in the agencies are torn two ways, risking estrangement from the White House if they get too close to Congress and risking clashes with Congress if its interests are neglected in favor of the White House.

The Inner and Outer Cabinets

A President typically enters office endorsing the idea of Cabinet government, even though the idea of a Cabinet is nowhere mentioned in the Constitution, and the duties of the Presidency cannot be delegated. Reciprocally, if an act of Congress makes a department secretary or a bureau chief within an agency responsible for a problem, this cannot be shifted to the White House. Presidential references to Cabinet government are meant to flatter senior appointees and raise their status. Insofar as the term has real meaning, it implies giving individual Cabinet secretaries substantial discretion to direct their department, and consulting the Cabinet as a group about major problems facing the administration.

Every President soon abandons any commitment to the symbols or practice of Cabinet government. The White House learns that when Cabinet secretaries follow the subgovernment agendas relevant to their department, conflicts arise with the views of the Oval Office. When the Cabinet does meet as a group, the President finds that the members have very little in common and that most of the members have nothing worthwhile to contribute to the imperatives of the postmodern Presidency. A President is better off investing time in talking with Congress than meeting with the Cabinet because members of Congress have something he needs, votes on legislation and appropriations. Cabinet secretaries tend to bring the President problems, and seek Oval Office support for their political agendas. Every President soon reduces the number of Cabinet meetings to a minimum, regarding them as a waste of time. No President has ever left office speaking in praise of Cabinet government.

A Prime Minister, by contrast, has practical reasons to meet regularly and frequently with Cabinet ministers. Responsibility for directing foreign affairs and the economy is in the hands of Cabinet colleagues; the Prime Minister's job is to balance conflicting claims between senior ministers and the Cabinet and its committees are used to resolve subgovernment conflicts in the name of government. Maintaining Cabinet solidarity is also important because the political future of the Prime Minister depends on maintaining the coalition of party interests that the Cabinet reflects. While George Washington sought to use the Senate as a body of councillors like the Cabinet in an eighteenth-century parliamentary system, the Senate believed that it should advise at arm's length and refused to discuss matters in his presence (Corwin, 1957: 209).

Although all Cabinet secretaries are formally equal, in practice the thirteen departments that they head can be divided into an Inner Cabinet and an Outer Cabinet (Cronin, 1980: 274ff). The distinction is political, reflecting the importance of issues, not the amount of money that a department spends (cf. table 9.1). *Inner Cabinet* departments deal with matters of high priority to the White House: State, Defense, Treasury, and Justice. Justice is important because the statutory and constitutional basis of the President's authority is so complex that the President often needs legal advice about how to find (or invent) the authority for doing what he wants to do. Because these offices deal with abiding concerns, they date from the time of George Washington.

TABLE 9.1

THE INNER AND OUTER CABINETS

Department	Created (present form)[a]	Budget ($ bn)	Personnel (000)
Inner Cabinet (4)			
State	1789	3	25
Treasury	1789	179[b]	130
Justice	1789 (1870)	4	63
Defense	1789 (1949)	286	3,221[c]
Outer Cabinet (9)			
Interior	1849	5	70
Agriculture	1862 (1889)	59	103
Commerce	1903 (1913)	2	32
Labor	1903 (1913)	24	18
Health and Human Services	1953 (1979)	334	128
Housing and Urban Development	1965	14	11
Transportation	1966	27	60
Energy	1977	11	16
Education	1979	18	4

a. Some departments formed by merger or by splitting.
b. Includes payment of interest on the debt.
c. Includes armed forces in uniform.

SOURCES: Principally, OMB (1987b) summary tables 3, 7, figures for 1986.

Presidential appointees heading Inner Cabinet departments are also involved in important subgovernments: the military-industrial complex; national and international leagues of diplomats, bankers, and financiers; and judges and law enforcement interests respectively. Many appointees to Inner Cabinet positions have held office in the department before and thus have a commitment to their department that is not shared with the White House.

The occupational hazard of Inner Cabinet secretaries is that their views will be trumped by the White House, because the issues they deal with are regarded as too important to be left in their hands. The risk of being trumped is greatest for the secretaries of state and of defense, who must compete with the assistant to the President for national security affairs. The Iran-*contra* affair showed that even a relatively weak national security staff could override the views of Cabinet secretaries. In such circumstances, a secretary of state can resign, as Cyrus Vance and Alexander Haig did, or can accept being cut out of important political initiatives run from the White House, as George P. Shultz and William Rogers did. The secretary of the treasury has no competitor within the White House, but he has no assurance that the Oval Office understands what he is doing. The attorney-general's problem is that he is often consulted only *after* White House action has created a mess that requires a lawyer to justify.

The reward for an Inner Cabinet secretary is to be designated the President's lead person on a matter of major White House concern. For example, Dwight D. Eisenhower gave John Foster Dulles, his secretary of state, substantial status and kept the White House national security adviser subordinate. President Reagan has allowed Treasury Secretary James A. Baker III to take the principal responsibility for dealing with the difficult task of finding an appropriate foreign exchange rate for the dollar. The President thus distances the White House from awkward problems and makes use of the skill of his appointees and the knowledge of their departments. The President can also detail a member of the White House staff to attend meetings chaired by the lead secretary, in order to make sure that nothing is done that would go beyond the President's wishes (cf. Porter, 1980; Odell, 1982).

The *Outer Cabinet*, in order of seniority, consists of the secretaries for agriculture, commerce, labor, health and human services, housing and urban development (HUD), transportation, energy, and education. The President must appoint people to head these agencies, which are established by law and represent important subgovernments in Washington. Even if the White House does not care about the secretary of agriculture, farm interests and members of Congress from rural districts care, just as congressmen from cities care about the direction of HUD. Collectively, these departments spend most of the money in the President's budget and have most of the federal government's civilian employees. Since five departments—Health and Human Services, HUD, Transportation, Energy, and Education—deal with programs favored by Democrats, these Outer Cabinet secretaries are often under suspicion by a Republican White House.

Neglect is the occupational hazard of a secretary in an Outer Cabinet department. The handshake that the President gives to a newly appointed secretary is likely to be his way of saying good-bye. A President does not want agencies dealing with issues remote from the Oval Office to turn their problems into his problems. When such a department faces a problem of presidential concern, the President is likely to tell one of his White House staff to sort things out, undercutting the authority of the secretary. The White House regards an Outer Cabinet appointee as good who avoids politically embarrassing actions and is loyal to White House pronouncements. A secretary is meant to satisfy, or at least, pacify, the department's subgovernment interests without running afoul of White House budget and legislative priorities. Satisfying subgovernments is much easier with a President who supports their goals than it is under a President who has trouble promoting new programs in Congress, such as Jimmy Carter, or a President wanting to cut budgets, such as Ronald Reagan.

Cabinet Secretaries: Natural Enemies and Intermittent Allies

A Cabinet appointee usually enters office pleased with being offered a high-level appointment by the President and expecting that he and the President are politically in harmony. Before completing his period of office—which may be terminated by his own decision to resign, by the electoral defeat of the President, or by being fired—a secretary will understand why the first budget director referred to Cabinet secretaries as the "natural enemies" of the President. The conflict arises from what can be called a separation of interests. The Oval Office is usually interested in Outer Cabinet departments only insofar as they affect overall presidential priorities, for example, threatening a budget ceiling or affecting critical groups in the White House electoral coalition. The more or less vague mandate a President usually gives a secretary on appointment is subject to challenge by the specific interests of the department.

A secretary's political reputation depends on how well he or she responds to the pressures that go with the job. A secretary is only briefly in office; the normal period is about two years. Because of the difficulties in working in Washington, most people neither seek nor receive a second job in Washington; the general rule is "in and out and never in again" (Brauer, 1987: 182). Because a Cabinet appointee is not looking for promotion to another and more important agency, he lacks the incentive to be agreeable to the White House that a minister has in a parliamentary system, where a Prime Minister will promote those who are loyal to higher-ranking posts in Cabinet. In Washington the incentives are different:

> There is an increasing role of political appointments in providing credentials for public servants in pursuit of lucrative private positions. The political appointment, then, is not so much the crown of a long career in public service as it is a ticket to the greater financial rewards available in the private sector. (Fisher, 1987: 29)

The short duration of a secretary's time in office means that he or she is under pressure to score quick successes. Many of the pressures emanate from Congress. The first thing a would-be secretary learns is that the President's letter of appointment is not enough to secure the job. In addition, he or she must be confirmed by the Senate, a process in which senators with an interest in the department can extract commitments as the price of supporting a nomination. The laws that the department carries out are enacted by Congress, and congressional committees can use their power of oversight to question how a new secretary proposes to exercise statutory authority. While budget requests are reviewed by OMB, binding decisions about the department's appropriations are in the hands of congressional committees. Managing Congress is a high priority for every Cabinet secretary, and mismanaging Congress is a recipe for political disgrace.

A Cabinet secretary must also come to terms with a department in which his office is only one small part. The basic units of the department are bureaus, each concerned with clearly defined programs, and the subgovernments of which each is a part. The bureaus give tangible expression to the meaning of the term bureaucrat (rule by bureaus), for many are headed by persons who have far more knowledge of departmental programs and procedures than do presidential appointees. Moreover, bureaucrats often identify closely with their work and have the political connections to cause a secretary trouble in Congress, and in the department, if the Secretary asserts a White House view at variance with the established policies of the subgovernment. Bureau chiefs look first to Congress for their marching orders, not to the White House. Presidential appointees tend to give bureaus "a meagerness of direction" (Kaufman, 1981: 184). Even though the Reagan administration took office with conservative inclinations at odds with the views of many bureau chiefs, the right-wing Heritage Foundation concludes that conservative commitment was often shallow and disappeared as appointees "went native," adopting the outlook of the department to which they were appointed (Rector and Sanera, 1987).

A Prime Minister can normally communicate the problems of government to his Cabinet colleagues because they tend to view the world in terms of a common political outlook, fostered by years of working together in a party. A President cannot invoke party principles as justification for taking a broad view of national problems, for he is not elected as a party man, nor do American parties have many agreed upon principles relevant to government. When disagreement arises within the Cabinet in a parliamentary system, a Prime Minister can focus attention on what everyone agrees about, namely, the collective need to win the next election, and a minister must accept this obligation. A White House official who puts this case to a Cabinet secretary is likely to be told that what the department wants will help the administration with the interests of a particular subgovernment, such as farmers or labor. Each department head directs attention to a particular section of the electorate and not to the President's nationwide constituency.

Members of the Inner Cabinet are usually allies because they deal with problems of immediate Oval Office concern. For example, if the Attorney

General were to ignore White House interests in giving legal advice, the President would fire him and get another lawyer. But Defense and State often differ with each other in their views of policy and compete for the President's backing of their views. In the absence of a clear directive from the President, which is most of the time, members of the Outer Cabinet will cultivate sub-governments, assuming that what is good for the department is also good for the White House. Two Presidents, Richard Nixon and Jimmy Carter, were so displeased with the activities of their Cabinet secretaries that they requested that all of them tender their resignations in order that their loyalty could be reassessed before they were reappointed or sacked.

Balancing Partisan Zeal and Bureaucratic Expertise

The American tradition of government is amateur and partisan: To the victor belongs the spoils of office. By contrast, parliamentary systems have an elitist tradition: Only the best and the brightest graduates should serve the state. Americans believe that democracy means opening up office to everyone—or at least everyone who supports the winning party. Parties have organized by patronage as much as by appealing to principles. The President is central to the exercise of federal patronage, for the White House has the authority to make thousands of appointments in an average year. Patronage appointments may be made on the basis of commitment to the President's program, however vaguely defined this may be, or be given to a party loyalist supported by members of Congress whose goodwill can be obtained by rewarding their friends.

Presidential appointees work closely with career civil servants, who are numerically dominant in every executive branch agency except the White House Office itself. Civil servants are recruited for technical expertise in particular programs, whether soil conservation or the procurement of military weapons, and they are assured of a permanent job independent of changes in the White House. The negative connotations of the word bureaucracy hide the fact that the bureaucrat's concern with procedure is also a concern with seeing that the agency applies the law fairly and honestly, without cutting corners that can land the agency in trouble with Congress, the courts, or both. Making expertise a qualification for a post is intended to ensure that staff is effective. Every modern government is predominantly staffed by permanent civil servants recruited for their expertise.

A President wants the directors of executive agencies to be zealous in the pursuit of his goals. Traditionally, American government has drawn a sharp line separating political zeal, deemed to come from the President and partisan appointees, from expert knowledge of programs, the special responsibility of career bureaucrats. Political screening at the White House is designed to identify people who have political commitment, and civil service procedures to identify those bureaucrats who are program experts. But this distinction is not easy to maintain in practice. The White House soon learns that to be effective in government it must put forward proposals that are "do-able," that is, capable of being implemented administratively, as well as desirable (Rose, 1987a).

Political executives, the presidential appointees and top bureaucrats who run agencies, can have any of four different sets of attributes (see figure 9.1). *Zealots* exhibit the faults of too much commitment and too little technical knowledge. A zealot's chance of achieving the political goals can be frustrated by ignorance of actions needed to advance partisan goals within an existing structure of programs and subgovernment interests. Experts without political commitment are managerial *technicians*; their knowledge is valued by the White House only insofar as it can be used to implement presidential directives. Ideally, a President would like to place executive agencies in the hands of *policy entrepreneurs*, people committed to his political priorities and with program expertise (cf. Marmor with Fellman, 1986). The last thing a President wants is to have a lot of agencies directed by *political passengers*, people who lack both expertise and political commitment.

Program Expertise

	High	Low
High	Policy entrepreneurs	Zealots
Political Commitment		
Low	Technicians	Passengers

FIGURE 9.1

A TYPOLOGY OF POLITICAL EXECUTIVES

SOURCE: Adapted from Rose (1987a) figure 7.

A President wants political executives to show "responsive competence," producing do-able programs that reflect his political priorities (Moe, 1985: 239; cf. Heclo, 1975; Nathan, 1984). Incoming presidential staff suspect career civil servants because they have served opponents in previous administrations, and because expertise usually goes along with strong program commitment. These suspicions are often correct. A major survey of differences of opinion between pro-welfare civil servants and anti-welfare Republicans concludes: "Even paranoids may have real enemies" (Aberbach and Rockman, 1976: 458, 467; cf. Sanera, 1984; Pfiffner, 1985). The result is, according to Rourke (1987: 225): "The position of the Imperial Presidency today is in no small measure a product of a widely perceived need to prevent the emergence of an Imperial bureaucracy."

171

The President's problem is to locate individuals who are both politically committed and technically expert, or to combine these qualities in a team of persons directing an agency. In a parliamentary system, this is not so much a problem. Cabinet ministers combine the commitment of partisans with prior experience in the direction of large government departments. Expertise is provided by career civil servants who in most European countries can be party members able to go on leave to take ministerial posts for which political commitment is required. Civil servants who are nonpartisans, as in the British case, are expected to take a broad view of issues as servants of the Crown, a term emphasizing that the national interest is something more than the sum of conflicting subgovernment interests. Ironically, this conception of serving the state or the Crown is akin to the President's view of serving the nation as a whole.

When White House staffers seek people to take presidential appointments they ask: Will he or she do us any good? One way in which an appointee can help the White House is by mobilizing support from interest groups, such as farmers, business, labor, blacks, women, or regions. A second advantage is for appointees to be zealous in pursuit of presidential directives. A new administration can attempt to take control of the executive branch by swamping the bureaucracy, hoping that the greater the number of zealous partisans that it throws at an agency, the more it will respond to the President's wishes. When the critical problem is to field enough people to swamp an agency, political appointees will be recruited more for their zeal than for program expertise. The Reagan administration has been particularly successful in recruiting zealous appointees; 64 percent report that serving an admired President is one of their highest sources of job satisfaction, more than double the average for previous Presidents (cf. Fisher, 1986; Goldenberg, 1984; Lynn, 1984: 370). But swamping the bureaucracy creates a problem: It insulates the White House from what is going on inside the agencies by imposing many layers of committed but inexpert appointees between the Oval Office and civil servants expert in programs.

Every presidential appointee new to an agency must come to terms with the officials already in place there. The advice that appointees receive may not be congenial, but it is expert in the substance of programs and the procedures of government. For example, a zealot may be told that a proposal risks violating a federal law, or heavy criticism from Congress. However frustrating this advice may be, it warns those who listen of the pitfalls that amateurs are prone to fall into. The longer presidential appointees remain in office, the more they appreciate the technical expertise of civil servants. Career civil servants become viewed as useful members of the administration's team rather than as antagonists. Four-fifths of presidential appointees come to view career officials as competent, and five-sixths regard them as responsive to political directives (NAPA, 1985). However, more than half think bureaucrats are not so good at dealing with Congress, and two-thirds that they are not so good at anticipating political problems (Pfiffner, 1987: 101).

Presidential appointees often become frustrated because their political faith is insufficient to remove mountains of obstacles that bureaucrats point out to them. They can be disillusioned as White House officials offer little support for their efforts to achieve what they see as presidential objectives, and intermittently issue peremptory orders about what the agency must do (NAPA 1984: 40ff). In default of frequent contact with the White House, presidential appointees are under great pressure to go along with the subgovernment of which their agency is a part. After two years, many presidential appointees have had enough of Washington and resign.

At mid-term, the White House faces a fresh set of choices. Political passengers can be dismissed or left in positions of no consequence. Zealots will either have learned how to become policy entrepreneurs by using the expert knowledge of bureaucratic staffs or have made sufficient mistakes to earn dismissal. The difficulty is keeping in place policy entrepreneurs committed to the President's goals and preventing the rise of policy entrepreneurs who advance their department's interest contrary to the President's wishes. They make the White House appreciate the advantages of managerial technicians, whose expertise promises a relatively trouble-free agency, although one that does not contribute much to the President's political goals.

A President who comes to Washington expecting to captain a team in which everyone is playing on the same side soon learns that subgovernments divide his appointees, and the turnover of appointees at the rate of nearly half each year further reduces the administration's cohesion and effectiveness. Presidential appointees learn that they do *not* need to hang together; each needs to cooperate with one specific part of the whole. In his evocatively named *A Government of Strangers*, Heclo (1977: 111) describes the situation thus:

> Political interaction is less like regularly scheduled matches between competing teams of partisans (President versus Congress, Republicans versus Democrats) and more like a sandlot pick-up game, with a variety of strangers, strategies and misunderstandings.

Yet a President has no choice but to come to terms with the heads of executive branch agencies.

> A President may not like his Cabinet members; he may disagree with them and suspect their loyalty; but he cannot destroy their power without seriously undermining his own. It is the agency heads, not the President, who have the men, money, material and legal powers. (Seidman and Gilmour, 1986: 78)

The President as a Policy Taster

Presidential appointees can follow only if the Oval Office gives a lead. Congress starts its annual legislative task, after the State of the Union message, and subgovernments lobby for and against proposals that the President puts forward. The media are full of stories about problems facing the nation, and about ideas being considered by the White House. Foreign nations and foreign investors also look to the White House for clues about what American government proposes to do next. In such circumstances, the basic Oval Office problem is: What to say?

A President enters office proclaiming a generalized vision of the American dream. But the vision is likely to be a very dreamy one, expressed in a vague, directionless slogan, such as John F. Kennedy's "Get American Moving Again" or Ronald Reagan's TV commercial celebrating the attractions of "Morning in America." In campaigns, a general slogan has more potential appeal to the very broad coalition of people and interests that a candidate seeks to attract in order to get elected.

Campaign rhetoric is a poor source of substantive policy direction. Congress wants to know in what direction the President wants to go, before it will decide whether to follow his lead, and presidential appointees want to know what the President wants them to do. Very few of the proposals that the President puts to Congress derive from campaign pledges. For example, during the term of office of John F. Kennedy, more than 800 domestic policy proposals were submitted by the White House to Congress. Of these, only 59 were wholly or partly carrying out campaign promises (Fishel, 1985: 38-42). Nearly 95 percent of the proposals that President Kennedy put to Congress were *not* campaign promises made when he ran for the White House.

A Prime Minister enters office as the leader of a party with a stronger commitment to programs than the catchall electoral coalition of a President. A European party's commitment is likely to be expressed in a statement of long-term principles, the support of a relatively stable coalition of voters, and a party manifesto prepared especially for each election. A party devotes a substantial amount of time in opposition to preparing more or less detailed proposals for action once in government. As a condition of becoming party leader, the Prime Minister will have pledged to uphold party principles. Once in office, ministers can look to the manifesto for guidance, and invite criticism if they go against important party commitments. A study of British party manifesto pledges found that they numbered nearly 100 at each election, and the great majority were put into effect by the winning party (Rose, 1984b: chap. 4).

The Oval Office as Focal Point

The White House has no problem in assembling a vast menu of ideas that the President can consider adopting as his own. The Oval Office is a focal point for many pressure groups seeking action by the federal government. Some pressures are generalized demands for action, for example, that the President "do something" about America's international trade deficit. The President is left with the problem of deciding what to do. Often, groups press solutions on the President, actions that the White House should take in their interest. These may be academic ideas that are the brainchild of a professor with a flair for publicity or measures that provide clear benefits for identified political interests. In response, the President must decide whether the action addresses a real national problem or is simply in the group's interest and if it is in the White House interest.

Most of the ideas considered within the White House come from outside the White House (see table 9.2). Three sources are particularly important to White House staff: Congress, executive branch agencies, and events and crises. Public opinion ranks fourth in importance. Only one-sixth of White House staff members regard the President himself as an important source of ideas. Institutions outside the White House are important sources of three-quarters of the ideas placed on what is formally described as the President's domestic policy agenda.

TABLE 9.2

SOURCES OF WHITE HOUSE IDEAS

	Percentage Mentioning Source (more than one possible)
External to White House	
Congress	52
Events and crises	51
Executive branch agencies	46
Public opinion	27
Party	11
Interest groups	7
Media	4
Within the White House	
Campaign and platform	20
President	17
Staff	16
Task forces	6

SOURCE: Light (1982) table 8. Replies by 118 White House officials to the question: Generally speaking, what would you say were the most important sources of ideas for the domestic agenda?

When a President goes Washington, he does not have to bring a new set of policy proposals with him. There are lots of ideas circulating in executive agencies and Congress. The subgovernments that link these institutions can formulate proposals in ways that government can adopt and mobilize support for them. From the viewpoint of a President who is a professional campaigner and an amateur in government, it is just as well that a pile of ideas awaits him for sorting when he arrives in the Oval Office, for he does not bring with him the knowledge or commitment to generate all the policy initiatives expected from the White House today.

Initiatives

Washington is a vast shopping mall in which many different subgovernments are promoting their products in hopes that something will be to the President's taste. Since there are far more ideas floating about than a President can digest in a single State of the Union message, timing is very important. Most proposals that are floating around town are neither accepted nor rejected; they are left to simmer until an appropriate time arises when they might be adopted as part of the President's program (cf. Kingdon, 1984). Many White House initiatives are based on ideas that have been incubating in subgovernments for years (cf. Polsby, 1984: 158ff).

Crisis events in the international system often preempt White House discussion by creating pressures for prompt action. Whether or not a President would like to act, he must respond to imperative international events that become headline news in the United States. In economic policy, the President is at the mercy of international market trends, which push the trade deficit up and down. Interest rates also move quickly—and independently of White House plans. Crisis events reduce the time devoted to deciding whether to act; they also reduce the time available to evaluate the likely success or failure of policy options.

By contrast, most domestic policy issues involve a seemingly interminable process of incubation in which there is disagreement about whether a problem exists, what its causes are, and alternative solutions. Some policy proposals current in Washington might be enacted by Congress this year (e.g., amending a clause in an existing act), whereas others take years to carry out (a major tax reform or alterations in social security). At the start of the annual policy review cycle, hundreds of ideas will be available for White House consideration. When Joseph Califano was in charge of President Johnson's State of the Union message, he kept a list of 500 "possibles" for inclusion in the annual address to Congress. Task forces were assembled to investigate what could be done about the topics that appeared politically most attractive. Task forces usually involve agency officials, outside experts, and a budget official to keep an eye on costs. President Johnson would only indicate whether he was for or against a proposal after months had been spent in testing the political costs and benefits of an idea.

A President samples the menu of domestic policy proposals with four criteria in mind (cf. Light, 1982: 72). First, what effect would this proposal have on going public? Second, how likely is this proposal to appeal to the taste of Congress? No President wants to offer a menu of legislation that is not to the taste of Congress. President Kennedy was notoriously cautious about putting forward domestic policy initiatives, for he reckoned his support in Congress was as weak as his 1960 election majority. Third, is this policy good in itself? Every President has some personal views about what measures are to his taste, independent of electoral calculations. Good policy is usually defined in terms of good intentions; other agencies of government are left to worry about implementation. A final consideration is whether a measure will add to the President's reputation in history, a particular concern of second-term Presidents. Historic achievements are few, but each President wants to leave his mark on history before he leaves office. A Prime Minister resembles a President in being concerned with electoral calculations, good policy, and a place in history. But a Prime Minister does not have to worry about Parliament as the White House must worry about Congress, thanks to disciplined party voting there. Because government measures are put forward collectively in the name of the Cabinet and government party, a year's legislative program is meant to reflect a balance of views within the Cabinet and to be enacted as a package by Parliament.

A postmodern President's view is particularly subject to economic constraints. Budget problems have caused a Democrat such as Jimmy Carter as well as Republican Ronald Reagan to ask: How much will it cost? (cf. Light, 1982: 150; Stockman, 1986). Measures involving substantial budget increases are likely to be dismissed by the White House without regard for congressional calculations. Following Black Monday on Wall Street in 1987, the world economy became a visible partner in the calculation of the money costs of policies. A postmodern President must consider policies in terms of their impact on America's position in the world economy, as well as the domestic costs of measures.

In order to secure broad support for a White House initiative, a President looks for consensus policies. In Cronin's phrase (1985: 52), a President supports the separation of brain and state. The originality of intellectuals often reflects minority views, or ideas whose time has not yet come. By definition, a consensus idea it not a fresh idea; it has been incubating for a while in executive agencies, in Congress, and in the press. As the idea moves into the public spotlight, the White House begins to take notice too, first in a noncommittal fashion and then with an opportunistic interest in giving presidential endorsement, if it is popular and does not cost too much. By the time a specific proposal comes forward to the Oval Office, it will be familiar to everyone concerned. The less novel the idea, the more likely the President is to be attracted, as it will be easier to secure adoption.

A President is not a maker of policies but a policy taster, sampling a wide variety of offerings put before him before deciding what he does and does not want. White House staff prepare the alternatives placed before the President, just as restaurant cooks prepare a menu and then a meal. Robert Gallucci explains:

> The President makes policy only in the sense that the customer in a restaurant makes dinner when he orders his food. He chooses from a limited menu prepared for him by the establishment and usually must accept the interpretation of his choice as it is reflected in the execution of his order. (Quoted in Greenstein, 1988: 350f)

Keeping Out of Trouble

"To govern is to choose and to choose is to cause discontent" (Will, 1987). When a problem arises, the first question facing a President is not which side to take, but whether he should get involved at all. Why should a President engage in battles with subgovernments that existed long before he arrived at the White House and will continue long after he has gone? The argument for opening what may be an indigestible can of worms is that the President has no choice; he is the prisoner of first things first, and imperative issues must be faced even if they place the President in a no-win position. But to have the political resources to respond to problems that the Oval Office must deal with, a President also must heed a negative imperative: Keep out of trouble whenever you can (Rose, 1977: 11ff).

The greater the emphasis on a few compelling priorities, the stronger the argument for avoiding involvement in secondary issues. A President who often invokes Samuel Goldwyn's motto—"Include me out"—does not appear as a heroic figure. But like the prudent English general who said that many of his greatest military successes were battles he never fought, he is a politician who avoids the political costs of trying to take charge. Even Lyndon Johnson, who prided himself on his ability to wheel and deal, knew there were limits to what he could achieve. When a staffer asked President Johnson what should be done about a quarrel between leading House Democrats and the secretary of agriculture, Johnson simply replied: "Get the President out of this" (Mansfield, 1983: 68).

Keeping out of trouble means that the President is using his discretion by deciding *not* to take a decision. Avoiding involvement in tedious arguments and no-win conflicts conserves political capital. As President Calvin Coolidge explained: "If you see ten troubles coming down the road, you can be sure that nine will run into the ditch before they reach you, and you have to do battle with only one" (quoted in Hughes, 1973: 97). By stalling before making a commitment on an issue, a President can avoid being on the losing side and, if he endorses the winning side, can claim a consensus victory. The less often the President rushes into a problem when the risks are not yet known, the more political capital he conserves to invest in high-priority issues in which he must be involved.

While the President's strategy makes sense to him as an individual politician, it is not a recipe for responsible government because it leaves sub-governments to pursue interests without interference by the head of government, and disputes may fester for years without resolution. In a parliamentary system, a Prime Minister cannot act like the President, passing the buck to the head of a Cabinet department, for the Prime Minister's political fortunes depend on Cabinet ministers being successful too. If a minister is not successful, the Prime Minister must find someone who will deal with a problem effectively. While a President may blame Congress for a budget deficit, a Prime Minister cannot dump blame on Parliament, for the budget that Parliament approves is the document that the Cabinet has approved with the Prime Minister in the chair.

A President has three basic strategies for keeping out of trouble. The first is to refuse to create offices in the White House that will attract troublesome issues there. Second, a President can monitor and buffer an issue. Third, he can stall by endorsing vague goals.

What the White House Does Not Do

One way to avoid a problem is not to assign White House staff to a subject. If staff members are assigned to a problem, then sooner or later what they deal with will reach the President's desk. The readiness of the President to avoid being the action officer for every problem of government is indicated by considering an impressive list of institutional functions that could be, but are *not*, normally found in the White House.

1. *Planning.* No President has the political incentive to commit himself to long-term coherent plans; his agenda is much more ad hoc, responding to opportunities as they present themselves and refusing to follow through if the political timing appears inopportune. The National Resources Planning Board, abolished by Congress in 1943, was the last planning branch in the Executive Office. President Nixon established the Domestic Council with the recommendation that it engage in long-term planning, but it saw that there was no demand for planning in the White House. The Domestic Council soon got involved in firefighting as problems broke out. The director of President Nixon's National Goals Commission to identify long-term priorities said, only half in jest, that his principal achievement was to win the right to use White House stationery. The commission could not get the President to say anything about the report because the Oval Office did not want to risk appearing committed to a discussion of long-term ideas.

2. *Program implementation.* No President has ever sought to become involved in the day-to-day delivery of federal programs; this is regarded as beneath the notice of the White House. The decisions that White House

staffers implement are directly related to the President's own priorities: relations with Congress and the agencies; publicity; and nonroutine communication with other countries. The restyling of the old Bureau of the Budget as the Office of Management and Budget in 1970 was ballyhooed as a sign of raising management concerns to the President's attention. But neither the White House nor senior OMB officials could be bothered to keep in place a simple management-by-objectives program to monitor whether agencies were implementing nonurgent objectives, and management has had low status since. (Rose, 1976b).

3. *Program evaluation.* The President is primarily concerned with evaluating what the government *ought* to do, not what it is doing. This is true even though most public money is spent on the operation of routine programs. President Johnson asked OMB to introduce evaluation in the form of PPBS (Program Planning Budgeting Systems), and President Carter sought to promote evaluation through ZBB (Zero-Based Budgeting). Each evaluation initiative has been abandoned, for there is not the political demand in the White House to evaluate established programs (Wildavsky, 1984).

4. *Intergovernmental coordination.* Because of the role of state and local governments in delivering many programs authorized by Congress and largely financed by federal funds, the Heineman Commission established by President Johnson declared: *"Policy coordination in Washington will be relatively meaningless unless programs are operated in harmony in thousands of communities across the nation"* (1967: 13; italics in the original). But proposals to link the White House with state and local governments do not make political sense. A unit placed in the White House to coordinate federal programs with states and cities would bring local disputes to the White House doorstep. As one aide remarked: "It's bad enough being President without having to be Governor of Alabama and Mayor of New York City too."

Monitoring and Buffering

A President does not seek information for its own sake, but information that can be used to his advantage. Given information, a President can decide whether to probe more deeply into a matter because he spots an opportunity for positive action or because he sees signs of trouble ahead. The monitoring of what is going on in Washington, nationally and internationally, is an integral part of White House work. Much of the material that the President receives each day, particularly about the international situation and about the economy, is not for action but for information. Monitoring buys time for a President who is not sure whether he wants to become involved in an issue, or what to do about it. President Eisenhower used to admonish eager staff: "Let's not make our mistakes in a hurry."

The President is not expected to manage the international system, but he is expected to be informed about trends that affect his imperative concerns.

180

Within the Executive Office three agencies, the National Security Council, OMB, and the Council of Economic Advisers, routinely monitor these concerns. Nearly all the information that goes into OMB is kept there, as it concerns specific budget items not worthy of presidential notice. Information from the State Department, the Defense Department, and the CIA is digested by the National Security Council, and selected items are included in a daily report of the national security adviser to the President. The chairman of the Council of Economic Advisers often prepares a one-page summary of economic data. White House staff monitoring Outer Cabinet domestic agencies soon learn to think that "no news is good news"; a trouble-free domestic agency is deemed a well run agency.

Interagency committees can be used to filter issues, deflecting from the Oval Office disputes about problems of limited consequence and undertaking the necessary spadework to decide what, if anything, requires the President's intervention. The Reagan administration established seven Cabinet councils to filter issues: Economic Affairs, Commerce and Trade, Human Resources, Natural Resources and Environment, Food and Agriculture, Legal Policy, and Management and Administration. Each council included as members the heads of the agencies primarily concerned. While the President was nominally the Chairman of each council, he attended less than one-fifth of the meetings. Only the Cabinet Council on Economic Affairs frequently engaged the President's attention (Newland, 1983, 1985; Campbell, 1986). Most of the councils dealt with issues such as the disposal of surplus cheese or the federal employee benefits program. Only one in seven of Cabinet council agenda items was eventually linked with a presidential decision; more than 85 percent were disposed of without bothering the President.

When a President does see trouble ahead, he can keep his political distance by *buffering* a problem, putting other officials and other institutions between himself and the problem looming on the horizon. From the President's perspective, the value of Outer Cabinet departments is that they are buffers keeping subgovernment problems from becoming White House problems too. If a buffer succeeds, then the President can claim a victory after the fact. If a buffer fails, the blame is not deposited on the President's desk. President Eisenhower was particularly adept at using others as buffers. His press secretary, James Hagerty, explained:

> President Eisenhower would say, 'Do it this way.' I would say, 'If I go to that press conference and say what you want me to say, I would get hell.' With that he would smile, get up and walk around the desk, pat me on the back and say, 'My boy, better you than me.' (quoted in Greenstein, 1982: 91f)

The Iran-*contra* affair illustrates how White House staffers can protect the President by placing their fingerprints, rather than his, on controversial acts or acts of dubious legality. Lieutenant Colonel Oliver North's phrase for acting as a buffer for the President was that he was ready to "take the spear" in his chest to protect the commander-in-chief. His superior as director of the National Security Council, Admiral John Poindexter, said it was his duty *not* to tell the President about illegal activities undertaken in pursuit of ends that the President endorsed. In that way, the President secured deniability; he could say that he knew nothing of illegal acts, while reaping political benefits if staff actions proved successful.

When a problem requires the authority of the White House, the President can designate a senior White House staffer to knock together the heads of the disputants in order to arrive at an outcome. A headknocker must have enough authority to deal with people of the status of Cabinet secretaries. This status was enjoyed by individuals such as H.R. Haldeman in the Nixon White House. A headknocker must also have enough status within the White House that the officials offered his ruling will accept it rather than appeal over his head to the President. As long as the President gives private guidance about how he would like the dispute resolved, the headknocker's decision will normally be final.

Keeping Objectives Vague

When the President is forced to speak out on an issue about which he prefers to remain uncommitted, he can do so in vague phrases that avoid commitment or defy logic. A President's stand on an issue involves a compromise between the incentive to be vague in order to appeal to the maximum number of voters as against being specific to appeal strongly to particular elements within the government coalition (Fishel, 1985: 18ff). Ambiguity gives the President room to maneuver. In the words of a senior presidential assistant:

> Presidential statements should be soft, fluid, vague, even tricky. There should be nothing in them to attract flak. We spend hours constructing paragraphs so that afterwards we can interpret them differently to different clients. (Quoted in Rose, 1976b: 5)

President Reagan's remarks often exploit purposeful vagueness. He is accustomed to talk in terms of generalities and anecdotes, and his reasoning is as likely to reveal non sequiturs or contradictions as it is to show logical consistency. Since being President is not an examination in logic and clarity, Reagan has often benefited. According to presidential analyst Stephen Wayne (1982a: 59f):

> This lack of specificity may be part of the strategy. In addition to being consistent with Reagan's personal style, it reduces his burden and, most important, his risk. Verbal blunders, poor judgment and costly errors can be and have been blamed on subordinates. The President avoids responsibility and ridicule by not having been informed about the details. All accomplishments, of course, result from his leadership.

182

Evasive tactics are not unique to Washington. A Prime Minister has Cabinet ministers who act as buffers against trouble. But the Prime Minister cannot avoid involvement in difficulties of government. In a Cabinet, problems as well as rewards are distributed collectively. Colleagues who share in taking the slings and arrows of government also share in the rewards. By standing up in Parliament to shield erring colleagues, a Prime Minister gains the loyalty of ministers, just as ministers are expected to show their collective solidarity by supporting the Prime Minister.

Influencing Organized Anarchy

Organized anarchy is a term that can characterize a large, complex organization with a high degree of uncertainty about the problems facing the organization, its goals and the means of achieving them, and the people participating in the making of the organization's policies. The concept was developed by Cohen and March (1974: 3) in a study of university presidents; it is also appropriate to describe Washington. The speed and complexity with which problems confront the President make it difficult for people in the White House to disentangle the resulting confusion. Actions that can be justified in retrospect are often uncertain or unclear in prospect. Uncertainty about how others will respond greatly compounds the confusion. In Washington there is a simple answer to the inquiring journalist's question: Who's in charge here? The correct constitutional answer is: No one.

Policymaking in an organized anarchy can be characterized as a "garbage can" process, in which different people at different times dump problems demanding actions, and others dump measures that they describe as solutions (Cohen and March, 1974: chap. 5; see also Cohen et al., 1972). Groups of participants deal with more or less unrelated problems and solutions. For reasons that may be accidental or are a by-product of other considerations, problems have a solution stuck to them. The important point is that the contents of the garbage can, and even more, the way in which things are thrown in and pulled out, is not the result of any individual's intent, whether President, Cabinet secretary, bureaucrat, or member of Congress.

Subgovernments introduce an element of organization and order because they consist of organizations that share common interests, are narrowly defined and stable. Participants in subgovernments know one another well and can usually anticipate what others will do, settling differences by bargaining among themselves. Subgovernments are not looking for central direction; their participants are prepared to coexist through a process of partisan mutual adjustment (cf. Lindblom, 1965). Subgovernments work hard to maintain stability within the area they dominate. Their leaders oppose intervention by the White House and fear the intrusion of free-floating uncommitted participants who may turn their cozy arrangements into a more open and less predictable issue network (cf. Heclo, 1978: 102ff; Freeman and Stevens, 1987).

The contrast with a parliamentary system of government is sharp. In a parliamentary system, many subgovernments operate, but they do so within a centralized system of authority that limits their scope for action. The Cabinet can collectively limit or repudiate the actions of an individual minister. The Prime Minister is a chief *with* an executive. More than that, the fusion of legislative and executive authority means that subgovernments cannot use Parliament to undermine the authority of the Cabinet. Political authority is organized so that anarchy is replaced by the collective responsibility of the Cabinet to Parliament.

Why Intervene?

A President surrounded by agencies that organize to exclude his influence or place obstacles in his way has good reason to ration involvement in the activities of Washington. Until the advent of the modern Presidency, most occupants of the White House believed, as a matter of principle, that they should not intervene in many matters deemed the concern of Congress, the states, or the people (cf. Tulis, 1987). The modern President has been expected to give leadership in domestic policy, and the postmodern President faces difficult international responsibilities. The Oval Office retains its freedom and makes government workable by selective intervention in Washington politics.

The President *must* uphold his oath to "preserve, protect and defend the Constitution of the United States." This oath emphasizes a few but fundamental concerns of sovereignty: maintaining national security, a sound economy, and law and order (cf. Rose, 1976a: 151ff). A postmodern President is therefore obligated to go international, even though he may find, in the international system, that organization and anarchy are both obstacles to the achievement of White House goals.

National security problems tend to select the President, for he is not only the head of state communicating with heads of other governments but also commander-in-chief of the armed forces. An unexpected crisis anywhere in the world will be noticed in the White House communication room. Yet the White House cannot be the action station on every problem in every country in the world. The President selects those issues that he and his staff will deal with, for example, arms-control negotiations with the Soviet Union or relations with China. Simultaneously, the White House screens out matters for other agencies to worry about, such as civil wars in Africa, the debt crisis in Latin America, and diplomatic relations with India.

Economic problems, like air pressure, are part of the atmosphere that the President breathes; it is instantly noticeable when oxygen (money) is in short supply. The state of the economy immediately affects taxing and spending measures contained in the budget that the President must send to Congress. The federal deficit is not only a budget problem but is also important for its impact on foreign loans needed to fund the budget deficit and the trade deficit. In turn, this influences domestic American interest rates, the price of imported goods, and values on the stock market. The problem for the White House is not whether to try to influence the economy; the problem is finding out how to do so effectively.

The President's responsibilities for law and order are best discharged when he has nothing to do. A President is not concerned with daily problems of crime on city streets, whether in Newark, Chicago, or Washington, D.C.; that is a local police responsibility. The seamy side of urban politics is one trouble spot that every President wants to keep out of. The President is concerned only with political challenges to public order, for example, the intentional violation of local laws in protest against the Vietnam war, nonviolent civil rights demonstrations seeking to uphold federal laws against local discrimination, or the disorder of an urban riot. Disorder stimulated by national political issues forces the President to act when judicial action is not an adequate response. In the 1980s, disorder has claimed much less presidential time than in the 1960s and early 1970s, thus enabling a postmodern President to concentrate nearly all his time on issues that are problems of the international system.

The President's job is to respond to imperative problems in the international system, when action is required on behalf of the United States. To do this, he does not need to mobilize the whole of the executive branch of the federal government. Only by traveling light, and selecting staff and institutional help from a small number of sources, can a President concentrate on the things that he must do in an increasingly open international system.

PART THREE

Problems of Leadership without Hegemony

10. The Economy: An Open Market for Policy

No President can have an economic policy; all his policies must be political.
—Richard E. Neustadt

If economics is what economists do, then politics is what the President does. The President's job is not to manage the economy but, as Richard Neustadt emphasizes, to stay on top of the political system (quoted in Rose, 1985c: 269). Concern with the economy is a by-product of the President's concern with the polity. Economic conditions affect the President's business; a booming economy is likely to boost his popularity, and a rise in inflation or unemployment puts pressure on the President to do something. Presidential initiatives on taxing and spending affect the nation's business. In an open international system, the confidence of foreigners is important too, for what the White House and Congress together do affects confidence in the dollar abroad.

Whether a President is going public, going Washington, or going international, economic conditions impose constraints on what the White House can do. A President cannot expect to be popular if the economy is in a mess. A President presiding over a booming economy will have more influence on political events, for he has more money to spend and gains political capital to invest in other fields. When the economy is in trouble, the President is criticized as part of the problem. A President's influence abroad is constrained if the American economy depends on foreign lenders to maintain the nation's standard of living.

There is widespread agreement among politicians about the goals of economic policy. Economic growth is good, inflation is bad, unemployment is undesirable, and a big international trade deficit is also undesirable. Differences of opinion usually concern the priority to be given each of these goals. In the heyday of Keynesian economics in the 1960s, there was a widespread belief that the economy could be managed to produce success on all four counts. Today, there is neither consensus nor confidence about the impact of government on the economy.

The central political questions are both normative—What should the President do about the economy?—and instrumental—What can the President do? The Constitution requires the federal government to levy taxes for the common defense and general welfare of the United States, to borrow money, to regulate trade and commerce, to coin money, to impose customs and excise taxes, to register patents, and to appropriate money. A contemporary President is expected to give a lead to Congress on economic policy. Even a free-market economist such as Milton Friedman recognizes that the federal government must underwrite order in the market. When the federal government taxes and spends one-fifth of the national product, its role goes well beyond that of a passive nightwatchman. When many billions of dollars are traded in international money markets each day, a postmodern President must also attend to the international economy.

Political calculations are central in determining what the President does. This is as it should be, for politics is about placing values on competing goals, whereas economic analysis is meant to identify the most efficient means to goals given by political choice. When the country cannot simultaneously enjoy growth, price stability, full employment, and a trade surplus, deciding between these competing goals is a legitimate function of politicians.

The dominance of politics can be demonstrated by comparing how a President and his economic advisers evaluate an issue. A politician will assess alternative policies in terms of their political attractiveness, and an economist by their economic effectiveness (see figure 10.1 on page 191). When the President and his economic advisers agree, the President can follow his political instincts, and economic advisers will offer technical support. When economic advice points in a politically undesirable direction, however, the President is likely to ignore it, and if it is frequently repeated, to ignore the adviser as well. The President can embrace a politically attractive course of action even when the economic reasoning is dubious.

Economic policy is the outcome of activities in an open market. Political desires are insufficient to make the economy do what the President would like. The state of the economy reflects the interaction between what government does and what happens in the market, plus random and unpredictable events. The actions of business, unions, workers, and consumers have always imposed constraints on the policies of a modern President. The international system is an increasingly important constraint too; a postmodern President cannot make the American economy boom in the midst of a world recession or expect the rest of the world to finance the federal deficit without profiting in return. Every time the President seeks an economic benefit, he must also pay a political cost. The first thing economic advisers teach a President about their subject is: There is no such thing as a free lunch.

To meet responsibilities for the economy, the President has four sets of institutions at hand: the Council of Economic Advisers (CEA), concerned with such broad macroeconomic issues as economic growth and inflation; the Office of Management and Budget (OMB), which prepares the federal budget on behalf of the President; the Treasury Department, particularly concerned with taxation and international economic policy; and the Federal

190

Economic Appraisal

President's Appraisal	Effective	Ineffective
Desirable	Doubly desirable	Economically dubious
Undesirable	Politically awkward	Doubly undesirable

FIGURE 10.1

COMPARING POLITICAL AND ECONOMIC APPRAISALS OF POLICIES

SOURCE: Adapted from Rose (1987c), 294.

Reserve Board (often simply called the Fed), the government's central bank. The CEA and OMB, as part of the Executive Office of the President, are closest to the Oval Office. But while they have the President's ear, they do not have their hands on the action. The CEA's role is purely advisory and OMB is principally concerned with making recommendations that Congress may reject. Although outside the White House, the Treasury and the Fed do have their hands on important pieces of economic action, collecting taxes and looking after interest rates and the nation's money supply.

Trying to Manage a Bucking-Bronco Economy

The economic theory of managing the economy resembles that of managing a spaceship. It assumes that economics is a science like astrophysics and that economists agree about where they want the economy to go, just as space crews agree about the destination of their mission. *Given these assumptions* it is considered a straightforward task to manipulate the dials that steer the economy to arrive at the desired destination. The only problem with this theory is that it is a model for economic management in outer space; it omits such earthlings as politicians. On earth, politicians must be treated as endogenous variables, that is, they must be incorporated in a model, if only as the joker in the pack (Lindbeck, 1976).

Policy analysts often speak of the President as managing the American economy, without regard to the origin of the word. The verb "to manage" is derived from the Latin word for *hand*. This sense is retained when one speaks of managing a horse, that is, having the reins in one's hand. When the economy is booming, the President may feel as if he is holding the reins of a thoroughbred, but in a recession, he has to whip a nag that has seen better days. In the contemporary international system, a President must often hold on tight to avoid being thrown off the back of a wildly bucking bronco. Whatever ride the economy offers, the President needs help in staying on top.

Supplying Economic Science

The Council of Economic Advisers was created by act of Congress in 1946 to advise the President on major matters of macroeconomic policy, such as economic growth, full employment, and stable prices. The creation of the CEA with a small staff was an expression of the American progressive idea of science in the service of society, and a vote of confidence in new economic techniques which assumed the economy was manageable (Flash, 1965). Lawrence Klein, who subsequently won a Nobel Prize in economics, wrote at the time: "The Keynesian economic system is essentially a machine which grinds out results according to where the several dials controlling the system are set" (Klein, 1947: 153; cf. Bailey, 1950). The CEA has no authority to turn dials, and it advises a President whose desk does not display the dials that economists would like it to have.

The first CEA chairman, Edwin Nourse, viewed economics as a technical rather than a political science, and the CEA was seen as operating at a distance from the White House, making detached analyses of economic trends and identifying policies for dealing with employment, inflation, and the national product (Nourse, 1953). The second chairman, Leon Keyserling, sought to develop a more activist role; the consequence was that Congress nearly abolished the council. It was kept in place by President Eisenhower to provide him with a confidential adviser, CEA Chairman Arthur F. Burns, who saw himself as a technical expert (Hargrove and Morley, 1984: chaps. 1-3).

Supplying the President with Help

The CEA became more closely integrated in the politics of the White House in the Kennedy administration. Walter Heller, the CEA chairman, was a staunch Keynesian economist and a skilled policy entrepreneur. His confidence that "modern economics is a source of national strength and presidential power" caused him to endorse "a growing political and popular belief that modern economics can, after all, deliver the goods" (Heller, 1967: 1, 3). When the economy started moving into recession, Heller promoted vigorously an idea that was as unconventional in Washington as it was normal in Keynesian textbooks: Stimulate economic recovery by increasing consumer demand through cutting taxes and letting the federal deficit go up. Since a faster rate of economic growth would increase tax revenues and reduce spending on such measures as unemployment compensation, the deficit would fall, thanks to the fiscal dividend of a higher rate of economic growth. This Keynesian prescription suggested actions that promised politically attractive benefits with few costs. President Kennedy took the advice and sold the idea of a tax cut to Congress. Because it then worked, the prestige of the CEA chairman was boosted.

Heller was a policy entrepreneur selling economic policies. He described his marketing techniques thus:

The idea was to get all of these people to understand that we knew what we were talking about, that Kennedy would make better policy if he listened to us, that they ought to be clued in on what we were trying to do in spite of the fact that this was an arcane subject to a bunch of lawyers. In that sense, the first job was to become an accepted part of the inner circle. If I had simply stood on my dignity in my office as Chairman of the Council and said, "Let them come to me," I'd have waited a hell of a long time. One had to prowl the corridors of the White House, those corridors of power. (Hargrove and Morley, 1984: 186)

Heller realized that private advice was not enough; he had to go public too.

I found out fairly early in the game that you couldn't operate just inside, that to get the kind of political leverage that you wanted on the President you had to have an outside presence. After we got our feet on the ground, I began to accept television invitations. (Hargrove and Morley, 1984: 188)

Most of the things that the President wants done are best described as political staff work; they do not require a Ph.D. in economics (Allen, 1977). Following the assassination of John F. Kennedy, Heller (1963) produced overnight a memo for President Johnson headed "The Services of Your Council of Economic Advisers." The helpful services listed, in descending order of importance, are:

1. Personal service to the President (information, speechwriting, writing economic policy round-ups, legislative reviews and staffing our programs, ad hoc activities).
2. Joint advisory services with OMB, the Treasury, and the Federal Reserve.
3. Chairing interagency committees and membership of committees.
4. Attendance at international meetings.
5. Meetings with business, labor and consumer advisory groups.
6. Preparing the statutorily required Annual Economic Report and its presidential message.
7. Testimony in Congress and speeches around the country.

Heller's successors at the CEA have accepted that their job is not to write economic papers in a form conventional for academics, but to apply economic analysis in ways helpful to the President.

While Prime Ministers are concerned with economic issues too, they do not need a Council of Economic Advisers on the Heller model, for the institutions of Cabinet government integrate economic ministries and the office of the Prime Minister. A British Prime Minister has no economic council attached to Downing Street. The Treasury, with its large staff of economists and an important politician at its head, remains of first importance in economic policymaking. In Germany, the Chancellor receives a public analysis of the state of the economy each year from "five wise men," economists who constitute a Committee of Experts, but the German Chancellor does not have economists prowling his corridors, trying to sell economic advice. Nor could he buy advice without first securing the agreement of his economics ministers and the Cabinet.

Difficulties in Producing What the President Wants

For the past two decades, economic advisers have not been able to give the President the help he has desired. In reaction against the optimism of Walter Heller, Milton Friedman (1972: 17) told his fellow economists:

> We economists in recent years have done vast harm—to society at large and to our profession in particular—by claiming more than we can deliver. We have thereby encouraged politicians to make extravagant promises, inculcate unrealistic expectations in the public at large, and promote discontent with reasonably satisfactory results because they fall short of the economists' promised land.

Computer models of the American economy are today far more sophisticated than they were two decades ago, but the actual outcomes are far less attractive. Inflation and unemployment have at times risen together to produce "stagflation." The economy has grown more slowly than previously, and in some years actually contracted; deficits in the federal budget have risen to unprecedented heights; and the United States has run up a mammoth trade deficit with the rest of the world. Presidents now recognize that economists sometimes offer only hard choices. For example, in 1980, an election year, President Carter supported an increase in interest rates even though it would boost unemployment, because the alternative was regarded as even worse, a rise in an already high inflation rate.

Economists today disagree in diagnosing the economic problems facing the country and prescribing what the government should (or should not) try to do. Neo-Keynesians give first priority to promoting economic growth and full employment, even at the cost of a higher rate of inflation. Monetarists see inflation as the country's biggest problem and tend to regard government intervention as a major cause of economic difficulties. International economists emphasize that trade deficits and borrowing from abroad have a major influence on the state of the American domestic economy.

As the economy has faced more troubles, CEA chairmen have been increasingly articulate about the fact that economics is not a science producing predictable results. It is a social science, in which the relationship between abstract theories and actual events is a matter of probabilities. As economic outcomes differ from what economic theories often predict, policy-oriented economists have become increasingly skeptical about the helpfulness of theoretical models. Former chairmen of the CEA (quoted in Hargrove and Morley, 1984) commented thus:

194

Arthur Burns: Models are bankrupt; they pay little attention to the real world.
Arthur Okun: We don't know as much as we used to think we knew.
Herbert Stein: Our experience really confirmed how little economists know, especially in the rather new conditions we face.

The bottom line for politicians is: "Economists cannot deliver what politics requires" (Sawhill, 1986: 109; see also Leontief, 1985; Klamer, 1983).

Today, the President faces a wide choice between economic ideologies with contrasting assumptions about how the economy works. The choice ranges from the views of neo-Keynesians to supply-side economists. There is no consensus among economists about which perspective is most appropriate. Major universities award top posts to Keynesian and anti-Keynesian economists. The Swedes display their political neutrality by giving Nobel prizes to economists of each faction.

Ronald Reagan, the first President with a degree in economics (Eureka College, 1932), has sought to proclaim the emancipation of the White House from the so-called dismal science of economics (every benefit has its costs) by making supply-side economics central to his policy. Supply-side economics opposes the Keynesian prescription to increase demand by increasing public spending, as well as the monetarist concern with keeping the federal deficit down. It is argued that the President should not worry about the budget deficit. A cut in tax rates should stimulate investment and the resulting boost in the economy should yield greater total tax revenues from lower rates. In 1981 supply-side arguments justified Reagan's program to cut taxes while pushing up federal expenditure on defense. Its policy prescriptions were "simple, self-confident, and politically saleable" (Sawhill, 1986: 100; cf. Roberts, 1984). By 1988, the ideas remain simple, but they are no longer so saleable.

Economic analysis can explain why a President would rather buy advice from a person who offers what he wants to hear than from an economist who offers a politically unpalatable analysis. A review of the evolution of CEA, from emphasizing arm's-length technical advice to policy entrepreneurship, concludes:

> Once the CEA members and staff decided to assume an advocacy role in the political and bureaucratic process, they left themselves vulnerable to the question: Is the President better served by economic advisers with some knack for politics, or perhaps better by politicians with some knack for economics?
> The CEA is in effect driven to be highly political in order to have enough impact to justify its continued existence, but at the same time an important—if declining—part of its political support is derived from the claim that it is a non-political expert professional group. (Nelson, 1987: 68)

The Treasury's Place
In parliamentary systems, being in charge of the Treasury is one of the top

jobs of government and it can be a stepping stone to becoming Prime Minister. For example, the chancellor of the exchequer, the minister in charge of the British Treasury, is responsible for: the macroeconomic forecasting policies undertaken in Washington by the CEA; decisions about budget spending undertaken by OMB; taxation, a U.S. Treasury concern; and relations with foreign institutions such as the International Monetary Fund (in Washington also a responsibility of the Treasury Department); and influencing the Bank of England (less distant from the Cabinet than the Federal Reserve Board). Furthermore, the British chancellor of the exchequer is normally a contender to be the next Prime Minister.

In Washington the secretary of the treasury is a buffer protecting the White House from involvement in economic problems and interest group concerns. The secretary is the President's representative to the banking community and Wall Street; in a Democratic administration this characteristic may make an individual suspect to liberals on the White House staff. A treasury secretary usually has no political weight as an individual. The autonomy of the job makes it attractive to a specialist in the field, but the independence of the Treasury from the White House means that the secretary of the treasury can be ignored when he wants the President's ear. The relatively low status of the Treasury is also indicated by the paucity of attention given it by students of the Presidency who comment on the CEA and OMB (for an exception, see Porter, 1980, 1983).

The White House Office normally has no senior staff person interested in and well informed about the technical concerns of the Treasury with tax policies and with the international monetary system. White House staffers tend to see economic issues as political problems. Technical studies by Treasury staff are not so relevant to pending legislation as are estimates by the President's congressional liaison staff of what members of Congress will endorse if the President puts it forward. CEA staff members understand what the Treasury is about, but they have their own political position to consider. A CEA chairman will be more concerned with the big picture of macroeconomic policy than with the day-to-day operational anxieties of the Treasury. Nor will a CEA chairman want to use his limited political influence with the President to fight another organization's battle.

The Treasury has risen in importance with the decline of the dollar internationally, for the secretary of the treasury is the front-line defender of the dollar (cf. Odell, 1982; Funabashi, 1988). In 1971 John Connally achieved brief prominence by taking the dollar off the gold standard and devaluing it. Connally's action reflected America's capacity to use its political power to impose economic outcomes abroad. In the 1980s, James A. Baker III has been in a different position, seeking cooperation from foreign governments, especially Germany and Japan, for actions intended to reduce the value of the American dollar in order to reduce America's trade deficit. But when Baker has been asked by foreign governments to do something about the federal

Central Directive Capability

Economic Policy	High (Parliamentary)	Low (Washington)
High interventionist	Satisfaction	Frustration
Minimal intervention	Satisfaction	Satisfaction

FIGURE 10.2

HOW POLITICAL INSTITUTIONS INFLUENCE ECONOMIC POLICY

budget deficit, he is handicapped, for making the budget is not a responsibility of the Treasury.

Shared Difficulties, Different Institutions

The economic difficulties facing the President exist from Tokyo to Bonn and everywhere economists disagree about how the economy works and what should be done to improve it. The White House is distinctive because the President has less authority to carry out economic policies; the fusion of powers in a parliamentary system is a great institutional asset for giving centralized direction. The Cabinet consists of a group of ministers who collectively are responsible for what happens to the economy; they thus have an incentive to cooperate. Advisers are usually chosen for their expertise and experience; they are civil servants who have learned to judge doctrines by their impact on the economy as well as on the standing of the government.

Since a single economic measure can be counter-productive if it is not supported by other measures making up a coherent economic policy, the integration of authority in the Cabinet is particularly important. The parliamentary system's fusion of executive and legislative authority greatly increases the capacity of an elected government to give direction to the economy by sustaining a coherent combination of policies. By contrast, the American system divides authority between Congress and the White House, and places the Federal Reserve Board and the Treasury in the middle. Because there is no central capability in the American system, the making of economic policy can produce an uncoordinated set of policies, as a consequence of organized anarchy.

When the capacity to make central decisions is high, as in a parliamentary system, then the government of the day has a pair of satisfactory alternatives (see figure 10.2). A social democratic Cabinet can pursue an active interventionist policy because the political institutions give government the capability to follow a coherent plan. A conservative administration can adopt a policy of minimal intervention; advocates of planning cannot subvert this policy because they lack the votes in Parliament and in the Cabinet. By contrast, the separation of powers in Washington is a framework for double frustration.

The President lacks the authority to determine taxing, spending, and money supply, thus frustrating those who wish coherent central direction, and Congress lacks the capacity to make a consistent economic policy because its responsibilities are fragmented among many committees. A President who wants government to do less may also be frustrated, since Congress has the power to pass spending and taxing measures against the opposition of the White House. After serving as secretary of the treasury, George P. Shultz concluded:

> In the United States fiscal policy is an unwieldy tool that can be applied to the economic machine only with the greatest clumsiness, however refined the mental processes of the policymakers. Perhaps in the land of Keynes a chancellor of the exchequer can execute spending and taxing decisions with precision and promptness. If so, the explanation lies in the structure of British institutions. In the United States both the theory and the reality are different. The President proposes but can hardly dispose. (Shultz and Dam, 1978: 23f)

Given the lack of central directive capacity in Washington, the easiest economic policy for the White House is that of minimal intervention. But a postmodern President finds it difficult to avoid a show of activity on the economic front when there are national and international pressures for the White House to do something about the economy. Lacking the fusion of powers that Keynes took for granted in Britain, a President who proposes the adoption of an interventionist economic policy risks frustration because of the low capability of the White House.

Adding Up Numbers That Don't Add Up

A budget has three sides: a spending side that registers the "good" goods and services that government provides; a taxing side that shows the costs of government; and a bottom line that registers the difference between taxing and spending, whether a surplus or a deficit. A budget registers a surplus if revenues exceed spending, and a deficit if they do not. While surpluses were frequent in the laissez-faire era of the traditional Presidency, the spending increases associated with the modern and postmodern President have created deficits in six of every seven years since 1950 (Peterson, 1985: 576; Buchanan and Wagner, 1977). Budgeting is a political process reconciling the competing claims of spending departments, the guardians of the public purse, and the nation's economy.

The basic elements of the budget process are common in every modern system of government, for they reflect the hard constraints of the great identity: Revenues must equal expenditures (Crecine, 1971). At the initial stage, a top-level agency makes a forecast about the total amount of spending and taxing deemed acceptable for the nation, bearing in mind both political and economic commitments and consequences. Individual departments make proposals for spending lines in the budget, reflecting the interests of their subgovernments in spending on established programs, and creating new programs. Since the numbers usually do not add up because spending exceeds revenue, a third stage is necessary, reducing expenditure and/or increasing revenue in order to arrive at a budget that everyone can live with politically.

All budgets express political power as well as economic necessity. Subgovernments, led by Cabinet secretaries, bureau chiefs, and interested members of Congress, press for more spending for their particular programs. Since they are not responsible for the taxation that finances programs, they are indifferent to the sum of all requests. Budget officials, at the center, worry when taxing and spending totals do not add up, thus creating a need to borrow to finance the resulting deficit. But budget technicians lack the political authority to overrule subgovernment interests. To do this requires something stronger than subgovernments; it requires the collective authority of government.

A century ago, Woodrow Wilson wrote a scholarly polemic attacking the practice of Congress scrutinizing the budget line by line, without regard to broad government concerns. He and other reformers proposed centralizing responsibility for compiling the federal budget in the Presidency (Caiden, 1987: 85f). The campaign for budget reform succeeded in creating a major role for the Presidency in budgeting, consistent with the responsibility of the Oval Office for government as a whole. But the authority to determine the final budget figures remains in the hands of Congress, which can alter any budget item if it chooses. In the words of a leading budget scholar, Allen Schick (1981b: 85): "The President makes the budget, but that does not mean that he controls it."

Budgeting with the Authority of Government

The budget is an excellent example of the authority of a parliamentary system, for its collective institutions resolve disputes between different subgovernments. Whereas the President can only make budget proposals to Congress, in a parliamentary system, the executive actually writes the document that becomes law and Parliament is largely a rubber stamp (Heclo and Wildavsky, 1981; Barnett, 1982; Mosley, 1984; and Wildavsky, 1975b).

The Cabinet binds ministers representing subgovernments to accept the constraints of government. The annual budget cycle starts with the finance minister presenting totals for taxing, spending, and the deficit to the Cabinet for its endorsement. Since the figures have usually been agreed upon with the Prime Minister beforehand, individual spending ministers are politically too weak to reject them. Room is left for political negotiations, for the allocation of money between departments is decided only after totals are agreed on. At the second stage, bilateral bargaining takes place between spending departments and the Treasury, whose officials try to squeeze cuts out of departmental budgets, while departmental officials argue that many increases are mandated by law (e.g., cost of living adjustments in social security), and other increases are justified by political priorities.

Disputes that cannot be settled at this stage are carried forward to a Cabinet committee consisting of politically strong individuals. This *Kern-kabinet* (core cabinet, in German) or Star Chamber (an English term referring to a medieval tribunal regarded as exercising oppressive power) resolves nearly all disputes. The Prime Minister's absence from this appeal body saves her or him the political cost of forcing cuts on stubborn ministers. If the sum total of cuts imposes a great political strain, the Prime Minister and Cabinet can endorse a few more spending increases and direct the finance ministry to "reheat," if not cook, the books in order to make the budget more palatable politically. Spending departments and finance officials represent conflicting subgovernments, but as members of the government they are also bound to accept collective decisions,

The Cabinet's decision *is* the budget because parliamentary approval is assured by party discipline. A minister who does not want to accept the Cabinet decision cannot do an end run by appealing to Parliament against the Cabinet. His only alternative is to resign, with all this implies in terms of loss of status and power within the governing party.

Budgeting by Concurrent Jurisdictions

Budgeting in Washington takes place without the central authority of government. Three institutions—the Presidency, spending departments, and Congress—have a concurrent interest in parts or the whole of the budget.* Each has a different perspective and reflects a different set of political values and interests. The final totals in the budget are not a deliberate choice of a collective authority, as in a parliamentary system; they are the outcome of a year-long struggle between competing interests.

The White House sees the budget as a legislative problem, for it must come to terms with what Congress will vote for. The budget process is a story of White House attempts to create the authority needed to prevail against Congress's ability to look after the interests of subgovernments. Given the initial weakness of the President, the long-term trend has been to give the White House more influence. The overall concern of the White House is with balancing competing political claims, such as the tax implications of propos-

---

*Because the Internal Revenue Service, technically a bureau within the Treasury Department, collects taxes and receives the complaints of individual taxpayers, it tries to distance itself from congressional pressures. Treasury Department officials concerned with tax issues lack the political clout of congressional committees and the White House.

als that increase spending; the spending cuts required to secure tax cuts; and the political and economic effects of a deficit. The President tends to be isolated because he is concerned with the overall budget picture.

Spending departments focus on increments, that is, more or less small changes that can add to or subtract from the money available to spend on the programs within their immediate jurisdiction (cf. Wildavsky, 1988). Executive agencies are concerned with budget lines that control spending in their departments; so too are congressional committees that oversee their programs. Advocates of spending more on their particular pet programs argue that the little bit of straw that they are proposing to place on the camel's back of the budget is not enough to break it. Taken in isolation, each statement is true. But the Oval Office cannot view individual spending items in isolation from one another. The President is concerned with the total impact of lots of seemingly small increases that can add up to a big budget deficit.

Broad political values influence budget judgments, for decisions about how much is enough are first and foremost questions of political priorities. Liberals tend to favor spending as evidence of government doing more good through public programs providing benefits and stimulating the economy to a higher rate of growth. Conservatives dislike public spending as evidence of government interfering with people and imposing higher federal taxes or bigger deficits on the economy. Divisions occur within parties as well as between them. For example, when President Jimmy Carter, a Democrat, recommended budget cuts as an anti-inflation measure, he was challenged by a fellow Democrat, Senator Edward Kennedy, in words that illustrate the importance of political values in budget conflicts:

> I support the fight against inflation. But no such fight can be effective or successful unless the fight is fair. The party that tore itself apart over Vietnam in the 1960s cannot afford to tear itself apart today over budget cuts in basic social programs. There could be few more divisive issues for America and for our party than a Democratic policy for drastic slashes in the federal budget at the expense of the elderly, the poor, the black, the sick, the cities and the unemployed. (Quoted in Cutter, 1984: 481)

The *Office of Management and Budget* is the budget arm of the Executive Office of the President. OMB has a staff of more than 500 civil servants with substantial knowledge of the practice of budgeting, including the art of raising or lowering spending by varying the assumptions and procedures used in calculating figures. Because OMB staff are responsible for monitoring spending in the agencies, they have a continuing interest in spending programs and knowledge that can be put at the service of the White House (Committee on Governmental Affairs, 1986).

The traditional mission of OMB has been to keep the increase in spending (and therefore in taxation or deficits) within limits that the President regards as politically tolerable. But its traditional role was eroded by Presidents who favored expanding the federal government. President Johnson undermined the conception of budgeting as a device for keeping spending down when he turned to budget officials for help in designing Great Society programs to spend more money. Budget officials were relied on because they were knowledgeable about programs, had a good sense of fiscal limits and, not least, because they were Executive Office staff rather than working for agencies integrated in subgovernments. Under Presidents Nixon and Carter, OMB became more concerned with management matters; more than half its staffers today are involved in nonbudget activities, such as management systems or monitoring agency regulations.

As the White House has identified OMB more closely with its priorities of the moment, it has been more anxious to increase political direction. This has meant imposing layers of partisan appointees at the top of OMB, people who are expected to share the President's zeal in altering the budget. Presidential appointees usually lack the specialized knowledge of budget practices and politics that are the stock in trade of career examiners. The White House has increasingly relied on zealots more than expert technicians in developing its budget position.

At the end of the budget process the critical question is: What amount of money is Congress prepared to vote? Individual members of Congress pay particular attention to spending for federal programs important in their home district. The authority of Congress is fragmented among many committees and subcommittees, covering all fields of government activity from agriculture to transportation. The Appropriations Committee, through its many subcommittees, decides the annual allocation of money for established programs and newly authorized programs. The House Ways and Means Committee is responsible for tax legislation. Each congressional committee consists of a few dozen individuals; subcommittees usually have a dozen or fewer members. Hence, there is great scope for variability in outlook from subcommittee to subcommittee. None of these committees has a view of the budget as a whole (Shuman, 1984).

In the early 1970s, members of Congress recognized that their inability to form a view of the budget as a whole was a political weakness. The 1974 Congressional Budget Act established a new set of appropriation procedures, intended to make Congress focus on budget totals as well as particular expenditure items, and a Congressional Budget Office to provide technical advice on macroeconomic implications of the "micro" measures that congressmen usually focus on. The act requires Congress to vote in the spring on a first budget resolution that sets targets for taxing and spending totals, itemized by major categories of programs. The resolution does not require the President's endorsement. Appropriation committees then mark up budgets for programs within their jurisdiction. When all the appropriation recommendations have been made by the end of the summer, Congress then has an opportunity to vote a second budget resolution to reconcile the discrepancy between the target figures it first set and the totals initially proposed by the appropriation committees. Reconciliation can occur by accepting higher spending totals, by instructing appropriation committees to reduce proposed increases, or by a compromise between the two (Schick, 1980, 1983).

Budget disputes are confined to altering expenditures at the margin, for more than $900 billion in federal expenditures is effectively uncontrollable, being mandated by law or contractual obligations (see table 10.1). Social security and retirement benefits totaling $264 billion a year are guaranteed by law and by contributions made in expectation of receiving benefits. Medicare and Medicaid payments of more than $100 billion a year are statutory entitlements of elderly and indigent citizens who fall ill. National defense accounts for $282 billion, including salary and pension obligations to career service personnel, the maintenance of military equipment, and contracts for new military equipment extending for several years ahead. Interest payments of $139 billion are a contractual obligation that the federal government must honor in order to continue borrowing money to finance the next year's deficit.

Given the political inertia of laws authorizing a trillion dollars of federal spending each year, the annual budget battle concentrates on "fringe tuning," that is, incremental changes at the margin, confined to sums of about one-tenth of 1 percent of the total (i.e., $1 billion) or occasionally approaching 1 percent (up to $10 billion). Changes at the margin are important because they can cumulatively create substantial changes in total spending

TABLE 10.1

UNCONTROLLABLE PROGRAMS DOMINATE THE BUDGET

	Billions of dollars	Percentage of total
Immediately Uncontrollable		
National defense[a]	282	27
Social security, retirement benefits	264	26
Net interest	139	13
Major medical programs	106	10
Other mandatory	148	14
Sub total	939	91
Discretionary		
Civilian programs, administration	97	9
Total budget	1,036	100

a. Includes $113bn of prior year obligations.

SOURCE: Calculated from OMB (1988), summary table 216. Figures for fiscal year 1988.

and the bottom-line deficit. As the budget examiner's saying has it: "A billion or two here, a billion or two there; pretty soon it all adds up to real money."

The Reagan Years

Modern Presidents have usually limited their concern with the budget, emphasizing defense and foreign policy instead. A postmodern President, however, cannot ignore the constraints of the budget, for the government's overall taxing and spending capacity today, not only affects domestic politics but also the country's position in the international system.

The Reagan administration arrived in Washington with a proclaimed commitment to cutting federal expenditures stronger than anything seen since President Herbert Hoover was defeated by Franklin Roosevelt in 1932. In the words of President Reagan's first inaugural address: "Government is not the solution to our problem. Government is the problem." The President also had a theory, supply-side economics, that claimed that cutting taxes would stimulate the economy and thus increase tax revenues. It did not allow for the prospect that spending on defense and other programs would also rise. Republican critics such as former CEA chairman Herbert Stein (1984: 235ff) called this painless approach to tax cutting "the economics of joy." Instead of following the dismal science of economics in assuming that all benefits have costs, Reaganomics concentrated on benefits without costs.

Because it developed an effective political strategy to reduce taxation, the Reagan administration has made a big impact on the budget. The directorship of OMB was given to David Stockman, who, as an ex-congressman, brought to the job a knowledge of the tricks of the Hill, as well as an unusual command of tricks of the budget. Stockman weakened the ties of executive branch agencies with subgovernments by imposing cuts on agencies before their political heads could be appointed. OMB took responsibility for negotiating departmental budgets with congressional committees to make sure that the agencies did not undertake end runs by getting Congress to restore cuts imposed with the authority of the White House.

The White House turned the new congressional budget procedures into a device to impose budget ceilings consistent with the Reagan view of what government should do, rather than subcommittee views of what subgovernments would like. Instead of limiting OMB's role to that of advising the President, Stockman developed OMB as the chief negotiator with Congress, using the political popularity of the President and the technical capacity of OMB to sustain White House recommendations. Stockman did not treat the budget as a document expressing government priorities, but as a bill that had to be marketed to congressmen. As a member of the White House Legislative Strategy Group, a normal role for an ex-congressman but not for a budget director, he was able to mobilize White House support for his own high-visibility role as a budget cutter (cf. Johnson, 1984; Stockman, 1986).

By hitting the ground running, the Reagan administration scored two big budget successes in 1981. With the help of southern boll weevils (conservative Democratic congressmen), the Reagan administration carried a budget with more cuts and fewer spending increases than normal, albeit without the radical spending cuts that Stockman favored. Concurrently, the White House entered into competition with Congress to see which could claim most credit for cutting taxes, resulting in the Economic Recovery Tax Act of 1981, in which subgovernments that had not had their interests favored by White House proposals lobbied Congressmen to add tax cuts to the bill. The act was a typical congressional "Christmas tree," ornamented by giving tax cuts to many different interests; it aimed at reducing federal revenue by $250 billion by 1988.

The Reagan administration has had a "top-down" approach to budgeting. Only a lead from the Executive Office could produce a set of budget recommendations offering substantially less to domestic spending departments than they would like and simultaneously offering a lot more to the Department of Defense. Only clear direction from the top could prevent the package of cuts recommended by the President from being sunk by subgovernments boring below the waterline in subcommittees on the Hill. Only a lead from the top could focus attention on the significance of votes that Congress takes to reconcile particular appropriations with overall spending totals.

The speed and skill of the 1981 Reagan budget operation could not easily be repeated, nor was it. For most of the Reagan administration, the President has been engaged in trying to circumvent the checks of Congress and balance pressures from the Hill against his own inclinations, being without the centralized authority of a parliamentary leader. Bargaining within a system of checks and balances often leads to stalemate. Stalemate was evident in 1982 when a big budget deficit not anticipated by supply-siders required tax increases, an action that the President did not want to propose and that Congress did not want to be blamed for on its own. Reagan's "practice of deciding to fight and take his case to the people when the bargains began to encroach on the ideological core of his program severely damaged his credibility as a trustworthy negotiator" (Burke, 1985: 83).

In 1985 Congress enacted the Balanced Budget and Emergency Deficit Control Act, asserting that this would progressively reduce the federal deficit. A more immediate purpose of the act was to allow members of Congress to wash their hands of responsibility for doing what was unpopular—cutting expenditures or increasing taxes—and to pass the buck to the Reagan White House. The Gramm-Rudman Act, as it is often called, was designed to eliminate the budget deficit in the medium term by mandating annual cuts in spending if the deficit rose above a gradually lowered ceiling. Budget cuts were meant to exclude social security, but to include defense. The more or less arbitrary procedures for making automatic cuts have been challenged on constitutional grounds, but the device prompted Congress and the White House to agree on a package of budget cuts and tax increases rather than suffer arbitrary automatic cuts.

The Reagan administration claimed a second major budget success in the 1986 Tax Reform Act, but this was a victory it had to share with Congress, where the critical decisions were made that turned a wide variety of proposals to do something about taxation into a binding statute. In response to political pressures for tax reform, the 1986 tax act produced $160 billion in alterations in tax laws. Because the cuts in tax rates were matched by the repeal of tax exemptions (so-called tax expenditures), total government revenues remained the same as before. The fact that the reform was revenue neutral meant that the Reagan administration could not celebrate another tax cut, but the law was popular because it reduced the basic rate of income tax to 15 percent and struck out deductions of greatest benefit to the well-to-do. The new act did not reduce the budget deficit, for it altered total tax receipts by less than one-tenth of 1 percent.

By 1987 the steam had run out of the Reagan budget initiative; David Stockman had moved to a job with a New York bank and published memoirs detailing how 1981 budget tactics had been based on a crass manipulation of figures that the White House knew were misleading (Stockman, 1986; Greider, 1982). The increased involvement of OMB in lobbying for the President's budget on the Hill had, according to Heclo (1984: 291), "increased its political power while its institutional strength has eroded." President Reagan was no longer interested in sending Congress a budget document that could be the basis for negotiating a budget that was a reasonable compromise between White House and Congress. Instead, he put the blame on Congress for the deficit resulting from previous spending commitments and tax cuts. In February 1987, congressional leaders denounced the President's budget proposals as "dead on arrival."

The extent of the Reagan administration's impact on the budget can be summarized by comparing the 1981 fiscal year, effectively determined by Congress under President Carter, with the most recent fiscal year figures for 1987. Federal spending has risen by more than $330 billion; the federal budget is now over $1 trillion a year. The 49 percent increase in spending has not been matched by a comparable increase in tax revenues, which are up 42 percent. In 1984, an election year, for every $100 that the federal government spent, it borrowed $28 and financed the rest by taxes. In consequence, the annual federal deficit went above $200 billion in 1985 and 1986, before Gramm-Rudman began to have some effect; in 1987, the deficit was one-quarter higher as a proportion of federal spending than in 1981 (OMB, 1987a: summary table 22).

In autumn 1987, the President and Congress faced a normal budget crisis in abnormal circumstances. Congress had refused to enact a budget by the start of the fiscal year on 1 October. Federal agencies were being financed by temporary appropriations. The estimated deficit exceeded the Gramm-Rudman ceiling for the year ahead and threatened $23 billion in arbitrary spending cuts if Congress and the White House could not agree. Black Monday on Wall Street shook the world's confidence in the American economy. Foreign financial leaders watched as the White House and Congress gave a textbook example of how separated powers arrive at a budget, by practices that sometimes make accounting look like a branch of creative literature. For example, an estimated $29 million saving was achieved by a requirement for truth in frozen pizza marketing. Federal cheese subsidies were assumed to fall by that amount in consequence of requiring frozen pizza manufacturers to label their products' artificial cheese if they do not use real cheese. The two ends of Pennsylvania Avenue failed to find enough such devices to agree on a 2 percent budget adjustment within the initial thirty-day deadline imposed by the Gramm-Rudman Act. With the aid of continuing resolutions and by working over a weekend in which the government could not default because banks were closed, Congress finally enacted a budget at 4 a.m. on 22 December.

In Washington, the ability of Congress and the President to agree on the federal budget three months after the start of the fiscal year and a month after arbitrary cuts were meant to start was hailed as an achievement of the political process. As one official told a journalist from abroad: "You Europeans just don't understand how a real democracy works" (Hogg, 1987). But one-liners that can stop criticism in the nation's capital are inadequate to answer the questions posed by international markets from London and Zurich to Tokyo and Hong Kong. The chief international economist of Goldman Sachs, an established New York investment house, drew a different moral for investors:

> When it gets down to the nitty gritty, the bottom line is that America can't make major budget decisions. This may be democracy gone wrong.
> The nonsense of what is proposed is flashed across the screen and feeds sceptical markets each day. The markets are so unsure of what will go through that they are not going to give the dollar the benefit of the doubt. (Quoted in Shamoon, 1987)

When a parliamentary system faces a budget crisis, the problem is basically money. The political system has the authority to make a decision, and everybody knows where the metaphorical buck stops. In Washington, the problem of the budget is political, for nobody wants to admit where the buck stops. The President denies responsibility for the faults of a budget enacted by Congress, and Congress blames the President for presiding over a government that cannot keep its accounts in order. Blame avoidance is the name of the game (Weaver, 1986), and it is particularly attractive to a Republican President facing a Democratic Congress. But avoiding blame for what has gone wrong is not the aim of government. The object is to prevent things going wrong in the first place.

Living with Your Banker

Like it or not, every President has to live with a banker, namely, the chairman of the Federal Reserve Board, an institution that is the government's bank, since it engages in financial activities on behalf of the government and funds the government's operating deficits. While the Federal Reserve is involved in highly technical operations, its responsibility for the money supply and interest rates means that its activities can have visible political consequences, such as a rise or fall in house prices or the cost of buying a car, and an impact on inflation, economic growth, and employment.

Prime Ministers must also learn to live with their central banker, for every modern government needs a central bank to maintain the credibility of the government's currency, internationally as well as domestically. A Prime Minister who has gained office by going government will usually be familiar with the role the central bank plays, and the finance minister will be close both to the central bank and the Prime Minister. By contrast, an American President normally enters office without any understanding of the Federal Reserve system. Even when the President does understand what the central bank does, he must face the fact, as a former adviser said bluntly, "for a very important instrument of macro policy, namely monetary policy, you don't have the dials in the President's office" (Paul McCracken, quoted in Woolley, 1984: 110).

What the Fed Does

The Federal Reserve System was established by act of Congress in 1913, and Congressional committees take a continuing interest in it. The system consists of a Washington headquarters, and twelve Federal Reserve banks distributed regionally from Boston to San Francisco. It is headed by a seven-member Board of Governors, appointed by the President for fourteen-year terms, subject to the approval of the Senate; board members cannot be removed by a newly elected President. The Fed is an independent agency; it is not part of the Executive Office of the President (see Woolley, 1984). The chairman of the board is appointed by the President for a four-year term, but the date of the appointment is not synchronized with the four-year term of the Presidency.

The Federal Reserve System makes and administers policy for the nation's monetary system, both domestically and in the international system. In an economy in which the government was not expected to influence economic conditions, its role as a central bank would be deemed technical and nonpolitical. This was the view of many of the early governors of the system. It is an argument often advanced by central bankers seeking to maintain their independence from elected officials or escape blame for the political consequences of actions they have taken. In an era in which control of the money supply is linked with larger economic issues, such as inflation, economic growth, employment, and the dollar's international position, its actions inevitably affect politically hot topics.

The Federal Reserve system relies on three main economic policy instruments (Melton, 1984). It determines the proportion of total deposits that commercial banks must keep in reserve, usually on deposit in a Federal Reserve bank. Increasing the reserve requirement reduces the amount of money available for lending, and thus the money supply; decreasing the requirement expands the money supply. Second, the Fed sets the discount rate, the interest a commercial bank must pay to borrow money from it. Doing this influences interest rates nationally and internationally. Third, it buys and sells U.S. government securities in the open international economy, moving money between its accounts and commercial banks, and between the United States and foreign central banks and commercial banks. The international operations of the Fed affect the foreign exchange value of the dollar.

How monetary policy should be conducted is a subject of debate among economists as well as politicians. Debates among economists are particularly important in the Federal Reserve system because it must justify itself publicly to a politically diverse audience in Washington, in the nation, and internationally. Economic reasoning provides a logical and seemingly scientific way of doing so, independent of political values. But politicians are less interested in economic theory than in agreement between the Fed's policies and their own political values. This is particularly true for the President, who appoints people to the Federal Reserve Board in the hope that they will support what he wants done.

For the first half of the postwar era there was a high degree of consensus among economists and politicians about interest rates in the conduct of monetary policy. There were differences of opinion among economists about the best technical means of conducting monetary policy, among Republicans and Democrats about the appropriate level of interest rates, and between the Federal Reserve and the White House and Congress, but these disagreements started from an acceptance of the importance of interest rates (see, e.g., Mayer, 1978; Kettl, 1986).

In the past two decades, a fundamental division has opened up between Keynesian and monetarist economists about the best way to achieve economic goals (Woolley, 1984: chap. 5; Sbragia, 1986: 224ff). Monetarists, led by the Nobel laureate Milton Friedman, have emphasized that money matters most, that is, changes in the money supply are of major importance in determining levels of inflation, employment, and output. Since the Federal

Reserve Board is responsible for managing the nation's money supply, monetarist economists have a clear prescription for policy at the Fed: Pay much less attention to interest rates and more to controlling money supply by adhering to a fixed rate of expanding credit, which incidentally is likely to boost interest rates. Keynesians have argued that they are not indifferent to the money supply and inflation while claiming to have a better set of policy prescriptions to meet consensual goals.

The debates between Keynesians and monetarists are not matters of science but concern fundamental assumptions about society and politics, as well as economics. This is illustrated by the split among economists on monetary issues. When a sample of American economists was asked whether or not the Fed should increase the money supply at a fixed rate, a fundamental tenet of monetarists, 61 percent rejected this view, as against 39 percent expressing at least qualified agreement (Kearl et al., 1979: 30). Policymakers can thus choose the policy that they find most congenial on political grounds and expect to find many established economists to endorse it.

In 1979 the Federal Reserve Board, under Chairman Paul Volcker, committed the bank to a policy of giving priority to the total supply of money in the economy. It was not alone in doing so; Margaret Thatcher had turned Britain in that direction following the Conservative election victory earlier in the year. The first thing that the Fed learned was that measuring money is not so easy as it looks because credit takes many forms, American dollars are held in many places, and foreign banks loan substantial sums to Americans. The political consequences were also unsatisfactory, for interest rates to business rose above 20 percent in 1981. The neoconservative economist Irving Kristol concluded in a *Wall Street Journal* article on 12 October, 1982: "Monetarism is an elegant and persuasive economic theory that is not working." By the end of 1982, the Fed was no longer making money supply its primary target.

Federal Reserve policy today is described by Woolley (1984: 106) as "an arena for resolving academic disputes by political means." Under the leadership of Paul Volcker the Federal Reserve pursued an eclectic and even incoherent set of policies, sacrificing strict economic logic in order to gain room for maneuver in the face of conflicting political pressures. By experimenting with monetarism, the Fed recognized the political and economic strength of the advocates of this approach. Because the consequences were politically unpalatable, on Wall Street, as well as to Keynesians, the Fed used its eclectic philosophy to justify a shift from monetarism. Changes in policies and rationales for policies were justified by Anthony Solomon, president of the Federal Reserve Bank of New York, as follows: "My own instinct is that there is no single approach to monetary policy that is best for all times and places. As conditions change, the approach will probably have to change too" (quoted in Woolley, 1984: 103).

Whose Bank Is the Fed?

Like the White House itself, the Fed's independence is limited by other powerholders in Washington. It is part of the subgovernment of money, which involves the White House, Congress and the Treasury Department, plus American banks, free-floating academic economists, international investors, and central banks in other nations. While in theory the Federal Reserve Board is independent of both Congress and the President, it cannot work in isolation from other institutions interested in money. It needs to influence the White House, just as the White House wants to influence its policy.

The President and the chairman of the Federal Reserve normally try to accommodate their actions to each other. There is frequent communication at staff level between White House economic advisers and Fed officials. As both groups are normally in the mainstream of economic opinion, differences are likely to be matters of emphasis. When conflicts do occur, they often involve balancing monetary goals of special concern to the Fed against broader economic goals of particular White House concern. The White House recognizes that the Fed may deem it necessary to take politically unpopular measures. When this happens, the President can use the Fed as a whipping boy. But the Fed tries to avoid making itself unpopular. Woolley (1984: table 6.1) found that the Fed took less visible policy actions in election years than in nonelection years. Moreover, 61 percent of its visible activities in election years eased money supply, an action agreeable to an incumbent of the White House. In nonelection years, 58 percent of its visible activities made money tighter, a politically less attractive policy.

Chairmen of the Federal Reserve have differed in their approach to their work and to the Oval Office. William McChesney Martin, chairman under Presidents Eisenhower, Kennedy, and Johnson, saw himself as an aloof banker in a city full of politicians, restricting White House contacts to the discussion of narrow monetary issues and relying on Wall Street support. Fed Chairman Arthur F. Burns, a former chairman of the Council of Economic Advisers, was much readier to discuss a host of economic issues with President Nixon and White House staff, and to offer policy recommendations about matters well beyond the immediate responsibility of the Fed. Paul Volcker, chairman from 1979 to 1987, walked a tightrope to accommodate Keynesians and monetarists, successfully traversing a swing to monetarism and back again. Volcker was also notable in cultivating the support of foreign central banks, whose role has become increasingly important in supporting the dollar. Alan Greenspan, named his successor in 1987, is a former CEA chairman with good Republican party credentials; he knows Congress, as well as the White House and Wall Street.

After reviewing fifty years of relations between the White House and the Federal Reserve chairman, Donald Kettl (1986: 198) concludes that for at least three-quarters of this period there has been a mutually satisfactory accommodation between the two institutions. The last big controversy is identified as in the mid-1960s when Martin disagreed with President Johnson's attempt to finance the Vietnam war by extensive borrowing, because he feared this would fuel inflation. From 1979 to 1982, the Fed was prepared to take the political heat for experimenting with monetarism, which neither President Carter nor President Reagan was prepared to do.

The Federal Reserve Board is relatively remote from Congress. The technical nature of its activities and lack of visibility to the electorate make the board less visible publicly and therefore less of a public target to attack. Specialist congressional committees concerned with the Fed usually confine particular interest to spasmodic discussion at times of economic crisis. When Congress does use its oversight power to ask awkward questions, the Fed chairman can deflect criticism by hiding behind a screen of obscure and technical language; lobby to select congressmen for support, work through banks in the home districts as well as directly; or use a hardball confrontation strategy in which the Fed policy is aggressively defended (Woolley, 1984: chap. 7; Kettl, 1986: 203).

As the American economy has had its dominant position in the international system eroded, the chairman of the Federal Reserve Board like a postmodern President, has increasingly had to cope with international as well as domestic pressures. When America runs a big trade deficit and the government borrows tens of billions of dollars from foreigners, the Fed has the awkward task of looking after a vulnerable dollar internationally. Federal Reserve staff must watch currency markets worldwide, and discuss developments daily with major central banks in Germany and Japan, which are immediately affected by changes in the exchange rate between the dollar, the deutsche mark, and the yen. In these discussions, the Fed cannot dictate what happens, nor can other central banks; all are part of an interdependent international money market.

Notwithstanding the important role of the Federal Reserve in looking after the dollar's international position, domestic priorities come first. The appointment of Alan Greenspan as chairman in 1987 was welcomed by Democrats as well as Republicans because he knew Washington well, and he knew how to communicate to the financial public from Wall Street to San Francisco. The internationally read London *Economist* took a different view. It noted on 6 June 1987: "Although a staunch free-trader, Mr. Greenspan has relatively little experience with the international financiers whose markets now finance America's deficit."

The heads of central banks in parliamentary systems are better able to combine an international and domestic political role. The dialogue between the central bank, the Prime Minister, and Cabinet can be carried on free from legislative pressures. The central bank knows that a Prime Minister has the full authority of government at hand. Whereas the Fed must balance non-White House as against White House pressures, in parliamentary systems:

Political pressures are channeled almost exclusively through the head of government and his chief economic ministers. Thus, the central bank has an even greater incentive to cooperate with the head of government than in the United States. (Woolley, 1983: 182)

Selective Intervention in the Marketplace.

An organizational approach views economic policymaking as a problem of coordination. How can the three horses of the *troika*—the CEA, OMB, and the Treasury—be made to pull together rather than pulling apart? Even more ambitiously, how can the *quadriad*—the *troika* plus the Federal Reserve Board—be made to track together? To prescribe coordination reflects the logic of an organization perceived as a single system with interdependent parts. However, the President does not see the economy as a whole. Nor does the White House have the political authority to coordinate the economic policy of the federal government, let alone the national economy in an open international system.

Modern Presidents have usually followed a policy of selective intervention in government economic policy, allowing individual horsemen in the *quadriad* to pull their burdens alone. A President can—and many Presidents do—delegate the hard work of budgeting to OMB and White House staff. A President can use the Treasury and the Federal Reserve as buffers, taking the political heat to act in the face of difficulties. The chairman of the CEA can privately keep the President advised about economic difficulties while publicly seeking to promote confidence in the wisdom of whatever is being done (or not done) by the White House at the moment.

The political incentives are strong for the White House to let other Washington powerholders look after economic policy. When the economy is booming, the President can go public, taking credit with the electorate for economic trends that are popular in the nation. When foreign confidence in the dollar plummets, the President can express confidence in the capacity of his secretary of the treasury to handle awkward foreigners. If unemployment is rising, the secretary of labor can be pushed forward to deal with the bad news, and if inflation is rising, the spotlight can be directed at the Federal Reserve Board. If all else fails, a Republican President can try to dump the blame on a Democratic Congress. By having buffers to confront difficulties and providing "hidden-hand" support as appropriate, the President can try to exert influence without exposing himself to the risk of failure in the event of economic difficulties.

To pursue a political strategy of selective intervention, the President needs to monitor the economy continuously. The files in presidential libraries show that most of the economic papers coming into the Oval Office are not asking for presidential action, but, giving information about what is happening to the economy nationally and internationally. Subgovernments concerned with taxation, spending, banking, or employment carry on without presidential intervention. Markets are even less dependent on White House initiatives. When a President does decide to intervene on an economic issue, he typically has "relied on a trusted adviser or group of advisers settling many issues bilaterally with the interested parties" (Porter, 1983: 415).

A postmodern President finds himself in the position of a Prime Minister of a major nation, but without the Prime Minister's political authority. A Prime Minister cannot walk away from economic difficulties by blaming Parliament, for the collective nature of parliamentary government means that the buck is sure to stop at the Cabinet table. Nor can a Prime Minister allow different economic policymakers to go their own ways, with all this implies in confusion, contradiction, and wasted effort. The job of a Prime Minister is to maintain a political strategy that relates economic necessities to political goals favored by the electorate.

The postmodern President must become increasingly involved in America's economic problems. As the American economy becomes more and more a part of the international system, the distinction between domestic and international politics begins to dissolve. For example, is the number of foreign cars bought by Americans a matter of domestic or international politics, or both? Concurrently, conventional distinctions between foreign policy and economic policy are also dissolving. What links, if any, does the White House wish to develop between America's trade deficit with Japan, and Japan's defense deficit, leading to reliance on U.S. troops for its own national security? A postmodern President can go Washington and go public effectively only if he also deals effectively with America's economic problems, which have now gone international.

11. National Security: One Country but Many Voices

*I've always thought this country could run itself domestically without a President·
all you need is a competent Cabinet to run the country at home. You need a President
for foreign policy; no Secretary of State is really important. The President makes
foreign policy.*

—Richard M. Nixon

*When the Administration itself is divided on its own foreign policy it cannot hope
to convince the world that the American people have a foreign policy.*

—James F. Byrnes

The President rightly sees national security, the object of diplomacy and
military policy, as a unique concern of the White House, for the United States
is a superpower, and he is the chief political voice of the United States. Every
President gives at least half his time to national security. Going international
also has political attractions: It allows the President to act with much more
authority than in domestic affairs. The issues involved are awesome. President Nixon was not the only occupant of the Oval Office to regard national
security issues as all-important. John F. Kennedy told him: "Foreign affairs
is the only important issue for a President to handle.... I mean, who gives a
shit if the minimum wage is $1.15 or $1.25 in comparison to something like
the Bay of Pigs?" (quoted in Cronin, 1980: 146).

A modern President such as Kennedy or Nixon started from the assumption that America was *the* dominant power in the world. But he soon
learned that while America's strength is great, the world is large and
complicated; many different nations compete for Oval Office attention. The
White House deals diplomatically with the Russians while maintaining
NATO military strength for protection against a Soviet attack. The President
must consider what, if anything, the United States can do about troublespots
in the Middle East, about many small independent countries of Africa, and
about conflicts within South Africa. Relations with Japan reflect the American need to adapt a relationship transformed by the rise of Japanese economic power. The White House is also interested in cultivating good
relations with the representatives of 1 billion Chinese people. There are

always troublespots of concern to the United States, where forces are fighting or a war could break out.

No President can dominate American government, as a Prime Minister may speak for the whole of government in a parliamentary system. In Washington there are many competing institutions concerned with national security, each linked with subgovernments in international affairs and often differing in the advice they offer the White House (Allison, 1971; Crabb and Mulcahy, 1986: chap. 2). The State Department views the world through diplomatic lenses; the Defense Department sees armed force as primary; and the Central Intelligence Agency has a bias in favor of secret information and operations. Public opinion is a significant factor too, because a President's success in going international is related to his success in going public. When allowance is made for the views of 535 members of Congress, their committees and subcommittees, and the interest groups that cluster around them, the number of self-appointed White House advisers expands exponentially.

A postmodern President faces even greater difficulties in going international. The linkage of economic with diplomatic and security issues broadens the number of Washington institutions that have an interest in what the White House does internationally. The Treasury Department and the Federal Reserve have a special concern with the international position of the dollar; the Commerce Department and the President's special trade representative are concerned with America's foreign trade deficit; the Agriculture Department wants to boost exports of farm products, while the Department of Labor is concerned about restricting foreign imports. The President must judge to what extent military power remains most important, in which case the Pentagon comes first at home, and Russia is the nation of most concern abroad. Alternatively, if the President decides that the economy is of primary importance in international relations, then America must compete with Japan and Germany, and reduce the extent to which American investment is directed to military weapons.

In a dire national emergency, such as the attack on Pearl Harbor in 1941, there is a consensus about what needs to be done, but a postmodern Presidency cannot rely on a foreign policy consensus. The Vietnam war has left a lingering distrust of the international actions of an Imperial President. When the countries of the world can no longer easily be divided into groups of good guys and bad guys, uncertainties arise about the direction of American foreign policy, and about the kinds of arms required, for a jungle war is fought differently from a war to protect sea lanes or deter a nuclear attack. Interest groups lobby Congress about nations with whom some segment of the American electorate feels sympathy, and right-wing and liberal causes lobby on opposite sides of foreign policy issues. The controversy between Congress and the Reagan administration about American aid to *Contra* rebels in Nicaragua illustrates how institutions of American government can disagree with one another about the best way to protect the nation's security.

With many different people and institutions voicing opinions about American foreign policy, it is difficult for foreign ambassadors in Washington to know what the U.S. government wants, and for federal agencies to follow the President's lead (cf. Byrnes, 1947: 241). Serving in Washington after being British ambassador to Germany and France, Sir Nicholas Henderson (1986) concluded that the system of checks and balances was a handicap in making foreign policy.

> The lack of any clearly defined authority on foreign policy leads not only to the kind of hugger-mugger operations, false disclosures, public recrimination and congressional hearings such as we have been witnessing in Irangate, but to continuing unpredictability and weakness in safeguarding the national interest.

A foreign nation seeking to do business with the United States must go Washington in the fullest sense of the term, spreading its efforts throughout the subgovernments of Washington. Foreign embassies must follow the public too, studying opinion polls and traveling outside the Beltway.

While Prime Ministers must also juggle many different international problems, their task is much more manageable, thanks to the fusion of authority within the parliamentary system. Once domestic differences of opinion are resolved by asserting the authority of government against subgovernments, a Prime Minister can speak with a single voice abroad as well as at home. Prime Ministers are usually much more experienced than a newly elected President in going international, dealing with foreign countries in other government posts held on the way to the top. Individually, no one parliamentary system of government is as strong as the United States. But collectively, the major nations of Europe plus Japan have a much bigger population and gross national product than America.

Before a President can go international, he must go Washington, listening to what many different voices want him to do, and seeing what they can do for the White House. Meetings with ambassadors from foreign countries sometimes present fewer difficulties than discussions with members of Congress, for ambassadors cast no votes in the American system. Yet a postmodern President soon learns that going Washington is not sufficient, for foreign nations do not always follow Washington opinion. In order to gain freedom from domestic political constraints and deal directly with the most pressing international imperatives, the President develops a White House capacity to conduct his own foreign policy, making his national security adviser in the White House of equal or greater importance than the secretary of state a few blocks away. In order to understand the President's position, this chapter looks first at the network of foreign policy agencies that surround the White House and then at how the President uses the White House as a center for conducting his own foreign policy.

Allies and Enemies within Washington

A newly elected President may assume that all Washington agencies concerned with international affairs are allies, cooperating in formulating policies for his administration. He soon learns that many different institutions represent the United States to foreigners. From the White House perspective, each is part of a particular subgovernment, linked with other institutions that share their particular view. There are always differences of opinion about what is or ought to be the policy of the U.S. government; this can lead the White House to see other institutions of the federal government as the enemy.

While seeking to represent the U.S. government to foreigners, the President must struggle to control government at home. For a Prime Minister this is a matter of winning an election once every few years. Most of the time a Prime Minister worries about the substantive problems that must be faced when going government. The President's difficulty is not a shortage of agencies and advisers, but a surplus; many different groups, within the executive branch and outside it, offer him their telescope in the hope that the President will see the world through their circumscribed lens.

The Constitution: Friend or Foe?

The multiplicity of voices with which America speaks to the world is a by-product of the Constitution. James Madison recognized that in time of war a President would need substantial discretionary authority, but he was also concerned that "a standing military force, with an overgrown executive will not long be safe companions to liberty. The means of defense against foreign danger have been always the instruments of tyranny at home" (quoted in Nathan and Oliver, 1987: 298). Alexis de Tocqueville, an early French friend of nineteenth-century America, had his doubts about the capacity of a democracy to conduct foreign relations, believing it to be "decidedly inferior to other governments" because lacking the capacity to "regulate the details of an important undertaking, persevere in a fixed design and work out its execution in spite of serious obstacles. It cannot combine its measures with secrecy or await their consequences with patience" (Tocqueville, 1954: 1: 243).

The survival of the American system, while every European monarchical and authoritarian regime perished, is evidence of the stamina of the Constitution. But past success is no guarantee of future prosperity. Three foreign policy experts, I.M. Destler, Leslie Gelb, and Anthony Lake (1984), describe the system for making American foreign policy as *Our Own Worst Enemy*, arguing that changes within American domestic policy, such as the rise of media influence, and the growth of White House staff, have made the system of government an obstacle in advancing the country's interests internationally.

Foggy Bottom: Less a Place and More a State of Mind
The State Department is the ranking department in the President's Cabinet, and the secretary of state is nominally the President's leading adviser on foreign affairs. The State Department has embassies in more than a hundred different countries, and its office in the Foggy Bottom district of Washington is a hub of communication with all the troublespots of the world. State Department officials also monitor the many dull spots, countries where nothing of great concern to America appears to be happening at the moment, but where problems can blow up on short notice or ripen and drop with a thud at the door of the Oval Office.

While foreign governments regard it as normal to communicate with other nations through foreign ministries, the White House does not. The history of modern American foreign policy is largely the story of presidential initiatives. While the State Department is nominally the lead agency in foreign affairs, less than one-quarter of the American officials serving abroad are State Department personnel (Crabb and Mulcahy, 1986: 61).

The State Department's strength is its weakness; its specialized knowledge of every member country of the United Nations is a commodity for which the Oval Office has little demand. A President does not want to be told by veteran State Department officials about all the commitments to foreign countries that his various predecessors have made. A President wants new initiatives that *he* can take. The characteristic State Department response to a bright idea in the White House is likely to be a memorandum that calls attention to all the obstacles in the way of realizing it. State Department diplomats learn about such obstacles by serving abroad, where it soon becomes obvious that foreigners do not think like White House staff. The fact that State Department advice is always full of cautions and qualifications gives rise to the gibe that Foggy Bottom is less a place and more a state of mind.

The State Department suffers two severe political handicaps: It lacks propinquity to the White House and it lacks clout in Congress. The secretary of state does not work down the hall from the President, as does the President's national security assistant. The memos that the State Department sends to the President are usually given to him with a cover note from the national security adviser. The more important the subject is to the White House, the less likely it is to want independent assessments, and the more it wants reassurance about the President's policy, whether justified or not by the knowledge of people on the spot. If the President wants to communicate with other countries, he can do so directly through the White House telecommunication network. When the President telephones the head of a foreign nation, the American ambassador in that city will normally hear of the phone call *after* the foreign ministry of that country—and sometimes weeks afterward.

While the State Department is represented throughout the world, it represents no constituency of concern on Capitol Hill. Whereas the Agriculture Department has congressmen from farm states supporting it, and HUD has the backing of big-city congressmen, no member of Congress represents the continents where the State Department has its staff and interests. Congressional critics often attack the State Department for doing its job, that is, knowing more about the politics of Gabon or Bolivia than about Alabama or Iowa. There is realism in the pessimistic assertion: "It is more important for senior diplomats to learn to speak the language of domestic politics than it is to learn a foreign language" (Goshko, 1987). Because the State Department's duty is to report what is happening in foreign countries, where there is inevitably some bad news, the department is always vulnerable to the accusation that it is "disloyal" because it says things that members of Congress do not want to hear.

Occasionally an individual can make the office of secretary of state important in the White House. Henry Kissinger could do this when secretary under President Ford, only because he was continuing to act as the de facto White House security adviser and neglecting duties in the State Department. John Foster Dulles did so under Dwight D. Eisenhower; one of Dulles's roles was to absorb public criticism by putting forward, in his own name, ideas that the President wanted to float as trial balloons. Since President Kennedy's time, most secretaries of state have arrived in office confident of the importance of their post, and have departed unhappy with how little influence they could have on the President and foreign policy. The testimony that Secretary of State George P. Shultz gave about the Iran-*contra* affair—he wasn't told much about what was going on, and when he objected, he was ignored—was accepted by Congress as a perfectly normal way for the White House to treat the official nominally responsible for administering America's dealings with foreign countries.

By contrast, in a parliamentary regime the Foreign Office is *the* center of communication between a government and foreign governments; its diplomats are consulted routinely by political leaders; and the foreign secretary is normally among those closest to the Prime Minister politically. The Prime Minister's office may even be incapable of sustaining communication with foreign governments. In Britain, for example, the Prime Minister normally has only one person concerned with foreign affairs working in Downing Street, a mid-career Foreign Office official who keeps his ministry briefed about what is happening in Number 10, and vice versa. The foreign secretary cannot commit the government without prior consultation with the Prime Minister, and the Prime Minister carries on negotiations with foreign countries through the diplomatic staff of the foreign ministry.

The Pentagon: Many Sides and a Hole in the Middle

The Pentagon, the five-sided office of the Department of Defense (DOD), is one of the largest buildings in the national capital, in keeping with the position of the department as the largest federal employer; DOD has more than 1 million civilian employees and 2 million uniformed servicemen. It also claims one-quarter of the federal budget.

The Pentagon has many sides politically as well as architecturally. While all the armed services fight under a common flag, there are interservice rivalries. The army, the navy, the air force, and marines are each a separate service with their own traditions, career structures, leaders, weapons systems, capabilities, and therefore, interests. The army is prepared to regard land forces as America's first line of defense; the navy to regard oceans as primary in strategic thinking, the air force to emphasize aerial weaponry, and the marines to stress their capacity to fight the little wars that often erupt unexpectedly in remote corners of the globe. The U.S. Army maintains the world's third largest air force because it does not trust the U.S. Air Force to maintain a helicopter fleet suited to the needs of an army in the field. Differences are reflected in competition between services for defense dollars, and in competing strategic doctrines that stress the unique importance of the service propounding it. The budget is central to defense because of the cost in money and time to develop new weapons systems. A decision to back a new air force missile could cost the navy many ships or the army a new type of tank, since there is not enough money to develop every potential weapons system.

The secretary of defense must wage a war on two fronts. First of all, he must assert his authority within the Pentagon. This is no easy task, given that he is a transient appointee, and most Pentagon staff are career military officials with considerable expertise in bureaucratic politics as well as weaponry. For more than a decade after the department was established in 1947, the secretary was weak as against his own army, navy, and air force staffs. In 1961, Robert S. McNamara became secretary, and created a strong Office of the Secretary of Defense, based on the command of analytic budgets and brainpower rather than military firepower. The recommendation of weapons systems is a responsibility of the secretary, reflecting political and strategic as well as technological considerations. The need for a weapon depends on the definition of America's most likely enemy and the circumstances in which arms are likely to be used.

The Pentagon has substantial clout, independent of the White House. The views of the military are always given consideration in the White House, for the President, as commander-in-chief, normally has a number of career military officers attached there. When making judgments about America's relations with foreign countries, frequently a military appreciation of contending forces is required. In going public and going Washington a President is well advised to remain on good terms with his secretary of defense. The DOD is regarded as a nonpolitical department, patriotically defending America's interests worldwide. A President who quarrels with his military advisers can lose popularity. On Capitol Hill, DOD is viewed as a formidable political department. Military bases are pork-barrel benefits for congressional districts, and so too are tens of billions of dollars spent each year on military contracts. DOD lobbyists know how to enlist the support of the senator from Boeing or the congressman for the Brooklyn Navy Yard when defense appropriations are threatened.

By contrast, European defense ministries are not a tail that can wag the civilian dog. In parliamentary regimes, the Ministry of Defense must accept whatever amount of money the Cabinet is collectively prepared to allocate. The unimportance of Parliament in decision making means that military officials cannot lobby individual MPs as the Pentagon lobbies members of Congress. In Germany and Japan, the reaction against being on the losing side in World War II has resulted in a strong commitment to civilian control of a military force that is strictly limited in size and commitments. The leaders of the armed forces are precluded from going public or lobbying Parliament by the conventions of national parliamentary systems.

The hole in the center of the Department of Defense symbolizes the absence of legitimate authority to act on its own. America's military force is meant to support policies laid down by popularly elected officials. The Defense Department is supposed to follow where the President leads. The Pentagon can enjoy popular support only as long as it does not produce a shooting war with unwelcome American casualties. Popular support for a strong defense is also lower when the Pentagon is thought to be wasting money. When the demand to curb public spending or cut the deficit grows, the Pentagon is a prime target because it receives such a large portion of the total federal budget.

The President's task is to subject the Pentagon to checks and balances so that the policies it enunciates support the Oval Office (cf. Korb, 1980). By appointing to the Joint Chiefs of Staff military officers who are sympathetic to his views, a President can gain the visible support of expert officials. By appointing a secretary of defense who is also an expert in weapons systems and defense budgeting, the President can place in the Pentagon an individual who is able to win arguments with the military. An expert such as Robert McNamara presented another advantage to the President: He had no political base independent of the White House. The capacity of the President to influence the Pentagon is contingent. A President who is unpopular in Washington can be quietly disobeyed by Pentagon officials who have the strong support of the defense subgovernment.

The Reagan administration illustrates how the relationship between the White House and the Pentagon can shift. Because Ronald Reagan entered office committed to a big defense build-up, this gave the Department of Defense enormous clout. At a time when other agencies were having their budgets cut, the Pentagon had the President's backing for a major increase. Defense Secretary Caspar Weinberger exploited this so much that Budget Director David Stockman ruefully complained that Cap the Knife (a reference to Weinberger's former role as director of OMB) had become Cap the Shovel, throwing money into the defense budget. When President Reagan decided to make arms-control negotiations with the Russians a major priority of his second term, the influence of the Defense Department waned. While its budget remained big, the White House turned elsewhere for advice about reducing spending on arms. The shift in White House priorities was symbolized in November 1987 by appointing a former State Department diplomat, Frank Carlucci, to succeed Weinberger as secretary of defense.

Secreting Intelligence: The CIA

There is no doubt about the centrality of the Central Intelligence Agency to the President's view of the world. The director of the CIA is one of the few presidential appointees of Cabinet rank who is frequently in contact with the Oval Office and senior White House officials. No President can be indifferent to reported efforts of foreign sabotage of American policies, and most Presidents express an interest in CIA proposals to make life difficult for unfriendly foreign governments. The frequent references to the late CIA director William J. Casey in the Iran-*contra* hearings provide a striking public example of CIA collaboration with White House staff in pursuit of presidential goals.

The CIA offers the President two advantages not enjoyed by its competitors. As against the State Department, the CIA can claim that its reports are based on secrets, that is, information that foreign governments want to keep hidden from the United States. Secret information is usually read with more interest than formal State Department reports, even though CIA reports are harder to corroborate and therefore more likely to be misleading or even false. By contrast with the Defense Department, the CIA can act on its information in a secret way. Pentagon forces are far larger than the CIA special operations staff, but any commitment of American troops must be done publicly, and this can stir up political controversy. By contrast, the CIA is able to act without public acknowledgment of its role. A President who wants something done about a troublesome country can turn to the company (as the CIA is familiarly known), asking it to do something about a troublesome foreign nation. The CIA also volunteers proposals to destabilize unfriendly regimes.

Secrecy is the weakness as well as the strength of the CIA. Because what it offers as intelligence is *not* subject to public scrutiny, it may give the White House reports that are misleading. Because its field operations are covert, it can go into business for itself to the subsequent great embarrassment of the White House. For example, the continuation of U-2 spy plane flights over the Soviet Union before a planned 1960 summit meeting with the Russians was a major embarrassment for President Eisenhower, and the enthusiastic support by William J. Casey for *Contra* operations in Nicaragua sowed the seeds for President Reagan's harvest of problems in the Iran-*contra* affair.

Congress: An Awkward Ally

In the American system of checks and balances, the President must make an ally of Congress, for if it becomes his enemy, the administration will be hobbled and harassed. Congress can influence foreign policy through the Senate's powers for approving treaties and confirming presidential appointees, and its general powers of oversight, budget, and legislation. Members of Congress cite many examples of action by an Imperial President to support their belief that the President is not to be trusted fully in foreign policy. They want to warn the President off what they regard as wrong policies. Foreign policy often provides an occasion for the extension of domestic political battles to another arena.

The critical difference between the conduct of American foreign policy and other countries is the role of Congress. Dictatorships as well as democracies are subject to pressures from subgovernments, and parliamentary as well as presidential democracies are subject to pressures from the electorate. But parliamentary democracies are not subject to pressures from Parliament, for MPs are disciplined by party loyalty to endorse the foreign policies of the government of the day. The foreign secretary and Prime Minister make statements to Parliament explaining their international activities, but they do not wait upon the vote of Parliament. Once the leaders of government have spoken, the nation is effectively committed.

As part of the government, Congress is necessarily implicated in whatever the White House does; a nuclear bomb that fell on 1600 Pennsylvania Avenue would also destroy the Hill. The immediate question is: What are the terms of the relationship? At the beginning of the modern Presidency, the White House showed deference. In the 1930s, President Roosevelt elaborately deferred to the isolationist sentiments of Congress, for he had seen Woodrow Wilson destroyed by congressional opposition to the League of Nations. After America entered World War II, the White House took the lead and kept the initiative in the cold-war era. Presidents Truman and Eisenhower continued to show deference to the position of Congress, but they kept the initiative in the Oval Office.

Until the late 1960s, Congress trusted the White House to act in the international system. The height of trust was registered in the 1964 Tonkin Gulf Resolution, approved unanimously by the House of Representatives and with only two dissenting votes in the Senate. It gave President Johnson a blank check to take any military action he saw fit in Vietnam. Senator J. William Fulbright, chairman of the then prestigious Foreign Relations Committee, argued for congressional deference to the President on the following grounds:

> The circumstance has been crisis, an entire era of crisis in which urgent decisions have been required again and again, decisions of a kind that the Congress is ill-equipped to make with what had been thought to be the requisite speed. The

President has the means at his disposal for prompt action; the Congress does not. When the security of the country is endangered, or thought to be endangered, there is a powerful premium on prompt action, and that means executive action. (Quoted in Nathan and Oliver, 1987: 110)

The resulting turmoil of the Vietnam war caused many congressmen to lose their trust in the White House, as Presidents Johnson and Nixon were deemed to have misled or lied to Congress. Watergate fueled more distrust. The 1987 Iran-*contra* hearings reinforced what many congressmen believed before they reached Washington, namely, that the White House cannot be trusted in foreign policy.

Contentiousness and uncertainty have become the norm in foreign as well as domestic affairs. Congress has sought "an entirely new framework of rules for power-sharing among the branches of government" (Frank and Weisband, 1979: 61). But talk of codetermination of foreign policy by the President and Congress is impractical, for the reasons that Senator Fulbright identified above. As congressional distrust of White House integrity has risen, Congress is less and less willing to give unquestioning support to the President. Before the 1968 Tet offensive, which signaled America's defeat in Vietnam, the President could expect Congress to respond compliantly to nearly half his requests. After the Tet offensive, compliant responses dropped to less than one-quarter (see table 11.1). Congress today is a forum for foreign policy "kibitzers," politicians who make comments about the conduct of foreign policy while looking over the shoulder of the President. A third of the time Congress pursues details, for example, reducing an appropriation while granting the White House most of what it wants. The percentage of cases in which Congress rejects what the President asks for is increasing, but it is still only one-sixth of the total. In addition, Congress occasionally takes initiatives to influence foreign policy.

TABLE 11.1

CONGRESSIONAL ACTION ON MEASURES OF INTERNATIONAL SIGNIFICANCE

(IN PERCENT)

Relation to President's Position	Pre-Tet Offensive 1946-67	Post-Tet 1968-82
Compliant	42	22
Resistant	28	35
Rejection	8	17
Independent	21	27
(Total number)	(360)	(288)

SOURCE: Carter (1986), table 2.

When Congress enacts laws to restrain the President's room for maneuver in the international system, it unintentionally illustrates the limited effectiveness of congressional action. For example, the 1973 War Powers Resolution restricted to sixty days, the period in which the President could deploy troops in combat without Congressional authorization. Having done this, Congress has repeatedly been hesitant to try enforcing the act against presidential claims that it was unconstitutional, or did not apply to the particular issue at hand. Congress follows what it reckons to be the mood of the public, which in foreign affairs is likely to be influenced not by the law but by "lack of early success" (Holland, 1984: 385). Sixty days is long enough to see whether American troops are moving quickly to victory, as in Grenada, or are in a virtually indefensible position, as in Lebanon.

In a parliamentary system, any member of Parliament can say what he or she thinks about the activities of government in the international system. But the existence of collective authority means that the capacity of the government to act is not hobbled by criticism in the legislature. At times British, French, German, and Japanese disagree among themselves about what the foreign policy of their government ought to be. But no one, whether a politician within the country or a diplomat from a foreign country, has any doubt about what the policy is: It is stated in a clear voice with the collective authority of the Prime Minister, the Foreign Secretary, and the Cabinet.

Frustration with the capacity of Congress to raise awkward questions about foreign policy has led successive Presidents to ask Congress to exercise self-restraint. Former President Gerald Ford (1986: 201ff) has attacked congressional attempts to become involved in foreign relations as unconstitutional, impractical, and obstacles to national security: "We cannot take the time to have 535 secretaries of state or secretaries of defense." The Reagan administration has gone further in asserting the White House's claim to exclusive powers. Ed Meese, a principal adviser of President Reagan, has argued: "It is the responsibility of the President to conduct foreign policy; limitations on that by the Congress are improper" (Destler et al., 1984: 156). Lieutenant Colonel Oliver North has gone further; he claims that the President or his advisers know what must be done in foreign policy regardless of acts of Congress. North told the 9 July 1987 congressional hearing on the Iran-*contra* affair that it was the duty of the White House to defend America's interests in Central America as it saw fit. North added that important foreign policy issues should not be subject to political controversy: "You can't treat the support of the Nicaraguan freedom fighters as you do the passage of a budget."

In the short term, the President can and often does take foreign policy initiatives without consulting Congress, relying on his prerogatives as head of state and commander-in-chief. The support or objections of Congress are registered after the fact. But many foreign policy measures of the President can only succeed after long-term negotiations with foreign governments. In

226

such circumstances, the White House needs the support of Congress to translate its initiatives into government policy, and Congress, unlike a Parliament, has substantial discretion to restrict or reject what the President proposes for national security.

Public Opinion: An Uncertain Echo

When international emergencies arise, a President cannot simply do what the people want because the views of the public are often not very clear or are easily changeable. The discretion given the President by public opinion is broad—as long as the results are not disturbing. When international events are unfavorable to America, however, because of White House action or influences outside American control, the postmodern President will be blamed for what has gone wrong. Surveys of public opinion* show:

1. The average American thinks first about problems of domestic politics. When people are asked about the biggest problems facing the country, 39 percent mention social problems, such as crime and drugs and 30 percent economic problems, as against 26 percent referring to international concerns. Moreover, people are inclined to think that government spends too much on defense and too little on domestic problems.

2. The foreign policy goals that Americans are most likely to endorse are directly related to America's standard of living. Asked to rank more than a dozen foreign policy priorities, 78 percent regard protecting the jobs of American workers as very important; securing an adequate supply of energy is second in importance. By contrast, helping to bring democracy to other nations is at the bottom of the list.

3. When asked whether or not the United States should take an active part or stay out of world affairs, internationalists outnumber isolationists by a margin of more than two to one. But the general public is not as activist as national leaders; 98 percent of national leaders favor America's taking an active role in world affairs, compared to 64 percent of the general public.

4. The public favors both a strong military force to defend the United States and, by a margin of more than four to one, negotiating an arms-control agreement with the Soviet Union. Schneider (1987: 49) explains: "The public does not favor peace over strength or strength over peace. It favors a policy that engages both values."

5. Americans are hesitant about committing troops overseas. When asked about sending troops elsewhere in the world, a majority would endorse doing so only in the case of a Soviet invasion of Western Europe or Japan. Two-thirds or more would *not* be in favor of sending U.S. troops to

*Public opinion data cited in this section are taken from the 1986 Gallup poll survey of the general public and of national leaders sponsored by the Chicago Council on Foreign Relations (Rielly, 1987). This and related surveys are discussed at length in Schneider (1987). For a conceptual overview and lengthy bibliography, see Russett and Graham (1988).

intervene in a war between countries in the Middle East, Central America, or Asia. On average, only 34 percent of Americans are prepared to endorse sending troops to intervene between two military combatants (see table 11.2).

6. National leaders often differ significantly from ordinary Americans in their views of foreign policy. Whereas most members of the public are normally against involving American troops, a majority of leaders favor sending troops to Western Europe, Japan, Nicaragua, Israel, and South Korea (see table 11.2). There is an average difference of 23 percent, between leaders and the general public, about the involvement of American troops abroad.

TABLE 11.2

PUBLIC AND LEADERSHIP ATTITUDES ON INVOLVING

AMERICAN TROOPS IN WARS ABROAD

(IN PERCENT)

Situation	General public	Approval by Leaders	Difference
Soviets invade Western Europe	68	93	25
Soviets invade Japan	53	82	29
Nicaragua allows Soviets to set up air strip	45	67	22
Arabs cut off oil to United States	36	n.a.	n.a.
Arabs invade Israel	33	57	24
Soviets invade China	27	14	13
Iran invades Saudi Arabia	26	n.a.	n.a.
El Salvador government losing to leftist rebels	25	n.a.	n.a.
Nicaragua invades Honduras to destroy *Contra* bases	24	17	–7
North Korea invades South Korea	24	64	40
China invades Taiwan	19	n.a.	n.a.
Average	34	56[a]	23

a. Based on replies to seven questions.

SOURCE: Derived from Rielly (1987), table V.3.

Clear or unclear, a President cannot ignore public opinion. In the two years before a Presidential election, the White House thinks about American-Soviet relations not only in terms of how an American initiative will play in Moscow, but also how it will play in Dubuque in the Iowa presidential caucus (Quandt, 1986: 832ff). Two critics of President Ronald Reagan (Ignatius and Getler, 1986) assert that he has reflected the contradictions of public opinion:

> The American public liked the President's rhetoric about standing tall, but not the reality of Marines getting killed in Lebanon. The public favored a defense buildup but not at the expense of arms-control talks. The public wanted tough talk on terrorism, but it also wanted hostages released. Reagan provided the sometimes contradictory mix that an America half-healed from the Vietnam era seemed to want.

Insofar as Americans are ambivalent about the nation's role in the world, policies reflecting public opinion will be ambivalent. A modern President could follow such an unsteady course because other nations had to adapt to what Washington did. But a postmodern President may reduce his influence by sending signals that seem contradictory and inconsistent. When the White House contradicts itself, as in its public posture of no dealings with terrorists while negotiating a swap of arms for hostages in Iran, the President loses the confidence of public opinion, and of Congress. The Tower Commission report on the Iran-*contra* affair (1987: IV-1) noted: "U.S. policy worked against itself." The Iranians noticed this too.

Pursuing Security from the White House

From the perspective of the Oval Office, the problem with foreign policy is that there are too many subgovernments, each wanting to advise or act in international affairs. The more important the issue, the greater the pressure that other powerholders in Washington direct at the Oval Office: "The more national security policy becomes salient, the more it becomes political, and the more it becomes political, the less Presidents will find national security policymaking exclusively within their jurisdiction" (Rockman, 1987: 26). The President wants to move from endless talk to action that he can command. In a parliamentary system, this is not difficult. Even if the Cabinet and Parliament have not formally endorsed a decision, the Prime Minister and foreign secretary can act confidently, knowing that party discipline will ensure endorsement after the fact.

The President believes that the White House is the "real" department of state, with the Oval Office having the authority to represent the United States in negotiations with foreign states and to act internationally. Foggy Bottom is regarded as the other State Department, part hindrance because of the objections it makes to bright ideas from the White House, and useful insofar as its officials deal with the boring side of diplomacy. Even if a postmodern President cannot take charge of the international system, he can try to take charge of American foreign policy.

For the President to take charge of important international affairs of state, he needs to create institutions that serve the White House independent of subgovernments. First, this requires creating within the White House the resources to monitor the problems that concern the Oval Office, and to formulate policies to deal with these problems. Second, the President needs the means to implement White House decisions, whether by negotiations conducted by a personal emissary or by invoking his authority as commander-in-chief of the armed forces. Third, the President can ignore a large number of issues, letting buffer agencies outside the Oval Office, including Foggy Bottom, absorb the troubles.

National Security without a Council

The formal status of the National Security Council (NSC) is that of a collegial body, like a Prime Minister's Cabinet, bringing together the heads of the principal agencies concerned with international activities. Like a Cabinet, the National Security Council was given a secretary and small staff to coordinate papers moving between the member agencies and the White House; to do staff work for the council; and to make sure that NSC decisions were carried out.

In practice, the National Security Council has not worked as a collective body. A major shortcoming is its representative nature. Because its members head the major Washington agencies concerned with foreign affairs, a council meeting is bound to reflect all the conflicts of opinion within an administration. Even when the NSC met frequently, there was a tendency for its conclusions to be couched in terms of increasing vagueness and generality as the importance of an issue increased, in order to secure formal consensus among agencies that would continue to disagree outside this forum. A council that regularly arrived at clear, precise, and practical recommendations would be doing the President's job in his place.

The President does not want a Council but a counselor, an individual to whom he can turn for assistance in assessing foreign policy independent of the subgovernments whose leaders are members of the NSC. The person to whom the President can readily turn is his assistant for national security affairs. The role of national security assistant was brought to the peak of prominence when Henry Kissinger served President Nixon. Zbigniew Brzezinski, the national security assistant to President Carter, explains the basis of his and Henry Kissinger's importance as follows:

> How the U.S. national interest is perceived and defined gets very much influenced by narrow institutional interests. The typical response of the Defense Department to a problem is to try and obtain an increase in the defense budget, while at the same time often being very reluctant to use force once that budget is increased. The institutional response of State is to rely on diplomacy and to be rather skeptical of the use of power even for demonstration purposes.

> That is why ultimately the President does need some sort of a coordinating framework or organ within which a broader vision is generated. This is one reason why, over the years, a presidential office for national security affairs emerged…. The office emerged because of the logic of America's engagement in the world and the President's need for a perspective that integrates the different institutional divisions. (Quoted in Nathan and Oliver, 1987: 303f)

The immediate asset of the national security assistant is proximity; he sees the President each morning and often several times later in the day. All papers relating to national security matters— whether from State, Defense, the CIA, or other agencies— go across his desk. The national security assistant can write comments on top of these papers, indicating how the President might react, or he can give the President a partial resume or withhold the paper. A second advantage is being in charge of the National Security Council staff, a group of about fifty people with varied experience of civilian, diplomatic, military, and intelligence work. Most of the staffers, are "irregulars" from outside the career bureaucracy; they are people whose career is advanced by acting on behalf of the President (cf. Rockman, 1981: 919ff; Destler et al., 1984).

If the President wants to act as his own secretary of state, formulating and carrying out foreign policy initiatives himself, then his assistant for national security and the NSC staff are at hand to help. The fact that the staff is small is not a major handicap, for the number of people actually working on a particular diplomatic problem in Foggy Bottom is usually very few. The State Department has a large staff because it routinely monitors more than a hundred countries with thousands of problems. Using in-house staff means that the President does not have to run the gauntlet of time-consuming and often frustrating bureaucratic procedures. The secretaries of state and defense do not even have to be told what the White House is doing. Information required from their departments can be obtained through" back channels," with subordinates instructed that they are not to tell their superiors what the White House is doing. Through his national security assistant, the President can keep track of developments on a daily basis.

The basic question that the President must ask himself is: Do I want to turn the White House into an institution running foreign policy on its own? A President has four broad alternatives (see figure 11.1). First, he can be a *delegator*, giving responsibility for formulating and carrying out major policies to the secretary of state and the State Department. Insofar as this is done, a President does not need to build up an alternative department of state in the White House. The job of the President's assistant for national security thus becomes that of a low-profile administrator, responsible for the flow of paper between executive agencies and the Oval Office. Although a postmodern President cannot delegate to Foggy Bottom major international responsibilities, he can save time and avoid trouble by delegating what he does not want to bother with—for the time being at least.

231

Policy Involvement	National security assistant's role	
	High	Low
High	Initiate and Implement (Adviser and agent)	Balancer (Policy Counselor)
Low	Consensus-Seeker (Coordinator)	Delegator (Administrator)

FIGURE 11.1

ALTERNATIVES FOR PRESIDENTIAL DIRECTION OF FOREIGN POLICY

SOURCE: Freely adapted by the author from Mulcahy and Crabb (1987).

A second presidential alternative is to be a *consensus-seeker*, adopting policies that have a broad base of support in the Pentagon, the CIA, and other institutions of government, as well as in the State Department. The President can encourage subgovernments to seek agreement among themselves by endorsing whatever they recommend as a reasonable compromise. If a President does this, then the National Security Council can become active as a council, holding meetings in which the heads of different agencies put forward their views and continue discussing a problem until a consensus emerges. In such circumstances, the role of the assistant for national security affairs is that of a coordinator or broker. As Lieutenant General Colin Powell, President Reagan's sixth appointee as assistant for national security, has described his role:

> I am a great believer that the interagency process works best when everybody has a chance to say his piece and get his positions out on the table, that when we forward the final decision package to the President or present it to him orally, everybody who played knows he has been properly represented and had his day in court. (Quoted in Cannon, 1987)

The attraction of this strategy is that it reduces conflict within the executive branch. It does not end conflict for, unlike a parliamentary system, disputes can continue in Congress. A second disadvantage is that if a consensus is agreed without the President's involvement, it is very difficult for a President to overrule without repudiating all his advisers.

To avoid having policy options foreclosed, a President can adopt the role of a *balancer*, taking disparate views from different agencies with an interest in major international issues, weighing them in the balance in terms of Oval Office costs and benefits, and himself making decisions about major foreign policies. In doing this, the President does not have to formulate a compromise; he may endorse one department's position, produce a fresh synthesis of disparate views, or may ask the agencies involved to take another look at a problem to see if they can come up with something better. In a crisis situation involving diplomatic negotiations and troops, the President will almost certainly want to hear from State, Defense, and the CIA—and, after weighing everything in the balance, to make the decision himself. In such circumstances, the national security assistant is likely to become the President's policy counselor, offering advice privately in daily Oval Office briefings or forcefully telling agencies what the President wants to hear from them. A limitation of this approach is that the implementation of policy is left in the hands of departments that may not energetically pursue the President's wishes.

To be confident that a major policy is carried out as he wishes, a President may try to become both an *initiator and implementor*, identifying a problem, canvassing policy options, making a decision, and carrying it out from the White House. From the President's perspective, this role is very attractive, for it allows him to play a creative role rather than simply react to files in his "In" tray. The opportunity to initiate and implement a major policy is also attractive to a national security assistant, for he will be the President's chief spokesman for the policy, and his staff will be responsible for implementation. When an initiative is successfully carried out, for example, the decision to restore diplomatic relations with China, carried out by Henry Kissinger for President Nixon, the result is a historic achievement for which the White House can take full credit. But when things go wrong, as in the Iran-*contra* affair, directed by national security assistant John Poindexter, then the White House rightly gets the blame.

Because there is a lot to be said for each of these roles, a President can follow more than one during a four-year term of office. For example, President Nixon was very happy to delegate to the State Department all those matters that he considered beneath White House notice, so that he could have more time to initiate and implement the big policies of special interest to himself, and his national security assistant, Henry Kissinger. President Eisenhower appeared to delegate major responsibilities to his secretary of state, John Foster Dulles, but he was capable of using the machinery of the National Security Council to encourage consensus when disputes arose, or to strike a balance on matters that he deemed suitable for personal and public involvement. President Reagan has been prepared to delegate to Defense as well as to State, carrying noninvolvement to the point of allowing disputes between agencies to continue indefinitely. On occasion he has made a judgment between competing agencies, initially favoring a big increase in the defense budget and then diplomatic negotiations with the Soviet Union on arms control. The Iran-*contra* affair was a spectacular warning of the dangers of the White House initiating and implementing foreign policy.

Once we appreciate that the President wants to combine involvement and noninvolvement in national security matters, we understand why the role of the national security assistant is a variable, not a constant (cf. Mulcahy and Crabb, 1987). The role varies within a given administration, for the President (and therefore, his assistant) will not be interested in every national security issue. Some issues will be left in the hands of the agencies, at least in the first instance. The job also varies with the President. Zbigniew Brzezinski's description of his job made sense only in a White House in which the President, Jimmy Carter, wanted to initiate policies, and take an active part in balancing (his critics would say, second-guessing) many more. McGeorge Bundy served John F. Kennedy, who took his own counsel on foreign policy matters, but welcomed Bundy's role in actively coordinating the disparate views put forward by agencies competing for Oval Office endorsement. Because Ronald Reagan has not wanted to be deeply involved in the conduct of foreign policy, he has had six national security assistants, none of whom could establish a personal ascendancy over major officials at State and Defense, nor was this desired. Reagan defined the national security assistant's job as that of a coordinator and administrator for a President who likes to delegate and see consensus around him.

Commanding Force

The President is most likely to see his decisions promptly obeyed when he acts as commander-in-chief of the armed forces. The capacity of the military to respond promptly to a request to bomb a target or move an aircraft carrier into a troubled area is in marked contrast with the way in which Congress responds to a presidential request. An action-oriented President will always find the armed services readier for action than any other agency in government. The development of modern telecommunication makes it possible for the White House to be the command post in a military action on the other side of the globe. For example, President Gerald Ford could give directions to ships in action in Asia, engaged in the rescue of the crew of an American freighter, the *Mayaguez*, captured by Cambodian forces in 1975. When a President steps into the role of commander-in-chief, he expects to strengthen his position in Washington, and with the American public, who are likely to rally round the flag, momentarily at least (cf. Edwards, 1986).

Many problems facing a postmodern President require considering military action to reinforce diplomatic action or as an alternative to diplomacy. When the President's attention is directed toward a problem where force is already in use, for example, in the Middle East or Central America, the influence that the United States can exert is limited if it is not prepared to contemplate the use of force. Force may be used on an "in-out" basis, such as the bombing of Libya in retaliation for Libyan assistance to terrorists; or it may involve a commitment of indefinite length, as in the dispatch of ships to protect oil tankers in the Persian Gulf in 1987.

By contrast with leaders of other Western nations, the American President considers the use of troops relatively frequently. Because of defeat in World War II, Germany and Japan are hesitant about any use of their military forces. The French and British governments have abandoned nearly all the military bases that they once maintained overseas in their days of empire, and rarely send troops into action abroad. The biggest military engagement of a NATO ally in the past two decades is Britain's attempt to cope with internal violence in Northern Ireland, continuous since 1969.

If keeping out of trouble is the second rule of the postmodern President, then he must be wary about acting as commander-in-chief, for every military action involves the risk of an enemy counterattack and big domestic political costs if military actions go wrong. The asymmetry of forces between the United States and many combative nations can be a handicap, for example, in a confrontation between the United States and a relatively small military force enjoying operational advantages on its own ground, such as North Vietnam or Nicaragua. A second kind of problem is a conflict between two forces already in action against each other, as in Lebanon. Even if a President orders military action in the belief that a brief engagement may do good for America, there is the risk that a venture that starts in high hopes and bold rhetoric may sink in ground as treacherous as the jungles of Southeast Asia or the streets of Beirut.

Selective Nonintervention
A President who concentrates attention on a single issue can command attention for his solo performance, but a soloist cannot cover the full repertoire of international problems. What the White House does not do is as important as what it does do. By practicing selective intervention, the President conserves his time and political capital for imperative concerns. For example, Presidents usually give minimal attention to Latin American affairs. The surest way for these matters to come to the attention of the Oval Office is if they ride on the back of another problem, such as American banks being threatened by bankruptcy if Latin American governments default on loan payments. When black congressmen committed to a strong stand against South Africa create difficulties for White House efforts to collect votes on the Hill, the President recognizes that sanctions can be applied along Pennsylvania Avenue as well as to South Africa.

Many decisions in favor of nonintervention are easy to make because of the limited scope for presidential influence. Crises, such as what to do about an attack on an American ship in the Middle East, maximize the President's opportunity to exert leadership, for a decision is needed fast. Strategic decisions intended to give long-term direction to policy, for example, about arms-control negotiations with Russia or economic relations with Japan, involve a much wider group of powerholders. Even if the President decides to articulate a clear strategy, the White House can have problems in seeing that its directive is consistently followed by other agencies. When subgovernments are much involved, for example, in a decision about a new weapons system affecting congressional districts where military equipment is produced, there is an incentive for the President to avoid getting caught in the crossfire of intensive lobbying on the Hill (cf. Ripley and Franklin, 1984: 28ff, 238ff).

The State Department makes a major contribution to presidential non-involvement by routinely monitoring conditions in the majority of nations of the world. The secretary of defense protects the President from much criticism concerning particular weapons systems, for after the White House rules on the size of the total military budget, it is the job of the defense secretary to apportion the money available between competing claims of the armed services and their civilian suppliers.

NSC staffers save the President time by screening out people and memoranda that are not of immediate interest to the Oval Office. The national security assistant quickly learns to gauge what topics do interest the President, what his total appetite for information is, and how long or short is his attention span. The President need only make a marginal comment on a document or ask why he has not been briefed about a problem discussed on TV, for the assistant to register the remark as a guideline for future screening. The national security assistant protects the President by trying to prevent agencies from acting in ways that would embarrass the White House. In the words of ex-NSC official, William Quandt: "A lot of what the NSC job is about is damage limitation, to prevent any more screwups" (Kirschten, 1987: 469).

Nonintervention and noncommunication are two-way streets. When the President keeps within the White House issues that he deems of highest importance, doing so makes it difficult to cooperate within government. Excluding agency heads from the preparation of major policy initiatives deprives the White House of agency knowledge, and especially warnings about the difficulties in carrying out a bright idea originating in the White House. In the words of an NSC staff person: "Political appointees seem to want to accomplish goals quickly while careerists opt to accomplish things carefully" (quoted in Rockman, 1981: 915). The commitment of officials will be diminished if they learn only after the fact what the policy is. In the absence of involvement, excluded officials are more likely to continue advocating their views after the White House gives a lead. As Secretary of State George P. Shultz said in 1987: "Nothing ever gets settled in this town. It is a seething debating society in which the debate never stops; nobody ever gives up, including me."

12. The International System Is Stronger Than the President

We shall pay any price, bear any burden, meet any hardship, support any friend, oppose any foe to assure the survival and the success of liberty.
This we pledge—and more.

—John F. Kennedy

The dollar is our currency but your problem.

— John Connally

But the problem is the—the deficit is—or should I say—wait a minute, the spending, I should say, of gross national product, forgive me—the spending is roughly 23 to 24 percent. So that it is in—it is what is increasing, while the revenues are staying proportionately the same and what would be the proper amount they should, that we should be taking from the private sector.

—Ronald Reagan

The postmodern President must work in a postimperial world in which the United States is not the only elephant in the international system. As nations have become more interdependent, the policies and politics of other nations affect the President when he goes Washington and when he goes public. In 1961, John F. Kennedy could make the politically proud and economically false boast that America had the resources to pay any price to maintain its world role. A decade later, President Nixon's treasury secretary, John Connally, could boast that America was passing to other nations a buck depreciated by inflation. Black Monday on Wall Street in 1987 revealed the vulnerability of the postmodern Presidency to an open international economy. Confronted with demands from abroad for action on the federal government's deficit, President Reagan had difficulty in replying coherently to a press conference question about American policy.

The United States has lost its former position of dominance in the international system but no other country has taken it over. Under certain conditions, oil-rich nations, guerrillas fighting in jungles, revolutionary regimes of the Right and Left, or staid central bankers can make their influence felt. In today's international system, impersonal economic forces are more important than the imagination and personality of heads of government. When the leaders of advanced industrial nations meet in the annual world summit, they bemoan the fact that the system is stronger than each of them.

President Reagan has shared with John F. Kennedy the desire to make America stand tall in the world. The Reagan doctrine asserted that America should develop overwhelming military superiority worldwide. Yet the Soviet Union under Mikhail Gorbachev is no longer viewed as an "evil empire." The historic meeting of the two leaders in Washington on 7 December 1987 underlined the interdependence of the two nations in pursuit of arms control. Supply-side tax reductions were to make the market dominate the world economy, and America the market leader. A turning point in the economy came in 1985 when the United States became a world debtor; it now borrows more money from foreigners than any nation has ever before borrowed. Yet President Reagan has not wanted to face the implications of losing hegemony: "The United States is the world's largest debtor but it continues to think like a creditor" (Bergsten, 1987: 772).

There is no turning back to an era of splendid isolation, just as there is no return to the steam train or lengthy stump speeches by campaigning politicians. A postmodern President must go international in order to meet his responsibilities for national security and directing the economy. Even if a President won immediate cheers from the public and Congress by proposing to return America to its isolationist past, the resulting shock to the internationally oriented U.S. economy would be so great that there could be no return to the isolationist prosperity of the 1920s.

In order to understand how the world has closed in on the White House, we must first look at the way in which military power is exercised in an interdependent world. The second section of this chapter examines the end of American hegemony in the world economy, a reflection of rapid growth in other nations. The continued growth of Japan has replaced American hegemony with what could be called *bigemony*,* an international system in which America and Japan are the two leading nations.￼ The political implications of this are examined in the third section. As America's relative power in the international economy declines, the postmodern President has become more vulnerable internationally, while it is also more important to succeed in going international.

Keeping the Military Balance

Military concerns have been central to the Presidency for half a century, and the need for a global system of defense is accepted by the public and by

---

*When Bergsten (1987: 790) initially coined this term a decade ago, he had in mind domination by the United States and Germany. So quickly has Japan risen to world prominence that it is now the appropriate partner.

Congress, as well as by the Oval Office. American patriotism is much higher than in other major nations (Rose, 1985d) and provides popular support for maintaining a strong military force. Because Americans proclaim a dislike of big government, the armed services and the military budget are somehow not seen as really part of government.

One Partner in a Balance

The maintenance of national security does not require the United States to dominate all other nations in the world, nor is such a goal realistic. A classic national security strategy is to maintain a balance-of-power through military force sufficient to prevent an unfriendly nation or coalition of nations from dominating the United States. The balance-of-power doctrine is consistent with the philosophy of the Founding Fathers, who built checks and balances into the Constitution to prevent the President, or any branch of government from securing domination. In a balance-of-power system, no nation, even if it is number one, can be strong enough to impose its will on all other nations. America assumed a global role in two world wars in order to maintain a balance of power. It sought to prevent German and Japanese forces from becoming dominant.

Since shortly after World War II, the Soviet Union has been the focus of American strategic concern; the goal has been containment, not conquest. Containment of the Soviet Union has been sought by means of a balance among the powers, in order that none of them should effect the subjugation of the others. Only for a brief period after 1945 could the United States be described as uniquely powerful, as the sole nation with the capability to wage nuclear war. The Soviet Union soon developed its own nuclear capability, resulting in the rough parity of power expressed in the strategic doctrine of MAD (Mutual Assured Destruction). America's nuclear weapons today are meant to be sufficient to deter a Soviet attack—and the same is true of Soviet weapons.

The cold war implied that no one side wins, thus achieving global hegemony. Whatever the campaign rhetoric, the object of successive American Presidents has been to keep the cold war "cold," that is, to avoid a war in which American troops fight Soviet troops. The White House has recognized the Soviet leader as a partner in a nuclear balance of power; the hot-line telephone between the White House and the Kremlin represents the need of the two leaders to keep in touch with one another. The acceptance of Soviet strength is not an endorsement of the Soviet system any more than Soviet negotiations with the United States are an endorsement of Reagan Republicanism.

Whether the measure is military expenditure or manpower, both the United States and the Soviet Union are undoubtedly still superpowers today. Each country spends more than eight times the amount of the third biggest military spender, Saudi Arabia. Even with difficulties in comparing Soviet and American military budgets, each superpower undoubtedly spends a large amount of money on defense. America's advantage is that it can finance hundreds of billions of dollars of defense spending from a more prosperous economy. To maintain rough parity in spending with the United States, the Soviet Union must try nearly twice as hard, spending more than 11 percent of its GNP on defense, as against more than 6 percent in the United States (see table 12.1). While the Soviet Union maintains more people under arms, 2.2 million American servicemen constitute a large and very professional fighting service.

Both the United States and the Soviet Union are leaders of alliances that seek to mobilize other nations to add weight on their side of the balance. The Soviet Union enjoys hegemony within its system of military alliances. It is by far the biggest nation of the seven Warsaw Pact countries in Eastern Europe. The Soviet Union accounts for an estimated 92 percent of military expenditures and more than three-quarters of total manpower (see table 12.1). Moreover, the Soviet Union dominates the governments of Warsaw Pact nations, as the Communist party governing each country is subject to discipline from Moscow. The presence of Soviet troops reinforces the Soviet position and these troops have been used in Poland, Czechoslovakia, East Germany, and Hungary to assert the supremacy of political directives from Moscow.

The United States is undoubtedly dominant in the 16-nation North Atlantic Treaty Organization (NATO) alliance established under American leadership in 1949 to protect Western Europe against Soviet aggression and the United States from Europe's being dominated by an unfriendly power. It accounts for two-thirds of military spending by NATO nations, and its military manpower is by far the largest force within the alliance. America's much greater population, and thus much larger national product, assures it a permanent position of leadership in military resources. Britain, France, and Germany each have a substantial armed force, and Britain and France are independent nuclear powers. Western European nations make a far greater contribution to NATO military expenditure than Eastern European nations add to Soviet expenditure (see table 12.1).

Within NATO, the United States can exercise leadership but it cannot expect major European nations to be client states, like poor Third World countries or banana republics. NATO allies have accepted America's military leadership, but they have carefully circumscribed the claims of the United States to impose its views on all their relations with the Soviet Union. European nations have viewed increased trade with neighbors in Eastern Europe as mutually beneficial, a view consistent with free-market values. Trade with the Soviet bloc is regarded as a positive measure to support *détente*, reducing cold-war tensions and making the Soviet Union more open to the West. Western European nations thus considered it reasonable to reduce dependence on Middle East oil by constructing a pipeline across the Soviet Union to transfer natural gas from Siberia. When the Reagan admin-

TABLE 12.1

U.S. MILITARY EFFORT COMPARED TO ALLIES AND THE SOVIET UNION

	Military Expenditures			Military Manpower	
	Percent GNP	$bn	Per-cent	(000)	Percent Total
NATO countries					
United States	6.5	217	66	2,222	37
Other NATO countries	3.6	112	34	3,712	63
Total	5.1	$329	100	5,934	100
Warsaw Pact countries					
USSR	11.5	212	92	3,800	76
Other Pact countries	5.8	18	8	1,168	24
Total	9.6	$230	100	4,968	100

SOURCE: Sivard (1986, 33); data for 1983.

istration sought to interfere with the trade patterns of its military allies, European nations showed the limits of American dominance by rejecting American criticism of their Soviet trade (Blinken, 1987; Nau, 1987).

Outside Europe, the United States finds itself in situations where its military power is unable to produce the outcome that the White House favors. In Central America, the President has always had the military capacity to dominate nations, sometimes by the dispatch of a small number of marines, so-called gunboat diplomacy. But the White House usually considers it inappropriate on political grounds to invoke the full weight of America's military force in Central America. Presidents did commit United States troops in large numbers to Vietnam; the result, however, was defeat. Although the United States and the Soviet Union each support nations in the Middle East, neither has been able to add the region to its sphere of influence, or achieve a stable balance within the region. America's relationship with postwar China has had a military element, first as an enemy and now as a check on the Soviet Union in Asia. But China is too large and too remote for the United States to treat it like a European member of NATO.

The Soviet Union has similarly found that there are limits to the power of a superpower. It has had as much difficulty suppressing rebellion in Afghanistan as Hitler had in putting down similar mountain-based resistance by the Yugoslavs in World War II. The defection of China from the Soviet sphere of influence has escalated Russia's need for defense forces, given the long land boundary of the Soviet Union and China. The rise of fundamentalist Islamic forces in Iran is a further check, for the Soviet Union has not only a land boundary with Iran but also tens of millions of Muslims in its population. The international system is stronger than the Kremlin as well as stronger than the White House.

Interdependence with an Enemy

In confronting the Soviet Union, the President is in a paradoxical position. Russia is viewed as the primary enemy against whom the United States must arm. Yet because war with the Soviet Union is ruled out by nuclear deterrence, the White House cannot seek victory over the enemy as in a traditional war. When the President thinks about national security, he must simultaneously think of reactions within the international system, and especially the Soviet Union. The Oval Office views defense expenditures and diplomatic negotiations as complementary. Since President Eisenhower first met a Soviet leader at a summit meeting, the White House has recognized that it must negotiate with the Soviet Union as well as arm against it.

Like John F. Kennedy, Ronald Reagan ran for the Presidency denouncing his opponent for alleged failure in maintaining America's defense, claiming that the Soviet Union had achieved superiority over the United States in strategic nuclear weapons in the 1970s. Notwithstanding opposition to government spending in general, President Reagan has supported a high level of military spending and has been ready to invoke "Rambo" images when going public. Furthermore, President Reagan has endorsed plans for a novel Strategic Defense Initiative ("Star Wars") intended to provide a new and untested level of deterrence against Soviet missiles.

The Reagan administration has more than doubled the amount of money spent on defense in the 1980s. When Ronald Reagan entered office in 1981, defense spending stood at $157 billion; by 1987, it had risen to $282 billion and is scheduled to rise to $320 billion by 1990 (OMB, 1988: summary tables 20, 21). When allowance is made for the effects of inflation, this is an increase of nearly 50 percent in real spending on the American military in the 1980s. Defense's share of the total federal budget went from 23 percent in 1981 to 28 percent in 1987. This boost has increased the dominance of the United States within NATO, as European nations have not followed suit.

Concurrently with diplomatic negotiations with the Soviet Union, President Reagan has had to impose a policy on the agencies and subgovernments concerned with America's national security. The Defense Department, under Caspar Weinberger and with Richard Perle as an articulate skeptic about Russian intentions, has pressed for increased defense expenditures. By contrast, the State Department has stressed the value of negotiating with Russia in hopes of achieving limited but real agreements on matters of mutual concern, for example, the risk and cost of escalating defense expenditures. Viewing Washington from the bicultural perspective of American specialists on the Soviet Union, Alexander Dallin and Gail Lapidus (1987:206) conclude: "The American political system creates considerable obstacles to the conduct of a coherent foreign policy."

The behavior of the Soviet Union has sent conflicting signals. A long war of suppressing nationalist rebels in Afghanistan and the coercion of Poland have contrasted with talk of *glasnost*, that is, openness and good feeling. The accession of Mikhail Gorbachev to the leadership of the Soviet Union was followed by a sustained Soviet initiative for summit meetings with the President to negotiate about arms control.

Preparation for a summit places a great political strain on a President, who must trust negotiators acting in his name because he himself is without previous experience in international diplomacy. When a President does try to negotiate one on one with a Soviet leader, the results can be confusion or worse. If a summit meeting does not turn out successfully, then a President risks losing support domestically, a fact known to Russian negotiators as well as White House staff. Presidents Eisenhower and Kennedy each had a summit encounter become a public relations disaster. President Reagan was thus in good company in having the 1986 Reykjavik summit meeting with Mikhail Gorbachev end in confusion. Because a downbeat outcome was viewed as bad for the President's image just before mid-term congressional elections, White House staff sought to dispel disappointment by propagating a fresh statement of administration goals, but this was shot down by critics in Washington—and the Republicans did badly in the congressional elections too (cf. Mandelbaum and Talbot, 1987: Oberdorfer, 1987).

A summit meeting gives the President the opportunity to take the initiative in making American foreign policy and the White House can keep close control on what negotiators say on behalf of the President. U.S. officials know that if they misrepresent the President, then their views and their careers can be quickly squashed. But the announcement of negotiations leading up to a summit meeting does not end disputes between sub-governments. For example, the Pentagon viewed planning for the 1985 Geneva summit between President Reagan and Mikhail Gorbachev as a victory by the "enemy," that is, the State Department. During the weeks leading up to that meeting, Secretary of Defense Weinberger occupied a role that "some would describe as sentinel and others would describe as spoiler" (Dallin and Lapidus, 1987: 234).

The Reagan-Gorbachev arms-control agreement demonstrated both the President's capacity for leadership within the American political system and the extent of White House interdependence in the international system. The agreement was the culmination of seven years of America's steadily increasing defense effort and intermittent discussions with the Soviet Union. It was an achievement to which President Reagan could make a unique contribution, for his position as an opponent of the "evil empire" of the Soviet Union gave him good credentials for mobilizing Republican support in its favor, and the substance was difficult for liberal Democrats to criticize. The President thus secured agreement with the Soviet leader, and also endorsement in Congress.

The treaty between the two superpowers is a textbook example of interdependence, for the accord could not have been reached without the readiness of Soviet leader Mikhail Gorbachev to take initiatives too. The ceremonies surrounding the signing of the treaty in Washington reflected interdependence, with each national leader ready to support what the other said, realizing that without their continued cooperation, the treaty could not succeed. Even if each superpower can dominate its allies militarily, it cannot dominate the other superpower.

The End of American Hegemony

In addition to enjoying global military eminence, modern and postmodern Presidents have been affected by the dollar being in a class by itself as a world currency. This was true when the dollar was the solution to the international demand for a currency that was literally as good as gold. It is still true when the dollar is America's problem as well as its currency.

Economic strength has pervasive political implications. McGeorge Bundy, national security assistant for Presidents Kennedy and Johnson, approvingly quoted Dean Acheson's view: "In the final analysis the United States is the engine of mankind, and the rest of the world is the train." America's leadership was assumed to be permanent. In the U.S. Treasury's annual report for 1963, Robert V. Roosa wrote that the idea that America should abandon its role as world banker because of the burdens involved was no more than "the Wordsworthian nostalgia of an adult wishing he could be a child again" (quoted in Odell, 1982: 100f).

America's Economy: Absolute Growth, Relative Decline
Although no postwar President has fully understood the intricacies of the international economy, Presidents from Truman through Nixon benefited from America's international economic strength. The great majority of Americans have also benefited as the absolute growth in the American economy provided more jobs, new products, and wealth on a scale previously unimagined. Americans are not the only people far better off materially than in 1945. America's growth has been part of a worldwide economic boom, benefiting the British, French, Germans, Japanese, and people in many newly industrializing countries.

America's loss of economic hegemony has occurred because other countries have grown much more. In 1953 the United States accounted for nearly half of the world's gross national product (GNP). America's GNP was then more than double that of twelve major European nations, ten times that

TABLE 12.2

AMERICA'S CHANGING SHARE OF THE GROSS WORLD PRODUCT

(AS PERCENTAGE OF TOTAL)

	1953	1960	1970	1983
Developed countries [a]				
United States	46.9	37.4	33.8	29.4
European Community [b]	20.7	21.1	23.2	22.3
Japan	2.4	3.2	6.8	10.4
Other	8.6	7.3	7.8	8.8
Total	78.6	69.0	71.6	70.9
Communist countries [c]				
USSR	4.5	2.7	11.1	6.4
China	1.2	4.2	n.a.	2.7
Other	7.0	10.8	4.0	2.4
Total	12.7	17.7	15.1	11.5
Third World countries	8.7	13.3	13.3	17.6
Total $ trillion	0.7	1.4	2.9	11.2

a. Europe, Canada, Australia, New Zealand, Israel, Japan, South Africa.

b. The 12 current member nations of the European Community: Belgium, Denmark, France, Federal Republic of Germany, Ireland, Italy, Luxembourg, Netherlands, United Kingdom, Portugal, Spain, and Greece.

c. USSR 1953: 1958 data; China 1953, 1952 data. Other: Czechoslovakia, Hungary, Yugoslavia, German Democratic Republic, Bulgaria, and Poland.

SOURCES: UN (1971a, 1983a, 1984a); UN (1964b, 1967b, 1977b); IMF (1974). Exchange rates for communist countries before 1960: UN (1960: I:9). Chinese GNP in 1983: Sivard (1986: 34); China, 1952, 1960: Yuan-li Wu (1973: tables 19.3, 19.4).

of the Soviet Union and nearly twenty times that of Japan. America stood tall in the world economy, because no other country was then a major industrial power (see table 12.2). The value of America's national product was equivalent to $2325 per person.

In the three decades since, the American economy has grown slowly but steadily because of the effect of compounding a seemingly small annual growth rate. The national product is now worth more than $4 trillion. After taking into account the effect of inflation, the gross national product is now double what it was a quarter-century ago. The value of the national product in 1988 is nearly $20,000 per person—and it is still growing.

Other countries have experienced faster rates of economic growth than the United States. This was true in the boom years of the early 1960s, when America's national product grew at an average annual rate of 4.6 percent, but the European Community countries and the Soviet Union grew at a rate of 4.7 percent and Japan at a rate of 6.8 percent. In the first half of the 1970s, when the world moved into recession, the relative gap widened between the United States—where the economy expanded at 2.2 percent annually—and other countries. Growth in the European Community averaged 2.8 percent; the Soviet Union, 3.0 percent; Japan, 4.7 percent, and developing countries 7.0 per cent (*Economic Report of the President*, 1987: table B-108).

Today, the United States is a rich country, but it is no longer the only rich country in the world. Among advanced industrial nations, standards of living now differ in degree, not kind (Rose, forthcoming). When economies are measured in terms of gross national product per capita, some European nations and some small, oil-rich sheikdoms produce more per person than the United States. America's share of the world national product has declined to less than 30 percent of the total. In 1983 Western Europe, Japan, and other industrial nations, such as Canada, accounted for 41 percent of the world's national product, more than the American share. Whatever the rate at which the American economy grows in the future, it is likely to account for a continually diminishing share of the world's national product.

Winning at Hardball: The Proof of Hegemony
Even when America was the dominant economy in the world, the dollar's role as an international currency was a source of trouble. Foreign demand was such that the dollar was overvalued, threatening America's balance of payments with other nations. President Kennedy rejected the idea of devaluing the dollar on political grounds. It would "call into doubt the good faith and stability of this nation and the competence of its President" (Sorensen, 1965: 408). Foreign nations began to test whether Washington had resources to defend the dollar, converting dollar reserves into gold, which the Federal Reserve was then obliged to pay out on demand. The United States demonstrated its power by defending its economic interests in a decade-long challenge to the dollar (see Odell, 1982).

The pressure on America came from abroad, particularly from France, which started a massive conversion into gold of dollars it held. Without consulting foreign nations or many Washington officials concerned with economic policy, President Johnson announced in July 1965 that the United States was ready to confer with other nations about reforming the Bretton Woods international monetary system. The upshot was the creation in 1969 of Special Drawing Rights at the International Monetary Fund (IMF), a step in line with White House intentions. The problems of the dollar worsened, however, because of inflationary pressures created by the Johnson and Nixon administrations financing the Vietnam war by increasing the money supply. As the dollar was overvalued, foreigners holding dollars had an economic incentive to convert their dollars into gold.

Faced with economic difficulties outside his knowledge and interest, President Nixon used as a buffer John Connally, a Texas Democrat whom he appointed secretary of the treasury with the instruction "Go ahead and do what you think you have to do" (Porter, 1982: 185). Connally was suitable for an era of American hegemony, for he was an economic nationalist prepared to use America's strength to do what he believed made sense for the United States, even if this was unpopular abroad and with others in the administration (Cohen, 1982: 165f). The power of the United States to impose its policy unilaterally on the international system was visibly demonstrated on 15 August 1971. President Nixon announced a New Economic Policy, which took the dollar off the gold standard and imposed a 10 percent temporary tax on goods imported into the United States. Shortly after taking the dollar off gold, Connally stated his outlook bluntly to a group of academic economists who advised him of the advantages of international economic policy coordination. Seeing the international economy as a game of hardball, Secretary of the Treasury Connally told the economists:

> I appreciate your coming in today. And since you have shared with me, I think I should give you an idea of where I am going. My basic approach is that foreigners are out to screw us. Our job is to screw them first. (Quoted in Odell, 1982: 263)

In 1971 the U.S. secretary of the treasury could play hardball in the international currency markets and win. In consequence of its aggressive policy stance, Washington succeeded in removing what was then seen as a major cause of the weakness of the American economy; it did so by unilateral action taken in what was deemed America's national interest without consultation with foreign governments. That is the privilege of a hegemonic power. America has that power no longer.

The Postmodern President Tries to Pass the Buck

In retrospect, the continuing problems of the dollar can be seen as an indicator of the loss of hegemony; the emergence of the postmodern Presidency is the result. Keohane (1984: 32) defines hegemony as based on four sources of economic power: control over raw materials, capital, markets, and competitive advantages in the production of highly valued goods. Evidence of America's loss of hegemony has been accumulating under each heading.

The 1973 OPEC-induced oil price rise made evident that the United States was not able to control one of the world's most critical raw materials. Although America is a major oil-producing nation, it does not produce sufficient oil to break the OPEC cartel. Nor was the United States ready to use its military force to seize foreign oil fields, as might have happened in an imperialist age. Because oil-producing Arab countries in the Middle East already were important in national security calculations, their economic leverage became doubly important. Middle East oil exporters have gained hundreds of billions of dollars, and this has reduced the power of American capital, as Middle East dollars have been invested in ways that have given foreign countries great leverage on Wall Street.

For decades after World War II, America had no difficulty expanding markets as world demand grew, for the United States was by far the largest industrial nation. Expansion involved the export of American-produced goods, and the export of capital to establish factories abroad owned by American multinational firms. Today, the United States no longer dominates world markets. The growth of European nations and Japan has created competition for the United States in the production of such goods as automobiles, where America was once supreme. Economic growth in newly industrializing nations such as Korea, has created competition in the production of basic industrial commodities such as steel. The creation of the European Economic Community, paying high subsidies to European farmers, has created difficulties for American agricultural exports. Japanese growth has been fueled by imports to America.

America has lost its unique advantage as the source of many highly valued goods, and other nations have become producers of goods that Americans value highly. The result is that the United States has changed from being a nation that exports more than it imports, to a nation that imports more than it exports. From 1946 to 1981, the United States had a net surplus in trade in goods and services. Since 1983, however, the United States has run a trade deficit, rising to well over $100 billion a year. Although the value of America's exports grew from 6 percent of the national product in 1965 to 13 percent in 1980 before declining to 9 percent by 1987, America's imports have grown even more. Imports were 4.6 percent of the national product in 1965 and rose to 12 percent in 1987, thus creating a mammoth trade deficit (*Economic Report of the President,* 1988: table B-1).

As the first fully postmodern President, Jimmy Carter was forced to seek cooperation with other nations, often from a position of relative economic weakness. President Carter was unprepared for an economy that was not as good as his intentions. Inflation accelerated, thus eroding much of the benefit from economic growth and leading to a balance-of-payments crisis. Benjamin J. Cohen (1987: 121) concludes: "Initially inclined toward an activist reaffirmation of America's influence over economic events, the Carter administration ended by stressing the advantages of compromise and collaboration with our key allies in Europe and Japan." But President Carter's efforts were largely unsuccessful as foreign nations reacted against what they saw as displays of economic "incoherence," "insensitivity," and "indifference" in Washington. At the 1978 Bonn summit meeting of leaders of major economies, the United States successfully lobbied the German government to act as an engine of growth, reflating its economy in the hope that this would pull other nations, including the United States, along in its train. But by autumn 1979, Chancellor Helmut Schmidt declared: "This ridiculous little locomotive theory has withered away now, and correctly so" (Putnam and Bayne, 1984: 99). German unwillingness to import American inflation by supporting the dollar was a strong force impelling the Federal Reserve Board to deflate the American economy late in 1979, an unusual step for the Fed to take, and for a President to accept, in the twelve months before a presidential election. The White House had no choice, since America lacked the hegemonic power to impose its terms on other nations, and the White House had no power to impose any coherent economic policy on the federal government. The Federal Reserve contracted the money supply and in 1980 the American economy actually shrank in size (cf. Tufte, 1978; Gilpin, 1987: 331).

Ronald Reagan owed his election as President in 1980 as much to foreign nations as to his own campaign. Pressures from abroad led to an election-year recession that cost the Democratic President votes, and the seizure of American hostages at the U.S. Embassy in Tehran showed every TV-watcher the limits of White House power in a posthegemonic world.

The Reagan administration entered office with a "Rambo" attitude, disregarding the views of foreign nations in the international system. The proponents of supply-side economics were primarily concerned with domestic policy and politics. Cutting taxes was the first priority, and this was a matter of winning votes in Congress. Nothing that foreigners could do affected votes on the Hill for the 1981 tax cuts, or the 1986 Tax Reform Act. President Reagan told the International Monetary Fund at its 29 September 1981 meeting: "The most important contribution any country can make to world development is to pursue sound economic policies at home." A senior White House adviser, Henry Nau (1984, 1985; cf. Bergsten, 1985), has described this policy as *domesticism*, that is, a belief that getting the national economy right is the best way to contribute to an improved international economy. A healthy domestic economy, especially an economy as big and important as that of the United States, is reckoned to have a positive impact on the international system as a whole. Critics described the Reagan administration as pursuing its economic policies "in almost total disregard for the outside world" (Cohen, 1987: 126).

In domestic politics, the immediate impact of Reagan's economic policy was favorable. The economy expanded by 16 percent in real terms in the first six years of the Reagan administration, notwithstanding a recession in 1982. At the start of 1988, the Reagan administration could boast of the longest period of sustained economic growth in the postwar era. Unemployment and inflation rates have improved, and compare favorably with the late 1970s. Tax cuts have allowed the federal government to reduce its taxes on the national product to less than 20 percent. But major federal spending programs such as social security and defense have continued to expand.

TABLE 12.3

STRUCTURAL CHANGES IN THE AMERICAN ECONOMY UNDER PRESIDENT REAGAN

	1980	1987	Change
Gross National Product (GNP)			
Current $ billion	2732	4486	Up $1.75 tr (64%)
Constant value $ billion	3187	3816	Up $629 bn (20%)
Taxes as % GNP	20.2	19.0	Down 1.2%
Spending as % GNP	22.5	22.4	Down 0.1%
Federal deficit $ billion	74	150	Worse by $76 bn
Interest on debt $ billion	52	139	Worse by $87 bn
(of which, interest			
paid to foreigners)	12.6	24.0	Worse by $11.4 bn
Balance in current accounts	2	−162	Worse by $164 bn
$ billion			
Net foreign investment	13	−157	Worse by $170 bn
$ billion			

SOURCE: *Economic Report of the President, 1988* (1988), tables B1, 2, 20, 78, 102.

Federal spending as a proportion of the national product has remained high; for every $5 raised in taxes, government is spending almost $6 (see table 12.3).

The popularity of Reaganomics is easy to understand: The United States has been consuming more than it produces. From 1981 through 1984, America's capacity to consume rose by more than 10 percent due to temporary changes in America's relation to the world economy, especially the rise in the value of the dollar, which made imports cheaper. Americans have not had to reduce consumption to pay the full cost of the federal deficit, because of the readiness of foreigners to lend money to the United States. Windfall gains from abroad contributed more to the increase in consumption than the actual growth in output in the domestic economy (Marris, 1985: 51ff).

Reaganomics has confirmed the end of American hegemony. The cut in taxes and the rise in spending have meant a federal deficit that has increased by magnitudes. A leading advocate of the domesticist policy, Henry Nau (1984: 29), wrote at the halfway mark in the Reagan administration: "Massive U.S. budget deficits cannot continue much longer without deleterious domestic and worldwide results." Nau suggested raising taxes in the budget presented immediately after the 1984 election; this was not done.

The impact on the international system of America's rising trade and budget deficits has been described as "the third shock," for it created as big a disequilibrium in the world's investment and savings as the two OPEC oil shocks of the 1970s (Marris, 1985: figure 1.8). The shock has affected the American economy too. The high interest rates required to finance the deficit kept the value of the dollar artificially high up to 1985. This priced many

250

American exports too high to sell abroad and imports were relatively cheap to Americans with overvalued dollars. In consequence, the trade balance reversed; the United States now runs the biggest trade deficit in world history. A portion of this deficit has been offset by selling American assets to foreigners. Whereas in 1980 Americans invested $13 billion more abroad than foreigners invested in the United States, by 1987 there was a $157 billion American deficit in international investment. Foreigners have been using their extra dollars to buy American assets, such as shares, real estate, and U.S. Treasury bonds, in anticipation of future earnings that can be withdrawn from the United States. As foreign loans to finance the federal deficit have increased, the annual interest paid by the U.S. government to foreign lenders has nearly doubled. The United States has become a much bigger debtor nation to the world than Mexico or Brazil.

Maintaining a high level of consumption in the United States depends on the continued support of Japan and Germany, the two nations capable of supplying credit on the scale that America now requires. As foreign debt and foreign investments rise, the cost of continuing as before rises. In its second term, the Reagan administration has recognized a need to internationalize America's economic problems. Official recognition that the United States no longer had the power to do what it liked with the dollar was given at the Plaza Hotel in New York on 22 September 1985 when the finance ministers of Germany, Japan, France, Britain, and the United States arrived at an agreement intended to bring about a gradual devaluation of the dollar against other currencies, in hopes that this would provide a "soft" rather than a "hard" landing for an American economy with global problems. The position was reaffirmed in a meeting at the Louvre in Paris in February 1987. Skeptics christened this a "Lourdes" agreement, on the grounds that only a miracle would prevent the troubles of the dollar from disrupting the world economy, especially the American economy (Funabashi, 1988).

Black Monday on Wall Street in October 1987 triggered worldwide falls in stock markets, an indication of the interdependence of national economies. It also triggered a massive fall in confidence in the dollar. The White House treated the problem as none of its responsibility, thus encouraging the dollar to fall further, a drop accelerated by the painfully slow process by which budget cuts were made to satisfy the requirements of the Gramm-Rudman Act for mandatory reductions in the federal deficit. Economic forecasters treated the fall in the value of the dollar as grounds for expecting a reduction in the trade deficit. But the fall also meant that foreign investors and central banks were suffering losses on sums loaned to the American government, loans that would be repaid in devalued dollars. This is likely to make foreigners less willing to finance public and private consumption by Americans, and raise the cost of financing the consumption that has marked the boom years of Reaganomics. A review of the Reagan administration's economic policies concludes:

Whatever the defense buildup has done to restore America's stature in the world, the nation is not standing tall among its trading partners. The United States may be winning the arms race but losing the economic marathon. (Sawhill, 1986: 106)

Toward American-Japanese Bigemony

The economic rise of Japan demonstrates how changes outside the United States can affect the Oval Office just as much as changes inside the United States. When John F. Kennedy was inaugurated President, there was no doubt that the United States was number one economically. America's gross national product per capita was more than double the average for advanced industrial nations, and six times that of Japan. Today, the two nations have economies that are nearly equal in GNP per capita; the critical element in comparisons is the exchange rate between the dollar and the yen. If one takes Inauguration Day 1989 rather than the date that Ronald Reagan entered office, the picture is much more favorable to Japan. Because Japan's economic growth has involved an enormous expansion of its exports to the United States, relations with Japan are of concern when going Washington and going public, as well as when going international.

Like it or not, America and Japan are yoked together, as American hegemony in the world economy is replaced by bigemony, that is, two nations exercising leadership in the international system. Like partners in a three-legged race, each nation might regard the other as a handicap, and prefer not to be joined as they are. But there is no way in which the two countries could break the relationship without a costly upheaval that would upset each nation—and also upset the international system.

From American Hegemony to Interdependent Bigemony

Japan's defeat by the United States in 1945 was the foundation of the postwar relationship between the two nations. American occupation authorities endorsed Article IX of Japan's postwar constitution, which contains an explicit prohibition against reconstituting a Japanese army. With the outbreak of the Korean war in 1950, the American occupation force became a shield protecting Japan (and indirectly the United States) from attack from Japan's close neighbors, China and the Soviet Union. Japan has made no attempt to form a large defense force; in 1976 the Japanese government imposed a ceiling of 1 percent of GNP on defense spending, and it mobilizes less than one-eighth the manpower of the United States in what is called its self-defense force (see table 12.4).

If an American President is anxious about the Soviet Union because it has a large military force notwithstanding the limitations of its economy,

Japan creates concern because it makes so little military effort by comparison to its economic strength. The fact that Japan spends only one-sixth the proportion of its national product on defense as does the United States is seen as an economic advantage to Japan and produces criticism in Washington that Japan is a "free rider" in the American-led and financed Western military alliance. For example, although much of Japan's oil supplies come from the Persian Gulf, Japan has been slow to contribute to the cost of Western naval patrols intended to maintain the free flow of oil from the war-torn Gulf in 1987 (cf. Mochizuki, 1987: 335ff; Olson and Zeckhauser, 1966).

TABLE 12.4

AMERICA AND JAPAN COMPARED IN RESOURCES

	United States	Japan	Japan as % of United States
Population	241 mn	121 mn	50
National Product	$4436 bn	$2379 bn	54
GNP per capita	$17,324	$16,136	93
Annual growth in GNP, 1980-86	3.0	3.6	120
Net savings as % GDP	2.5	18.4	643
Trade balance as % GDP	−3.3	+4.0	—
Yen/dollar exchange rate			
20 January 1981	—	202	—
20 January 1988	—	128	—
Defense expenditure			
Total	$275 bn	$ 19.5 bn	7
% GDP	6.6	1.0	15
Military manpower (000)	2,198	245	11

SOURCES: Principally OECD (1988). GNP for 1987 at current exchange rates.

Concurrently, the Japanese economy has grown enormously and Japan is now an economic superpower. In 1952 its GNP per capita was less than one-quarter the average for advanced industrial nations, and less than one-tenth that of the United States. By 1964, Japanese GNP was only half that of the average OECD nation, and one-quarter that of the United States. Japanese per capita income surpassed the OECD average in 1978. Today it contends with the United States for the claim to be the richest major industrial society in the world. If Japan continues to maintain a higher rate of economic growth than America in the next seven years, it will pull ahead of the United States in GNP per head. Because the population of Japan is half that of the United States, the total American national product will remain much greater for the foreseeable future. But Japan's population of 121 million people is double that of the largest European nation. Its GNP is thus the second largest in the OECD world, and also much greater than the Soviet Union.

The interdependence of the two countries is most evident in trade. Whereas major European countries such as Germany and Britain trade with a diversified range of countries, Japan's growth has been linked to a rapid and concentrated increase in exports to the United States. Japan's exports to the United States have not been balanced by an equivalent amount of imports; hence the United States runs a large trade deficit with Japan. In 1976 Japan exported $17 billion of goods to America and imported $10 billion, producing an American trade deficit with Japan of $7 billion. Today, America is running a trade deficit of about $150 billion a year, and Japan's trade surplus accounts for more than $50 billion of this sum. Viewed from Tokyo, the figures show that America is Japan's best customer, accounting for 40 percent of its exports. The moral is clear: "The Japanese need a healthy American economy as much as Americans do" (Packard, 1987: 353).

Japan can use the surplus dollars it earns to buy goods from third countries, such as Middle East oil exporters, or it can invest the dollars in the United States, buying government bonds that finance the federal deficit, starting up American branches of Japan-based companies, or buying American real estate, and shares. Given the size of its dollar surplus, Japan can and must do all these things. Japan now invests more than twice as much in America as America invests in Japan.

America and Japan today are economically interdependent. Wall Street must now operate on an around-the-clock basis, for the Tokyo Stock Exchange opens at 7 p.m. New York time. When dealers arrive in Wall Street in the morning, they want to be briefed about what happened in Tokyo while they slept. American consumers and Japanese workers are interdependent too. American consumers would face severe shortages in the absence of many familiar Japanese products, such as Sony radios or Toyota cars, and unemployment would soar in Japan if Americans lost their taste for these imported goods. If Japanese investors liquidated dollar holdings in order to convert them back into yen, they would suffer a loss because of the depreciation of the dollar against the yen. An unwillingness of Japanese investors to purchase U.S. government bonds would force Americans to finance a larger portion of the federal deficit by paying higher taxes and reducing personal consumption.

While Japan remains totally dependent on the United States for military defense, the economic relationship has been heading in the reverse direction. The federal deficit is no longer just a debt that we owe to ourselves; it is increasingly a debt that Americans owe to foreign nations, especially Japan. Together, the American public and private sector have net obligations of more than $400 billion compared with having had a credit balance of $141 billion as recently as 1981 (Peterson, 1987: 49). Gilpin concludes (1987: 314): "The third era of international finance came to a close in 1985. In that year the United States itself became a debtor, and Japan displaced it as the world's foremost creditor nation."

Adjusting to the Pacific Tilt

The President inaugurated in 1989 must look west, for the past quarter-century has seen a shift in the world economy from a trans-Atlantic to a trans-Pacific focus. When John F. Kennedy was inaugurated President, he looked to Europe, which, along with the United States, accounted for more than half the world's economy. Today, America, Japan, and other countries of the Pacific Basin, such as Taiwan, South Korea, Hong Kong, and Singapore, account for more than half the product of the world economy. Moreover, America's trade with Pacific Basin nations now exceeds its trade with European nations. As the only major industrial nation with both an Atlantic and a Pacific orientation, the United States is, in principle, well-positioned to take advantage of a Pacific tilt in the world economy (cf. Linder, 1986).

Many arguments can be advanced in favor of the advantages of American-Japanese interdependence in providing bigemonic leadership in the international system. Whatever their nationality, liberal economists endorse free trade. Japan's growth as a trading nation is deemed a benefit to the world economy, making it operate more efficiently and bringing better or cheaper goods to consumers. Political affinities between the two countries are considerable. Prime Minister Noboru Takeshita stresses *furosato*, or hometown politics. Like Congressman Tip O'Neill, the Japanese Prime Minister says that all politics are local, and his home district in Shimane prefecture now receives more government grants per head than any other district in Japan! The dominant Liberal Democratic party of Japan is similar to the Republican and Democratic parties in rejecting the socialist or social democratic mixed-economy welfare state (cf. Rose and Shiratori, 1986). While both civilizations have been much influenced by Europe, each stands outside it. Japanese society has imported modernity, and after its military defeat in 1945, looked to the United States as a model.

The increasing contacts arising from interdependence inevitably create frictions. Insofar as the White House was prepared for challenges to American hegemony, it expected this to come from Europe or the Soviet Union. Ignorance of Japan is one thing that a President shares with other powerholders in Washington, and with the American public as well. Congressmen whose constituents are said to be losing jobs because their firms cannot compete against Japanese imports engage in "Japan-bashing" and lobby to restrict Japanese imports to protect American industries (Destler et al., 1976; Destler, 1986). A former Reagan assistant, Richard Darman, offers an alternative diagnosis, blaming America's trade deficit with Japan on American business leaders being "bloated, risk-averse, inefficient and unimaginative" (quoted in Rowan, 1987). But Darman said this only after he left the White House. An American President cannot easily blame the country, and therefore himself, for relative economic decline without expecting to suffer political consequences.

Interdependence creates interests within the American political system supporting close ties across the Pacific. To a substantial extent, the Frostbelt versus Sunbelt division within the United States parallels the difference between a European and a Pacific orientation within the American economy. California, the nation's largest state, is preeminently oriented across the Pacific as both importer and exporter. Much trade is complementary, for example, the purchase of Japanese electronic components for American products. An estimated 30 percent of Japan's current exports are structurally linked to the production and marketing activities of American firms. Every member of Congress has Japanese car dealers in his district, and to remind him of this, one in five of all Washington lobbyists have Japanese clients (Calder, 1985: 603). The imposition of major tariffs on Japanese goods would raise the prices of many products, from TV sets to automobiles. The strength of free-trade sentiment in the White House is derived from the fact that no President wants to be accused of putting up the price of goods in the shop or preventing Americans from spending money as they like.

The Japanese are very conscious that their well-being is linked with that of the United States, but they are not certain about what to do with their newly acquired strength. Japan is increasingly turning attention to economic and political links with other nations in the Pacific, but it cannot escape from the fact that America is its biggest export market for its manufactures, and for its capital. Nor can Japan ignore the contribution that U.S. armed forces make to its military defense. Japan's present trade surplus of $90 billion a year is an unstable asset. The longer it continues the more there is the risk of "either Japan being shut out of the export markets on which it depends for its own growth or the weakening of some of the big industrial economies which are those markets. Either way, Japan loses; so would the rest of the world" (Maidment, 1987: 4).

As Japan becomes more important internationally, the Japanese Prime Minister learns the costs of being part of a system that is stronger than any one country. For Japan to reduce its surplus by importing more food sounds good to American farmers, but bad to Japanese farmers, who would be put out of work by more efficient American farmers. It sounds even worse to LDP members of Parliament who represent these farmers. To pay America more for Japan's defense might make sense to Washington, but it is open to criticism from nationalists within Japan.

One thing is certain: The Japanese government is much better equipped to deal with the United States than Washington is to deal with Japan. A Japanese-speaking American expert, George R. Packard (1987: 361f) explains this as the result of the proliferation of subgovernments without government:

In Washington, it is hard to discover a Japan policy. There is no part of the executive branch whose mission it is to oversee all aspects of the relationship.

...Today, a welter of intergovernmental working groups, task forces and coordinating bodies share bits of the action, but no one department or agency can be said to be in charge.

To this disarray one must add the growing power and interest of Congress, or more precisely, of individual members, committees and staff members concerned with particular aspects of the relationship. To this mix must also be added an ever-increasing army of lobbyists and special interest groups, some representing Japanese interests and some working for American corporations.

None of this is particularly new to Washington or unique to the U.S.-Japan relationship, but the result of all the tugging and pulling is that U.S. behavior toward Japan is eccentric, episodic and devoid of any long-term vision of where this important relationship should be headed and how it will get there. Japanese negotiators cannot be blamed for failing to understand or act upon American priorities, for no one can say at any moment what these priorities are.

Packard (1987: 362) contrasts Washington with Tokyo, where the authority of government in a parliamentary system and the accumulated Japanese expertise in dealing with the United States make Japan "better equipped to negotiate complex issues and manage the relationship according to an overall strategy."

In Washington, there is still debate about whether or not America should accept that it no longer has the hegemony it once enjoyed internationally. Experienced White House hands disagree. Peter G. Peterson (1987: 58) argues that no President can indefinitely pursue a military policy of "standing tall on bended knees." Herbert Stein, chairman of the CEA under President Nixon, views the process of adaptation calmly: "We will have to get used to living in a world in which we are no longer number one, or at least not number one by much." But Richard Darman, involved in the White House and Treasury under the Reagan Administration, takes the opposite view: "The day you accept being number two, psychologically you are on the way down" (quoted in Auerbach and Behr, 1987).

The White House in an Open Market

In an era of American hegemony other nations had the problem of being in bed with an elephant; today America has the problem of no longer being the only elephant in the bed. This is not a fatal condition, for most nations have enjoyed national security and economic prosperity without hegemonic power. The replacement of military concerns by economic problems can even be regarded as an indication of progress in achieving international security in a nuclear age. Just as the United States has learned that it can achieve national security without winning a shooting war with the Soviet Union, so it must learn how to conquer economic difficulties that cannot be blamed on a foreign enemy.

The political problem facing the postmodern President is to adjust the country's diplomatic, military, and economic policies to an international system in which the United States must sometimes follow instead of leading. The initial reaction of many Americans is a sense of estrangement from a world that is harder to predict or control—an attitude supporting a return to the isolationism of the traditional Presidency. But America can no longer isolate itself from the rest of the world. In the White House and at the work bench, in the office and at home, Americans are now part of an open international system. The decision to go international was made forty years ago—and there is no turning back now.

Washington as an Open Market for Policy

In a representative system of government, questions about what to do turn into the question: Who decides? While the President is the highest-ranking person in government, he has never had the authority of a Prime Minister in a parliamentary system. Instead, the Oval Office is only one among many institutions influencing America's place in the international system. The fragmentation of authority in the Washington marketplace rules out a policy of economic nationalism in which the state takes the lead in restructuring an economy to compete internationally. To take the lead in revitalizing the economy would require the President to have powers normal in parliamentary regimes from Stockholm to Tokyo but lacking in the United States.

When a foreign leader with sufficient authority to speak for the nation as a whole tries to negotiate with Washington, he or she often hears the sound of one hand clapping. An authoritative proposal by a foreign government may be met by American officials fumbling to respond with a gesture that will not be ignored or repudiated by the Oval Office, by Congress, or by conflict between the two. Watching the President and Congress wrangle about relatively small reductions in the budget deficit in autumn 1987, a British journalist concluded that the participants thought that America's financial problems were a national problem, not an international problem. The complementary mistake of foreign observers was "to clamor for something that it is peculiarly hard for Washington to deliver—international financial leadership" (Binyon, 1987).

Constitutional limitations are compounded by the President's inclination to ignore questions of economic policy, particularly international economic policy. Economic advisers find that their first task is to try to educate the President in basic economic relationships (cf. Hargrove and Morley, 1984). To do this, they must engage his interest. Most Presidents learn little about international economic policy because they do not want to bother. Even though President Nixon was in office during the critical period when the U.S. dollar was taken off the gold standard, White House tapes recorded him talking as follows during a 1972 briefing on a report of the White House Council on International Economic Policy:

I don't care about it. Nothing we can do about it. It's too complicated for me to get into [re: floating the British pound].

There ain't a vote in it. Only George Shultz and people like that think it's great [re: a trade quota measure].

I don't give an [expletive deleted] about the lira [report on Italian currency].

A President starts much lower on the learning curve of international economic policy than does a Prime Minister, and is likely to rise less high. At each change of administration, the turnover of White House personnel is so great that there is little of the institutional learning found in a parliamentary system, where civil service advisers continue in office from administration to administration. Most incoming advisers share the President's ignorance and lack of interest in international economic issues. For example, even though Henry Kissinger had been a Harvard colleague of many leading economists with Washington experience, he ignored international economic issues, confessing, "to put it mildly, it had not been a central field of study for me." He added ruefully: "Only later did I learn that the key economic policy decisions are not technical but political" (Kissinger, 1979: 950).

If events force a President to become interested in international economic policy, he can make a critical contribution to the development of a policy by emphasizing priorities or ruling some options out of bounds (Odell, 1982). For example, President Reagan has endorsed free trade, notwithstanding congressional pressures for protection, and he has set tax increases out of bounds, thus increasing American dependence on foreign borrowing. International economic policy is usually an orphan with no one in the White House looking after it. National security staff are concerned with military and diplomatic power, and CEA follows the President's lead in concentrating upon the domestic side of the economy. For example, the lengthy statistical appendix in Herbert Stein's (1984) informed review of *Presidential Economics* contains no reference to trade deficits, balance of payments problems, or foreign exchange rates of the dollar.

The problem of serving the President is not organizational but motivational. "Presidents are inclined to devote their time and energies to those areas where they have the greatest interest and where they feel they have the greatest opportunity to influence events" (Porter, 1982: 189). Hence, national security issues make first claim on the President's attention.

The President delegates investigating what should (or can) be done about international economic problems to agencies outside the White House. Typically, the secretary of the treasury is asked to look after the dollar, as international economic policy may be colloquially described. Up to a point the secretary of the treasury has no difficulty in doing this, for he has some familiarity with monetary policy, and the Treasury Department maintains a substantial staff of experts especially concerned with international economic policy. What the secretary of the treasury lacks is political authority. Unlike the representatives of other governments with whom he deals regularly, the American secretary of the treasury cannot be sure whether what he says to foreign governments will become government policy. A senior Treasury Department official concludes:

> In a world in which we are increasingly interdependent economically—in which most of the other top economic spokesmen are finance ministers who want to consult with and negotiate with their counterparts who have equal authority— the U.S. government is not really geared up to participate in that process. (Quoted in Campbell, 1983: 123)

Foreign governments incorporate experts in international economic policy at the top of government. A Prime Minister will see his treasury minister privately, as well as publicly, several times a week, and the two will keep close watch on the budget and the central bank, as well as fluctuations and trends in the international economy. Economic advisers of foreign governments also keep a close watch on what is happening in the American economy. Reflecting on his experience as CEA chairman in representing the White House at international meetings, Herbert Stein noted: "When I went to the OECD meetings in Paris, people from all the other countries seemed to know more about the United States than I knew about any of the other countries" (Hargrove and Morley, 1984).

A Market without Political Community

A political community is based on a long-term legal commitment to common action, whether or not in the immediate self-interest of every participant. The creation of the United States was a commitment by the thirteen colonies to create a political community. A group of people who simply meet together to exchange policies in pursuit of the self-interest of each constitutes a market, for they are bound by no common allegiance. International economic policy is today conducted in a market rather than a political community. Cooperation for mutual benefit *is* possible, but only when there are incentives to cooperate, and when each national government has the political resources to act in harmony with others.

The saga of summit meetings between the American President and the leaders of Britain, Canada, France, Germany, Italy, and Japan illustrates the extent and the limits of international consultation and cooperation. The modern Presidency was characterized by the pilgrimage of leaders of other nations to Washington (Plischke, 1986). The postmodern Presidency is characterized by the annual spring summit of leaders of the major advanced economies, at a meeting place that rotates between its seven member countries, symbolizing the fact that no one nation can dominate the international system today. The first summit meeting was called in 1975 in an attempt by national leaders to find common ground in responding to a severe world recession (Putnam and Bayne, 1987; Merlini, 1984).

Summits have been particularly valuable for an American President, who usually has not known his opposite numbers in other countries before taking office. By contrast, Prime Ministers in the European Community nations meet at least twice a year for collective discussion about Community policies. Before each summit meeting, there are preliminary discussions between representatives of the leaders, called *sherpas* after the native guides to the summit of Mount Everest. The sherpas prepare papers that focus on common concerns for discussion. Summit meetings can also be used for domestic political purposes. The White House press secretary will approach the summit as a grand opportunity for the President to go public, even if scoring points at home may sometimes offend foreign leaders.

While summit discussions focus on common concerns, the results are limited by the diversity of national interests. Each national leader brings to the summit particular concerns—and things that will not be discussed or conceded to other nations. The President takes a position on behalf of the United States and other leaders similarly take positions on behalf of their countries. Planners and participants are under no illusion that summit discussions reflect underlying policy agreements:

> You can't expect spectacular decisions from a meeting like that. It's naive to believe that that is possible.
>
> We are all convinced of the value of an international trading system, so there is some attempt to take the world view, but basically we are most concerned about our own domestic problems.
>
> Every nation goes there, first of all, to explain its own problems, and secondly, to see how far it can get others to help it with its own problems. (Quoted by Putnam, 1984: 52)

At a minimum, the annual summit provides consultation between national leaders on matters of international economic importance. Cooperation occurs when two or more countries each see it in their mutual interest to act. This form of cooperation is a weak ad hoc agreement, analogous to a transaction in a marketplace. The test of political community is the willingness of national leaders to coordinate policies, that is, "to make a significant modification of national policies in recognition of international economic interdependence" (Wallich, 1984: 85). Coordination may require two countries acting in opposite ways, for example, the United States cutting its budget deficit to reduce demand for foreign imports while Germany and Japan increase their deficits to stimulate demand for American exports (Putnam, forthcoming).

The communique from the 1987 Venice summit emphasized the desirability in principle of "economic policy coordination...essential to achieving stronger and sustained global growth, reduced external imbalances and more stable exchange rate relationships." While computer programs exist to model the coordination of the national economic policies of summit nations, political agreement is lacking (cf. Artis and Ostry, 1986: 68ff; Williamson and Miller, 1987). In practice, summit meetings emphasize that national political leaders normally put immediate national interests ahead of international policy coordination (cf. Pelkmans, 1984). Only in 1978 did a summit meeting produce a major act of policy coordination between the United States and another power, Germany. However, the circumstances could not easily be repeated—particularly as German politicians subsequently concluded that following American advice had caused inflation, and then recession, in Germany.

Whereas a generation ago the White House saw the United States as the engine of mankind, today it looks to Germany and Japan to be the locomotives of economic growth. President Reagan does not want to raise taxes to reduce the federal deficit. Instead, the Reagan administration wants Germany and Japan to increase their deficits in order to raise demand for American exports. But German and Japanese leaders do not want to take steps that they fear will import inflation or lead to a recession in their economies. In the absence of either American hegemony or a political community, German and Japanese leaders are under no obligation to do what the White House requests. As the President of the European Community, Jacques Delors, complained publicly just before the 1987 summit: "It seems the economically weaker the United States becomes, the more of a dominating position the Americans try to exercise over their Western partners."

Markets Clear—But at a Cost

The international economy can operate without positive leadership from the White House. Banks, multinational corporations, national and international traders, and major producers can simply carry on their business as normal. But markets are influenced by government policies. Government makes its presence felt by introducing what economists regard as imperfections in the marketplace. When so-called imperfections are purposeful political actions, they can bring benefits. But when an imperfection is a by-product of ignorance or neglect, costs are likely to rise.

An apparent imperfection in the international system today is that the system seems stronger than any President or Prime Minister; everywhere power is somewhere else. This is not a new experience for European nations or Japan, which for decades were subject to American hegemony. The present situation is novel only in America, as the postmodern President is unable to impose a solution on other nations. Following Black Monday on Wall Street in 1987, the British chancellor of the exchequer, Nigel Lawson, spoke for the leaders of many nations in announcing that they would be glad to cooperate with Washington—once there was evidence of positive action there.

The key requirement is to get talks going in the United States—to bring the administration and Congress together to work for a solution. When the administration has succeeded, then that will be the time to hold an international meeting.

It would be folly to rush into such a meeting now, before the Americans are in a position to announce their policy. The markets would just say "this is ridiculous," and that would be quite counter-productive in rebuilding market confidence.

The American end has to be solved first, and of course that is tricky, because any changes—reductions in spending, increases in taxation—have to be approved by Congress. So there has to be an agreement before the package is credible. If the administration were just to say, "This is what we propose," no one would have any idea whether they could achieve it. Until Congress is locked in to the deal, it will not have market credibility. (Quoted in Anderson, 1987)

Just as economists note that, sooner or later, markets clear, so political scientists can claim that, sooner or later, Washington deals with every problem facing the country. The question is not whether the system works, but at what price? While there is nothing new in American domestic politics holding the key to international affairs, what is new in the postmodern Presidency is the rising cost of inaction.

PART FOUR

Evaluation

13. How Popular Should a President Be?

A statesman is a dead politician.
—Harry S Truman

The paradox of democracy is that everyone is expected to accept how the country is governed but to disagree about who should govern. The President faces a dilemma: As head of state, he is President of all the people; but as an elected officeholder, he has the support of little more than half the voters. The President wants all Americans to support measures that he proposes for the country, but if he is to be more than a figurehead, pronouncing the views of the lowest common denominator of opinion, then any policies that he advocates are likely to divide Congress and the country. Anticipating the judgment of history, President Truman recognized that only after a politician is dead will the controversies that he stirred up be forgotten and his reputation as a statesman secured.

Only a constitutional monarch can hope for nearly unanimous approval by public opinion: abstention from policymaking is the price that a King or Queen pays for so positive an evaluation (Rose and Kavanagh, 1976). A Prime Minister who serves a monarch symbolizing unity does not seek popularity at the price of political irrelevance. A Prime Minister's aim is to enjoy 100 percent of the authority of government with 51 percent of the popular vote. By contrast, a President is always concerned with going public; in the Oval Office there is no such thing as too much popularity; a President can use nationwide popularity to influence other powerholders in Washington. In an era of frequent and widely reported public opinion polls, both the President and his critics are always aware of how popular or unpopular he is.

Whatever the President's current level of popularity, he always wants more, for the alternative to an increase in popularity is a fall. Politicians are concerned with trends; the uncertain result of the next election is as important as the last election. Whatever the absolute level of popularity registered by the latest poll, it makes a big difference whether it can be headlined as the President's popularity going up 4 percent, a sign of growing popularity, or going down 4 percent, evidence of growing unpopularity. In the course of a four-year term of office, a President must expect both ups and downs in popularity; a postwar President is about as likely to be defeated in a bid for reelection as to win endorsement twice. Prime Ministers too are frequently frustrated by the electorate when they seek reelection (cf. Rose and Mackie, 1983).

The difficulties that Presidents have in maintaining popularity have led some political scientists to argue that we have entered an era of the "no-win" Presidency or of presidential "insolvency." The President is insolvent if he cannot generate the support needed to discharge the responsibilities of his office (Berman, 1987: chap. 1). If a decline in presidential popularity is sure to follow after a postinauguration honeymoon, the President is in a no-win situation, incapable of effectively going public or going Washington (Light, 1982: chap. 9; cf. Brody, 1982). Both theories should be particularly applicable to the postmodern Presidency, which is vulnerable to shocks from abroad as well as to the erosion of domestic support.

One way to answer the question, How much is enough popularity? is to compare approval of successive Presidents with popular approval of Prime Ministers. While we cannot expect a President to be as popular as the Queen of England, we can expect a President to be as popular as a British Prime Minister. Therefore, the first section of this chapter compares postwar American Presidents and Prime Ministers in order to test whether any decline in popularity is a general feature of leadership today or is distinctive to Washington. The second section examines whether a high or low popularity rating is deserved, going up when the economy booms and political events are favorable, and going down when the economy turns down and events abroad and at home are unfavorable. The concluding section considers whether the shift from the traditional through the modern to the postmodern Presidency has created a long-term decline in great Presidents. The answer is a reassuring no.

How Much Approval?

Comparing popular approval of the President with popular approval of Prime Ministers can test whether or not there is a crisis of confidence distinctive to the United States. Insofar as the average President rates as high or higher than a Prime Minister, the person in the Oval Office is doing well. Insofar as both sets of politicians have a low or declining level of public approval, this implies that the cause of unpopularity is a general characteristic of advanced industrial nations. Insofar as the President is much more unpopular than leaders in other nations, this implies uniquely American causes, such as the Vietnam war and Watergate.

Comparing public opinion about the President with the British Prime Minister is appropriate, for in Britain, attention is centered on one place, Parliament, and the Prime Minister is the central figure in Parliament. While the Cabinet remains collectively responsible for government, increased media attention to Prime Ministers, intensified by Margaret Thatcher's personality, has led some British writers to allege that British politics is being "presidentialized" (King, 1985). Just as Presidents have varied in their popularity, so too have Prime Ministers. Mrs. Thatcher has won three straight elections since 1979, and Harold Wilson won three of his four campaigns, whereas Sir Alec Douglas-Home and James Callaghan lost the one election that each fought after taking office in the middle of a Parliament.

In both the United States and Britain, the respective Gallup poll organizations have asked similarly worded questions about the popularity of the nation's political leader for four decades since the end of World War II. We can thus compare the popularity of eight American Presidents since Harry Truman and the nine British Prime Ministers since Clement Attlee took office after the Labour party's 1945 victory. There is ample data to test whether the American public is as likely to approve its leader as is the British public. Trend data can answer the question: Is there a tendency for the popularity of leaders to decline because of the responsibilities of office, or does popularity fluctuate up and down as leaders change, or within one leader's term of office?

Presidents Are More Popular

Americans are readier to give popular approval to the President than Britons are to express satisfaction with the Prime Minister (see table 13.1). This is true for the most popular as well as for the least popular Presidents. A wartime hero such as General Dwight D. Eisenhower had an average approval rating of 65 percent in his Presidency; Sir Winston Churchill, the heroic leader in wartime Britain, averaged 52 percent approval in his postwar period in Downing Street. "Give 'em hell" Harry Truman was prepared to accept unpopularity in order to campaign for what he thought right; his average Gallup rating is the lowest for any postwar President, 43 percent. Margaret Thatcher is also prepared to reject consensus politics; her average rating is lower still, 40 percent.

There are very great differences in the way in which the public evaluates particular Presidents. John F. Kennedy averaged endorsement by 71 percent of Americans, a figure two-thirds higher than the average approval rating of Harry Truman. In Britain, Sir Anthony Eden, a polished diplomat, had a popularity rating 20 percent greater than that of Edward Heath, Britain's least popular postwar Prime Minister.

Overall, postwar Presidents have normally had the approval of 53 percent of Americans compared to 46 percent of Britons approving the Prime Minister. In both countries, the average figure is close to 50 percent, exactly what would be expected in a competitive party system in which electoral support swings between the party in office and the opposition. The President is not only elected by a majority vote but also keeps the approval of more than half the electorate for most of his term of office. The average British Prime

TABLE 13.1
POPULARITY OF PRESIDENTS AND BRITISH PRIME MINISTERS SINCE 1945

Leader, years in office	President (% approval)		Prime Minister (% satisfaction)	
	Average	High/low	Average	High/Low
John F. Kennedy, 1961-63	71	83 - 56	-	
Dwight D. Eisenhower, 1953-60	65	79 - 48	-	
Sir Anthony Eden, 1955-57	-		57	73 - 41
Lyndon B. Johnson, 1963-68	56	80 - 35	-	
Ronald Reagan, 1981-Dec. 1987	52	68 - 35	-	
Sir Winston Churchill, 1951-55	-		52	56 - 48
Harold Macmillan, 1957-63	-		51	79 - 30
Richard Nixon, 1969-74	49	67 - 24	-	
Gerald Ford, 1974-76	47	71 - 37	-	
Clement Attlee, 1945-51	-		47	66 - 37
Jimmy Carter, 1977-80	46	75 - 21	-	
Harold Wilson II, 1974-76	-		46	53 - 40
James Callaghan, 1976-79	-		46	59 - 33
Harold Wilson I, 1964-70	-		45	69 - 27
Sir Alec Douglas-Home, 1963-64	-		45	48 - 42
Harry Truman, 1945-52	43 -	87 - 23	-	
Margaret Thatcher, 1979-Dec. 1987	-		40	53 - 25
Edward Heath, 1970-74	-		37	45 - 31
Average	54	76 - 35	47	60 - 35

NOTE: In the United States the question is: *Do you approve or disapprove of the way in which ——— is handling his job as President?* In Britain: *Are you satisfied or dissatisfied with ——— as Prime Minister?*

SOURCE: Calculated by the author from publications of the Gallup poll, Princeton, N.J. and of the British Gallup poll, London. Two entries are given for Harold Wilson, since his time in office was interrupted by a period in opposition.

Minister is just short of popular approval by an absolute majority. Because of third party competition, no British party has gained more than half the popular vote since 1935. In the postwar era, the winning candidate for the Presidency has averaged 54 percent of the vote; the winning party in Britain has averaged 47 percent.

Although the personality of an individual politician is more or less constant, the popularity of a politician goes up *and* down during his or her term of office. Americans are much more fickle than the British in evaluating a national leader (see table 13.1). Succeeding to office following the death of Franklin D. Roosevelt, Harry Truman initially enjoyed the approval of 87 percent of the public. Subsequently, his rating fell to 23 percent during the darkest days of the Korean war. The public evaluation of President Carter swung greatly too. Near the start of his term of office Jimmy Carter had the approval of three-quarters of Americans, but by July 1980, less than one-quarter approved of Carter. The distance between the peak and trough of a President's approval averages 41 percent (see table 13.1). While a Prime Minister cannot match a President in scaling the peaks of popularity, neither does a British politician descend so far into the pit of unpopularity. The gap between the peak and pit for a Prime Minister averages 25 percent.*

If generalizations about the popularity of a leader were made at his peak of popularity, a President would appear a public hero. If generalizations focus on a President at the trough of his popularity, he looks unworthy. The media often seize upon current popularity ratings without regard for what was happening twelve months earlier, or what could occur in another year's time. For example, Ronald Reagan's big dip in popularity at the time of the Iran-*contra* affair was not his first fall; his popularity had also tumbled in 1982 with the advent of a big recession. Journalistic lack of perspective tends to subject politicians to hero or bum evaluations, highlighting each extreme in turn.

Evidence from other countries supports conclusions from American and British comparison. In the French Fifth Republic, public approval of leaders tends to be lower than of Presidents and to fluctuate up and down, as in Britain and America (cf. Lafay, 1981: 143; Hibbs and Vasilatos, 1981). The German public is less ready than Americans to invest big hopes in a popular leader, reacting against the cult of the leader (in German, *Fuehrer*) in Hitler's Third Reich. More than 40 percent of Germans said they were undecided when initially asked to evaluate the first postwar Federal Chancellor, Konrad Adenauer. The proportion without an opinion remains about one-quarter today. Because those expressing an opinion are fewer, usually less than half the German electorate positively endorses the Chancellor; those in favor usually outnumber critics.**

The evidence rejects the argument that the President is politically insolvent because of a deficit in public support. The President is usually approved by more than half the American people, and his rating is noticeably higher than that for Prime Ministers considered solvent by critics of the Presidency. The greater popularity of an American President and the greater stability of a British Prime Minister's public rating reflect three major causes. First, a Prime Minister is a symbol of party, whereas the President campaigns without emphasizing a party label. Partisanship limits the depth to which a

* Greater stability is also shown by the lower coefficient of variation for the monthly popularity rating of Prime Ministers; the median figure is 0.11. By contrast, the median, coefficient of variation for presidential popularity is nearly twice as high, 0.20.

**The key term in the standard German question refers to *einverstanden* (agreement) with the Chancellor, implying a policy and partisan judgment different from the more personal measure of approval used in America and Britain. Copious data on German public opinion are available in the Zentralarchiv, University of Cologne.

Prime Minister will fall, and also imposes a ceiling on popularity. Winston Churchill was less popular than Dwight D. Eisenhower because Churchill was perceived as the Conservative party leader by Labour and Liberal as well as Conservative voters, and supporters of the opposition parties are not so likely to approve of the governing party's leader. By contrast, most Americans have a weak party identification or see themselves as independents, and are thus readier to evaluate Presidents by their individual performance.

A second reason for greater stability is that before entering Downing Street, she or he has been in the public eye far longer than the average President. A party leader who has served as foreign secretary or chancellor of the exchequer is one of the best-known politicians in the country, speaking frequently in Parliament and on television (Rose, 1987b: table 4.2). An opposition leader has years of exposure on television, for public broadcasting authorities are obligated by law to balance reporting of the parties. By contrast, the out party in America has no leader. At the start of the primary season, most candidates are virtually unknown nationally. Jimmy Carter was greeted at the start of the primary campaign that won him the Presidency with the question: "Jimmy who?" The candidates for the Democratic nomination in 1988 were so little known that the press dubbed them the Seven Dwarfs.

A third reason why a President can be more popular is because he tries so much harder to court popularity. While a Prime Minister would prefer to be popular, this is not a necessary condition of remaining in office. Parliamentary party support is virtually certain, independent of the leader's standing in the opinion polls. By contrast, a President must always be going public in order to sustain his influence in Washington. When things go wrong in the American system, the President suffers more unpopularity because he is so much in the public eye. By contrast, when things go wrong in a parliamentary system, public opinion turns against the governing party.

Power without Popularity
Public opinion and the power of the Presidency are often discussed together because the President's ability to influence Washington is affected by his ability to persuade others. Popularity with the electorate is an important asset for a President dealing with other Washington officials who lack his media potential. But influence derived from popularity is much less secure than that conferred by institutions, for public opinion shows far greater fluctuations than institutions.

The authority of a Prime Minister is not diminished by lacking the approval of a majority of the voters, for in a parliamentary system power is derived from institutions of government. Victory at a general election gives the governing party a majority in Parliament, and this majority is virtually certain whatever the ups and downs of public opinion. The critical point is not the leader's popularity, but the governing party's popularity. Cabinet colleagues and MPs share with the Prime Minister a desire for the governing party to remain popular in order to secure their own reelection in a system in which elections depend on party competition, not personalities. A leader's personal standing influences very few votes at a British general election (Graetz and McAllister, 1987).

Governing is the first priority in a parliamentary system, and authority is concentrated in the governing party in order to insulate the government from fleeting changes in public mood. A British election is an infrequent event, whereas a President must be perpetually campaigning outside Washington in order to hold his own inside Washington. Because a Prime Minister has the power to choose the date of a general election, many ups and downs in the opinion polls can be taken in stride. For example, the government of Margaret Thatcher could trail the opposition in polls for most months of a Parliament and could still win reelection by choosing an election date when the governing party's popularity was high. Success in policy, rather than success in personal publicity, is the first priority. An opposition leader who concentrates on boosting his personal popularity—running a presidential-style campaign, as it is called in Britain—can expect little reward. In 1987 Labour leader Neil Kinnock, ran a personal campaign with American-style media sophistication and evasion of difficult policy questions. The Labour party received less than one-third of the popular vote.

Because a Prime Minister is assured of power without popularity, the government can embark on a series of measures that will be unpopular in the short run but that are expected to produce popular results in the medium term. In Britain, a governing party can use a general election victory as an opportunity to undertake actions which it knows will stir up immediate controversy but that it believes will be good for the country. It can plan ahead for several years, thanks to the security of its parliamentary majority.

The popularity that a President demonstrates by winning an election is only good for a short time in Washington. Within a year of an election, Congress, the agencies, and the media begin to look for fresh evidence of popularity. When the American electorate withdraws its approval of the President, he loses influence as well as popularity. In a parliamentary system, a fall in party popularity is a warning shot across the bow; in the American system, it is a direct hit, making it harder for the President to steer the ship of state.

When a President Should Be Unpopular

In a democracy, a President should always be unpopular with a portion of the electorate, for democracy is about the articulation of competing views concerning the government of the country. The *losing* candidates for the White House win an average of 46 percent of the popular vote. In three postwar elections with more than two candidates, the President won the election with a minority of the vote. Furthermore, people whose votes have elected a President have a right to change their minds when they see what happens in office. A slump in popularity warns the President that he is a short-term representative of the people, not a ruler for life. Only if voters change their minds from time to time will elections be truly competitive, alternating control of the White House. Moreover, a change in leadership can create the opportunity for new policy initiatives (cf. Bunce, 1981; Roeder, 1985; Rose, 1984b).

To err is human, and a President's humanity is demonstrated by political mistakes. The bigger the mistake, the more the media turn the tables on the White House. Instead of the President exploiting the media by going public, the media exploit the President by going White House in search of a story about White House blunders. Some things that make the President unpopular, such as a recession in the economy or inflation, cannot be dismissed as media events. Voters do not need to turn on the TV to find out if something is wrong with the economy; they can learn this at work or at a shopping center.

When people think there is something wrong with the way the country is being governed, then there is good reason for the President to be unpopular. Mistakes and misfortunes confirm the judgment of those who voted for his opponent and weaken the loyalty of those who supported him with reservations or have no ties to the President's party. Moreover, a President will not want to hoard popularity indefinitely; he will want to consume some of it promoting his political goals. A President who pushes measures that he deems important will lose some support by the resulting controversy (Kernell, 1986: 186). The critical point for a first-term President is to manage a high level of approval in his fourth year in office in order to have a good chance for reelection.

The no-win theory of the Presidency predicts a very different course of events: Every President is expected to undergo a substantial and steady decline in popularity because of fundamental defects in the American system of government. Paul Light (1982: chap. 9) argues that a President finds it difficult to achieve his policy goals because of the increasing obstacles placed before him by other powerholders in Washington. Moreover, the time when he can be most effective, just after inauguration, is when he is least capable of making wise choices about policy, because of inexperience in government. In order to achieve success in going Washington, a President will concentrate on securing short-term advantages. The crisis of the Presidency literature, sparked by the Vietnam war and further fueled by Watergate and the Iran-*contra* affair, is consistent with this no-win theory of the Presidency (cf. Caddell, 1979; Miller, 1979; Sundquist, 1980).

Whereas the conventional democratic theory of presidential unpopularity sees public attitudes toward the Oval Office going up as well as down, the no-win theory assumes that the President is always on the down escalator.

Moreover, no-win theories explain presidential unpopularity by reference to persisting characteristics unique to the American system rather than as a reflection of specific Oval Office shortcomings and mistakes. The complaints Light and others voice about Congress could not arise in a parliamentary system; thus the popularity of a Prime Minister should not show a decline in office.

No-Win Theory Loses

If a President is in a no-win situation, then we would expect public opinion data to show: (1) each President's popularity declining consistently during his term of office; (2) each President lacking the approval of a majority of the electorate for most of a term; (3) the downward trend so great that each President leaves office very unpopular; and (4) the decline in presidential popularity to be greater than that of Prime Ministers in parliamentary systems. The evidence of public opinion polls rejects each of these hypotheses.

1. The first hypothesis is rejected because there is no consistent trend in the popular assessment of a President. Although a President's popularity invariably falls from an initially high standing, it normally rises again. During a term of office, a President will undergo several up-and-down cycles of lesser or greater amplitude (see figure 13.1). When one looks at a graph of presidential approval since 1945, it resembles a mountain range full of peaks and valleys rather than a ski slope heading steadily down. The ups and downs in presidential popularity do not follow a simple mathematical formula; they reflect variable political influences. A President whose popularity has dipped down can recover by taking actions that the public judges successful, just as a President high in public esteem can fall abruptly.

The Reagan adminstration illustrates the ups and downs of a President, for Ronald Reagan is the first President in a generation to serve two terms in the White House without interruption (see figure 13.2). By comparison with many Presidents, Ronald Reagan did not enter office with a high rating in public opinion, winning only 50.7 percent of the popular vote in 1980; President Carter's unpopularity propelled him into the White House (Wattenberg, 1986). There was a great deal of skepticism among the electorate about Ronald Reagan's capacity for the Oval Office and the direction in which he wanted to lead. Television familiarity, boosted by sympathy after an assassination attempt, soon brought the President the approval of 68 percent of Americans. Shortly thereafter, his support started falling, going below 50 percent by the end of 1981 and dropping to 35 percent following the 1982 economic recession. Presidential popularity then started to climb with improvements in the economy, exceeding 50 percent at the start of 1984, an election year.

Following reelection in November 1984, popular views of the President again went down, and then rose again as the economy boomed. Just before

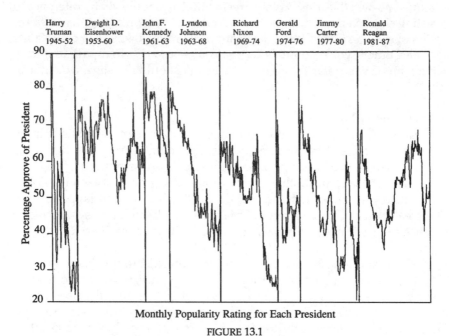

| Harry
Truman
1945-52 | Dwight D.
Eisenhower
1953-60 | John F.
Kennedy
1961-63 | Lyndon
Johnson
1963-68 | Richard
Nixon
1969-74 | Gerald
Ford
1974-76 | Jimmy
Carter
1977-80 | Ronald
Reagan
1981-87 |

Monthly Popularity Rating for Each President

FIGURE 13.1

UPS AND DOWNS IN THE POPULARITY OF AMERICAN PRESIDENTS SINCE 1945

SOURCE: Gallup poll, Princeton, N.J.

the news of the Iran-*contra* affair broke in autumn 1986, the President was approved by 63 percent of the electorate; his popularity registered a 16 percent drop in Gallup support in the following month, and fell to 40 percent after the release of the critical Tower Commission report. The continued boom in the economy and the conclusion of an arms-control agreement with Soviet leader Mikhail Gorbachev brought the President's rating above 50 percent by the end of 1987. The several recoveries in the President's popularity reject the no-win theory, which predicts a steady decline in popularity. Nor can the fluctuations be explained by personality factors, for President Reagan's character has been consistent. The changes reflect ups and downs in policies and events associated with the Presidency.

2. If a President is in a no-win position, he should be unpopular with a majority of the public for most of his time in office. Since there are tens of millions of Americans who do not vote, a President does not need approval by an absolute majority of the adult electorate. To win reelection, he needs a majority only among the 60 percent or less who actually turn out to vote. In 1980 Ronald Reagan was elected President with the support of less than 28 percent of the total electorate.

In fact, a President usually enjoys the approval of an absolute majority of Americans. For three-quarters of his time in office, a President is approved

276

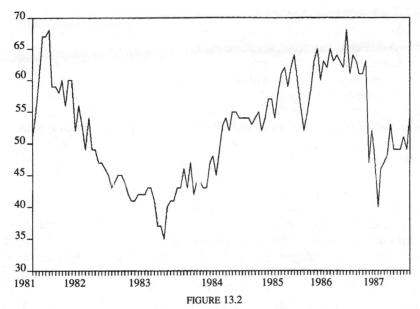

FIGURE 13.2

UPS AND DOWNS IN THE POPULARITY OF RONALD REAGAN

SOURCE: Gallup poll.

by more people than express disapproval. A President has actually had majority approval in every monthly Gallup poll on five different occasions: Dwight D. Eisenhower's two terms of office, John F. Kennedy's term, Lyndon Johnson's abbreviated first term, and the first term of Richard Nixon. While Presidents Jimmy Carter and Gerald Ford had their ups and downs, in three-quarters of the polls President Ford was endorsed by a majority, and in more than half President Carter had this support. Ronald Reagan has usually kept his popularity above the 50 percent mark too. Only twice has a President usually been unpopular in monthly polls; this happened to Harry Truman from 1949 to 1952, and in the truncated Watergate term of Richard Nixon.

3. As the President is endorsed by an average of 68 percent of the public in his first month in office, he can only go down from this peak. But the downward movement is not so much a repudiation of performance in office as it is an adjustment to reality. In the course of four years a President will show his faults as well as his strengths. Some actions that he takes will mobilize opposition from those who voted against him and will be disliked by some of his supporters. The changes result in the President's popularity being less high, but the ratings are more realistic, based on performance.

Most Presidents leave office enjoying majority approval in the Gallup poll. A President who is successful in winning a bid for reelection is sure to be popular; Dwight Eisenhower's rating stood at 79 percent at the end of his first term, and Lyndon Johnson at 69 percent after winning election in 1964.

277

Since the creation of the Gallup poll, only Presidents Nixon and Carter have left office with more people disapproving than approving. Gerald Ford, although defeated in his bid for reelection, still enjoyed the approval of more than half the electorate. On average, a President has the approval of 52 percent of the electorate at the end of his term of office.

4. Because the no-win theory emphasizes the use or abuse of congressional powers as a cause of White House popularity, the absence of an independent Congress should enable a leader in a parliamentary system to maintain a higher level of popularity throughout a term of office. In addition to having a very subordinate legislature, a Prime Minister also has at least three of the four resources that Light (1982: 225ff) recommends to make the Presidency "winnable": the ability to plan ahead, appoint experienced people to office, and receive expert policy advice.

In fact, Prime Ministers have just as much difficulty as a President in maintaining a consistently high level of popularity with their national electorate. Harold Wilson rose and fell sharply in public esteem several times, and Margaret Thatcher, too, has had her ups and downs (Butler and Butler, 1986: 254ff). A British Prime Minister does not expect or need to be continuously popular with the public. The strategic objective of a Prime Minister is to see that the governing party is more popular on the one day in every few years when a general election is held.

During a term of office, a British Prime Minister is less likely than a President to enjoy the endorsement of a majority of the electorate, and is often less popular than the leader of the opposition party in Parliament (Rose, 1980a: table 1.3). Because of a greater foundation of partisan support, no postwar British Prime Minister has left office, as much disliked by the public, as were Truman, Nixon, or Carter. Nevertheless, no Prime Minister, since Macmillan retired in 1963, has had Gallup poll approval by more than half the electorate for the majority of his or her period in office. Notwithstanding three successive election victories, Prime Minister Thatcher had the approval of half the electorate in only eight months during her nine years in office.

Accounting for Variations
The ups and downs of presidential popularity are multiple and the patterns diverse. Four different sets of influences affect the fluctuations in approval of the President: the logic of a four-year term; a core of partisan backing; economic conditions; and distinctive and usually unexpected events in the international system and at home.

1. *The logic of a four-year term.* A President enters office enjoying a honeymoon effect, for his popular approval is almost invariably greater than the share of the votes won in the election that takes him to the White House. The extent of the boost can be substantial; for example, John F. Kennedy was elected with less than half the popular vote in 1960, but as soon as he became

President, his rating in the Gallup poll rose to 72 percent. In the postwar period, a President has received an average boost of 14 percent in his approval rating in the immediate aftermath of election victory.

Before the Vietnam war and Watergate, David Sears (1968:424ff) argued that there is a "positivity" bias in popular views of public figures, that is, an inclination to express positive views of people who occupy important public positions. If this were so, then the bonus in public approval that a President enjoys on entering the White House would remain with him throughout his term of office. But this is not the case. At some point in his term of office, the President's popularity will decline well below the share of the vote that won him election. The boost that a President enjoys on entering office is a short-term boost, not a permanent addition of support, lasting as long as he is in the Oval Office.

One explanation for loss of popularity is that during an election campaign, the winner builds a broad coalition of support, encouraging many different groups to believe that he will do what they want (Mueller, 1973). Problems of government result in the President's having to disappoint some of his supporters, as he cannot command the political and economic resources to give everybody what they want. If a candidate raises contradictory expectations among supporters during a campaign, then postelection approval is bound to fall as actions taken in the White House resolve contradictions to the dissatisfaction of some supporters.

The logic of Mueller's theory of declining popularity is partially substantiated by the evidence. Since a new President enters office on a high, he is very likely to go down from there. But a decline in popularity from a momentary peak is not evidence of a loss of confidence by the American people. Statistically, it is no more than a statement that abnormally high support will subsequently regress to the mean. Furthermore, Mueller does not allow for the conditions in which a President can increase his support by restoring his coalition or building a new coalition.

2. *A core of loyal partisans.* Even in an era of declining partisanship, some voters will always support a President on the basis of "my party, right or wrong." One big difference between the winner and loser in an election is that the winner can continue to mobilize party support from the White House, as the party's standard-bearer. By contrast, the loser often fades from view because he is a failed standard-bearer. In a parliamentary system, the opposition party leader can regularly challenge the Prime Minister in Parliament and can benefit from appearing as the alternative Prime Minister. The President however does not have to compete with an active and ambitious opposition leader.

A President on average enjoys the approval of 74 percent of those who identify with his party, 53 percent of independents, and 38 percent of those who identify with the opposing party (Kernell, 1986: table 7.3). It is difficult for a President to boost further the already high popularity that he has among the minority of the electorate who identify with his party. Increased support is more likely to be gained by boosting approval among independents, and decreasing criticism from those identifying with the opposition party.

Party identification affects whether voters give the President a favorable or unfavorable first hearing, but partisans as well as independents change their views about the President during his term of office (Edwards, 1983: table 6.1). A President who wants to keep majority support does not have to target his appeal at a single partisan group; he is most likely to remain popular if he does what is approved by both partisan and nonpartisan voters. While differences in approval are substantial between loyal Democrats, independents, and loyal Republicans, opinion in all three groups tends to change in response to the same sorts of influences. When President Richard Nixon's popularity went down among Democrats because of Watergate, it also went down among Republicans and Independents, and when Jimmy Carter's approval went down among Republicans, it also went down among Democrats.

3. *Economic conditions.* Although few American voters are economic determinists in the Marxist sense, voters can hold the President responsible for the state of the economy and alter their opinion of the White House with fluctuations in the economy. We would expect approval of the President to rise when inflation and unemployment fall, and approval to fall when economic conditions worsen. As the international system increasingly influences the American economy, a postmodern President is more and more subject to economic changes beyond the control of Washington.

The influence of the economy on the President's popularity can occur in a number of ways. Inflation, unemployment, and economic growth are each significant indicators of the conditions of the national economy, but they need not be of equal influence on the opinions of electors. The benefits of economic growth and the anxieties of inflation are likely to be widespread, whereas the impact of unemployment tends to be concentrated. Voters can define their political interests narrowly in terms of personal income or form political judgments reflecting conditions in the national economy (cf. Kinder and Kiewiet, 1981; Kiewiet, 1983). A presidential candidate asks to be judged on pledges for future action, but this can be qualified by his party's performance in the past. An incumbent in the White House will run on his past record if it is good; if it is unfavorable, an incumbent will emphasize promises for the future and will attack the alleged incompetence of opponents.

Studies of presidential popularity usually conclude that in one or another way, the economy exerts some influence on presidential popularity. Studies also find that the influence is limited (see, e.g., Monroe, 1984; Edwards, 1983: 226ff; MacKuen, 1983; Kernell, 1986: 203; Alt and Chrystal, 1983: chap. 7). To some extent and under certain circumstances, such economic conditions as inflation, unemployment or economic growth affect a President's popularity. People think about the well-being of the national economy as well as their own pocketbook. Retrospective judgments of a President's record can be important when an election offers a chance to choose between candidates or parties with established and different records. A variety of economic influences also exert some influence on the popularity of Prime Ministers (cf. Paldam, 1981; Whiteley, 1980; Hibbs and Fassbender, 1981). Because the links are contingent, we must consider the specifics of the political situation before concluding that economic influences determine the outcome of a particular election.

4. *Political events*. Although it sounds obvious to say that political events influence presidential popularity, the point can easily be overlooked in writings that concentrate solely on a President's personality, party loyalties, or economic determinants. Major political events, whether foreign or domestic, positive or unwelcome, immediately claim the attention of the President and of the electorate. A statistical analysis by Michael MacKuen (1983) of the effect of economic conditions and political events on presidential popularity from Johnson through Carter, concludes that inflation, unemployment and political events are each significant and substantial influences on the popularity of a President; together they explain about three-quarters of the fluctuations in the popularity of the President (see also Ostrom and Simon, 1985).

Unlike economic conditions, which are continuing and often change slowly, political events can make an immediate and unexpected impact; the effect of a political event also declines with each month that passes. Just as media people tend to forget yesterday's news, so the public soon forgets many events that had some impact when first headlined. The longer a President remains in office, the harder it is for any particular event to alter substantially, judgments formed by a host of previous events and experiences of a President. Of eighty-six varied events salient to the White House over a seventeen-year period, MacKuen (1983: table 1) found that nearly two-thirds had less than a 5 percent immediate impact on presidential popularity. International events such as Soviet invasions of Czechoslovakia and Afghanistan had little effect upon popular views of the White House, and the same was true of such domestic events as President Carter's address to Congress describing energy as a problem equivalent to war.

The involvement of the modern and the postmodern Presidency in the international system has been paralleled by events abroad becoming a major influence on the President's success in going public. Eighteen of the thirty events that changed the public's view of the President, by at least 5 percent in a month were international events (see table 13.2). In the Johnson and Nixon Presidencies, events in Vietnam were particularly important; the Carter Presidency was particularly affected by Iran. President Reagan's Presidency has not been marked by a major shooting war, but it has faced recurrent problems in the Middle East and in Central America. Of the international events having a major impact on public opinion, more than

TABLE 13. 2

IMPACT OF EVENTS ON PRESIDENTIAL POPULARITY

	Type	Immediate impact on popularity in percent
Johnson		
Great Society speech	Domestic	5.8
Intervene, Dominican Republic	Foreign	7.0
Gallbladder operation	Personal	5.8
Escalates Vietnam war	Foreign	6.4
Urban riots	Domestic	−6.6
Glassboro summit	Foreign	8.3
Nonproliferation weapons treaty	Foreign	7.4
Christmas message from Vietnam	Foreign	5.1
Pueblo ship seized	Foreign	−6.8
Nixon		
Midway meeting about Vietnam	Foreign	−7.9
Silent majority speech	Foreign	11.8
Invasion of Laos	Foreign	−6.7
Mining Haiphong	Foreign	5.1
Return to bombing Hanoi	Foreign	−10.4
Vietnam peace announcement	Foreign	15.3
Price freezes	Domestic	−5.3
Vice-President Agnew resigns	Scandal	−6.2
John Dean Watergate testimony	Scandal	−6.4
Watergate[a]	Scandal	−24.5
Ford		
Nixon pardon	Domestic	−8.0
Tax cut proposal	Domestic	7.0
Mayaguez ship rescue	Foreign	12.9
Captures Republic nomination	Domestic	6.6
Carter		
Bert Lance hearings	Scandal	−9.4
Panama Canal Treaty signed	Foreign	−8.7
Camp David peace treaty	Foreign	11.7
National malaise speech	Domestic	8.9
Iran embassy takeover	Foreign	6.6
Permits Shah to enter United States	Foreign	11.4
Failed hostage rescue mission	Foreign	10.1

a. Cumulative impact of Watergate over 17 months
SOURCE: Adapted by the author from MacKuen (1983), table 1.

two-thirds boosted the President's popularity. This is true of successful military actions (President Ford's role in rescuing the *Mayaguez*, popularity up 12.9 percent); peaceful initiatives (President Nixon announcing the end of the Vietnam war, up 15.3 percent); and cases of international adversity (President Carter's involvement in the Iranian hostages ordeal, popularity up 6.6 percent on seizure of hostages). A President cannot be confident that military action will necessarily produce a boost in public approval, as demonstrated by the Vietnam war, for President Nixon's popularity went down 10.4 percent after the bombing of Hanoi.

The American people view international events more in terms of national interests than immediate personal interests. People do not need a direct personal link between international events and their own or their family's well-being, to be influenced by what happens abroad. For example, families with a member serving in Vietnam had virtually the same view of events there as those without this personal contact with the war (Edwards, 1983: 236).

Domestic events are as likely to contribute to a President's unpopularity as give him a boost. This is most evident when a scandal breaks out involving the White House, such as President Carter's unsuccessful backing of Bert Lance for the directorship of OMB while Lance's financial dealings were being publicly criticized, or Vice-President Agnew's resigning because of corruption charges. Watergate is the event that has had the greatest recorded impact on popularity, depressing President Nixon's popularity by 24 percent over a period of seventeen months. In view of the great effort invested by the President and White House staff in preparing domestic policy initiatives, it is striking that only once every few years will a domestic political event alter the President's popularity substantially. President Carter's popularity went up 8.9 percent after his national malaise speech, and President Nixon's went down 5.3 percent after the imposition of price controls. In seventeen years, only one personal event, President Johnson's gallbladder operation, had a major impact on public opinion.

No Long-Term Decline

Understanding the conditions that make a President unpopular is important in order to avoid the mistake of inferring that just because the President has made a bad mistake there is a long-term decline in popular confidence in the Presidency and in American political institutions. The evidence shows that the ups and downs of postwar Presidents are not signs of a long-term decline in the Presidency or in American government as an institution.

The Myth of a Golden Age

The Presidency has changed enormously in two centuries, but there has been no decline from a Golden Age of great Presidents. The traditional role of the Presidency was not intended to attract great men. Most nineteenth-century occupants of the White House were "postage-stamp" Presidents; having their portrait placed on a stamp was their main lasting achievement and the space occupied in the history books, by such Presidents, has been of postage-stamp size. The rise of the modern Presidency created the expectation that a President would be an active leader. Even though the postmodern President is less powerful internationally, he is far more important to the nation than the President was at the beginning of the twentieth century.

When historians are asked to rank all the country's Presidents according to their performance in office, scholars are as ready to give a high place to such twentieth-century Presidents as Franklin D. Roosevelt, Theodore Roosevelt, and Woodrow Wilson as to Presidents of earlier eras, such as George Washington, Thomas Jefferson, and Abraham Lincoln (see figure 13.3). The past has seen weak or discredited Presidents, such as Benjamin Harrison and Ulysses S. Grant, and so too, has this century, in Warren Harding and Calvin Coolidge. The correlation between the recency of a President and whether historians rate him high or low is statistically insignificant, 0.17.

Rankings by historians and public opinion polls reject the idea of a long-term postwar decline in public approval of Presidents. Public approval of Presidents tended to rise for two decades, from Truman through John F. Kennedy. Presidents since then have been less popular, but it is misleading to interpret this as a long-term decline in public confidence. If a President errs in office, the electorate has the democratic right to withdraw approval. For example, President Johnson campaigned in 1964 as a man who would secure peace. When Johnson ordered an escalation in the Vietnam war, it was reasonable for peace-loving voters to withdraw their approval. Similarly, Richard Nixon campaigned in 1972 as a proponent of law and order. After his Vice-President resigned when facing corruption charges and Nixon himself was found to be lying about his part in the Watergate cover-up, it was reasonable for law-abiding voters to withdraw their approval.

The Reagan Presidency is particularly important in demonstrating that a postmodern President can successfully go public and make use of personal popularity in going Washington and going international. In his years in office President Reagan has averaged approval by more than half the American people. While Reagan has not reached the height in popularity of Kennedy and Eisenhower, neither has he fallen to the depths of Carter or Nixon. The ups and downs in President Reagan's popularity have reflected events and economic conditions in his terms of office. Reagan shows that there is no inevitable decline in the popularity of a postmodern President, just as Carter demonstrated that the Rose Garden strategy of looking presidential could not sustain the popularity of a President held responsible for undesirable conditions.

If a President is associated with popular events and favorable economic conditions, then his popularity should and does go up. If a President is

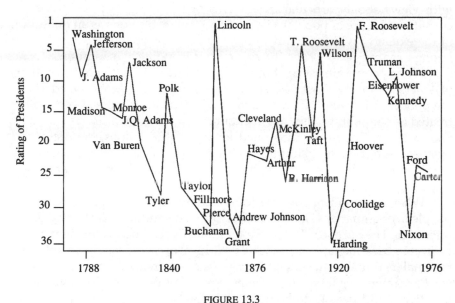

FIGURE 13.3

HISTORIANS TRACE THE UPS AND DOWNS OF PRESIDENTS

SOURCE: Rankings by 846 American historians surveyed by Murray and Blessing (1983), 540.

associated with unpopular events and unfavorable economic conditions, then his popularity should and does go down. A President may plead that the country's difficulties are not his fault, but this is inconsistent with the President's taking credit for good news for which he may not be responsible. Many of the most damaging events, such as the Vietnam war or Watergate, are measures for which the President is very much responsible. The conclusion is clear; insofar as a President is not as popular as he would like, *"the shortfall is one of competence rather than confidence"* (Sigelman, 1982: 257, italics added).

Blame the Man, Not the Institution

In any system of government, it is easy to confuse individuals and institutions. When we look at the White House, we see not only the Presidency as an institution but also a particular person in office, such as Ronald Reagan or Jimmy Carter. There is a fundamental difference between the institution and the individual. Whereas every President is a transitory occupant of the White House, the institution endures.

Does the unpopularity of a particular President, at a particular moment in American history, represent widespread popular dissatisfaction with America's political institutions? We cannot ask people to evaluate the Presidency as an institution because such evaluations are inevitably confused with views about particular incumbents of the office. We can, however, consider evidence of popular views of political institutions as an indication of the extent to which the difficulties of recent Presidents are matched by strong negative feelings about America and its political institutions.

When people are asked about their confidence in different institutions of American society, those that receive the highest ratings—the armed forces, the police, and the education system—are public institutions. Even if often treated as nonpolitical, they are maintained by public laws and financed by tax revenues. The institutions rated lowest—labor unions, the press, and business—are private institutions. This is bad news for businessmen and media writers who like to attack the government as lacking popular respect (Lipset and Schneider, 1983).

When the confidence of Americans is compared with the confidence that people in other nations show in their national institutions, the United States rates high. The European Values System Study asked people in many European countries and Japan to indicate their level of confidence in ten different national institutions: the armed forces, police, church, education, civil service, Parliament, legal system, business, press, and unions. No comparative question could be asked about the President and Prime Ministers, since Parliament normally symbolizes democratic government outside the United States. On average, 59 percent of Americans expressed confidence in major institutions of society; this was the highest of any country surveyed (Rose, 1984a: table 6.4; Parisot, 1988: 18).

In a book that concentrates attention on the White House, it is easy to forget a fundamental feature of public opinion: Most people do not see the President playing a big role in their lives. When things go wrong in Washington, as is sure to happen from time to time, the news is not personally disturbing, for Americans do not look to the President or Congress to see to their personal concerns. Personal problems are not politicized. Most people do not believe that government is responsible for solving problems that they face in everyday life. Whereas a presidential race is of dramatic importance to those involved in the campaign, the lives of ordinary people tend to be insulated from such media events (cf. Brody and Sniderman, 1977; Sniderman and Brody, 1977; Rose, 1980c).

When disapproval is directed at the White House, as inevitably happens from time to time, it does not represent popular rejection of political institutions. Equally, a rise in approval, such as that registered in the honeymoon period of a newly inaugurated President, is not a sign of a big shift in popular evaluations of the American system as a whole. After a careful evaluation of mass opinion data, Citrin and Green (1986: 453) conclude: "The level of political trust among citizens is more a function of what government does than a constraint on what it can do." A President who wants to be popular must earn his popularity by his performance in office.

14. As the World Closes In

Foreign relations begins at home
—Richard E. Neustadt

Political leaders must be judged in relative, not absolute, terms. A traditional President could succeed in his symbolic office simply by being white, male, and Protestant. The postmodern President must meet much more demanding standards. Responsiveness to the electorate is a necessary condition of going public, and responsiveness to Congress is necessary for success in going Washington. As the world closes in on the White House, the President must also be successful when there are pressures to put the international system first.

The proposition "Foreign relations begins at home" is true for every nation. As long as America was the only elephant in the international system, the President could be confident of being effective abroad. In a world without hegemony, however, other nations do not have to follow the White House. When American actions are in harmony with the interests of allies, unity is assured. But when America appears to be backing a losing cause, then allies can distance themselves from U.S. policy. Given the choice between losing money by following White House exhortations or making money by speculating against the dollar, foreign banks and corporations would prefer to profit at America's expense.

To avoid basing policies on misperceptions, a national leader needs to understand how other major nations perceive the world. This is particularly important for the President, who is usually a latecomer in dealing with foreign nations. Unless the President develops the gift of seeing America as others see us, he is in danger of projecting on to everyone—Margaret Thatcher, Mikhail Gorbachev, and the Speaker of the Iranian Majlis—the psychology and political outlook of a Washington newshound, a member of Congress, or a Pentagon official. The fact that so much diplomatic business is now conducted in English may encourage the President to believe that people who speak the same language will also see the world through Oval Office spectacles. This is not the case: "What seems cockeyed from abroad is rational when viewed in terms of home" (Neustadt, 1970: 61).

At the start of the third century of the United States, there is a need to adapt the way we look at American government. A century ago, Woodrow

Wilson rejected as unnatural the idea of a political system remaining static because of a mechanical set of checks and balances: "Government is not a machine but a living thing. It is modified by its environment, necessitated by its tasks, shaped to its functions by the sheer pressure of life" (quoted in Tulis, 1987: 121). By contributing to the development of the modern Presidency, Wilson demonstrated that the Constitution is not static.

As the world closes in on the White House, the challenge is to create an effective postmodern Presidency. The President inaugurated on 20 January 1989 will find that interdependence has replaced independence. This chapter's first section explains why a change of faces in the Oval Office will not change the problems that confront a postmodern President. The legacy of the Reagan administration includes budget and trade deficits that have made the dollar a global problem. When dealing with problems in the international system, a new President faces a great asymmetry: Other nations understand what the White House is doing better than the United States understands what the rest of the world is doing. Moreover, foreigners who have no vote in American elections judge the President by how effectiv̧e he is in the international system. The conclusion considers alternative ways in which the postmodern Presidency can address the problems that face us in a century of global interdependence.

After Reagan

After Ronald Reagan leaves the White House, most of American government will go on as before. Washington in the 1990s will reflect the abiding legacy of the past. Institutions ordained in the Constitution limit how a postmodern President can respond to pressures in the international system. The force of political inertia carries forward every public policy ordained by law, organized by federal agencies, and supported by congressional appropriations. Political inertia also carries forward obligations to pay foreigners interest on hundreds of billions of dollars borrowed from abroad to finance Reaganomics. A new President hopes that his personality and ideas will be strong enough to make changes, but a new President can no more repudiate the legacy of past government commitments, for example, treaties with allies and with the Soviet Union, than a young adult can ignore the influences of family upbringing.

Institutions: Not Much Room for Maneuver

An incoming President must work with institutions that are at hand. The American Constitution has survived for two centuries while every other major power in the world has had major upheavals affecting its territory and system of government. The survival of the American Constitution is proof of the durable genius of the Founding Fathers. It is also proof of the adaptability of its institutions to a world that the Founding Fathers never foresaw. As Reinhold Niebuhr has emphasized, the strategic problem has been to distinguish between features of government that can, and should be, changed and those that must be accepted as given.

A Constitution with a great history can nonetheless have contemporary shortcomings. Criticisms are sometimes faulty because the diagnosis and prescription for cure are superficial, or alternatively, because proposals for change are so fundamental that their prescriptions are not practical politics. Many proposals for constitutional amendment are oversold as a quick technological fix or are irrelevant to the central problems of the postmodern Presidency. A single institutional change, for example, the replacement of the electoral college by the direct popular election of the President, is unlikely to have much impact on the nation's economy or on foreign nations. Why should the General Secretary of the Communist party of the Soviet Union, the Ayatollah Khomeini, or the Japanese Prime Minister alter his nation's foreign policy simply because the electoral college is abolished?

Fundamental criticisms raise serious issues—but not always in ways that are convincing. For example, former White House Counsel Lloyd Cutler (1980: 32) declares: "In parliamentary terms, one might say that under the U.S. Constitution it is not now feasible to form a government." The charge ignores the fact that in the eighteenth century, Parliament was meant to act as a check on the authority of an overmighty monarch, and Congress was assigned this role in the American Constitution, a role that it still plays. The fact that the parliamentary system has changed, so that Parliament is now usually a rubber stamp in the hands of a Prime Minister and Cabinet, is not an argument for changing the American system. In Britain, some politicians and scholars argue that Parliament should become a stronger check on the executive, as Congress is in the United States.

Constitutional amendments are proposed to make the American system resemble more closely a parliamentary system, for example, by electing Congress and the President with a single vote, allowing the President to speak in Congress or allowing members of Congress to serve in the President's Cabinet (Sundquist, 1986; Robinson, 1985, 1987). The intent is to give more power to the President and make the man in the White House more like a British Prime Minister, or even a Gaullist French President. Yet there remain grounds of principle for defending the separation of powers. In the words of professor James Q. Wilson (1987: 51), "It helps preserve liberty and it slows the pace of political change." A lot of ordinary Americans think it is a good thing to maintain checks on the powers of the executive branch. After reviewing a host of surveys about public opinion regarding constitutional amendments, Austin Ranney (1985: 287) concludes that there is popular support for "proposals intended to limit the reach and power of the national government in one way or another."

There are also practical arguments against expecting a major constitutional amendment. An amendment to the Constitution requires the endorsement of two-thirds of both Houses of Congress and three-quarters of the states. It is hardly conceivable that the great majority of members of Congress would willingly vote to reduce their independence in voting on White House proposals or have their electoral fate decided by the election of the President. While constitutional amendments have been proposed at the rate of more than 200 a year in the postwar era, less than 1 in 2000 is adopted. Controversial amendments can easily be blocked by the cumbersome amendment procedures. Even if a parliamentary system were introduced, there is no guarantee that it would produce disciplined party government, as its proponents desire. This would occur only if a two-party system remained in place. In fact, parliamentary elections in America could easily produce a three, four, or five-party system, like the broken-back parliamentary systems of Denmark, the Netherlands, or Belgium, characterized by endless haggling between parties about the terms of short-lived coalition governments. In such circumstances the occupant of the White House would be a broker of interparty coalitions, like leaders in the House and Senate today.

Major changes in American government have occurred without constitutional amendment, including the evolution of the modern and postmodern Presidencies. Changes in the conduct and rules of parties would contribute to the strengthening of political authority, and thus to the Presidency. Changes in Congress, such as strengthening its leadership sufficiently to prepare alternative policies or bargain with the White House, would go a long way to reduce the present fragmentation of authority in Washington. Every reformer of the American system has plenty of suggestions to make about changes within the existing Constitution. None of these proposals, however will do much for the next incumbent of the White House; he must work the system as it is.

Unfinished Business in the Oval Office

People change but problems persist. Just as Ronald Reagan inherited unfinished business from President Carter, so his successor inherits a mixture of assets and liabilities from President Reagan. The new President can leave to future historians the task of assessing Reagan's contribution to American history; he is more interested in what to do next. In response to the immediate imperatives to go international, the first thing a new President sees are the footprints and thumbprints of his predecessor.

One thing is certain: An incoming President will inherit a massive military establishment in 1989, claiming twice as much money as the defense budget left behind by Reagan's predecessor. Even more important, the incoming President inherits a series of multiyear commitments to the development of new weapons systems. Because of contractual obligations, these commitments can be canceled only after additional expenditure, and often after spending political capital as well. The most prominent and problematic of new defense plans, the Strategic Defense Initiative ("Star Wars"), has been a favorite of President Reagan and is therefore a particular challenge to anyone wanting to be a new broom in the White House.

The need for military defense depends on the definition of potential threats to America's national security. This is much more problematic today than in the cold-war era. The Soviet Union no longer stands as America's public enemy Number One. The 1987 arms accord with the Soviet Union was not a big step in itself, but it is big in its implications, raising expectations of further progress in arms control. A new President will be expected to make progress toward reducing threats of war, while maintaining the country's security in a balance of power with the Soviet Union. Arms-control negotiations with the Soviet Union are a prime example of interdependence; success for the White House depends on success for the Kremlin, and vice versa. While President Reagan demonstrated the advantages that could be gained by concluding an agreement in 1987, President Jimmy Carter learned about the risks of negotiating with the Soviet Union. The 1979 SALT-II (Strategic Arms Limitation) treaty was never approved by the Senate, whose doubts of Soviet intentions were confirmed by the Soviet invasion of Afghanistan.

In the Middle East and Central America, a new President will inherit a relatively well defined position: The United States has made enemies of regimes in Iran and Nicaragua. A new President may want to turn over a new leaf in troublespots where United States policy has yet to achieve its long-term aims. But will Iranians want to trust the emissaries of a White House in which one part of the President's staff does not always tell others what it is doing? Will either *Contra* rebels or the Sandinista government want to trust a government where Congress adopts one policy for Nicaragua and the White House pursues another? America's allies in NATO and Japan have reasons to be anxious too about the future contribution of the United States to mutual defense.

Even before taking the oath of office, the President-elect will be confronted with the unfinished business of Reaganomics. Financial markets in London, Wall Street, and Tokyo will react to the election result, starting at 4 a.m. New York time, the morning after, when the London market opens. As soon as the President-elect has enjoyed reading the election returns, he must begin to face far less attractive figures in the economic forecasts that shape the budget message, due a few weeks after inauguration (Rose, 1988). The two big problems that he will inherit are the federal deficit and the trade deficit, and the problems are cumulative.

Federal deficits are nothing new, but the size and scale of the Reagan deficits constitute a novel (and unwanted) inheritance for his successor. When Jimmy Carter turned over to Ronald Reagan, the deficit was 12 percent of federal expenditure. In the course of the Reagan administration, the

291

annual deficit rose to as much as 26 percent of federal spending. In 1984, an election year, the Reagan administration borrowed $1 for every $3 it raised in tax revenues. The deficit has fallen from that peak, but it is still double that when President Carter left office, and one-third bigger in relation to the national product (cf. table 14.1). A recession could add $50 to $100 billion more to an annual deficit, by reducing tax revenues and forcing up expenditures on measures such as Medicaid and unemployment benefits.

In the words of one Reagan budget specialist: "We're not a tax-and-spend crowd; we're the borrow-and-spend crowd." The advent of a fresh face in the White House stimulates lenders to take a fresh look at the books of the federal government and calculate afresh the value of buying more U.S. government bonds. As a former Reagan OMB official, Lawrence Kudlow, explains:

> Reagan paints such a positive picture that the negatives just don't seem as negative and the positives seem much more so. Reagan is a master at creating mood music. It's so soothing that it really calms fears of a lot of the malignant spirits, such as the deficit. People don't think about the bad; they tend to focus on the good. The 1988 candidates will not be as successful at painting this mellifluous picture. That's when the harder choices are going to emerge. (Quoted in Hoffman, 1986: 22)

A second novel feature of the deficit is that it has been financed to an unusual extent by foreign lending. Whereas modern Presidents normally funded the federal deficit by borrowing from Americans, the Reagan administration has exploited interdependence by borrowing heavily from abroad. The federal debt is no longer just money that we owe to ourselves; an increasing portion is money that we owe to foreign governments and investors: "During the 1980s we have decided that our biggest export should be IOUs" (Peterson, 1987: 46). By definition, foreign lenders are capable of withdrawing their capital from the United States, and the volatility of the dollar in relation to foreign currencies adds to the risk of lending to the United States. The risk can be overcome by paying relatively high rates of interest to attract foreign lenders, but high interest rates have negative effects on the American economy.

America's dependence on the rest of the world for maintaining its high standard of living, is also evident in the trade deficit, which is also a Reagan legacy (see table 14.1). In 1980, the United States ran an overall surplus in its balance of payment accounts, which measure the total effect of imports and exports of goods and services and the movement of capital. In that year, imports of manufactured goods and services exceeded exports, but this was more than offset by the flow of investment income from abroad. By 1982, there was a small deficit in the current account, consistent with the pattern of fluctuations in the postwar era to date. By 1984, the soaring dollar was promoting the import of goods and services, and hurting exports.

TABLE 14.1

THE REAGAN LEGACY OF DOUBLE DEFICITS

Year	Federal Budget Deficit $ billion	International Current Account $ billion
1980	74	+2
1981	79	+7
1982	128	–9
1983	208	–46
1984	185	–107
1985	212	–116
1986	221	–141
1987	150	–162
1988	146	n.a
Change	72	164

SOURCES: OMB (1988), summary table 24; *Economic Report of the President* (1988), table B-102; 1987 current account and 1988 budget deficits are estimated.

The current account deficit reached the unprecedented figure of $107 billion, as foreign imports ran ahead of American exports, and payments of interest increased to foreign holders of American investments. In 1986, for every $2 of goods and services that America exported, more than $3 was imported from abroad.

The budget deficit and the trade deficit are linked. Experts attribute the great bulk of the trade deficit to the high interest rates that the Reagan administration has had to pay to finance the budget deficit. Up to 1985, this led to a 70 percent rise in the value of the dollar in relation to foreign currencies (cf. Feldstein, 1987). Given a high dollar, American manufacturers, workers, and farmers have faced domestic competition from imports that have been relatively cheap because of the overvalued dollar. Concurrently, American exporters have had difficulty selling abroad, even though world trade is expanding, because the overvalued dollar made the price of American exports artificially high. The dramatic fall in the value of the dollar since 1985 has been intended to make American exports more competitive in price terms. But it also increases the cost of hundreds of billions of dollars of imported goods that American consumers are now accustomed to buying.

The budget and trade deficits are also cumulative. Last year's deficit is added to outstanding federal debt, thus increasing the total interest that the government must pay. The Reagan administration has added more than $1.5 trillion to the total federal debt. Since 1980, the debt has risen from one-third of the national product to more than half the national product. Simply paying interest on this additional debt adds upwards of $100 billion to federal spending in a year, and thus to the current deficit. The trade deficit presents both financial and industrial problems. Each year's trade deficit creates financial obligations to foreigners; interest payments to Japanese investors now add a further complication to America's already complicated international balance of payments. The longer the trade deficit persists, the more difficult it is for American exporters to regain markets by a decline in the value of the dollar, for customers lost have gone elsewhere, and are not always easy to win back.

Inside the Beltway, President Reagan may appear clever by passing to his successor, bills for rising living standards, financed by foreign borrowing. His successor cannot enjoy the fiscal prospect facing him "the morning after" his inauguration (Peterson, 1987). A pro-American British journalist concluded a review of the American economy, "Reaganomics Coming Home to Roost," with the statement: "The CIA has got nothing on the U.S. Treasury as an agent of destabilization" (Jenkins, 1987).

Abroad, things look different. The German and Japanese governments cannot view a new President as starting with a clean slate. They have something much more substantial than puzzlement at Reaganomics; they hold tens of billions of dollars in U.S. government bonds that have been devalued in relation to deutsche marks and yen by the fall in the dollar engineered to reduce the trade deficit. Reagan's treasury secretary, James A. Baker III, does not want to issue U.S. government bonds denominated in deutsche marks or yen, reasoning that this would show "a lack of confidence by the United States in its own currency" (Berry, 1987). Foreign lenders, however, could make it a condition of continued financing of the deficit that the U.S. government pay back loans in their national currencies rather than in depreciated dollars (Berry, 1987).

A Window for Change by Changing Leaders?

Every fourth year, Americans dissatisfied with the record of a President can eject the incumbent from office or reject the candidate most closely identified with an unpopular administration. Thus, Gerald Ford was defeated in 1976, and Jimmy Carter was elected in his place. In 1980, the electorate turned out Carter and put Ronald Reagan in office in his stead.

The extent to which a new President can change the direction of government is easily overestimated, especially by the President-elect. The President enters office almost blissfully ignorant of the problems that confront him in going international, for his experience has been in going public. Insofar as he has been concerned with going Washington, Congress appears to be the biggest enemy of the White House. Foreign nations are hardly taken into account. The names of foreign leaders and the acronyms of international relations are simply facts that have to be memorized from briefing books to avoid appearing ignorant when asked questions as part of the 64-million vote quiz that constitutes campaigning for the Presidency.

Before a President proclaims that a new day is starting in world affairs, he should consider what experienced leaders of other nations will make of his rhetoric. While foreign leaders are usually too polite to say what they think, a former German Chancellor, Helmut Schmidt, once broke this silence.

> As Chancellor, I worked under four Presidents, and it's quite an experience, I can tell you.... First Carter sent his Vice-President to tell us almost everything done by his predecessors was wrong and implied that our cooperation was in vain and something different had to start. Then, along comes Reagan and tells us the same thing. (Quoted in Destler et al., 1984: 13)

Although the style of an individual President can change the way in which the public and Washington perceive the Oval Office, the scope for change in the international system is much less for a postmodern President. The intangibles of personality are often literally lost in translation. Nor are foreigners particularly interested in following the ins and outs of struggles between the White House and Congress. Foreign leaders, who remain in office while the White House changes hands, focus on problems that continue from one administration to the next.

It is comforting to imagine that economic problems may be reduced to a crisis of political confidence, but it is also misleading. It implies that if foreigners have lost confidence in President Reagan's smile, his successor should look grim and determined when talking about America's budget and trade deficits. Yet there is no reason why foreign creditors of the United States should be satisfied with what plays in Peoria. At the end of the day, the material problems of the American economy can be addressed only by measures that have a material impact on the American economy. The new President has been left in no doubt about what actions are desired by foreign creditors. Finance ministers of OECD nations, meeting in Paris in May 1987, spelled out their goals for American economic policy thus:

> In the United States, the process of reducing the federal budget deficit—which is coming down from 5.2 percent of GNP in 1986 to less than 4 percent in 1987—*must and will continue in the years ahead. Holding firm to this course is essential for external and domestic reasons.* The confidence of economic agents in the United States and elsewhere depends heavily upon it. (OECD, 1987a: 19; italics added)

International pressures have continued since. Michel Camdessus (1988: 195), managing director of the International Monetary Fund, had no hesitation in identifying the initial step in improving the international economy: "The first point is the need for the United States to reduce its budget deficit substantially further."

It is an oversimple interpretation of democracy to think that each President is able to do what he wants and what the people want, just because popular election makes him the legitimate spokesman of the United States. Although all democratic politicians accept the importance of elections, leaders of other major nations want the White House to recognize that the international system must sometimes take precedence over the politics of going Washington and going public. The future of the postmodern Presidency depends on the Oval Office recognizing that many of the voices that influence America's place in the world today do not speak with American accents.

The Great Asymmetry

As the world closes in on the White House, it is not surprising that some people want to turn their backs on what is happening and be isolated from the world, as in the days of President Ulysses S. Grant. Even so cosmopolitan a policymaker as Henry Kissinger once evoked the language of romantic isolationism:

> Americans admire the cowboy leading the caravan alone astride his horse, the cowboy entering a village or city alone on his horse. Without even a pistol, maybe, because he doesn't go in for shooting. He acts, that's all, aiming at the right spot at the right time.... I've always acted alone. (Quoted in Nathan and Oliver, 1987: 68)

The heroism of a cowboy, whether riding the western plains or the situation room of the White House, has little effect on a world in which the cowboy's enemies can use their political radar to track him riding into their line of sight. A contemporary President can no more escape the implications of interdependence than European Prime Ministers could do so after the end of World War II. In an open international system, the White House *must* learn to get along with other elephants.

Misperceiving the World about Us

Because foreign policy begins at home, each national government perceives the world differently. What it sees—and what it tries to ignore—reflects its institutions, culture, and international commitments. As long as America existed in splendid isolation, it mattered little what America thought. When America could dominate the international system, other nations had to attend to Washington first. As America's influence on other nations becomes less certain, it is more important for Washingtonians to heed Neustadt's (1970: 117) dictum: "Influential action turns on accurate perception."

Changes within the United States are making it harder to perceive accurately America's place in the world. For most of American history, the East Coast was politically central, and American foreign policy was oriented toward Europe. The bulk of America's population was in the Northeast, and New York was the home of the foreign policy elite. The shift from the traditional to the modern Presidency was accompanied by a reversal of roles. Instead of America needing defense from Europe, America became central to the defense of Europe. The transition to the postmodern Presidency has been contemporaneous with a dramatic shift in the balance of the American electorate from the Frostbelt to the Sunbelt. In the Sunbelt, Caribbean and Latin American nations are closest in every sense; in the Southwest, Mexico and Mexicans are near at hand; and the Pacific Coast faces toward Japan and the rest of Asia. Immigration and trade give the Sunbelt a very different outlook on the world. A President who seeks to speak for America can do so by turning to Europe, to Latin America, or to Japan and Asia. In each instance, he can be speaking for a different part of America.

In the past quarter-century, tens of millions of Americans have traveled to all corners of the earth. But just as George Bernard Shaw once described America and Britain as two countries separated by a common language, so Americans and citizens of other nations can easily misperceive what they see. We would not want Europeans to judge America by cowboy films or *Rambo*, or citizens of Soviet or Third World nations to draw conclusions about this country from viewing "Dallas" or *The Grapes of Wrath*. So we should hesitate before judging other countries on the basis of package tours designed to provide all the comforts of home. Understanding foreign countries requires empathy, the psychological ability to put yourself in other people's shoes. Now that America cannot rely on hegemonic power, White House representatives need more empathy with foreigners.

Most people close to the President lack experience in dealing with foreign nations. White House jobs are held because of campaign credentials or skills in going Washington. The first test of a national security assistant to the President is who he knows; the confidence of the President is essential in doing the job. The frequent use of military personnel as National Security Council staff ensures that the White House has people who understand the Pentagon well. Nothing in the Naval Academy education of Vice Admiral John Poindexter and Lieutenant Colonel Oliver North prepared them for conducting negotiations with Iran. No one in the United States thinks it unusual that ambassadors to many foreign countries are ignorant of the country to which they are going. To argue that such ambassadors teach foreigners to understand how American politics works does not encourage foreign confidence in Washington.

Lack of knowledge of foreign countries does not mean lack of intelligence; it reflects a lack of experience outside the Beltway or outside the United States. People rise high in Washington because they are good at something, whether it is playing games with the federal budget, attracting favorable media publicity, or attending to very important persons. The typical high-ranking government official sees his job as knowing Washington inside out. Any travel, whether it involves going public or going international, is related to promoting policies and positions held within the Beltway. If it will help the President to see the Pope or the Emperor of Japan, then many people will volunteer to take their first trip to Rome or Tokyo to make advance plans for a meeting. If it won't, they don't.

The White House is not the only American institution that looks inward when making decisions about the rest of the world. Although America has many multinational corporations, boards of directors are usually not multinational. Ford, General Motors, IBM, and Mobil Oil are four of the world's largest corporations, selling from a third to one-half their output abroad. Yet, none of these companies has had a non-American on its board of directors (*Economist*, 25 April 1987). When such firms send senior officials abroad, the impression often left with foreign colleagues is that they do not understand how other cultures work: "They are like snails; they carry their house with them wherever they go." Other countries understand how America works; for example, it is the basis of their success in boosting imports to the United States.

To paraphrase the late Andy Warhol, any country can be famous in Washington for fifteen minutes; all that is required is to attack Americans violently and dramatically. This will gain instant attention in the White House and in the national media. A British journalist in Washington notes:

> There always seems to be one story in America; it may be the Middle East, or Central America, or the economy. When one disappears, another pops up. People run out of interest very quickly. Suddenly something else becomes the story. Radio-TV news bulletins concentrate on one or two topics; the rest of the world is ignored. (Quoted in Bonafede, 1982: 667)

If knowledge is power, then ignorance is a source of weakness. Fred Bergsten (1986: 8) describes the consequences for international economic policy: "Each administration either fails to learn the lessons of its predecessors or consciously chooses to ignore these lessons. Each thus has to proceed through a disruptive shift from one policy extreme to another." Learning from failure is an increasingly expensive form of education for everyone involved, and especially for the United States.

The World Watches Washington

Politicians in other countries are experienced watchers of America, for they have grown up in an era in which American hegemony was a fact of their existence. For example, Japanese Prime Minister Noboru Takeshita and German Chancellor Helmut Kohl each entered politics after their country was under American occupation. European Prime Ministers often find that the only language that they have in common is English. Leaders in other nations watch Washington to see what actions they can or should take in their own national interest. A cosmopolitan American journalist concludes:

> The result is an astonishing asymmetry: The minutiae of American politics and society are followed compulsively by others as a critical component of life in the real world, while the U.S. government and individual American citizens seem to show an ever declining knowledge of and interest in everyone else. (Ungar, 1985: 18)

Although a President may consider himself too busy to pay attention to what other nations do in the international economy, foreigners never cease watching the American economy. At every hour of the day and night, foreign exchange dealers somewhere—in Zurich or London, in Tokyo or Hong Kong—are trying to make a quick profit by speculating on the fluctuating value of the dollar against other currencies. Oil-rich nations that invest their surplus capital in dollar accounts in American banks are watching to see what happens to their wealth, and Third World countries that have borrowed more money from American banks than they can repay are watching to see if there is anything that the American government will or can do to help them.

The foreign media cover Washington intensively, but not as Washington hands expect. When Stephen Hess (1983) conducted an analysis of foreign press reporting, he assumed that foreigners would normally not be interested in American events for their own sake. Hess thought foreigners would seek what Americans often seek abroad, a local angle, that is, stories that directly linked their country with the United States, for example, "Greek Immigrant's Son Runs for President." This is not the case. Foreign papers report the stories that are big inside Washington, for such is the global significance of American politics that anything important in Washington, such as a change in the budget deficit, is also news abroad.

Foreign nations that follow Washington closely can act as political arbitrageurs, profiting from the difference between their knowledge of Washington and White House attention to them. Because of America's trade deficit with Japan, the Japanese Prime Minister must try to appease American critics of its trade policy, and this requires keeping informed about what is going on at both ends of Pennsylvania Avenue. The Japanese media maintain far more English-speaking journalists in Washington than the American media has Japanese-speaking journalists in Tokyo. By understanding American politics, the Japanese government can time statements in Tokyo and trips to Washington to influence trade protection measures being debated inside the Beltway. A Japanese politician can trade on the asymmetry of understanding by delivering more substance in Tokyo and more symbolic reassurances in Washington.

299

The Iran-*contra* affair is a textbook example of how actions of the White House are followed carefully abroad, and how foreign arbitrageurs profit, both politically and financially. The arms that Iran obtained for use in its war against Iraq were acquired because Teheran understood the White House, weaknesses and all. Accounts of the Iran-*contra* affair were read carefully in the Middle East. One photograph symbolized this, showing a guerrilla fighter in Beirut momentarily resting, his weapon at hand, reading *Time* magazine's cover story about the testimony of Lieutenant Colonel Oliver North. In Europe, straightforward reporting of what was said at congressional hearings inevitably showed American foreign policy in an unfavorable light. A middle-of-the-road London paper, *The Independent* (3 August 1987), simply quoted the judgment of Senator Daniel Inouye, chairman of the special investigating committee on the Iran-*contra* affair: "This was a rather sordid chapter in our history, a chapter of lies and deceit and deception. I jus hope that it will not happen again. But I suppose it will."

Foreign allies of the United States see these faults but take no pleasure in evidence of blunders and weakness in the White House. Former British Prime Minister James Callaghan (1986) commented on the Iran-*conta* affair: "A disabled President is as much a weakness and danger to Europe as to his own country. And although there will be occasions and policies on which we shall differ, Europe needs him to be effective while he holds his great office."

Nations long accustomed to living with interdependence want the White House to recognize that interdependence is a two-way street. The White House risks rebuffs if it does not consult with allies. The ability of other nations not to accept direction from a postmodern President is illustrated by the Reagan administration's failure to prevent Europeans from importing natural gas from the Soviet Union via a lengthy pipeline from Siberia. In the wake of the 1973 and 1979 oil price shocks, a group of European nations, including Germany, France, and Italy, negotiated an agreement to import gas from Siberia in order to reduce their dependence on the Middle East, and as a potential contribution to improved East-West relations. By the test of the market, a favorite catchword in Ronald Reagan's Washington, the agreement made sense. The Reagan administration, however, tended to view such trade as a boost to the Soviets—except for grain exports, which Reagan endorsed as a candidate when bidding for the farm vote in 1980.

The White House decided it would punish the Soviet Union by opposing the construction of the natural gas pipeline to Western Europe. When the Siberian gas pipeline was treated as a test case of America's power to control European allies, the White House failed the test. The administration unilaterally extended restrictions imposed on American firms exporting equipment for the pipeline and on foreign companies holding licenses from American firms. European governments ordered their firms to continue supplying the goods, on the grounds that contractual commitments of traders should be honored. European governments continued to believe that the trade made sense, and did not want to bow to unilateral White House action. A European Community statement rejected Washington's opposition thus:

> This action, taken without any consultation with the Community, implies an extra-territorial extension of the U.S. jurisdiction which, in the circumstances, is contrary to the principles of international law, unacceptable to the Community, and unlikely to be recognized in courts in the European Economic Community. (Quoted in Lieber, 1987: 188)

In November 1982, President Reagan lifted sanctions that had never been observed. A detailed study of the frustration of the White House concluded:

> A fact of life in the Western alliance is that no one member can issue marching orders to the others. To do so would be to make the alliance indistinguishable from the Warsaw Pact, which is based on a relationship of intimidation and domination decreed by the Soviet doctrine of limited sovereignty. Alliance policy, in short, must be the product of compromise, not coercion. (Blinken, 1987: 154)

For the Soviet Union, a crisis of confidence in Washington is an opportunity for action. In a period of *glasnost*, Mikhail Gorbachev can approach Western European leaders with proposals that appear attractive—if they can be believed. Concurrently, the United States is seen in a less favorable light. For example, in autumn 1987, a four-nation survey found that 62 percent of Americans trusted President Reagan more than Mikhail Gorbachev to reduce cold-war tensions. By contrast, less than one-quarter of Britons, French, and Germans trusted President Reagan more. Consistent with the growth in self-confidence among European leaders, the largest group in Britain, France, and Germany trusted neither foreign leader (see table 14.2).

TABLE 14.2

TRUST IN AMERICAN AND SOVIET LEADERS COMPARED

(IN PERCENT)

	More Trust in		Neither	Don't
	Reagan	Gorbachev	No difference	know
United States	62	17	13	8
Britain	19	39	30	11
France	23	16	43	18
Germany	16	24	42	17

SOURCE: Surveys taken for NBC News (Beeston, 1987).

A postmodern President cannot ignore foreigners when making foreign policy, for other nations are checks and balances on America's actions in the international system, and can send shocks through the system, impelling the President to react to problems he would prefer to ignore. Just because a presidential representative may be ignorant or inexperienced does not mean that foreign representatives are similarly uninformed. For example, a presidential appointee negotiating with the Soviet Union about technology learned that it was unusual for the Russians to meet the same American official at the negotiating table for two successive years, whereas Russian officials had continuity. The moral was clear: "They know everything about us, and we are learning about them. That puts us at a terrible disadvantage, however good our people are" (quoted in Brauer, 1987: 179).

The Future of the Postmodern President

At the signing of the Declaration of Independence, Benjamin Franklin recognized the interdependence of thirteen separate colonies, saying: "We must indeed all hang together, or most assuredly we shall all hang separately." Today, the question is not whether nations will hang together, but how.

There is plenty of goodwill between Washington and leaders of other major nations, for Prime Ministers are as aware as Presidents that their nation's fate is greatly influenced by what happens in the international system. Between the United States, Germany, and Japan, relations are particularly close. In national security, Germany and Japan are each front-line nations, only a few miles from Soviet troops in East Germany or in Siberia, and American troops provide front-line defense to Germany and Japan. The economic interdependence of America, Germany, and Japan is great too, but the terms of the relationship are reversed. Japan and Germany are major exporters, whereas the United States now runs a very large trade deficit. Germany and Japan have currencies that are strong, inflation is low, and savings and investment are high. The American economy is in the opposite shape; the dollar is weak, savings and investment are very low, and the trade and budget deficits increase the risk of inflation. Given interdependence, political decisions affecting the American economy can now be taken in Bonn and Tokyo, as well as in Washington.

Interdependence need not mean cooperation. There are politicians, such as former President Richard M. Nixon (1980: 32), who still believe that the White House enjoys the powers of two decades ago.

> Some say we are entering a period of collective leadership in the West, that because the United States has lagged in economic growth and lost its military

supremacy, we are going to have to consult our more prosperous allies and defer to them in the search for a Western consensus. This is nonsense. Consult, of course. But unless the United States leads, nobody will. And unless the President leads, nobody will.

While Ronald Reagan is a postmodern President, he often has not recognized the need for cooperation with other countries financing his deficits. President Reagan has seen the American economy purely in domestic terms, and his domestic political line is "Tax increases will only occur over my dead body."

Noncooperation can cut both ways. British Prime Minister Margaret Thatcher and French President François Mitterrand have each had to take politically unpopular steps to resolve economic problems created by their fiscal mistakes. Each can ask the question: Why should we have sympathy with an American President who claims to be too weak to take unpopular decisions that we have had to take? There is little sympathy abroad when the United States appears to be calling for expansionary policies in Japan and Europe simply to help solve its own problems. The Japanese and Europeans are inclined to respond that since American policies have caused international monetary instability, the solution to the problem must be found in Washington (Marris, forthcoming: 59; see also Nau, 1985). Nor does any nation want to sacrifice its export markets or export-led growth simply to enable the next President to look good by a reduction in the United States trade deficit.

"If you can't beat them, join them" is an old American adage. Since 1985 Treasury Secretary Baker has been meeting with his counterparts of other major nations in an effort to resolve worldwide economic problems (Funabashi, 1988). But financial leaders in other nations have learned that an agreement with the secretary of the U. S. Treasury is not an agreement with the government of the United States. Treasury reflects the position of only one subgovernment in an open market for policy. The White House and Congress have continued to demonstrate the difficulty of agreeing to a coherent economic policy, as can be done in a parliamentary system. Moreover, economists themselves disagree about what the government should do, and about how certain their advice is to produce benefits from international economic policy coordination (cf. Tanzi, 1988; Frankel, 1988).

Writing two decades ago, Richard Neustadt (1970:144) described a modern President as enjoying a "wide latitude for ignorance; it scarcely seemed to matter whether we guessed right or wrong." The hegemonic power of the United States meant that allies would have to accept whatever the White House chose to do. For a postmodern President, ignorance is a luxury. Just as going Washington and going public have become increasingly linked, so the line between what was once considered domestic politics (e.g., grain prices in Iowa) and foreign policy (negotiations with the Soviet

Union) has dissolved. Increasing pressure from the international system on the United States makes the White House even more the focal point for the linkage of international and domestic politics.

As the world closes in on the White House, the scope and range of the President's concerns widen, while the influence of the White House in the international system is not so certain as before. To make interdependence work on behalf of the United States does not require novel policies. The measures needed to deal with deficits in the economy and adapt national security to the 1990s are in principle similar to those taken by other major nations. Nor is a radical transformation of American society required. As Calleo (1987: 126) emphasizes: "Solutions that call for heroic changes in American character and practice seem less promising than solutions proposing that America adapt itself to the real world."

When John F. Kennedy spoke a quarter-century ago of America paying any price to assure the survival of liberty, the price was measured both in dollars and in military force. The United States was then the banker of the world. Dollars went abroad for profitable investments, as foreign aid to underdeveloped countries, and to support military alliances. The United States was also the supreme military force in the world.

The price that a postmodern President must pay is different: It is the price of abandoning illusions. The biggest illusion is the belief that we can turn the clock back to the era when Franklin D. Roosevelt created the modern Presidency, and Dwight D. Eisenhower could rely on American wealth and military force to sustain a global *Pax Americana*. All the rhetoric of a Kennedy, the wheeling and dealing of a Johnson, and the imperial ambitions of a Nixon, could not maintain American dominance indefinitely. The modern Presidency was an institution of the American century, an era that lasted only a few decades after 1945.

A new century has now commenced, based on global interdependence. America's hegemonic influence is not sufficient to last to the year 2000. In this new era, the postmodern President is even more important, for the Oval Office is the best place to see the links between the international system and America's domestic concerns. While responsibilities are larger, resources are fewer, for the White House is now palpably subject to checks and balances on every continent. In this new world of interdependence, there is much less latitude for ignorance and luck. The postmodern President depends on power armed by an understanding of how the world now works.

Appendix

Presidents of the United States

President (Years)	Party	Percent Popular Vote
1. George Washington (1789-97)	Federalist	n.a.
2. John Adams (1797-1801)	Federalist	n.a.
3. Thomas Jefferson (1801-09)	Democratic-Republican	n.a.
4. James Madison (1809-17)	Democratic-Republican	n.a.
5. James Monroe (1817-25)	Democratic-Republican	n.a.
6. John Quincy Adams (1825-29)	Democratic-Republican	n.a.
7. Andrew Jackson (1829-37)	Democrat	56.0, 54.3
8. Martin Van Buren (1837-41)	Democrat	50.8
9. William Henry Harrison (1841)	Whig	52.9
10. John Tyler (1841-45)	Whig	V.P.
11. James K. Polk (1845-49)	Democrat	49.5
12. Zachary Taylor (1849-50)	Whig	47.3
13. Millard Fillmore (1850-53)	Whig	V..P.
14. Franklin Pierce (1853-57)	Democrat	50.8
15. James Buchanan (1857-61)	Democrat	45.3
16. Abraham Lincoln (1861-65)	Republican	39.8, 55.0
17. Andrew Johnson (1865-69)	Union	V.P.
18. Ulysses S. Grant (1869-77)	Republican	52.7, 55.6
19. Rutherford B. Hayes (1877-81)	Republican	48.0
20. James A. Garfield (1881)	Republican	48.3
21. Chester A. Arthur (1881-85)	Republican	V.P.
22. Grover Cleveland (1885-89)	Democrat	48.5
23. Benjamin Harrison (1889-93)	Republican	47.9
24. Grover Cleveland (1893-97)	Democrat	46.1
25. William McKinley (1897-1901)	Republican	51.0. 51.7
26. Theodore Roosevelt (1901-09)	Republican	V.P., 56.4
27. William Howard Taft (1909-13)	Republican	51.6
28. Woodrow Wilson (1913-21)	Democrat	41.9, 49.4
29. Warren G. Harding(1921-23)	Republican	60.3
30. Calvin Coolidge (1923-29)	Republican	V.P., 54.0
31. Herbert Hoover (1929-33)	Republican	58.2
32. Franklin D. Roosevelt (1933-45)	Democrat	57.4, 60.8, 54.8, 53.5

President (Years)	Party	Percent PopularVote
33. Harry Truman (1945-53)	Democrat	V.P., 49.6
34. Dwight D. Eisenhower (1953-61)	Republican	55.1, 57.4
35. John F. Kennedy (1961-63)	Democrat	49.7
36. Lyndon B. Johnson (1963-69)	Democrat	V.P., 61.1
37. Richard M. Nixon (1969-74)	Republican	43.4, 60.7
38. Gerald R. Ford (1974-77)	Republican	V.P.
39. Jimmy Carter (1977-81)	Democrat	50.1
40. Ronald Reagan (1981-88)	Republican	50.7, 58.8

NOTE: Where more than one figure given for percentage of vote, President elected more than once. V.P.: Presidency attained by succession from Vice-Presidency.

The Presidency in the Constitution

Section 1. The executive power shall be vested in a President of the United States of America. He shall hold his Office during the term of four years, and, together with the Vice-President, chosen for the same term, be elected as follows:

Each state shall appoint, in such manner as the legislature thereof may direct, a number of electors, equal to the whole number of Senators and Representatives to which the state may be entitled in the Congress: but no Senator or Representative, or person holding an office of trust or profit under the United States, shall be appointed an elector.

(The electors shall meet in their respective states, and vote by ballot for two persons, of whom one at least shall not be an inhabitant of the same state with themselves. And they shall make a list of all the persons voted for, and of the number of votes for each; which list they shall sign and certify, and transmit sealed to the seat of government of the United States, directed to the President of the Senate. The President of the Senate shall, in the presence of the Senate and House of Representatives, open all the certificates, and the votes shall then be counted. The person having the greatest number of votes shall be the President, if such number be a majority of the whole number of electors appointed; and if there be more than one who have such majority, and have an equal number of votes, then the House of Representatives shall immediately choose by ballot one of them for President; and if no person have a majority, then from the five highest on the list the said House shall in like manner chose the President. But in choosing the President, the votes shall be taken by states, the representation from each state having one vote; a quorum for this purpose shall consist of a member or members from two-thirds of the states, and a majority of all the states shall be necessary to a choice. In every case, after the choice of President, the person having the greatest number of votes of the electors shall be the Vice-President. But if there should remain two or more who have equal votes, the Senate shall chose from them by ballot the Vice-President.)[1]

1. Superseded by the Twelfth Amendment.

The Congress may determine the time of choosing the electors, and the day on which they shall give their votes; which day shall be the same throughout the United States.

No person except a natural-born citizen or a citizen of the United States at the time of the Adoption of this Constitution shall be eligible to the office of President; neither shall any person be eligible to that office who shall not have attained the age of thirty-five years, and been fourteen years a resident within the United States.

(In case of the removal of the President from office, or of his death, resignation, or inability to discharge the powers and duties of the said office, the same shall devolve on the Vice-President, declaring what officer shall then act as President, and such officer shall act accordingly, until the disability be removed, or a President shall be elected.)[2]

The President shall, at stated times, receive for his services a compensation, which shall neither be increased nor diminished during the period for which he shall have been elected, and he shall not receive within that period any other emolument from the United States, or any of them.

Before he enter on the execution of his office, he shall take the following Oath or Affirmation: "I do solemnly swear (or affirm) that I will faithfully execute the office of President of the United States, and will, to the best of my ability, preserve, protect, and defend the Constitution of the United States."

Section 2. The President shall be Commander in Chief of the Army and Navy of the United States and of the militia of the several States, when called into the actual service of the United States, he may require the opinion, in writing, of the principal officer in each of the executive Departments, upon any subject relating to the duties of their respective offices, and he shall have power to grant reprieves and pardons for offenses against the United States except in cases of impeachment.

He shall have power, by and with the advice and consent of the Senate, to make treaties, provided two-thirds of the Senators present concur; and he shall nominate, and by and with the advice and consent of the Senate, shall appoint ambassadors, other public ministers and consuls, judges of the Supreme Court, and all other officers of the United States, whose appointments are not herein otherwise provided for, and which shall be established by Law: but the Congress may by law vest the appointment of inferior officers, as they think proper, in the President alone, in the courts of law, or in the heads of departments.

The President shall have Power to fill up all vacancies that may happen during the recess of the Senate, by granting commissions which shall expire at the end of their next session.

Section 3. He shall from time to time give to the Congress information of the state of the union, and recommend to their consideration such measures as he shall judge necessary and expedient; he may, on extraordinary occasions, convene both houses, or either of them, and in case disagreement between them, with respect to the time of adjournment, he may adjourn them to such time as he shall think proper; he

2. Modified by the Twenty-fifth Amendment.

shall receive Ambassadors and other public ministers; he shall take care that the laws be faithfully executed, and shall commission all the officers of the United States.

Section 4. The President, Vice-President and all civil officers of the United States, shall be removed from office on impeachment for, and conviction of, treason, bribery, or other high crimes and misdemeanors.

Veto Power

Section 7. Every bill which shall have passed the House of Representatives and the Senate, shall, before it become a law, be presented to the President of the United States. If he approve he shall sign it, but if not he shall return it, with his objections, to that house in which it shall have originated, who shall enter the objections at large on their journal, and proceed to reconsider it. If after such reconsideration two-thirds of that house shall agree to pass the bill, it shall be sent, together with the objections, to the other House, by which it shall likewise be reconsidered, and if approved by two-thirds of that house, it shall become a law. But in all such cases the votes of both houses shall be determined by yeas and nays, and the names of the persons voting for and against the bill shall be entered on the journal of each house respectively. If any bill shall not be returned by the President within ten days (Sundays excepted) after it shall have been presented to him, the same shall be a law, in like manner as if he had signed it, unless the Congress by their adjournment prevent its return, in which case it shall not be a law.

Amendment XII (1804)

The electors shall meet in their respective states and vote by ballot for President and Vice-President, one of whom, at least, shall not be an inhabitant of the same state with themselves; they shall name in their ballots the person voted for as President, and in distinct ballots the person voted for as Vice-President, and they shall make distinct lists of all persons voted for as President, and of all persons voted for as Vice-President, and of the number of votes for each, which lists they shall sign and certify, and transmit sealed to the seat of government of the United States, directed to the President of the Senate. The President of the Senate shall, in the presence of the Senate and House of Representatives, open all the certificates and the votes shall then be counted. The person having the greatest number of votes for President shall be the President, if such number be a majority of the whole number of electors appointed; and if no person have such majority, then from the persons having the highest numbers not exceeding three on the list of those voted for as President, the House of Representatives shall choose immediately, by ballot, the President. But in choosing the President, the votes shall be taken by states, the representation from each state having one vote; a quorum for this purpose shall consist of a member or members from two-thirds of the states, and a majority of all the states shall be necessary to a choice. (And if the House of Representatives shall not choose a President whenever the right of choice shall devolve upon them, before the fourth day of March next following, then the Vice-President shall act as President, as in the case of the death or other constitutional disability of the President.)[3] The person having the greatest number of votes as Vice-President shall be the Vice-President, if such number be a majority of the whole number of electors appointed, and if no person have a majority, then from the two highest numbers on the list, the Senate shall choose the Vice-President; a quorum for the purpose shall consist of two-thirds of the whole number of Senators, and a majority of the whole number shall be necessary to a choice. But no person constitutionally ineligible to the office of President shall be eligible to that of Vice-President of the United States.

Amendment XX (1933)

Section 1. The terms of the President and Vice-President shall end at noon on the 20th day of January, and the terms of Senators and Representatives at noon on the 3rd day of January of the years in which such terms would have ended if this article had not been ratified; and the terms of their successor shall then begin.

Section 2. The Congress shall assemble at least once every year, and such meeting shall begin at noon on the 3rd day of January, unless they shall by law appoint a different day.

Section 3. If, at the time fixed for the beginning of the term of the President, the President-elect shall have died, the Vice- President-elect shall become President. If a President shall not have been chosen before the time fixed for the beginning of his term, or if the President elect shall have failed to qualify, then the Vice-President elect shall act as President until a President shall have qualified; and the Congress may by law provide for the case wherein neither a President-elect nor a Vice-President-elect shall have qualified, declaring who shall then act as President, or the manner in which one who is to act shall be selected, and such person shall act accordingly until a President or Vice-President shall have qualified.

Section 4. The Congress may by law provide for the case of the death of any of the persons from whom the House of Representatives may choose a President whenever the right of choice shall have devolved upon them, and for the case of the death of any of the persons from whom the Senate may choose a Vice-President whenever the right of choice shall have devolved upon them.

Section 5. Sections 1 and 2 shall take effect on the 15th day of October following the ratification of this article.

Section 6. This article shall be inoperative unless it shall have been ratified as an amendment to the Constitution by the legislatures of three-fourths of the several states within seven years from the date of its submission.

3. Superseded by the Twentieth Amendment.

Amendment XXII (1951)

No person shall be elected to the office of the President more than twice, and no person who has held the office of President, or acted as President, for more than two years of a term to which some other person was elected President shall be elected to the office of the President more than once.

But this Article shall not apply to any person holding the office of President when this Article was proposed by Congress, and shall not prevent any person who may be holding the office of President, or acting as President, during the term within which this Article becomes operative from holding the office of President or acting as President during the remainder of such term.

Amendment XXV (1967)

Section 1. In case of the removal of the President from office or of his death or resignation, the Vice-President shall become President.

Section 2. Whenever there is a vacancy in the office of the Vice-President, the President shall nominate a Vice-President who shall take office upon confirmation by a majority vote of both Houses of Congress.

Section 3. Whenever the President transmits to the President pro tempore of the Senate and the Speaker of the House of Representatives his written declaration that he is unable to discharge the powers and duties of his office, and until he transmits to them a written declaration to the contrary, such powers and duties shall be discharged by the Vice-President as Acting President.

Section 4. Whenever the Vice-President and a majority of either the principal officers of the executive department or of such other body as Congress may by law provide, transmit to the President pro tempore of the Senate and the Speaker of the House of Representatives their written declaration that the President is unable to discharge the powers and duties of his office, the Vice-President shall immediately assume the powers and duties of the office as Acting President.

Thereafter, when the President transmits to the President pro tempore of the Senate and the Speaker of the House of Representatives his written declaration that no inability exists, he shall resume the powers and duties of his office unless the Vice-President and a majority of either the principal officers of the executive department or of such other body as Congress may by law provide, transmit within four days to the President pro tempore of the Senate and the Speaker of the House of Representatives their written declaration that the President is unable to discharge the powers and duties of his office. Thereupon Congress shall decide the issue, assembling within forty-eight hours for that purpose if not in session. If the Congress, within twenty-one days after receipt of the latter written declaration, or, if Congress is not in session, within twenty-one days after Congress is required to assemble, determines by two-thirds vote of both Houses that the President is unable to discharge the powers and duties of his office, the Vice-President shall continue to discharge the same as Acting President; otherwise, the President shall resume the powers and duties of his office.

Inaugural Address of President John F. Kennedy, 20 January 1961

Vice-President Johnson, Mr. Speaker, Mr. Chief Justice, President Eisenhower, Vice-President Nixon, President Truman, Reverend Clergy, fellow citizens:

We observe today not a victory of party but a celebration of freedom—symbolizing an end as well as a beginning—signifying renewal as well as change. For I have sworn before you and Almighty God the same solemn oath our forebears prescribed nearly a century and three-quarters ago.

The world is very different now. For man holds in his mortal hands the power to abolish all forms of human poverty and all forms of human life. And yet the same revolutionary beliefs for which our forebears fought are still at issue around the globe—the belief that the rights of man come not from the generosity of the state but from the hand of God.

We dare not forget today that we are the heirs of that first revolution. Let the word go forth from this time and place, to friend and foe alike, that the torch has been passed to a new generation of Americans—born in this century, tempered by war, disciplined by a hard and bitter peace, proud of our ancient heritage—and unwilling to witness or permit the slow undoing of those human rights to which this nation has always been committed, and to which we are committed today at home and around the world.

Let every nation know, whether it wishes us well or ill, that we shall pay any price, bear any burden, meet any hardship, support any friend, oppose any foe to assure the survival and the success of liberty.

This much we pledge—and more.

To those old allies whose cultural and spiritual origins we share, we pledge the loyalty of faithful friends. United, there is little we cannot do in a host of cooperative ventures. Divided, there is little we can do—for we dare not meet a powerful challenge at odds and split asunder.

To those new states whom we welcome to the ranks of the free, we pledge our word that one form of colonial control shall not have passed away merely to be replaced a far more iron tyranny. We shall not always expect to find them supporting our view. But we shall always hope to find them strongly supporting their own freedom—and to remember that, in the past, those who foolishly sought power by riding the back of the tiger ended up inside.

To those peoples in the huts and villages of half the globe struggling to break the bonds of mass misery, we pledge our best efforts to help them feed themselves, for

311

whatever period is required—not because the communists may be doing it, not because we seek their votes, but because it is right. If a free society cannot help the many who are poor, it cannot save the few who are rich.

To our sister republics south of our border, we offer a special pledge—to convert our good words into good deeds—in a new alliance for progress—to assist free men and free governments in casting off the chains of poverty. But this peaceful revolution of hope cannot become the prey of hostile powers. Let all our neighbors know that we shall join with them to oppose aggression or subversion anywhere in the Americas. And let every other power know that this hemisphere intends to remain the master of its own house.

To that world assembly of sovereign states, the United Nations, our last best hope in an age where the instruments of war have far outpaced the instruments of peace, we renew our pledge of support—to prevent it from becoming merely a forum for invective—to strengthen its shield of the new and the weak—and to enlarge the area in which its writ may run.

Finally, to those nations who would make themselves our adversary, we offer not a pledge but a request: That both sides begin anew the quest for peace, before the dark powers of destruction unleashed by science engulf all humanity in planned or accidental self-destruction.

We dare not tempt them with weakness. For only when our arms are sufficient beyond doubt can we be certain beyond doubt that they will never be employed.

But neither can two great and powerful groups of nations take comfort from our present course—both sides overburdened by the cost of modern weapons, both rightly alarmed by the steady spread of the deadly atom, yet both racing to alter that uncertain balance of terror that stays the hand of mankind's final war.

So let us begin anew—remembering on both sides that civility is not a sign of weakness, and sincerity is always subject to proof. Let us never negotiate out of fear. But let us never fear to negotiate.

Let both sides explore what problems unite us instead of belaboring those problems which divide us.

Let both sides, for the first time, formulate serious and precise proposals for the inspection and control of arms—and bring the absolute power to destroy other nations under the absolute control of all nations.

Let both sides seek to invoke the wonders of science instead of its terrors. Together let us explore the stars, conquer the deserts, eradicate disease, tap the ocean depths, and encourage the arts and commerce.

Let both sides unite to heed in all corners of the earth the command of Isaiah— to "undo the heavy burdens... (and) let the oppressed go free."

And if a beach-head of cooperation may push back the jungle of suspicion, let both sides join in creating a new endeavor, not a new balance of power, but a new world of law, where the strong are just and the weak secure and the peace preserved. All this will not be finished in the first one hundred days. Nor will it be finished in the first one thousand days, nor in the life of this Administration, nor even perhaps in our lifetime on this planet. But let us begin.

In your hands, my fellow citizens, more than mine, will rest the final success or failure of our course. Since this country was founded, each generation of Americans has been summoned to give testimony to its national loyalty. The graves of young Americans who answered the call to service surround the globe.

Now the trumpet summons us again—not as a call to bear arms, though arms we need—not as a call to battle, though embattled we are—but a call to bear the burden of a long twilight struggle, year in and year out, "rejoicing in hope, patient in tribulation"—a struggle against the common enemies of man: tyranny, poverty, disease and war itself.

Can we forge against these enemies a grand and global alliance, North and South, East and West, that can assure a more fruitful life for all mankind? Will you join in that historic effort?

In the long history of the world, only a few generations have been granted the role of defending freedom in its hour of maximum danger. I do not shrink from this responsibility—I welcome it. I do not believe that any of us would exchange places with any other people or any other generation. The energy, the faith, the devotion which we bring to this endeavor will light our country and all who serve it—and the glow from that fire can truly light the world.

And so, my fellow Americans: Ask not what America can do for you—ask what you can do for your country.

My fellow citizens of the world: ask not what America will do for you, but what together we can do for the freedom of man.

Finally, whether you are citizens of America or citizens of the world, ask of us here the same high standards of strength and sacrifice which we ask of you. With a good conscience our only sure reward, with history the final judge of our deeds, let us go forth to lead the land we love, asking His blessing and His help, but knowing that here on earth God's work must truly be our own.

References

Aberbach, Joel D., Robert D. Putnam, and Bert A. Rockman. 1981. *Bureaucrats and Politicians in Western Democracies*. Cambridge, Mass.: Harvard University Press.

Aberbach, Joel D., and Bert A. Rockman. 1977. "The Overlapping Worlds of American Federal Executives and Congressmen." *British Journal of Political Science* 7(1): 23-48.

ACIR (Advisory Commission on Intergovernmental Relations). 1983. *Changing Public Attitudes on Governments and Taxes*. Washington, D.C.: ACIR S-12.

Adams, William C. 1987. "As New Hampshire Goes...." In Garry Orren and Nelson Polsby, eds., *Media and Momentum*, Chatham N.J.: Chatham House. 42-59.

Allen, William R. 1977. "Economics, Economists and Economic Policy," *History of Political Economy* 9(1): 48-88.

Alt, James E., and K. Alec Chrystal. 1983. *Political Economics*. Berkeley: University of California Press.

Anderson, Bruce. 1987. "How Lawson Will Save Us from the Slump." *Sunday Telegraph* (London) 8 November.

Anderson, James E., and Jared E. Hazleton. 1985. *Managing Macroeconomic Policy: The Johnson Presidency*. Austin: University of Texas Press.

Appleby, Paul. 1949. *Policy and Administration*. University, Ala.: University of Alabama Press.

Arnold, Peri E. 1986. *Making the Managerial Presidency: Comprehensive Reorganization Planning, 1905-1980*. Princeton: Princeton University Press.

Arterton, F. Christopher. 1984. *Media Politics*. Lexington, Mass.: Lexington Books.

Artis, Michael, and Sylvia Ostry. 1986. *International Economic Policy Coordination*. London: Routledge & Kegan Paul, Chatham House Papers No. 30.

Asher, Herbert B. 1984. *Presidential Elections and American Politics*. 3d ed. Homewood, Ill.: Dorsey Press,

Auerbach, Stuart, and Peter Behr. 1987. "America Faces a Rude Awakening." *Washington Post, National Weekly Edition*, 4 May.

Austin, Erik W., with Jerome M. Clubb. 1986. *Political Facts of the United States Since 1789*. New York: Columbia University Press.

Avery, William P., and David P. Rapkind, eds. 1982. *America in a Changing World Political Economy*. New York: Longman.

Baerwald, Hans H. 1986. *Party Politics in Japan*. Boston: Allen and Unwin.

Bailey, Stephen K. 1950. *Congress Makes a Law*. New York: Columbia University Press.

Bailey, Thomas A. 1966. *Presidential Greatness: The Image and the Man*. New York: Appleton-Century Crofts.

Barber, James David. 1972. *The Presidential Character*. Englewood Cliffs, N.J.: Prentice-Hall.

Barilleaux, Ryan J. 1985. *The President and Foreign Affairs: Evaluation Performance, and Power*. New York: Praeger.

Barnett, Joel. 1982. *Inside the Treasury*. London: Andre Deutsch.

Beeston, Nicholas. 1987. "Britons Regard Reagan As the 'Bad Guy.'" *The Times* (London) 8 December.

Bennett, Colin. 1985. "From the Dark to the Light: The Open Government Debate in Britain." *Journal of Public Policy* 5(2): 187-214.

Bergsten, C. Fred. 1985. "Reaganomics: The Problem?" *Foreign Policy*, no. 59:132-44.

Bergsten, C. Fred. 1986. "America's Unilateralism." In *Conditions for Partnership in International Economic Management*, 3-14. New York: Trilateral Commission Triangle Papers No. 32.

Bergsten, C. Fred. 1987. "Economic Imbalances and World Politics." *Foreign Affairs* 65(4): 770-94.

Berman, Larry. 1987. *The New American Presidency*. Boston: Little, Brown.

Berry, John M. 1987. "Dollar Gets a Pounding in Markets." *Washington Post*, 25 April.

Bessette, Joseph M., and Jeffrey Tulis, eds. 1981. *The Presidency in the Constitutional Order*. Baton Rouge: Louisiana State University Press.

Beyme, Klaus von. 1983. *The Political System of the Federal Republic of Germany*. Aldershot: Gower.

Beyme, Klaus von. 1987. *America as a Model*. Aldershot: Gower.

Bibby, John, Thomas Mann, and Norman Ornstein. 1980. *Vital Statistics on Congress, 1980*. Washington. D.C.: American Enterprise Institute.

Binyon, Michael. 1987. "U.S. Finding Price of Leadership Too High." *The Times* (London) 21 November .

Blinken, Antony J. 1987. *Ally vs. Ally: America, Europe and the Siberian Pipeline Crisis*. New York: Praeger.

Blondel, Jean. 1980. *World Leaders: Heads of Government in the Postwar Period*. London: Sage Publications.

Blundy, David. 1987. "Fuzzy Admiral Produces Lots of Smoke but No Fire." *Sunday Telegraph* (London) 19 July.

Bock, Joseph G., and D.L. Clarke. 1986. "The National Security Assistant and the White House Staff." *Presidential Studies Quarterly* 16(2): 258-79.

Bogdanor, Vernon, and D.E. Butler, eds. 1983. *Democracy and Elections*. Cambridge: Cambridge University Press.

Bonafede, Dom. 1982. "The Washington Press: Competing for Power with the Federal Government." *National Journal*, 17 April.

Brauer, Carl M. 1986. *Presidential Transitions: Eisenhower through Reagan.* New York: Oxford University Press.

Brauer, Carl. 1987. "Tenure, Turnover and Postgovernment Employment Trends of Presidential Appointees." In G.C. Mackenzie, ed., *The In-and-Outers*, 174-94. Baltimore: Johns Hopkins University Press.

Braybrooke, David, and C.E. Lindblom, 1963. *A Strategy of Decision.* New York: Free Press.

Broder, David S. 1985. "Between His Ears an Arid Desert." *New Orleans Times-Picayune*, 2 September.

Broder, David S. 1986. "All the President's Midgets." *Washington Post, National Weekly Edition*, 15 December.

Broder, David S. 1987a. "Pollsters and Parliaments." *Washington Post, National Weekly Edition*, 13 July.

Broder, David S. 1987b. "Our Peculiar Way of Picking Presidents." *Washington Post*, 1 March.

Brody, Richard A. 1982. "Public Evaluations and Expectations and the Future of the Presidency." In J.S. Young, ed., *Problems and Prospects of Presidential Leadership*, 1: 37-56. Washington, D.C.: University Press of America.

Brody, Richard A., and Paul Sniderman. 1977. "From Life Space to Polling Place." *British Journal of Political Science* 7: 337-60.

Browne, Eric C., and John C. Dreijmanis, eds. 1982. *Government Coalitions in Western Democracies.* New York: Longman.

Brownlow, Louis. 1937. President's Committee on Administrative Management. *Administrative Management in the Government of the United States.* Washington, D.C.: Government Printing Office.

Buchanan, Bruce. 1987. *The Citizen's Presidency.* Washington, D.C.: CQ Press.

Buchanan, James M., and Richard Wagner. 1977. *Democracy in Deficit.* New York: Academic Press.

Bull, Hedley. 1986. "The American Presidency Viewed from Britain and Australia." In K.W. Thompson, ed., *The American Presidency: Perspectives from Abroad.* Lanham, Md.: University Press of America.

Bunce, Valerie. 1981. *Do New Leaders Make a Difference?* Princeton: Princeton University Press.

Bureau of the Census. 1960. *Historical Statistics of the United States, Colonial Times to 1957.* Washington, D.C.: Government Printing Office.

Burke, John P. 1985. "Presidential Influence and the Budget Process." In George Edwards, Steven Shull, and Norman Thomas, eds., *The Presidency and Public Policy Making*, 71-94. Pittsburgh: University of Pittsburgh Press.

Burns, James MacGregor. 1978. *Leadership.* New York: Harper & Row.

Butler, David, and Gareth Butler. 1986. *British Political Facts, 1900-1985.* 6th ed. London: Macmillan.

Byrnes, James F. 1947. *Speaking Frankly.* New York: Harper.

Caddell, Patrick. 1979. "Trapped in a Downward Spiral." *Public Opinion* 2 (October-November): 2-7.

Caiden, Naomi. 1987. "Paradox, Ambiguity and Enigma: The Strange Case of the Executive Budget and the United States Constitution." *Public Administration Review* 47(1): 84-92.

Cain, Bruce, John Ferejohn, and Morris Fiorina. 1987. *The Personal Vote.* Cambridge, Mass.: Harvard University Press.

Calder, Kent. 1985. "The Emerging Politics of the Trans-Pacific Economy." *World Policy Journal* 2: 593-623.

Callaghan, James. 1986. "Why Europe Needs Reagan to Fight Back." *The Times* (London) 19 December .

Calleo, David P. 1987. *Beyond American Hegemony.* New York: Basic Books.

Camdessus, Michel. 1988. "Camdessus Proposes Seven Points of Action." *IMF Survey,* 13 June, 194-96.

Campbell, Angus, Philip, Converse, Warren, Miller, and Donald Stokes. 1960. *The American Voter.* New York: Wiley.

Campbell, Colin. 1983. *Governments under Stress.* Toronto: University of Toronto Press.

Campbell, Colin. 1986. *Managing the Presidency: Carter, Reagan and the Search for Executive Harmony.* Pittsburgh: University of Pittsburgh Press.

Cannon, Lou. 1987. "A Team Player for the NSC." *Washington Post, National Weekly Edition,* 16 November.

Carter, Jimmy. 1982. *Keeping the Faith.* New York: Bantam Books.

Carter, Ralph. 1986. "Congressional Foreign Policy Behavior: Persistent Patterns of the Postwar Period." *Presidential Studies Quarterly* 16(2): 329-59.

Cater, Douglass. 1964. *Power in Washington.* New York: Random House.

Ceaser, James W. 1979. *Presidential Selection: Theory and Development.* Princeton: Princeton University Press.

Ceaser, James W., Glen Thurow, Jeffrey Tulis, and Joseph Bessette. 1981. "The Rise of the Rhetorical Presidency." *Presidential Studies Quarterly* 11(2): 158-71.

Chancellor, Alexander. 1987. "A Lesson Left Unlearnt." *The Independent* (London) 3 August.

Chubb, John E., and Paul E. Peterson, eds. 1985. *The New Direction in American Politics.* Washington, D.C.: Brookings Institution.

Citrin, Jack, and Donald Philip Green. 1986. "Presidential Leadership and the Resurgence of Trust in Government." *British Journal of Political Science* 16(4): 431-54.

Cohen, Benjamin J. 1977. *Organizing the World's Money: The Political Economy of International Monetary Relations.* New York: Basic Books.

Cohen, Benjamin J. 1987. "An Explosion in the Kitchen? Economic Relations with Other Advanced Industrial States." In K. Oye et al., eds., *Eagle Resurgent,* 115-44. Boston: Little, Brown.

Cohen, Michael D., and James G. March. 1974. *Leadership and Ambiguity: The American College President*. New York: McGraw-Hill.

Cohen, Michael D., James G. March, and Johan P. Olsen. 1972. "A Garbage Can Model of Organizational Choice." *Administrative Science Quarterly* 17: 1-25.

Cohen, Michael D., James G. March, and Johan P. Olsen. 1976. "People, Problems, Solutions and the Ambiguity of Relevance." In J. G. March and J.P. Olsen, *Ambiguity and Choice in Organizations*, 24-37. Bergen: Universitetsforlaget.

Cohen, Stephen D. 1982. "Approaches to the International Economic Policy-Making Process." In William Avery and David Rapkin, eds., *American in a Changing World Political Economy*, 147-74. White Plains, N.Y.: Longman.

Committee on Government Operations. 1986. *Office of Management and Budget: Roles and Future Issues*. Washington, D.C.: Congressional Research Service, 94th Cong., 2nd sess.

Cooper, Chester L. 1970. *The Lost Crusade: America in Vietnam*. New York: Dodd, Mead.

Corwin, Edward S. 1957. *The President: Office and Powers*. 4th ed. New York: New York University Press.

Council of State Governments. 1982. *The Book of the States, 1982-83*. Lexington, Ky.: Council of State Governments. Vol. 24.

Crabb, Cecil V., and Kevin V. Mulcahy. 1986. *Presidents and Foreign Policy Making from FDR to Reagan*. Baton Rouge: Louisiana State University Press.

Crecine, J.P. 1971. "Defense Budgeting: Organizational Adaptation to Environmental Constraints." In R.F. Byrne et al., *Studies in Budgeting*. Amsterdam: North-Holland.

Cronin. Thomas E. 1970. "'Everybody Believes in Democracy until He Gets to the White House'—An Analysis of White House-Departmental Relations." *Law and Contemporary Problems* 35(3): 573-625.

Cronin, Thomas E. 1980. *The State of the Presidency*. 2d ed. Boston: Little, Brown.

Cronin, Thomas E., ed. 1982. *Rethinking the Presidency*. Boston: Little, Brown.

Cronin, Thomas E. 1985. "On the Separation of Brain and State: Implications for the Presidency." In Marc Landy, ed., *Modern Presidents and the Presidency*, 51-64. Lexington, Mass.: Lexington Books.

Cunliffe, Marcus. 1982. *George Washington: Man and Monument*. Rev. ed. New York: Mentor.

Cunliffe, Marcus. 1987. "The Invention of the Presidency." In *The Great Ideas Today: 1987*, 156-221. Chicago: *Encyclopaedia Britannica*, .

Curtis, Gerald. 1979. "Big Business and Political Influence." In E. Vogel, ed., *Modern Japanese Organization and Decision-Making*, 33-70. Tokyo: Charles Tuttle.

Cutler, Lloyd. 1980."To Form a Government." *Foreign Affairs* 59 (Fall): 126-39.

Cutter, W. Bowman. 1984. "The Presidency and Economic Policy: A Tale of Two Budgets." In Michael Nelson, ed., *The President and the Political System,* 471-93. Washington D.C.: CQ Press.

Dahl, Robert A. 1957. "The Concept of Power." *Behavioral Science,* 2(July): 201-15.

Dallin, Alexander, and Gail W. Lapidus. 1987. "Reagan and the Russians." In K. Oye et al., eds., *Eagle Resurgent,* 193-254. Boston: Little, Brown.

Darman, Richard. 1987. "Darman Reflects on the Reagan Era." *Washington Post,* 7 April.

Davis, Eric L. 1983. "Congressional Liaison: The People and the Institutions." In A.S. King, ed., *Both Ends of the Avenue,* 59-95. Washington, D.C.: American Enterprise Institute.

Denton, Robert E., Jr., and Dan F. Hahn. 1986. *Presidential Communication.* New York: Praeger.

Destler, I.M. 1980. *Making Foreign Economic Policy.* Washington, D.C.: Brookings Institution.

Destler, I.M. 1981. "National Security II: The Rise of the Assistant, 1961-81." In H. Heclo and L. Salamon, eds., *The Illusion of Presidential Government,* 263-86. Boulder, Colo.: Westview Press.

Destler, I.M. 1986. *American Trade Politics.* Washington, D.C.: Institute for International Economics.

Destler, I.M., P. Clapp, H. Sato, and H. Fukui. 1976. *Managing an Alliance: The Politics of U.S.-Japanese Relations.* Washington, D.C.: Brookings Institution.

Destler, I.M., Leslie Gelb, and Anthony Lake. 1984. *Our Own Worst Enemy: The Unmaking of American Foreign Policy.* New York: Simon & Schuster.

Deutsch, Karl W. 1963. *The Nerves of Government.* New York: Free Press.

Dickenson, James R. 1987. "To Some Predecessors, Howard Baker Appears as Prime Minister to Reagan." *Washington Post,* 8 March.

Dillon, Douglas. 1985. "Address at Tufts University." In D.L. Robinson, ed., *Reforming American Government,* 24-29. Boulder, Colo.: Westview Press.

Dror, Yehezkel. 1980. *Crazy States.* Millwood, N.Y.: Kraus Reprint.

Dror, Yehezkel. 1987. "Conclusions: Advising the Rulers." In W.J.E.L. Plowden, ed., *Advising the Rulers,* 185-215. Oxford: Basil Blackwell.

Duggan, Ervin, William F. Gavin, and Robert Shrum. 1987. "Word Perfect." *Public Opinion* 10(1): 6-9.

Economic Report of the President. Annual. Washington, D.C.: Government Printing Office.

Edwards, George C., III. 1980. *Presidential Influence in Congress.* San Francisco: Freeman.

Edwards, George C., III. 1983. *The Public Presidency: The Pursuit of Popular Support.* New York: St. Martin's Press.

Edwards, George C., III. 1986. "The Two Presidencies: Reevaluation." *American Politics Quarterly* 14: 247-63.

Edwards, George C., III. 1988. "Presidential Leadership of Congress: The Role of Legislative Skills." In B. Jones, ed., *Political Leadership from Political Science Perspectives.* Topeka: University of Kansas Press.

Edwards, George C., III, and Stephen Wayne, eds. 1983. *Studying the Presidency.* Nashville: University of Tennessee Press.

Edwards, George C., III, and Stephen Wayne. 1985. *Presidential Leadership: Politics and Policy Making.* New York: St. Martin's Press.

Entman, Robert. 1981. "The Imperial Media." In A.J. Meltsner, ed., *Politics and the Oval Office*, 79-102. San Francisco: Institute for Contemporary Studies.

Evans, Rowland, and Robert Novak. 1987. "At the White House, Japan-Bashing is Out." *Washington Post*, 29 April.

Farrell, Brian. 1971. *Chairman or Chief? The Role of the Taoiseach in Irish Government.* Dublin: Gill and Macmillan.

Federal Register. 1986. *United States Government Manual.* Washington, D.C.: Government Printing Office.

Feldstein, Martin. 1987. "Correcting the Trade Deficit." *Foreign Affairs*, Spring, 795-806.

Fenno, Richard F., Jr. 1978. *Home Style: House Members in Their Districts.* Boston: Little, Brown.

Ferejohn, John A., and Morris P. Fiorina. 1985. "Incumbency and Realignment in Congressional Elections." In John E. Chubb and Paul E. Peterson, eds., *The New Direction in American Politics*, 91-116. Washington, D.C.: Brookings Institution.

Finer, Herman. 1960. *The Presidency: Crisis and Regeneration.* Chicago: University of Chicago Press.

Fiorina, Morris P. 1981. *Retrospective Voting in American National Elections.* New Haven: Yale University Press.

Fishel, Jeff. 1985. *Presidents & Promises: From Campaign Pledge to Presidential Performance.* Washington, D.C.: CQ Press.

Fisher, Linda. 1986. "Appointments and Presidential Control: The Importance of Role." Paper presented at annual meeting of the American Political Science Association, Washington, D.C.

Fisher, Linda. 1987. "Fifty Years of Presidential Appointments." In G.C. Mackenzie, ed., *The In-and-Outers*, 1-29. Baltimore: Johns Hopkins University Press.

Flash, Edward S. 1965. *Economic Advice and Presidential Leadership.* New York: Columbia University Press.

Ford, Gerald R. 1979. *A Time to Heal.* New York: Harper & Row.

Ford, Gerald R. 1980. "Imperiled, Not Imperial." *Time*, 10 November.

Ford, Gerald R. 1986. "Congress, the Presidency and National Security Policy." *Presidential Studies Quarterly* 16(2): 200-205.

Frank, Thomas M., and Edward Weisband. 1979. *Foreign Policy by Congress.* New York: Oxford University Press.

Frankel, Jeffrey. 1988. "Obstacles to International Macroeconomic Policy Coordination." Paper presented to a conference on Blending Economic and Political Analysis of International Financial Relations, Claremont Colleges and the University of Southern California, Los Angeles, 24-26 May.

Freeman, J. Leiper. 1955. *The Political Process: Executive Bureau-Legislative Committee Relations.* New York: Doubleday.

Freeman, J. Leiper, and Judith Parris Stevens. 1987. "A Theoretical and Conceptual Re-examination of Subsystem Politics." *Public Policy and Administration* 2(1): 9-24.

Frey, Bruno. 1987. "Fighting Political Terrorism by Refusing Recognition". *Journal of Public Policy* 7(2): 179-88.

Friedman, Milton. 1962. *Capitalism and Freedom.* Chicago: University of Chicago Press.

Friedman, Milton. 1972. "Have Monetary Policies Failed?" *American Economic Review* 62(1).

Funabashi, Yoichi. 1988. *Managing the Dollar: From the Plaza to the Louvre.* Washington, D.C.: Institute for International Economics.

George, Alexander L. 1980. *Presidential Decisionmaking in Foreign Affairs.* Boulder, Col.: Westview Press.

Gergen, David R. 1976. *The Ford Presidency: A Portrait of the First Two Years.* Washington, D.C.: White House Office of Communications.

Gilpin, Robert. 1975. *U.S. Power and the Multinational Corporation.* New York: Basic Books.

Gilpin, Robert. 1987. *The Political Economy of International Relations.* Princeton: Princeton University Press.

Goldenberg, Edie N. 1985. "The Permanent Government in an Era of Retrenchment and Redirection." In L. Salamon and M. Lund, eds., *The Reagan Presidency and the Governing of America,* 381-404. Washington, D.C.: Urban Institute Press.

Goldstein, Joel K. 1982. *The Modern American Vice Presidency.* Princeton: Princeton University Press.

Goodnow, F.J. 1910. *City Government in the United States.* New York: Century.

Goodsell, Charles T. 1985. *The Case for Bureaucracy.* 2d ed. Chatham, N.J.: Chatham House.

Goshko, John M. 1987. "Sticking It to the Foreign Service." *Washington Post, National Weekly Edition,* 25 May.

Gowa, Joanne. 1983. *Closing the Gold Window: Domestic Politics and the End of Bretton Woods.* Ithaca: Cornell University Press.

Graber, Doris. 1980. *Mass Media and American Politics.* Washington, D.C.: CQ Press.

Graetz, Brian, and Ian McAllister. 1987. "Party Leaders and Election Outcomes in Britain, 1974-1983." *Comparative Political Studies* 19(4): 484-507.

Gramlich, Edward M. 1984. "How Bad Are the Large Deficits?" In G.B. Mills and J.L. Palmer, eds., *Federal Budget Policy in the 1980s*, 43-68. Washington, D.C.: Urban Institute Press.

Gray, William H. 1985. "Expect Chaos." *New York Times*, 19 December.

Greenstein, Fred. 1978. "Change and Continuity in the Modern Presidency." In A.S. King, ed., *The New American Political System*, 45-86. Washington, D.C.: American Enterprise Institute.

Greenstein, Fred. 1982. *The Hidden-Hand Presidency; Eisenhower as Leader.* New York: Basic Books.

Greenstein, Fred, ed. 1983. *The Reagan Presidency*. Baltimore: Johns Hopkins University Press.

Greenstein, Fred, ed., 1988. *Leadership In the Modern Presidency*. Cambridge, Mass.: Harvard University Press.

Greenstein, Fred, Larry Berman, and Alvin Felzenberg. 1977. *Evolution of the Modern Presidency: A Bibliographical Survey*. Washington, D.C.: American Enterprise Institute.

Greider, David. 1982. *The Education of David Stockman and Other Americans*. New York: E.P. Dutton.

Grogan, Fred I. 1977. "Candidate Promise and Presidential Performance, 1964-72." Paper presented at Midwest Political Science Association annual meeting, Chicago.

Grossman, Michael B., and Martha J. Kumar. 1981. *Portraying the President: The White House and the News Media*. Baltimore: Johns Hopkins University Press.

Gunlicks, Arthur B., ed. 1981. *Local Government Reform and Reorganization: An International Perspective*. Port Washington, N.Y: Kennikat Press.

Hadenius, Axel. 1985. "Citizens Strike a Balance: Content with Taxes, Discontent with Spending." *Journal of Public Policy* 5(3): 349-64.

Hall, Peter Dobkin. 1982. *The Organization of American Culture, 1700-1900*. New York: New York University Press.

Hargrove, Erwin C., and Samuel A. Morley, eds. 1984. *The President and the Council of Economic Advisers: Interviews with CEA Chairmen*. Boulder, Colo.: Westview Press.

Hargrove, Erwin C., and Michael Nelson. 1984. *Presidents, Politics and Policy*. New York: Knopf.

Hart, Gary. 1988. "Why Do the Media Miss the Message?" *Washington Post, National Weekly Edition*, 3 January.

Hart, Roderick. 1987. *The Sound of Leadership: Presidential Communication in the Modern Age*. Chicago: University of Chicago Press.

Hayao, Kenji. 1985. "The Japanese Prime Minister in the Policy Process." University of Michigan, Ann Arbor. Duplicated.

Hayward, J.E.S. 1983. *Governing France: The One and Indivisible Republic.* London: Weidenfeld and Nicolson.

Heclo, Hugh. 1974. *Modern Social Politics in Britain and Sweden.* New Haven: Yale University Press.

Heclo, Hugh. 1975. "OMB and the Presidency—the Problem of 'Neutral Competence.'" *Public Interest,* no. 38 (Winter).

Heclo, Hugh. 1977. *A Government of Strangers: Executive Politics in Washington.* Washington, D.C.: Brookings Institution.

Heclo, Hugh. 1978. "Issue Networks and the Executive Establishment." In A.S. King, ed., *The New American Political System,* 87-124. Washington, D.C.: American Enterprise Institute.

Heclo, Hugh. 1983. "One Executive Branch or Many?" In A.S. King, ed. , *Both Ends of the Avenue,* 26-58. Washington, D.C.: American Enterprise Institute.

Heclo, Hugh. 1984. "Executive Budget Making." In G.B. Mills and J.L. Palmer, eds., *Federal Budget Policy in the 1980s,* 255-91. Washington, D.C.: Urban Institute Press.

Heclo, Hugh. 1985. "The Executive Office of the President." In Marc Landy, ed., *Modern Presidents and the Presidency,* 65-82. Lexington, Mass.: Lexington Books.

Heclo, Hugh. 1986. "Reaganism and the Search for a Public Philosophy." In John L. Palmer, ed., *Perspectives on the Reagan Years,* 31-64. Washington, D.C.: Urban Institute Press.

Heclo, Hugh, and Lester Salamon eds., 1981. *The Illusion of Presidential Government.* Boulder, Colo.: Westview Press.

Heclo, Hugh, and Aaron Wildavsky. 1981. *The Private Government of Public Money.* 2d ed. London: Macmillan.

Heineman, Ben W., Jr. 1985. "Comment on Executive Office Policy Apparatus." In L. Salamon and M. Lund, eds., *The Reagan Presidency and the Governing of America,* 169-75. Washington, D.C.: Urban Institute Press.

Heineman Commission. 1967. *A Final Report of the President's Task Force on Government Organization.* Working Paper No. 1. Washington, D.C. Unpublished typescript. 15 June.

Heller, Peter, and Alan Tait. 1983. *Government Employment and Pay: Some International Comparisons.* Washington, D.C.: International Monetary Fund, Occasional Paper No. 24.

Heller, Walter W. 1963. "Memorandum for the President: The Services of Your Council of Economic Advisers." 1 December. LBJ Presidential Library, Austin, Administration History, CEA File, vol. 1.

Heller, Walter W. 1967. *New Dimensions of Political Economy.* New York: Norton.

Henderson, Sir Nicholas. 1987. "Of Unsound Constitution." *The Times* (London) 22 July .

Herbers, John. 1976. *No Thank You, Mr. President.* New York: Norton.

Hess, Stephen. 1976. *Organizing the Presidency.* Washington, D.C.: Brookings Institution.

Hess, Stephen. 1981. *The Washington Reporters.* Washington, D.C.: Brookings Institution.

Hess, Stephen. 1983. "How Foreign Correspondents Cover the United States." *Brookings Review,* no. 10: 3-5.

Hibbs, Douglas, and Heino Fassbender, eds. 1981. *Contemporary Political Economy.* Amsterdam: North-Holland.

Hibbs, Douglas, and Nicholas Vasilatos. 1981. "Economics and Politics in France." *European Journal of Political Research* 9. 191-212.

Hirschfield, Robert S., ed. 1973. *The Power of the Presidency.* 2d ed. Chicago: Aldine.

Hoffman, David. 1986. "A Flawed Legacy." *Washington Post Magazine,* 30 November.

Hogg, Sarah. 1987. "The Lessons of the Crash That America has Failed to Learn." *The Independent* (London) 11 November.

Holden, Matthew, Jr., 1986. "Bargaining and Command in the Administrative Process." Charlottesville, Va.: Working Papers in Public Administration No. 2.

Holland, Kenneth M. 1984. "The War Powers Resolution." In Gordon M. Hoxie, ed., *The Presidency and National Security Policy.* New York: Center for the Study of the Presidency.

Hoover, Irvin H. 1934. *Forty-two Years in the White House.* Boston: Houghton Mifflin.

Horowitz, Donald. 1987. "Is the Presidency Failing?" *Public Interest* 88: 2-27.

Hrebenar, Ronald J. 1986. *The Japanese Party System.* Boulder, Colo.: Westview Press.

Hughes, Emmet John. 1973. *The Living Presidency.* Baltimore: Penguin.

Hughes, T.L. 1967. "Relativity in Foreign Policy." *Foreign Affairs* 45 (July): 670-82.

Ignatius, David, and Michael Getler. 1986. "Ronald Reagan's Foreign Policy." *Washington Post, National Weekly Edition,* 1 December.

IMF (International Monetary Fund). 1974. *International Financial Statistics 1972: Supplement.* Washington, D.C.: International Monetary Fund.

Inter-Parliamentary Union. 1986. *Parliaments of the World.* 2d ed. Aldershot: Gower.

Jacob, Charles E. 1985. "The Congressional Elections." In Gerald Pomper ed., *The Election of 1984,* 112-31. Chatham, N.J.: Chatham House.

Jacobson, Gary C. 1983. *The Politics of Congressional Elections.* Boston: Little, Brown.

Jenkins, Peter. 1987. "Reaganomics Coming Home to Roost." *The Independent* (London) 21 October.

Johnson, Bruce E. 1984. "From Analyst to Negotiator." *Journal of Political Analysis and Management* 3(4): 501-15.

Johnson, Haynes. 1980. *In the Absence of Power: Governing America*. New York: Viking.

Johnson, Richard T. 1975. "Presidential Style." In Aaron Wildavsky, ed. *Perspectives on the Presidency*, 262-300. Boston: Little, Brown.

Jones, Charles O. 1974. "Doing Before Knowing: Concept Development in Political Research." *American Journal of Political Science* 18(1).

Jones, Charles O. 1981. "House Leadership in an Age of Reform." In Frank Mackaman, ed., *Understanding Congressional Leadership*. Washington, D.C.: CQ Press.

Jones, Charles O. 1982. *The United States Congress*. Homewood, Ill.: Dorsey Press.

Jones, Charles O. 1983. "Presidential Negotiation with Congress." In A.S. King, ed., *Both Ends of the Avenue*, 96-130. Washington, D.C.: American Enterprise Insitute.

Jones, Charles O. 1985. "A New President, a Different Congress, a Maturing Agenda." In L. Salamon and M. Lund, eds., *The Reagan Presidency and the Governing of America*, 261-87. Washington, D.C.: Urban Institute Press.

Jones, George W. 1987. "The United Kingdom." In W.J.E.L. Plowden, ed., *Advising the Rulers*, 36-66. Oxford: Basil Blackwell.

Jordan, A. Grant. 1981 "Iron Triangles, Woolly Corporatism or Elastic Nets? Images of the Policy Process." *Journal of Public Policy* 1(1): 95-124

Kahler, Miles. 1987. "The United States and Western Europe: the Diplomatic Consequences of Mr. Reagan." In K.W. Oye et al., eds., *Eagle Resurgent*, 297-334 Boston: Little, Brown.

Kataoka, Masaaki. 1988. "The Political Experience of Japanese Prime Ministers since 1955." University of Michigan, Ann Arbor. Duplicated.

Kaufman, Herbert. 1981. *The Administrative Behavior of Federal Bureau Chiefs*. Washington, D.C.: Brookings Institution.

Kearl, J.R., C.L. Pope, G.C. Whiting, and L.T. Wimmer. 1979. "A Confusion of Economists?" *Proceedings of the American Economic Association: American Economic Review* 69 (May).

Kelley, Stanley. 1956. *Professional Public Relations and Political Power*. Baltimore: Johns Hopkins University Press.

Keohane, Robert O. 1984. *After Hegemony: Cooperation and Discord in the World Political Economy*. Princeton: Princeton University Press.

Keohane, Robert O., and Joseph S. Nye, Jr. 1977. *Power and Interdependence*. Boston: Little, Brown.

Kernell, Samuel. 1985. "Campaigning, Governing and the Contemporary Presidency." In John E. Chubb and Paul E. Peterson, eds., *The New Direction in American Politics*, 117-43. Washinton, D.C.: Brookings Institution.

Kernell, Samuel. 1986. *Going Public: New Strategies of Presidential Leadership.* Washington, D.C.: CQ Press.

Kernell, Samuel, and Samuel I. Popkin, eds. 1986. *Chief of Staff: Twenty-Five Years of Managing the Presidency.* Berkeley: University of California Press.

Kessel, John H. 1974. "The Parameters of Presidential Politics," *Social Science Quarterly* 54: 8-24.

Kessel, John. 1975. *The Domestic Presidency.* North Scituate, Mass.: Duxbury.

Kessel, John H. 1983. "The Structures of the Carter White House." *American Journal of Political Science* 27(3): 431-63.

Kessel, John H. 1984a. *Presidential Campaign Politics.* 2d ed. Homewood, Ill.: Dorsey.

Kessel, John H. 1984b. "The Structures of the Reagan White House." *American Journal of Political Science* 28(2): 231-58.

Ketcham, Ralph. 1984. *Presidents Above Party: The First American Presidency, 1789-1829.* Chapel Hill: University of North Carolina Press.

Kettl, Donald F. 1986. *Leadership at the Fed.* New Haven: Yale University Press.

Key, V.O., Jr. 1949. *Southern Politics in State and Nation.* New York: Knopf.

Key, V.O., Jr. 1961. *Public Opinion and American Democracy.* New York: Knopf.

Key, V.O., Jr. 1964. *Politics, Parties and Pressure Groups.* 5th ed. New York: Crowell, .

Keynes, J.M. 1936. *The General Theory of Employment.* London: Macmillan.

Kiewiet, D. Roderick. 1983. *Macroeconomics and Micropolitics.* Chicago: University of Chicago Press.

Kinder, Donald, and Roderick D. Kiewiet. 1981. "Sociotropic Politics—the American Case." *British Journal of Political Science* 11(2): 129-61.

Kindleberger, Charles. 1973. *The World in Depression, 1929-1939.* Berkeley: University of California Press.

King, A.S., ed. 1983. *Both Ends of the Avenue.* Washington, D.C.: American Enterprise Institute.

King, A.S., ed. 1985. *The British Prime Minister.* London: Macmillan.

Kingdon, John W. 1984. *Agendas, Alternatives, and Public Policies.* Boston: Little, Brown.

Kirschten, Dick. 1985. "Once Again Cabinet Government's Beauty Lies in Being No More Than Skin Deep." *National Journal*, 15 June.

Kirschten, Dick. 1987. "Competent Manager." *National Journal*, 28 February.

Kissinger, Henry. 1979. *White House Years.* Boston: Little, Brown.

Klamer, Arjo. 1983. *Conversations with Economists.* Totowa, N.J.: Rowman and Allanheld.

Klein, Lawrence R. 1947. *The Keynesian Revolution.* New York: Macmillan.

Klein, Lawrence R., and A.S. Goldberger. 1955. *An Econometric Model of the United States, 1929-1952.* Amsterdam: North-Holland.

Kloeti, Ulrich, and Hans-Jakob Mosimann. 1985. "Cabinet Committees in Switzerland." In T. Mackie and B. Hogwood, eds., *Unlocking the Cabinet*, 155-79. Beverly Hills: Sage Publications.

Koenig, Louis W. 1975. *The Chief Executive*. 3d ed. New York: Harcourt Brace Jovanovich.

Korb, Lawrence J. 1980. "The Evolving Relationship between the White House and the Department of Defense in the Post-Imperial Presidency." In Vincent Davis, ed., *The Post-Imperial Presidency*, 101-10. New Brunswick, N.J.: Transaction.

Kozak, David C. 1980. "Review of Alexander L. George." *Presidential Studies Quarterly*. 10(3): 500-504.

Kraft, Tim. 1977. "Memorandum for the President: 1977: Your Schedule and Time." Washington, D.C.: White House. Duplicated.

Ladd, Everett Carll. 1986. "Republicans and Democrats." *Dialogue* 74: 71-72.

Lafay, Jean-Dominique. 1981. "The Impact of Economic Variables on Political Behavior in France." In D.Hibbs and H. Fassbender, eds., *Contemporary Political Economy*, 137-49. Amsterdam: North-Holland.

Lamar, Jacob V. 1987. "Prepping the President." *Time*, 30 March.

Lammers, William W. 1982. "Presidential Attention-Focusing Activities." In Doris Graber, ed., *The President and the Public*, 145-71. Philadelphia: Institute for the Study of Human Issues.

Langdon, Frank C. 1967. *Japan*. Boston: Little, Brown.

Lehmbruch, Gerhard. 1967. *Proporzdemokratie: Politisches System und Politische Kultur in der Schweiz und in Oesterreich*. Tuebingen: J.C.B. Mohr.

LeLoup, Lance, and S.A. Shull. 1979. "Congress versus the Executive: The 'Two Presidencies' Reconsidered." *Social Science Quarterly* 59(4): 704-19.

Leontief, Wassily. 1985. *Essays in Economics: Theories, Theorizing, Facts and Policies*. New Brunswick, N.J.: Transaction.

Lees, John D. 1987. "The President and His Party." In Malcolm Shaw, ed., *Roosevelt to Reagan: The Development of the Modern Presidency*, 46-82. London: C. Hurst.

Lieber, Robert J. 1987. "International Energy Policy and the Reagan Administration." In K. Oye et al., eds., *Eagle Resurgent*, 167-92 Boston: Little, Brown.

Light, Paul C. 1982. *The President's Agenda*. Baltimore: Johns Hopkins University Press.

Lindbeck, Assar. 1976. "Stabilization Policy in Open Economies with Endogenous Politicians." *American Economic Review*, 66(2).

Lindblom, Charles E. 1965. *The Intelligence of Democracy*. New York: Free Press.

Linder, Staffan B. 1986. *The Pacific Century: Economic and Political Consequences of Asian-Pacific Dynamism*. Stanford: Stanford University Press.

Lipset, S.M. 1960. *Political Man*. New York: Doubleday.

Lipset, S.M., and William R. Schneider. 1983. *The Confidence Gap*. New York: Free Press.

Lowi, Theodore J. 1985. *The Personal President: Power Invested, Promise Unfulfilled*. Ithaca: Cornell University Press.

Lynn, Laurence E., Jr. 1985. "The Reagan Administration and the Renitent Bureaucracy." In L. Salamon and M. Lund, eds., *The Reagan Presidency and the Governing of America*, 339-70. Washington, D.C.: Urban Institute Press.

MacDougall, Terry E., ed. 1982. *Political Leadership in Contemporary Japan*. Ann Arbor: University of Michigan Papers in Japanese Studies No. 1.

Mackenzie, G. Calvin. 1981. *The Politics of Presidential Appointments*. New York: Free Press.

Mackenzie, G. Calvin, ed. 1987. *The In-and-Outers: Presidential Appointees and Transient Government in Washington*. Baltimore: Johns Hopkins University Press.

Mackie, T.T., and B.W. Hogwood, eds. 1985. *Unlocking the Cabinet: Cabinet Structures in Comparative Perspective*. Beverly Hills: Sage Publications.

MacKuen, Michael B. 1983. "Political Drama, Economic Conditions, and the Dynamics of Presidential Popularity." *American Journal of Political Science* 27: 165-92.

Maass, Arthur. 1983. *Congress and the Common Good*. New York: Basic Books.

Maidment, Richard. 1987. "Japan: A Survey." *The Economist*, 5 December.

Malek, Frederic V. 1978. *Washington's Hidden Tragedy*. New York: Free Press.

Mandelbaum, Michael, and Strobe Talbott. 1987. *Reagan and Gorbachev*. New York: Vintage.

Mann, Thomas E. 1981. "Elections and Change in Congress." In T.E. Mann and N.J. Ornstein, eds., *The New Congress*, 32-54. Washington, D.C.: American Enterprise Institute.

Mansfield, Harvey C., Sr. 1983. "Presidential-Congressional Relations in the 1980s." In J.S. Young, ed., *Problems and Prospects of Presidential Leadership in the Nineteen-Eighties*, 2: 53-76. Lanham, Md.: University Press of America.

March, James G., and Johan P. Olsen. 1983. "Organizing Political Life: What Administrative Reorganization Tells Us About Government." *American Political Science Review*, 77(2).

Marmor, Theodore R., with Phillip Fellman. 1986. "Policy Entrepreneurship in Government." *Journal of Public Policy* 6(3): 225-54.

Marris, Stephen. 1985. *Deficits and the Dollar: The World Economy at Risk*. Washington, D.C.: Institute for International Economics.

Marris, Stephen. Forthcoming. *The Economics and Politics of Managing the World Economy*. Washington, D.C.: Institute for International Economics.

Massot, Jean. 1979. *Le Chef du Gouvernement en France*. Paris: La Documentation Francaise.

329

May, Ernest R. 1987. "Changing International Stakes in Presidential Selection." In A. Heard and M. Nelson, eds., *Presidential Selection*, 32-52. Durham, N.C.: Duke University Press.

Mayer, Thomas, ed. 1978. *The Structure of Monetarism*. New York: Norton.

Mayntz, Renate. 1980. "Executive Leadership in Germany: Dispersion of Power or *Kanzlerdemokratie?*" In R. Rose and E. Suleiman, eds., *Presidents and Prime Ministers*, 139-70. Washington, D.C.: American Enterprise Institute.

Medved, Michael. 1979. *The Shadow Presidents: The Secret History of the Chief Executives and Their Top Aides*. New York: Times Books.

Meltsner, Arnold J. 1981. "Politics and Governance." In A.J. Meltsner, ed., *Politics and the Oval Office*, 285-302. San Francisco: Institute for Contemporary Studies.

Merlini, Cesar, ed. 1984. *Economic Summits and Western Decision-Making*. London: Croom Helm.

Miller, A.H., M.P. Wattenberg, and O. Malanchuk. 1986. "Schematic Assessments of Presidential Candidates." *American Political Science Review* 80(2): 521-40.

Miller, Warren E. 1979. "Misreading the Public Pulse." *Public Opinion* 2 (October-November): 9-15.

Mochizuki, Mike M. 1987. "The United States and Japan: Conflict and Cooperation under Mr. Reagan." In K. Oye et al., eds., *Eagle Resurgent*, 335-58. Boston: Little, Brown.

Moe, Terry M. 1985. "The Politicized Presidency." In John E. Chubb and Paul E. Peterson, eds., *The New Direction in American Politics*, 235-72. Washington, D.C.: Brookings Institution.

Monroe, Kristen. 1984. *Presidential Popularity and the Economy*. New York: Praeger.

Mosher, Frederick C., W.D. Clinton, and D.G. Lang. 1987. *Presidential Transitions and Foreign Affairs*. Baton Rouge: Louisiana State University Press.

Mosley, Paul. 1984. *The Making of Economic Policy*. Brighton: Wheatsheaf.

Mueller, John. 1970. "Presidential Popularity from Truman to Johnson." *American Political Science Review* 64(1): 18-34.

Mueller, John. 1973. *War, Presidents and Public Opinion*. New York: Wiley.

Mulcahy, Kevin, and Cecil V. Crabb. 1987. "Presidential Management of National Security Policymaking, 1947-87." Paper presented at annual meeting of the Southern Political Science Association, Charlotte, N.C.

Muramatsu, Michio. 1987. "In Search of National Identity: The Politics and Policies of the Nakasone Administration." *Journal of Japanese Studies* 13(2): 307-42.

Muramatsu, Michio, and Ellis S. Krauss. 1984 "The Ruling Coalition and Its Transformation." Paper presented to Japan Political Economic Committee Conference, Tokyo.

Murray, Robert K., and T.H. Blessing. 1983. "The Presidential Performance Study: A Progress Report." *Journal of American History* 70: 535-55.

NAPA (National Academy of Public Administration). 1984. *Recruiting Presidential Appointees: A Conference.* Washington, D.C.: NAPA. Occasional Papers No. 4.

NAPA (National Academy of Public Administration). 1985. *Leadership in Jeopardy.* Washington, D.C.: NAPA. Final Report of the Presidential Appointee Project.

Nathan, James A., and James K. Oliver. 1987. *Foreign Policy Making and the American Political System.* 2d ed. Boston: Little, Brown.

Nathan, Richard A. 1983. *The Administrative Presidency.* Rev. ed. New York: Wiley,

Nathan, Richard. 1985. "Public Administration Is Legitimate." In L. Salamon and M. Lund, eds., *The Reagan Presidency and the Governing of America,* 375-79. Washington, D.C.: Urban Institute Press.

Nau, Henry R. 1984. "Where Reaganomics Works." *Foreign Policy,* no. 57: 14-37.

Nau, Henry R. 1985 "Reaganomics: Or the Solution?" *Foreign Policy,* no. 59: 144-53.

Nau, Henry R. 1987. "Trade and Deterrence" *National Interest,* Spring, 48-60.

Nelson, Anna Kasten . 1981. "National Security I: Inventing a Process, 1945-60." In H. Heclo and L. Salamon, eds., *The Illusion of Presidential Government,* 229-62. Boulder, Colo.: Westview Press.

Nelson, Robert H. 1987. "The Economics Profession and the Making of Public Policy." *Journal of Economic Literature* 25(1): 49-91.

Nettl, J.P. 1968. "The State as a Conceptual Variable." *World Politics* 20: 559-81.

Neuman, W. Russell. 1986. *The Paradox of Mass Politics.* Cambridge, Mass.: Harvard University Press.

Neustadt, Richard E. 1960. 1980. 3d ed. *Presidential Power.* New York: Wiley.

Neustadt, Richard E. 1970. *Alliance Politics.* New York: Columbia University Press.

Neustadt, Richard E. 1986. "Foreword." In S. Kernell and S. I. Popkin, eds., *Chief of Staff.* Berkeley: University of California Press.

Newland, Chester A. 1983. "The Reagan Presidency: Limited Government and Political Administration." *Public Administration Review* 43(1): 1-21.

Newland, Chester A. 1985. "Executive Office Policy Apparatus: Enforcing the Reagan Agenda." In L. Salamon and M. Lund, eds., *The Reagan Presidency and the Governing of America,* 135-68. Washington, D.C.: Urban Institute Press.

Nixon, Richard M. 1980 "Needed: Clarity of Purpose." *Time,* 10 November.

Nixon, Richard M. 1985 "Televised Interview with David Frost, 1977." Reprinted in Barbara Hinckley, *Problems of the Presidency,* 256-57. Glenview, Ill.: Scott, Foresman.

Nourse, Edwin G. 1953. *Economics in the Public Service*. New York: Harcourt Brace.

Nove, Alex. 1986. *The Soviet Economic System*. London: Allen and Unwin.

Oberdorfer, Don. 1987. "At Reykjavik, Soviets Were Prepared and U.S. Improvised." *Washington Post*, 16 February.

Odell, John S. 1982. *U.S. International Monetary Policy: Markets, Power and Ideas as Sources of Change*. Princeton: Princeton University Press.

OECD. 1984. *Japan: OECD Economic Surveys*. Paris: Organisation for Economic Cooperation and Development.

OECD. 1985. *Social Expenditure, 1960-1990*. Paris: Organisation for Economic Cooperation and Development.

OECD. 1986a. *Revenue Statistics of OECD Member Countries*. Paris: Organisation for Economic Cooperation and Development.

OECD. 1986b. *Historical Statistics*. Paris: Organisation for Economic Cooperation and Development.

OECD. 1987a. "OECD Council Meets at Ministerial Level: Communique." *OECD Observer*, no. 146: 19-22.

OECD. 1988. "OECD in Figures." *OECD Observer* 152 (June/July), supplement.

Olsen, Johan. 1980. "Governing Norway :Segmentation, Anticipation and Consensus Formation." In R. Rose and E. Suleiman, eds., *Presidents and Prime Ministers*, 203-56. Washington, D.C.: American Enterprise Institute.

Olson, Mancur. 1968. "Economics, Sociology and the Best of All Possible Worlds." *Public Interest*, no. 12.

Olson, Mancur, and Richard Zeckhauser. 1966. "An Economic Theory of Alliances." *Review of Economics and Statistics* 48(3): 266-79.

OMB. 1987a. *Historical Tables: Budget of the United States Government: Fiscal Year 1988*. Washington, D.C.: Government Printing Office.

OMB. 1987b. *Budget of the United States Government Fiscal Year 1988: Supplement*. Washington, D.C.: Government Printing Office.

OMB. 1988. *Budget of the United States Government Fiscal Year 1989: Supplement*. Washington, D.C.: Government Printing Office.

Ornstein, Norman J. 1983. "The Open Congress Meets the President." In A.S. King, ed., *Both Ends of the Avenue*, 185-221. Washington, D.C.: American Enterprise Institute.

Ostrom, Charles W., and Dennis M. Simon. 1985. "Promise and Performance: A Dynamic Model of Presidential Popularity." *American Political Science Review* 79(2): 334-58.

Oye, K.A. 1987. "Constrained Confidence and the Evolution of Reagan Foreign Policy." In K. Oye et al., eds., *Eagle Resurgent*, 3-40 Boston: Little, Brown.

Oye, K.A., R.J. Lieber, and D. Rothchild, eds. 1987. *Eagle Resurgent? The Reagan Era in American Foreign Policy*. Boston: Little, Brown.

Packard, George R. 1987. "The Coming U.S.-Japan Crisis." *Foreign Affairs*, Winter, 348-67.

Page, Benjamin I., and Mark Petracca. 1983. *The American Presidency*. New York: McGraw-Hill.

Page, Benjamin I., and Robert Y. Shapiro. 1985. "Presidential Leadership through Public Opinion." In G.C. Edwards III et al., eds., *The Presidency and Public Policy Making*, 22-36. Pittsburgh: University of Pittsburgh Press.

Page, Edward C., and M. J. Goldsmith, eds. 1987. *Central and Local Government Relations*. Beverly Hills: Sage Publications.

Paldam, Martin. 1981. "A Preliminary Survey of the European Theories and Findings on Vote and Popularity Functions." *European Journal of Political Research*, 181-200.

Parisot, Laurence. 1988. "Attitudes about the Media: A Five Country Comparison." *Public Opinion* 10(5): 18-20.

Patterson, Bradley H., Jr. 1976. *The President's Cabinet: Issues and Questions*. Washington, D.C.: American Society for Public Administration.

Patterson, Bradley H., Jr. 1982. "Comment." In B.L.R. Smith and J.D. Carroll, eds., *Improving the Accountability and Performance of Government*, 105-10. Washington, D.C.: Brookings Institution.

Patterson, Thomas. 1980. *The Mass Media Election: How Americans Choose their President*. New York: Praeger.

Pechman, Joseph A. 1983. *Federal Tax Policy*. Washington, D.C.: Brookings Institution.

Pelkmans, Jacques. 1984. "Collective Management and Economic Cooperation." In C. Merlini, ed. *Economic Summits and Western Decision-Making*, 89-136. London: Croom Helm.

Pempel, T.J. 1982. *Policy and Politics in Japan*. Philadelphia: Temple University Press.

Pempel, T.J. 1984. "Organizing for Efficiency; The Higher Civil Service in Japan." In Ezra Suleiman, ed., *Bureaucrats and Policy Making*, 72-106. New York: Holmes and Meier.

Pempel, T.J. 1986. "Uneasy toward Autonomy: Parliament and Parliamentarians." In Ezra Suleiman, ed., *Parliaments and Parliamentarians in Democratic Politics*, 79-105. New York: Holmes and Meier.

Pempel, T.J. 1987. "The Unbundling of Japan, Inc.: The Changing Dynamics of Japanese Policy Formation." *Journal of Japanese Studies* 13(2): 271-306.

Peppers, Donald A. 1975. "'The Two Presidencies': Eight Years Later." In Aaron Wildavsky, ed., *Perspectives on the Presidency*, 462-71. Boston: Little, Brown.

Peters, B. Guy. 1985. "The United States: Absolute Change and Relative Stability." In R. Rose, *Public Employment in Western Nations*, 228-61. New York: Cambridge University Press.

Peterson, Paul E. 1985. "The New Politics of Deficits." *Political Science Quarterly* 100(4): 575-601.

Peterson, Peter G. 1987. "The Morning After." *Atlantic Monthly*, October, 43-69.

Pfiffner, James. 1985. "Political Public Administration." *Public Administration Review* 45 (March/April).

Pfiffner, James, ed. 1986. *The President and Economic Policy.* Philadelphia: Institute for the Study of Human Issues.

Pfiffner, James P. 1987. *The Strategic Presidency: Hitting the Ground Running.* Homewood, Ill.: Dorsey.

Pious, Richard M. 1979. *The American Presidency.* New York: Basic Books.

Plischke, Elmer. 1971. "The President's Right to Go Abroad." *Orbis* 15(4): 755-83.

Plischke, Elmer. 1985. "Rating Presidents and Diplomats in Chief." *Presidential Studies Quarterly* 15(4): 725-43.

Plischke, Elmer. 1986. *Diplomat in Chief: The President at the Summit.* New York: Praeger.

Plowden, W.J.E.L., ed. 1987. *Advising the Rulers.* Oxford: Basil Blackwell.

Podhoretz, Norman. 1987. "Tory Lessons for Reagan," *The Times* (London) 18 June.

Polsby, Nelson. 1983. *Consequences of Party Reform.* New York: Oxford University Press.

Polsby, Nelson. 1984. *Political Innovation in America.* New Haven: Yale University Press.

Polsby, Nelson, and Aaron Wildavsky. 1984. *Presidential Elections.* 6th ed. New York: Scribner's.

Porter, Roger B. 1980. *Presidential Decision Making: The Economic Policy Board.* New York: Cambridge University Press.

Porter, Roger B. 1982. "Organizing International Economic Policy Making." In William Avery and David Rapkin, eds., *America in a Changing World Political Economy*, 175-90. New York: Longman.

Porter, Roger B. 1983. "Economic Advice to the President." *Political Science Quarterly* 93(3): 403-26.

Porter, Roger B. 1985. "Interview on How the White House Works." *Brookings Review*, Fall, 37-40.

Porter, Roger B. 1987. "Comment on the United States Presidency." In W.J.E.L. Plowden, ed., *Advising the Rulers*, 86-92. Oxford: Basil Blackwell.

Price, Don K. 1982. "The Institutional Presidency and the Unwritten Constitution." In James S. Young, ed., *Problems and Prospects of Presidential Leadership*, 1: 57-84. Washington, D.C.: University Press of America.

Public Opinion. 1987. "The Role of Government." 9(6): 21-40.

Putnam, Robert. 1984. "The Western Economic Summits: A Political Interpretation." In C. Merlini, ed., *Economic Summits and Western Decision-Making*, 43-88. London: Croom Helm.

Putnam, Robert. 1988. "Diplomacy and Domestic Politics: The Logic of Two-Level Games." *International Organization* 42, no. 3 (Summer): 427-69.

Putnam, Robert, and Nicholas Bayne. 1987. *Hanging Together: The Seven-Power Summits.* 2d ed. Cambridge, Mass. : Harvard University Press.

Quandt, William B. 1986 "The Electoral Cycle and the Conduct of Foreign Policy," *Political Science Quarterly* 101(5): 825-37.

Quirk, Paul J. 1984. "Presidential Competence." In Michael Nelson, ed., *The Presidency and the Political System,* 133-55. Washington, D.C.: CQ Press.

Randolph, Eleanor. 1987. "Changes in Tone, Technology Reflect Evolution of TV Newscasts." *Washington Post,* 9 February.

Ranney, Austin. 1978. "The Political Parties: Reform and Decline." In A.S. King, ed., *The New American Political System,* 213-48. Washington, D.C.: American Enterprise Institute.

Ranney, Austin. 1983. "The President and His Party." In A.S. King, ed., *Both Ends of the Avenue,* 131-53. Washington, D.C.: American Enterprise Institute.

Ranney, Austin. 1985. "What Constitutional Changes Do Americans Want?" In D. Robinson, ed., *Reforming American Government,* 280-87. Boulder, Colo.: Westview Press.

Rector, Robert, and Michael Sanera, eds. 1987. *Steering the Elephant.* New York: Universe Books.

Reedy, George L. 1970. *The Twilight of the Presidency.* New York: Mentor.

Richardson, Bradley M., and Scott C. Flanagan. 1984. *Politics in Japan.* Boston: Little, Brown.

Ridley, F.F. 1966. "Chancellor Government as a Political System and the German Constitution." *Parliamentary Affairs* 19(4): 446-61.

Rielly, John E. 1987. *American Public Opinion and U.S. Foreign Policy 1987.* Chicago: Chicago Council on Foreign Relations.

Ripley, Randall B., and Grace A. Franklin. 1980. *Congress, the Bureaucracy and Public Policy.* Rev. ed. Homewood, Ill.: Dorsey.

Roberts, Paul Craig. 1984. *The Supply-Side Revolution.* Cambridge, Mass.: Harvard University Press.

Robinson, Donald L., ed. 1985. *Reforming American Government.* Boulder, Colo.: Westview Press.

Robinson, Donald L. 1987. *To the Best of My Ability: The Presidency and the Constitution.* New York: Norton.

Robinson, Michael, and Margaret Sheehan. 1983. *Over the Wire and On TV.* New York: Russell Sage Foundation.

Roche, John P. 1985. "Comments on LBJ." In Marc Landy, ed., *Modern Presidents and the Presidency,* 187-91. Lexington, Mass.: Lexington Books.

Rockman, Bert A. 1981. "America's *Departments* of State." *American Political Science Review* 75(4): 911-27.

Rockman, Bert A. 1984. *The Leadership Question: The Presidency and the American System*. New York: Praeger.

Rockman, Bert A. 1987a. "Reforming the Presidency: Nonproblems and Problems." *PS* 20(3): 643-49.

Rockman, Bert A. 1987b. "Mobilizing Political Support for U.S. National Security." *Armed Forces and Society* 14(1): 17-41.

Roeder, Philip G. 1985. "Do New Soviet Leaders Really Make a Difference?" *American Political Science Review* 79(4): 958-76.

Roosevelt, Theodore. 1929. *An Autobiography*. New York: Scribner's.

Rose, Richard. 1976a. "On the Priorities of Government." *European Journal of Political Research* 4(3): 247-89.

Rose, Richard. 1976b. *Managing Presidential Objectives*. New York: Free Press.

Rose, Richard. 1977. "The President: A Chief but not an Executive." *Presidential Studies Quarterly* 7(1): 5-20.

Rose, Richard. 1980a. "British Government: The Job at the Top." In R. Rose and E. Suleiman, eds., *Presidents and Prime Ministers*, 1-49. Washington, D.C.: American Enteprise Institute.

Rose, Richard. 1980b. "Government against Sub-Governments: A European Perspective on Washington." In R. Rose and E. Suleiman, eds., *Presidents and Prime Ministers*, 284-347. Washington, D.C.: American Enterprise Institute.

Rose, Richard. 1980c. "Ordinary People in Extraordinary Economic Circumstances." In R. Rose, ed., *Challenge to Governance*, 151-74. Beverly Hills: Sage Publications.

Rose, Richard. 1984a. *Understanding Big Government*. Beverly Hills: Sage Publications.

Rose, Richard. 1984b. *Do Parties Make a Difference?* 2d ed. Chatham, N.J.: Chatham House.

Rose, Richard. 1985a. *Public Employment in Western Nations*. New York: Cambridge University Press.

Rose, Richard. 1985b. "From Government at the Center to Government Nationwide." In Vincent Wright and Yves Meny, eds., *Centre-Periphery Relations in Western Europe*, 13-32. London: Allen and Unwin. New Local Government Series No. 25.

Rose, Richard. 1985c. "Can the President Steer the American Economy?" *Journal of Public Policy* 5(2): 267-80.

Rose, Richard. 1985d. "National Pride in Cross-National Perspective." *International Social Science Journal* 27(1): 85-96.

Rose, Richard. 1985e. *Politics in England*. 4th ed. Boston: Little, Brown.

Rose, Richard. 1986a. "Law as a Resource of Public Policy." *Parliamentary Affairs* 39(3): 297-314.

Rose, Richard. 1986b. "British MPs: More Bark Than Bite?" In Ezra Suleiman, ed., *Parliaments and Parliamentarians in Democratic Politics*. New York: Holmes and Meier, 136-73.

Rose, Richard. 1987a. "Steering the Ship of State: One Tiller but Two Pairs of Hands." *British Journal of Political Science* 17(4): 409-33.

Rose, Richard. 1987b. *Ministers and Ministries: A Functional Analysis.* Oxford: Clarendon Press.

Rose, Richard. 1987c. "The Political Appraisal of Employment Policies." *Journal of Public Policy* 7(3): 285-305.

Rose, Richard. 1988. "Changing Markets." In James P. Pfiffner and R. Gordon Hoxie, eds., *The Presidency in Transition.* New York: Center for the Study of the Presidency.

Rose, Richard. Forthcoming. "How Big Is American Government?" *Political Science Quarterly*

Rose, Richard, and Terence Karran. 1987. *Taxation by Political Inertia.* Boston: Allen and Unwin.

Rose, Richard, and Dennis Kavanagh. 1976. "The Monarchy in Contemporary Culture." *Comparative Politics* 8(3): 548-76.

Rose, Richard, and Ian McAllister. 1986. *Voters Begin to Choose.* Beverly Hills: Sage Publications.

Rose, Richard, and T.T. Mackie. 1983. "Incumbency in Government: Asset or Liability?" In H. Daalder and P. Mair, eds., *Western European Party Systems*, 115-37. London: Sage Publications.

Rose, Richard and Rei Shiratori, eds. 1986. *The Welfare State East and West.* New York: Oxford University Press.

Rose, Richard, and Ezra, Suleiman, eds. 1980. *Presidents and Prime Ministers.* Washington, D.C.: American Enterprise Institute.

Rossiter, Clinton. 1956. *The American Presidency.* New York: Harcourt, Brace.

Rourke, Francis E. 1987. "Bureaucracy in the American Constitutional Order." *Political Science Quarterly* 102(2): 217-232.

Rowan, Hobart. 1987. "Japanese Critical of Nation's Slow Growth." *Washington Post, National Weekly Edition*, 8 April.

Russett, Bruce. 1985. "The Mysterious Case of Vanishing Hegemony: or, Is Mark Twain Really Dead?" *International Organization* 39(2): 207-31.

Russett, Bruce, and T.W. Graham. 1988. "Public Opinion and National Security Policy." In M. Midlarsky, ed., *Handbook of War Studies.* London: Allen and Unwin.

Salamon, Lester M., and Michael S. Lund, eds. 1985. *The Reagan Presidency and the Governing of America.* Washington, D.C.: Urban Institute.

Sanera, Michael. 1984. "Implementing the Agenda." In S. Butler, M. Sanera, and B. Weinrod, eds., *Mandate for Leadership.* Washington, D.C.: Heritage Foundation.

Sawhill, Isabel V. 1986. "Reaganomics in Retrospect." In J.L. Palmer, ed., *Perspectives on the Reagan Years*, 91-120. Washington, D.C.: Urban Institute.

Sbragia, Alberta. 1986. "Monetary Policy and Monetary Theory". In James P. Pfiffner, ed., *The President and Economic Policy*, 219-39. Philadelphia: Institute for the Study of Human Issues.

Scalapino, R.A., and Junnosuke Masumi. 1962. *Parties and Politics in Contemporary Japan.* Berkeley: University of California Press.

Scammon, R.M., and Alice V. McGillivray, 1985. *America Votes 16.* Washington, D.C.: CQ Press.

Schattschneider, E.E. 1935. *Politics, Pressures and the Tariff.* New York: Prentice-Hall.

Schick, Allen. 1980. *Congress and Money: Budgeting, Spending and Taxing.* Washington, D.C.: Urban Institute Press.

Schick, Allen. 1981a. "The Coordination Option." In Peter Szanton, ed., *Federal Reorganization: What Have We Learned?* 85-113 Chatham, N.J.: Chatham House, 85-113.

Schick, Allen. 1981b. "The Problem of Presidential Budgeting". In H. Heclo, H. and L. Salamon, eds., *The Illusion of Presidential Governance,* 85-111. Boulder, Colo.: Westview Press.

Schick, Allen, ed. 1983. *Making Economic Policy in Congress.* Washington, D.C.: American Enterprise Institute.

Schlesinger, Arthur M., Jr. 1965. *A Thousand Days.* Boston: Houghton Mifflin.

Schlesinger, Arthur M., Jr. 1974. *The Imperial Presidency.* New York: Popular Library.

Schlesinger, Arthur M., Jr. 1986. *The Cycles of American History.* Boston: Houghton Mifflin.

Schneider, William R. 1983. "Conservatism, Not Interventionism: Trends in Foreign Policy Opinion, 1974-82." In K. A. Oye, R.J. Lieber, and D. Rothchild, eds., *Eagle Defiant,* 33-64. Boston: Little, Brown.

Schneider, William R. 1987. "Rambo and Reality: Having It Both Ways." In K. Oye et al., eds. *Eagle Resurgent,* 41-75 Boston: Little, Brown.

Schumpeter, Joseph A. 1952. *Capitalism, Socialism and Democracy.* 4th ed. London: Allen and Unwin

Sears, David O. 1968. "Political Behavior". In G. Lindzey and E. Aronson, ed., *Handbook of Social Psychology: Applied Social Psychology,* vol. 5. Reading, Mass.: Addison-Wesley.

Seidman, Harold, and Robert Gilmour. 1986. *Politics, Position and Power.* 4th ed. New York: Oxford University Press.

Seligman, Lester G. 1980. "On Models of the Presidency." *Presidential Studies Quarterly* 10(3): 353-63.

Shamoon, Stella. 1987. "Markets: Where the Buck Stops." *The Observer* (London) 29 November.

Shapiro, Martin. 1981. "The Presidency and the Federal Courts." In A.J. Meltsner, ed., *Politics and the Oval Office,* 141-60. San Francisco: Institute of Contemporary Studies.

Shiratori, Rei. 1985. "Candidate Selection in Japan: Localism, Factionalism and Personalism." Paper presented at annual European Consortium for Political Research Workshop, Barcelona.

Shultz, George P., and Kenneth W. Dam. 1978. *Economic Policy Beyond the Headlines*. New York: Norton.

Shuman, Howard E. 1984. *Politics and the Budget*. Englewood Cliffs, N.J.: Prentice-Hall.

Sigelman, Lee. 1982. "The Presidency: What Crisis of Confidence?" In Doris Graber, ed., *The President and the Public*, 242-59. Philadelphia: Institute for the Study of Human Issues.

SIPRI Yearbook. 1986. New York: Oxford University Press.

Sivard, Ruth Leger. 1986. *World Military and Social Expenditures 1986*. 11th ed. Washington, D.C.: World Priorities.

Skowronek, Stephen. 1984. "Presidential Leadership in Political Time." In M. Nelson, ed., *The Presidency and the Political System*, 87-132. Washington, D.C.: CQ Press.

Skowronek, Stephen. 1986. "The Presidency in the Political Order." *Studies in American Political Development*, 1: 286-302. New Haven: Yale University Press.

Smith, Harold E. 1945. *The Management of Your Government*. New York: McGraw-Hill.

Sniderman, Paul A. 1977 "Coping: The Ethic of Self-Reliance." *American Journal of Political Science* 21: 50-122.

Sorensen, Theodore. 1965. *Kennedy*. New York: Harper and Row.

Speakes, Larry. 1987. "Speakes Aims Final Salvo at White House Practices." *Washington Post*, 31 January.

Sperlich, Peter W. 1975. "Bargaining and Overload: An Essay on *Presidential Power*." In Aaron Wildavsky, ed., *Perspectives on the Presidency*, 406-30. Boston: Little, Brown.

Stein, Herbert. 1984. *Presidential Economics: The Making of Economic Policy from Roosevelt to Reagan and Beyond*. New York: Simon and Schuster.

Steiner, Jurg. 1982. "Switzerland: Magic Formula Coalitions." In E.C. Browne and J. Dreijmanis, eds., *Government Coalitions in Western Democracies*, 315-34. New York: Longman.

Stockman, David A. 1986. *The Triumph of Politics*. New York: Harper & Row.

Storing, Herbert. 1981. *What the Anti-Federalists Were For*. Chicago: University of Chicago Press.

Strange, Susan. 1971. *Sterling and British Policy: A Political Study of an International Currency in Decline*. London: Oxford University Press.

Suleiman, Ezra, ed. 1984. *Bureaucrats and Policy Making*. New York: Holmes and Meier.

Sundquist, James L. 1980. "The Crisis of Competence in Our National Government." *Political Science Quarterly* 95 (Summer).

Sundquist, James L. 1986. *Constitutional Reform and Effective Government*. Washington, D.C.: Brookings Institution.

Szanton, Peter, ed. 1981. *Federal Reorganization: What Have We Learned?* Chatham, N.J.: Chatham House.

Taft, William Howard. 1916. *Our Chief Magistrate and His Powers*. New York: Columbia University Press.

Tanzi, Vito. 1988. "International Coordination of Fiscal Policies: Current and Future Issues." Washington, D.C.: International Monetary Fund. Duplicated.

Tarschys, Daniel. 1977. "The Soviet Political System: Three Models." *European Journal of Political Research* 5: 287-320.

Tatalovich, Raymond, and B.W. Daynes. 1984. *Presidential Power in the United States*. Monterey, Calif.: Brooks/Cole.

Taylor, Paul. 1987. "Is This Any Way to Pick a President?" *Washington Post, National Weekly Edition*, 13 April.

Thomas, Norman C. 1987 "The Presidency and Critical Scholarship in Perspective." Paper presented at American Political Science Association neeting, Chicago.

Thurow, Lester. 1981. "The Moral Equivalent of Defeat." *Foreign Policy*, Spring.

Times Mirror. 1987. *The People, Press & Politics*. Los Angeles: Times Mirror Corporation.

Tocqueville, Alexis de. 1954. *Democracy in America*. New York: Vintage ed., 2 volumes.

Tomita, N., A. Nakamura, and R.J. Hrebenar. 1986. "The Liberal Democratic Party: The Ruling Party of Japan." In R.J. Hrebenar, ed., *The Japanese Party System*, 235-82. Boulder, Colo.: Westview Press.

Toth, Robert C. 1986. "Managing the National Security Council," *International Herald Tribune*, 29-30 November.

Tower, John R. 1987. *Report of the President's Special Review Board*. Washington, D.C.: Executive Office of the President.

Truman, Harry S. 1949. *Public Papers of the Presidents of the United States*. Washington, D.C.: Government Printing Office.

Tsurutani, Taketsugu. 1977. *Political Change in Japan*. New York: Longman.

Tufte, Edward R. 1978. *Political Control of the Economy*. Princeton: Princeton University Press.

Tulis, Jeffrey. 1981. "On Presidential Character." In J. Bessette and J. Tulis, eds., *The Presidency in the Constitution Order*, 283-313. Baton Rouge: Louisiana State University Press.

Tulis, Jeffrey. 1987. *The Rhetorical Presidency*. Princeton: Princeton University Press.

Ullman, Richard H. 1983. "Redefining Security." *International Security* 8(1): 129-53.

Ullman, Richard H., and Mario Zucconi, eds. 1987. *Western Europe and the Crisis in U.S.-Soviet Relations*. New York: Praeger.

Ungar, Sanford J., ed. 1985. *Estrangement: America and the World*. New York: Oxford University Press.

United Nations. Annual-a. *Statistical Yearbook*. New York: United Nations.

United Nations. Annual-b. *Yearbook of National Accounts Statistics.* New York: United Nations.

United Nations. 1960. *Yearbook of International Trade Statistics 1958.* New York: United Nations.

U.S. Bureau of the Census. 1960. *Historical Statistics of the United States.* Washington, D.C.: Government Printing Office.

Van Mechelen, Denis, and Richard Rose. 1986. *Patterns of Parliamentary Legislation.* Aldershot: Gower.

Viguerie, Richard A. 1987. "Hello Baker, Bye-bye Reagan." *Washington Post,* 15 March.

Vogel, Ezra F., ed. 1979. *Modern Japanese Organization and Decision-Making* Tokyo: Charles E. Tuttle.

Walcott, Charles, and Karen M. Hult. 1987. "Organizing the White House: Structure, Environment and Organizational Governance." *American Journal of Political Science* 31(1): 109-25.

Wallich, Henry C. 1984. "Institutional Cooperation in the World Economy." In J. Frenkel and M. Mussa, eds., *The World Economic System.* Dover, Mass.: Auburn House.

Wattenberg, Martin P. 1984. *The Decline of American Political Parties.* Cambridge, Mass.: Harvard University Press.

Wattenberg, Martin P. 1986. "The Reagan Polarization Phenomenon and the Continuing Downward Slide in Presidential Candidate Popularity." *American Politics Quarterly* 14(3): 219-45.

Wayne, Stephen. 1978. *The Legislative Presidency.* New York: Harper and Row.

Wayne, Stephen. 1980. *The Road to the White House.* New York: St. Martin's Press.

Wayne, Stephen. 1982a. "Expectations of the President." In Doris Graber, ed., *The President and the Public,* 17-38. Philadelphia: Institute for the Study of Human Issues.

Wayne, Stephen. 1982b. "Congressional Liaison in the Reagan White House." In Norman J. Orstein, ed., *President and Congress: Assessing Reagan's First Year.* Washington, D.C.: American Enterprise Institute.

Wayne, Stephen. 1987. "The United States." In W.J.E.L. Plowden, ed. *Advising the Rulers,* 71-86. Oxford: Basil Blackwell.

Weaver, R. Kent. 1986. "The Politics of Blame Avoidance." *Journal of Public Policy* 6(4): 371-98.

Weihmiller, Gordon R., and Dusko Doder. 1986. *U.S.-Soviet Summits.* Lanham, Md.: University Press of America/Institute for the Study of Diplomacy.

Weinraub, Bernard. 1986. "How Donald Regan Runs the White House". *New York Times Magazine,* 5 .

Whiteley, Paul, ed. 1980. *Models of Political Economy.* London: Sage Publications.

Wildavsky, Aaron. 1975a. "The Two Presidencies." In A. Wildavsky, ed., *Perspectives on the Presidency*, 448-61. Boston: Little, Brown.

Wildavsky, Aaron. 1975b. *Budgeting: A Comparative Theory of Budgetary Processes*. Boston: Little, Brown.

Wildavsky, Aaron. 1988. *The New Politics of the Budgetary Process*. Boston: Little Brown.

Will, George F. 1987. "Why America Will Weather the Storm." *Daily Telegraph* (London) 10 November.

Williamson, John, and Marcus Miller. 1987. *Targets and Indicators: A Blueprint for the International Coordination of Economic Policy*. Washington, D.C.: Institute for International Economics Policy Analysis No. 22.

Wilson, James Q. 1987. "Does the Separation of Powers Still Work?" *The Public Interest*, no. 86: 36-52.

Woolley, John T. 1983. "Political Factors in Monetary Policy." In D.R. Hodgman, ed., *The Political Economy of Monetary Policy: National and International Aspects*, 178-203. Boston: Federal Reserve Bank Conference Series No. 26.

Woolley, John T. 1984. *Monetary Politics: The Federal Reserve and the Politics of Monetary Policy*. New York: Cambridge University Press.

Woolley, John T. 1985. "Central Banks and Inflation." In Leon N. Lindberg and Charles S. Maier, eds., *The Politics of Inflation and Economic Stagnation*, 318-48. Washington, D.C.: Brookings Institution.

Wooten, James T. 1977. "Pre-Inaugural Memo Urged Carter to Emphasize Style over Substance." *New York Times*, 4 May

Wright, Deil. 1982. *Understanding Intergovernmental Relations*. Monterey, Cal.: Brooks-Cole.

Wu, Yuan-Li. 1973. *China: A Handbook*. Newton Abbot, Devon: David and Charles.

Young, James S. 1966. *The Washington Community, 1800-1828*. New York: Harcourt, Brace.

Index

About the Author

RICHARD ROSE brings to the study of the Presidency a great breadth of knowledge about politics and public policy in the United States and in Europe. A native of St. Louis, he took his B.A. at Johns Hopkins University and, after further education at the London School of Economics and the *St. Louis Post-Dispatch*, his doctorate at Oxford.

For more than two decades Rose has been pioneering the study of comparative politics from a base at the University of Strathclyde, Glasgow, Scotland, where he is the founder and director of the Centre for the Study of Public Policy. Rose has viewed Washington close at hand as a visiting scholar at the Woodrow Wilson International Center of the Smithsonian, the Brookings Institution, the American Enterprise Institute, and the International Monetary Fund. In addition, appointments as a visiting professor have been held at Stanford University, Johns Hopkins University, the European University Institute in Florence, and the Wissenschaftszentrum, Berlin.

In addition to making innovative use of empirical data, Rose is also known for clear and witty contributions to television and print media on both sides of the Atlantic. He has addressed audiences in academic and public policy seminars in more than two dozen countries on five continents. Translations of his books and articles have appeared in French, German, Italian, Spanish, Swedish, Norwegian, Polish, Hebrew, Japanese, and Chinese.